OCR Classical Civilisation

AS AND A LEVEL

COMPONENTS 21 AND 22

OCR Classical Civilisation

AS AND A LEVEL

COMPONENTS 21 AND 22:
Greek Theatre and Imperial Image

ROBERT HANCOCK-JONES
JAMES RENSHAW
LAURA SWIFT

GENERAL EDITOR:
JAMES RENSHAW

BLOOMSBURY ACADEMIC
LONDON · NEW YORK · OXFORD · NEW DELHI · SYDNEY

BLOOMSBURY ACADEMIC
Bloomsbury Publishing Plc, 50 Bedford Square, London, WC1B 3DP, UK
Bloomsbury Publishing Inc, 1359 Broadway, New York, NY 10018, USA
Bloomsbury Publishing Ireland, 29 Earlsfort Terrace, Dublin 2, D02 AY28, Ireland

BLOOMSBURY, BLOOMSBURY ACADEMIC and the Diana logo are trademarks of
Bloomsbury Publishing Plc

First published in Great Britain 2017
Reprinted 2018 (twice), 2020, 2021, 2022, 2023, 2024, 2025, 2026

Cover design by Terry Woodley and Olivia D'Cruz
Cover image © Getty/Jim Zuckerman

A catalogue record for this book is available from the British Library.

A catalog record for this book is available from the Library of Congress.

ISBN: PB: 978-1-3500-1511-1
       ePDF: 978-1-3500-1513-5
       eBook: 978-1-3500-1512-8

Typeset by RefineCatch Limited, Bungay, Suffolk
Printed and bound in Great Britain

To find out more about our authors and books visit www.bloomsbury.com
and sign up for our newsletters.

For product safety related questions contact productsafety@bloomsbury.com.

ACKNOWLEDGEMENTS

The authors divided the text between them as follows:

Part 1: Greek Theatre by James Renshaw and Laura Swift
Part 2: Imperial Image by Robert Hancock-Jones

The authors would like to thank the many anonymous reviewers at universities, schools
and OCR who read and commented on drafts of this text. All errors remain their own.

CONTENTS

INTRODUCTION

Welcome to your textbook for OCR AS and A Level Classical Civilisation.

This book has been created to support two of the components from Component Group 2 Culture and the Arts: Component 21 'Greek Theatre' and Component 22 'Imperial Image'.

Through your reading of this textbook and your wider study in class, you will be able to gain a broad knowledge and understanding of a range of literary and cultural materials from the classical world. As well as learning about the culture, history and ideas of the ancient Greeks and Romans, you will read ancient texts in translation and study ancient art and objects from the classical world, together with the surviving remains of religious and domestic architecture.

The specification requires you to respond to the prescribed source material and assess content through analysis and evaluation. The box features (see pp. vii–viii) are designed to build up your skills and knowledge, while exam tips, practice questions, and chapters on assessment will prepare you for taking your final examinations.

A Companion Website, available at www.bloomsbury.com/class-civ-as-a-level, supports this textbook with further information, resources and updates. If you have any suggestions for improvement and additional resources please get in touch by writing to contact@bloomsbury.com.

We hope you will enjoy this wide-ranging and fascinating course, and that it will inspire you to go on to further study of the ancient world.

HOW TO USE THIS BOOK

The layout design and box features of this book are designed to aid your learning.

COLOUR

Box features that focus on assessment preparation and exam skills are coloured in blue.

Box features with Stretch and Challenge material are coloured in yellow.

All other box features are coloured in red.

ICONS

The Prescribed Source icon **PS** flags a quotation or image that is a source prescribed in the specification.

The Stretch and Challenge icon **S&C** indicates that an exercise extends beyond the core content of the specification.

The Companion Website icon **CW** highlights where extra material can be found on the Bloomsbury Companion Website www.bloomsbury.com/class-civ-as-a-level.

BOX FEATURES

In the margins you will find feature boxes giving short factfiles of key events, individuals and places.

Other features either **recommend** teaching material or highlight **prescribed** content and **assessment** tips and information.

Recommended teaching material is found in the following box features:

Activities
Debates
Explore Further
Further Reading
Modern Parallels
Study Questions
Topic Reviews

Prescribed content and assessment-focused tips and information are found in the following box features:

Exam Overviews
Exam Tips
Modern Scholarship
Practice Questions
Prescribed Sources

Material that extends beyond the specification is found in the Stretch and Challenge box features. Remember that the specification requires students to study extra sources and material not listed in the specification, so **S&C** information and exercises will provide a good place for you to start.

A NOTE ON QUESTIONS

Questions found in Topic Review boxes and Study Question boxes are not worded in the form you will find on the exam papers. They are intended to encourage investigation and revision of the material, but do not reflect the questions you will answer in the exam. Practice Questions at the end of each topic, and the questions found in the 'What to Expect in the Exam' chapters do mirror the format and wording you will encounter in the exam.

GLOSSARY

At the back of the book you will find a full glossary of key words. These words are also defined on pages in margin features.

Spellings of names and texts are formatted in line with the OCR specification.

On the Companion Website you will find a colour-coded glossary that highlights which components the words come from.

IMAGES

Illustrations give you the opportunity to see the ancient visual material you are required to study, flagged with the **PS** icon, but also illustrate other relevant aspects of the ancient world. Often what survives from the ancient world does not provide us with ways to illustrate what we study. Thus, art, drawings and reconstructions from later periods and the modern day may be used to illustrate this book. Don't forget that these are not sources like your prescribed texts and visual material – they are later interpretations of aspects of antiquity and do not represent evidence for analysis.

COMPANION WEBSITE

Resources will include

- links to the text of Prescribed Literary Sources
- further images and information on Prescribed Visual/Material Sources
- annotated further reading
- links to websites that give useful contextual material for study
- quizzes on key topics and themes
- worksheets to supplement Activity box features in the book

DON'T FORGET

Look out for cross references to other pages in the book – this is where you will find further information and be able to link concepts or themes.

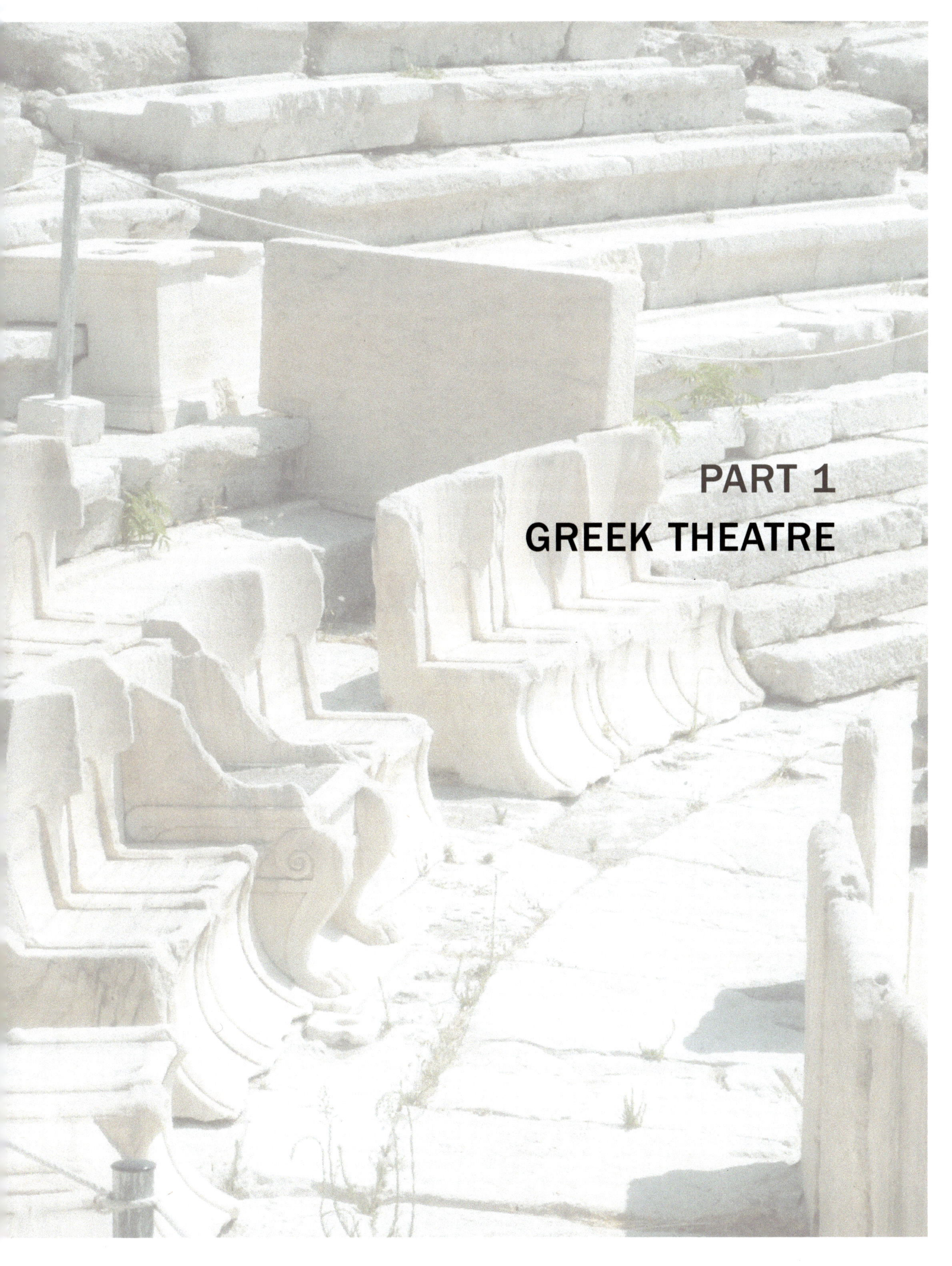

PART 1
GREEK THEATRE

Introduction to Greek Theatre

When drama emerged in Athens in the late sixth century BC, it was the first organised theatre in the western tradition. Indeed, it is fair to say that drama is one of ancient Greece's greatest gifts to civilisation, and one that has had a profound impact on the development of European drama ever since. One cannot fully understand the works of playwrights such as Shakespeare, Molière or Goethe without understanding the tradition from which they emerged. Athenian drama therefore continues to cast a long shadow today.

However, it is not just the influence that is important. The plays that have survived from the fifth century – some forty-three in all – continue to confuse, challenge and entertain today. In that sense, they are timeless. It is likely that whenever you are studying this course there will be more than one ancient Greek play being performed somewhere in the UK. Why do these plays continue to be performed? The short answer is that they engage with issues with which we still wrestle today, such as the conflict between the individual and the state, the nature of human relationships, the transience of human happiness and the nature of human suffering. Every human society has had to engage with issues such as these, and the Athenians managed to do so to a remarkable depth in their theatre.

This component asks you to read three great ancient plays, each written by a different playwright: two are tragedies (*Oedipus the King* and *Bacchae*) and one is a comedy (*Frogs*). Moreover, the component will allow you to learn about the dramatic culture in which they were first produced – at religious festivals in large theatres. In some ways, an ancient performance was very different from our own experience of watching a play today, and it is important to appreciate this. When we truly engage with an ancient play, we cannot but be enriched by it.

General bibliography

Cartledge, P. (1990). *Aristophanes and his Theatre of the Absurd* (London: Bloomsbury Academic).

Csapo, E. and W.J. Slater (1994). *The Context of Ancient Drama* (Ann Arbor: University of Michigan).

Dugdale, E. (2008). *Greek Theatre in Context* (Cambridge: Cambridge University Press).

Easterling, P.E. (ed.) (1997). *The Cambridge Companion to Greek Tragedy* (Cambridge: Cambridge University Press).

Gregory, J. (2005). *A Companion to Greek Tragedy* (Oxford: Blackwell).

Revermann. M. (ed.) (2014). *The Cambridge Companion to Greek Comedy* (Cambridge: Cambridge University Press).

Scodel, R. (2010). *An Introduction to Greek Tragedy* (Cambridge: Cambridge University Press).

Storey, I.C. and A. Allan (2013). *A Guide to Ancient Greek Drama*, Blackwell Guides to Classical Literature (Chichester: John Wiley & Sons).

Wiles, D. (2000). *Greek Theatre Performance: An Introduction* (Cambridge: Cambridge University Press).

Your assessment is a written examination testing AO1 and AO2. It is

| 50% of the AS Level | 1 hr 30 mins | 65 marks |

32 marks will test AO1: demonstrate knowledge and understanding of:

- literature, visual/material culture and classical thought
- how sources and ideas reflect, and influence, their cultural contexts
- possible interpretations of sources, perspectives and ideas by different audiences and individuals

33 marks will test AO2: critically analyse, interpret and evaluate literature, visual/material culture, and classical thought, using evidence to make substantiated judgements and produce coherent and reasoned arguments.

The examination will consist of two sections.

All questions in **Section A** are compulsory. There are three question types:

- short-answer questions
- 8-mark stimulus question using the prescribed sources
- 16-mark essay

Section B has one question type:

- 25-mark essay

There is a choice of one from two essays.

Your assessment is a written examination testing AO1 and AO2. It is

| 30% of the A Level | 1 hr 45 mins | 75 marks |

35 marks will test AO1: demonstrate knowledge and understanding of:

- literature, visual/material culture and classical thought
- how sources and ideas reflect, and influence, their cultural contexts
- possible interpretations of sources, perspectives and ideas by different audiences and individuals

40 marks will test AO2: critically analyse, interpret and evaluate literature, visual/material culture, and classical thought, using evidence to make substantiated judgements and produce coherent and reasoned arguments.

The examination will consist of two sections.

All questions in **Section A** are compulsory. There are three question types:

- short-answer questions
- 10-mark stimulus question using the prescribed sources
- 20-mark essay

Section B has one question type:

- 30-mark essay

There is a choice of one from two essays. In these essays, learners will be expected to make use of secondary sources and academic views to support their argument.

1.1 Drama and the Theatre in Ancient Athenian Society

- role and significance of drama and the theatre in ancient Athenian society, including the religious context of the dramatic festivals
- the organisation of the City Dionysia, including the make up and involvement of the audience
- structure of the theatre space, and how this developed during the fifth and fourth centuries BC, including:
  - machinery associated with the theatre: the crane and the wheel platform, and how they contributed to the staging of Greek drama
- the representation in visual and material culture of theatrical and dramatic scenes

The following prescribed sources are covered in this topic:

- Theatre of Dionysus at Athens
- Theatre of Thorikos, a coastal deme of Attica
- red-figure vase fragment: single actor possibly playing Perseus and 2 audience members/judges
- red-figure calyx krater depicting Medea's escape
- red-figure bell krater by Schiller Painter, depicting scene with wine-skin & boots from *Women at the Thesmophoria* (*Thesmophoriazusae*)

Don't forget that you will be given credit in the exam if you study extra sources and make relevant use of them in your answers.

KEY INDIVIDUAL

Dionysus the Greek god of drama, wine and revelry

This topic examines the context in which drama was performed in ancient Athenian society, first looking at the religious festivals in honour of **Dionysus** where drama was presented. It will then explore theatre buildings, with all the accompanying adornments. Finally, it will examine what visual and material record we can rely on for evidence of how drama was performed.

THE RELIGIOUS CONTEXT OF THE DRAMATIC FESTIVALS

The tradition of theatre in western civilisation was born in Athens during the second half of the sixth century BC, and this remains one of the ancient Greek world's most significant legacies. However, the context in which plays were performed in ancient Athens was quite different from our experience of the theatre today. Drama was performed only at religious festivals. An Athenian could not simply choose to go to a theatre on any given date as we might do. Moreover, a key element of the Athenian dramatic festival was an element of competition. A number of playwrights entered plays written for the occasion, and one of them was judged to be the winner.

The idea of the 'arts festival' is familiar to us – the Cannes Film Festival (which itself has a competitive ethos), the Hay Festival and the Glastonbury Festival all attract great crowds to watch performances of a high calibre. However, ancient Athenian dramatic festivals were intimately associated with the worship of Dionysus, the god of drama, wine and revelry. The plays were just one aspect of such festivals (albeit an important one), which typically included other events such as processions, sacrifices and revelry in honour of Dionysus.

These festivals were highly-organised and grand civic occasions. Indeed, it is important to be aware of their importance for the state – or **polis** – of Athens. (The Greek word 'polis' is often translated as 'city-state' since it described not only the physical city but also the political entity and the land it controlled – words such as 'politics' are therefore derived from it.) The polis of Athens encompassed a large region surrounding the city itself called Attica. Any free-born man from any part of it was automatically a full Athenian citizen, able to take part in civic events such as the democratic assembly or festivals. Moreover, as we see, festivals were not just limited to the city itself.

> **polis** (pl. **poleis**) the word for a Greek city-state. The polis of Athens consisted of the city and its surrounding region, Attica

Festivals of Dionysus were generally held in the winter months. The most important dramatic festival was the City Dionysia, held in late March, examined in detail below. In addition, the Athenian calendar contained two other important festivals of Dionysus at which plays were performed:

- the **Lenaea** was held in late January, and competitions for comedy and tragedy were introduced to it *c.* 440 – comedy seems to have been more important. The fact that it was held so early in the year made it open only to Athenians, since the seas were too rough for a journey from further afield (by contrast, the City Dionysia made a point of welcoming outsiders)
- the **Rural Dionysia** was held in mid-winter. Unlike the City Dionysia and Lenaea, it was a local festival celebrated in the rural communities of Attica, known as demes. A **deme** might be compared to a village today, although they varied in size; there were 139 in the fifth century. Some deme theatres have been identified, including a well-preserved one at Thorikos (see p. 14). The plays performed at the Rural Dionysia were probably revivals of those performed at the two main city festivals

> **Lenaea** a drama festival held in Athens in late January at which comedy took precedence
>
> **Rural Dionysia** a drama festival held in the rural demes of Attica in mid-winter
>
> **deme** a village or district of Attica

Despite being performed at religious festivals, it is unclear how drama related to the worship of Dionysus. Out of all our surviving Greek drama, he appears as a character only in *Bacchae* by Euripides and *Frogs* by Aristophanes. Indeed, one estimate reckons that only about 4 per cent of the plays we know of are directly concerned with Dionysus.

FIGURE 1.1

Attica in the fifth century BC.

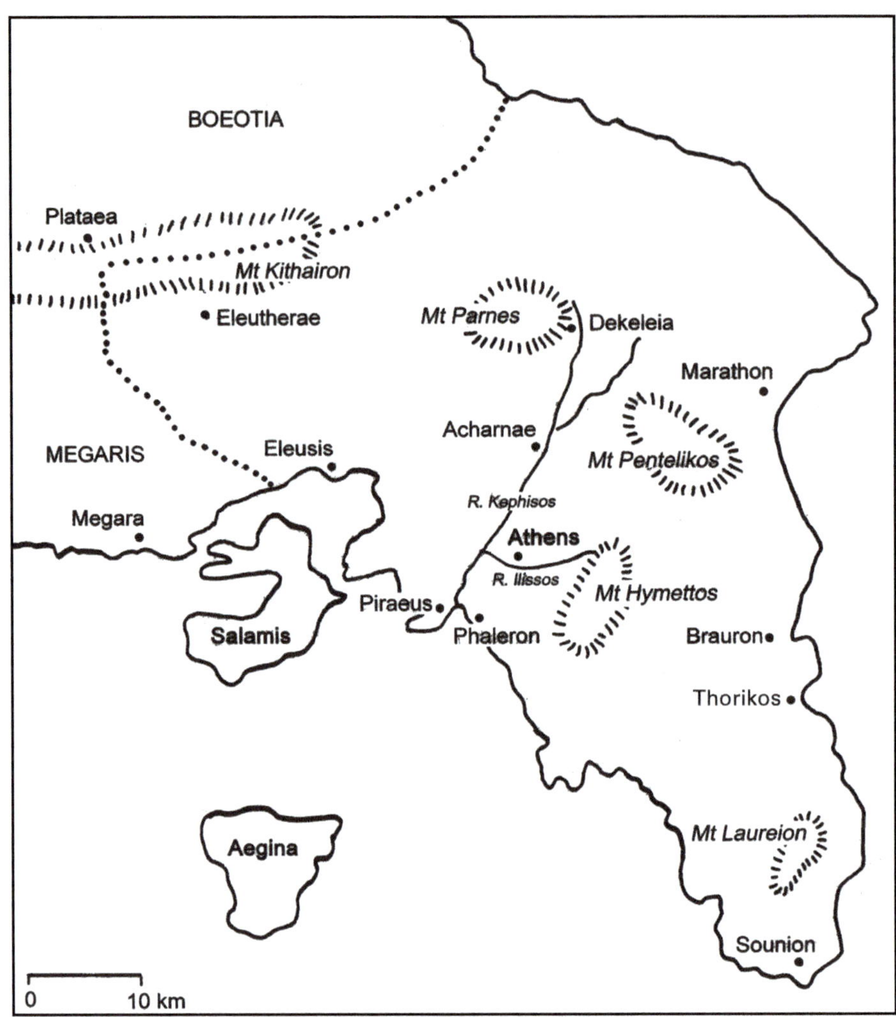

THE CITY DIONYSIA

For an Athenian, late March heralded the coming of spring, the reopening of the sea lanes and the festival of the City Dionysia. The three were connected: it was appropriate to worship Dionysus, a god who encouraged new growth, in the springtime. Moreover, the

MODERN SCHOLARSHIP

One scholar, Oliver Taplin, has gone so far as to say that 'there is nothing intrinsically Dionysiac about Greek tragedy'. Others have challenged this view; for Goldhill, Dionysus' role as a god of subversion was essential to tragedy.

To explore academic views about the role of Dionysus in the Athenian theatre, read pp. 24–34 of *A Guide to Ancient Greek Drama* and 'A Show for Dionysus', chapter 2 of *The Cambridge Companion to Greek Tragedy* (see p. 22).

start of the sailing season allowed the Athenians to show off their city and its festival to visitors from other parts of the Greek world. During the days of the festival, public business ceased and the law courts were closed; prisoners were even given day-release to watch the plays. In the later years of the fifth century, the festival ran for five days and, apart from the theatrical contests, contained a number of other events, including processions, sacrifices and choral competitions. The festival was organised by one of Athens' leading political figures, the **eponymous archōn**. Athenian citizens could take part in it in various ways and so it was truly a festival put on by the people for the people.

Preparations started during the summer of the preceding year. Any tragic playwright wishing to compete presented a synopsis of four plays (three tragedies and a satyr-play; see p. 25 for a description of satyr-plays) to the eponymous archōn. By contrast, comic playwrights needed only to present the synopsis of a single play. We do not know how the archōn made his choice, but he selected three tragic playwrights each to write three tragedies and a satyr-play, and five comic playwrights each to write a comedy. Another of the archōn's duties was to select a **chorēgos** for each playwright. The chorēgos ('chorus-director') was the financial backer of a set of plays and his input was vital. He was drawn from the city's wealthy elite, who were required to fund various public services called liturgies; serving as a chorēgos was one such **liturgy**.

A chorēgos needed a lot of money to make a success of the position: for example, records tell us that in 410, a chorēgos for tragedy spent 3,000 drachmas, and in 402 for comedy alone, the chorēgos spent 1,600 drachmas (for comparison, one drachma was the

eponymous archōn a leading politician of Athens who was responsible for running the City Dionysia. He is referred to as eponymous because the Athenian civil year was named after him

chorēgos the financial backer attached to a playwright to support the production of his plays

liturgy a tax on the super-rich requiring them to contribute to the functioning of Athens

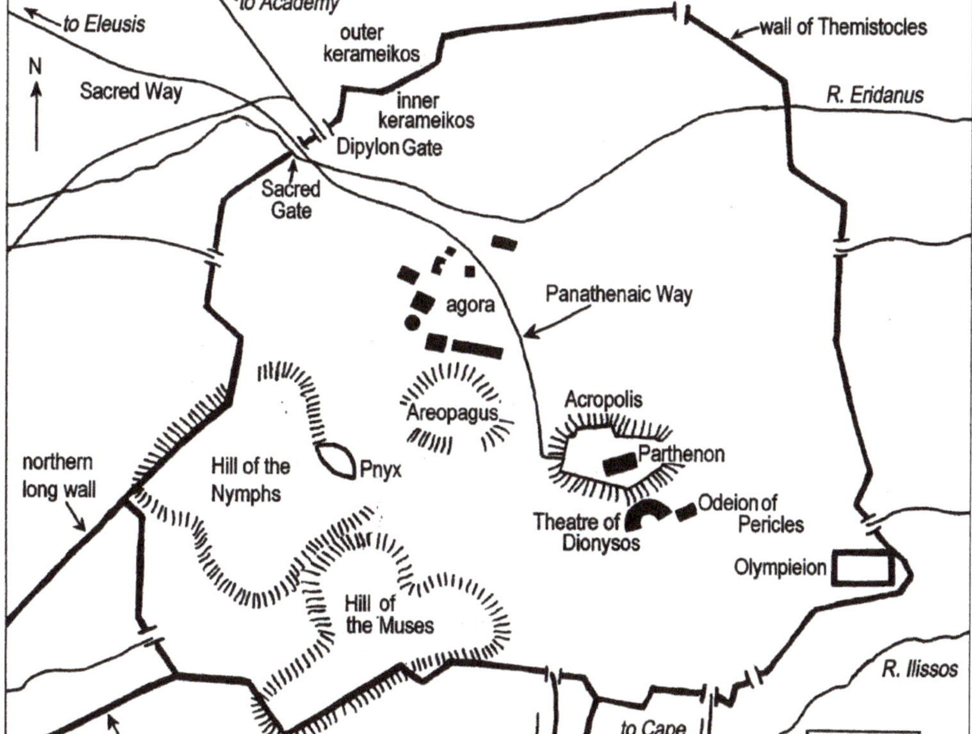

FIGURE 1.2
Fifth-century BC Athens.

daily wage of a skilled worker in Athens). The chorēgos paid for almost everything: costumes, props, masks, special effects, the payment for the chorus and their musicians. He also had to select the members of his chorus and provide them with food, a place to rehearse and sometimes even accommodation. Furthermore, if the playwright wasn't skilled enough to train his own chorus, then the chorēgos had to hire a professional trainer.

Despite this, many wealthy Athenians must have welcomed the opportunity to serve as a chorēgos: if they were associated with the success of such an important festival, it gave them prestige – in this sense, it could be compared to sponsoring a major public event today. One example of a chorēgos who went on to great things is the leading statesman Pericles who, early in his career, financed Aeschylus' plays at the City Dionysia of 472. The final expense for a chorēgos might well have been the most important as far as he was concerned: if his playwright won, he could pay for a victory monument, which would be inscribed with his own name, together with those of the eponymous archōn, the main actors and the musicians.

proagōn an event which acted as a preview and introduction to the festival

A day or two before the festival began, the **proagōn** ('pre-contest') was held in the Odeion, a covered concert hall next to the Theatre of Dionysus (see Figure 1.2). In this ceremony, the plays were announced and each playwright delivered a short synopsis; he might also introduce his chorēgos, actors and musicians, and have an actor read a short passage to give the audience a foretaste of a play. This was the only time that the actors would appear in character without their masks, so it was a chance for the audience to see who they were.

On the evening before the festival began, a wooden statue of Dionysus was brought into the city from a shrine just outside the city on the road to Eleutherae. This torchlight procession re-enacted Dionysus' arrival in Athens from the distant deme of Eleutherae. The statue was escorted to the theatre of Dionysus, where a sacrifice was made. Thereafter,

TABLE 1.1
The likely outline of events at the City Dionysia in *c.* 430

Day	Event
A few days before	proagōn
The eve of the festival	torchlight procession
Day 1	pompē dithyrambic contests kōmos
Day 2	opening ceremony 5 comedies
Day 3	3 tragedies, 1 satyr-play
Day 4	3 tragedies, 1 satyr-play
Day 5	3 tragedies, 1 satyr-play judging & prize giving
A few days later	the review

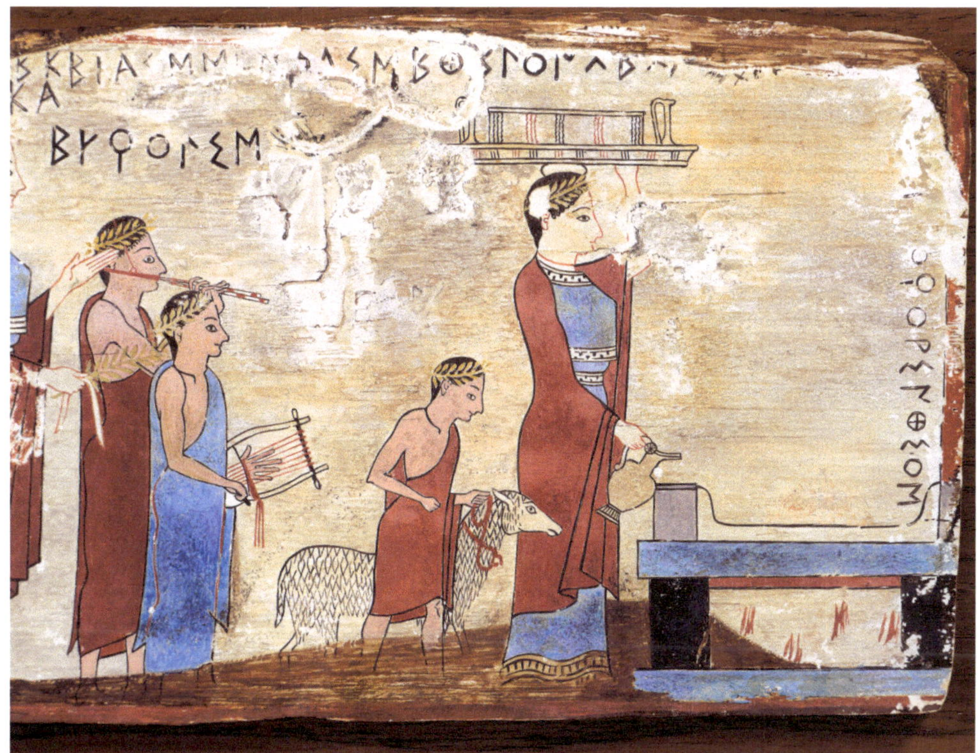

FIGURE 1.3
This sixth century BC painted panel from Pitsa (near Corinth) shows a procession leading to a sacrifice, with accompanying musicians.

the statue remained in the theatre throughout the dramatic performances, a symbol of the god's presence at his festival.

On the morning of day one, the grand procession, or **pompē**, took place. It started outside the city and made its way to the agora, then on to the Temple of Dionysus, where it culminated in the sacrifice of a sacred bull together with many other animals. In the afternoon, there were dithyrambic competitions in the theatre – the **dithyramb** was a choral dance in honour of Dionysus (see p. 25), and each **tribe** entered choruses for this event. (All Athenian citizens were members of one of ten tribes. Each tribe formed a political constituency in Athens, a regiment in the Athenian army, and had religious duties.) Each chorus had its own chorēgos and victory could bring great prestige. Later that evening, a revel (known as a **kōmos**, described on pp. 40–1) was held in the streets by the men of the city.

pompē a grand religious procession

dithyramb a choral dance sung in honour of Dionysus

tribe a political division in Athens. All Athenian citizens were members of one of the ten tribes

kōmos a loosely organised revel through the streets with song and dance

Days two to five (the play days)

Although the programme of events changed over the years, in the latter part of the fifth century day two was the day when five comic playwrights presented their play (it is possible that during the Peloponnesian War, 431–404, only three comic plays were presented, one on each of the other play days, so that the festival was a day shorter). On the following three days, the tragic plays were presented: each day saw three tragedies and satyr-play of one playwright. Lots were drawn to determine the order in which the sets of plays were performed. The action started early in the morning and continued into the afternoon.

Before the plays began on day two, there was a grand opening ceremony in the Theatre of Dionysus. The priest of Dionysus sacrificed a piglet on the altar in the acting area, and the city's ten generals poured libations to the twelve Olympian gods. Following this, three important presentations were made:

- **parade of tribute**. During the fifth century, when Athens controlled an empire, all the tribute from her subject-allies was due at this time of year. The money was brought into the theatre and paraded for the audience to view
- **proclamation of honours**. A herald announced the names of those who had done outstanding service for the city, and awarded them a crown
- **parade of orphans**. The boys and youths whose fathers had died fighting for Athens paraded into the theatre. The state paid for their education as a mark of respect for their fathers' sacrifice. Those who had turned eighteen that year were awarded a suit of armour and declared independent citizens

Each of these presentations emphasises the civic nature of the City Dionysia and suggest that the plays too were a way of reflecting on the Athenian polis.

The spectators

Entry to the theatre cost two obols per day. As this was roughly a day's wage for an unskilled worker, the poor were probably excluded from the festival in its early years. However, at some point in the second half of the fifth century (or possibly later), the Athenian state established the **Theoric Fund**, which paid for the poorest citizens to attend the theatre if they could not afford the entrance fee. This ensured that the dramatic contests were open to the full range of citizens; this once again emphasises the democratic nature of the festival.

Theoric Fund a fund provided by the Athenian state which ensured that poorer citizens could afford to attend the City Dionysia

At the City Dionysia, the seats in the front rows were reserved for important officials: the 500 members of the city's council, foreign and allied dignitaries, generals, other important magistrates and the priest of Dionysus. By the late fourth century, the seating area behind was divided by section to allow tribes to sit together. We do not know if spectators sat in similarly designated areas during the fifth century, but it is tempting to think that they did. The issue of seating also raises the thorny topic of whether women made up part of the audience at the festival – the sources are ambiguous and academic opinion remains divided.

Our sources suggest that the spectators were loud and opinionated when they wanted to be – perhaps like an audience in Shakespearean England. We hear of spectators hissing,

---

MODERN SCHOLARSHIP

The issue of whether women were allowed to watch plays at the City Dionysia is debated by scholars, and the arguments turn on a small number of ancient sources. Analyse the arguments for yourself by reading pp. 48–9 of *A Guide to Ancient Greek Drama* and 'The Audience of Greek Tragedy', chapter 3 of *The Cambridge Companion to Greek Tragedy*.

hooting or kicking their heels when unimpressed. A comic audience must have been especially lively and involved in the action, perhaps similar to a pantomime audience today. To keep things under control there was a theatre police force, the 'rod-bearers', who could beat badly-behaved spectators.

The judging

At the end of day five, the judging took place. The system for this was randomised to avoid bribery. The judges voted on the winning tragic and comic playwright in a process that ran as follows:

- before the festival began, the Athenian council drew up a list of names from the ten tribes of the city. The names from each tribe were sealed in an urn and the ten urns were stored on the Acropolis
- on the first morning of the plays, the ten urns were placed in the theatre and the eponymous archōn drew out one name from each urn. These ten citizens swore an oath of impartiality and sat as judges for the competition
- on the fifth day of the festival each judge wrote down his order of merit on a tablet. All ten tablets were placed in a single urn. The eponymous archōn drew out five of the ten tablets at random and the playwright with the most votes was declared the winner

An entertaining moment in Aristophanes' *Assembly-Women* gives us some insight into the judging process: in the following lines the chorus-leader breaks the dramatic illusion to address the judges directly:

> Just a word to the judges: are there any intellectuals among you? Judge our play by its wit and wisdom. Do you enjoy a good laugh? Judge us by the fun we've given you – that should ensure top marks from almost all of you. Oh, and don't let it make any difference that we were put on first; that's just how the lot fell out, and you'll have to remember it all, and keep your oath, always to judge the choruses fairly, and not to be like the sort of girl who can only remember the fellow she slept with last.

Aristophanes, *Assembly-Women*, 1154–62

Interestingly, these lines must have been put in once the festival had started and the order of plays had been decided, suggesting that lines could be changed right up until the moment of performance.

The review

A few days later, the Athenian assembly met in the Theatre of Dionysus to review the festival, and any citizen could make a complaint if he felt that it had not been run well. If a complaint was upheld, then the eponymous archōn could be fined. However, if the assembly felt that the festival had been a success, it could vote to award the archōn a crown in recognition of his services.

THE STRUCTURE OF THE THEATRE SPACE

Our image of a typical Greek theatre is formed by the many well-preserved ancient theatres dotted around the eastern Mediterranean. The most famous is probably the theatre at Epidaurus in the Peloponnese, which had a capacity of about 15,000 and where plays and concerts are still performed today. However, such stone theatres were first built only in the late fourth century BC. Before this, theatres were built from wood and so little trace of them has survived. All surviving Athenian tragedies and most of the comedies date from the fifth century (including your prescribed plays) and it is important to be aware that there is no conclusive evidence as to every detail of the theatre space at this time. None the less, it is possible to reconstruct an outline.

The main theatre in Athens was the Theatre of Dionysus, situated on the south-eastern side of the Acropolis, just above a religious sanctuary dedicated to the god. The remains of the theatre, which can be seen today, are dated to well after the fifth century: it was first built in stone in the 320s under the supervision of a leading Athenian statesman, Lycurgus, and so the theatre of this era is sometimes referred to as the Lycurgan theatre. From this time on, it had a capacity of some 17,000 spectators. The theatre continued to be remodelled over time, most notably in the first and third centuries AD, when Greece was under Roman control. The ruins today reflect this later period in the theatre's history.

The location of the theatre was important for both practical and symbolic reasons. Practically, the south side of the Acropolis was protected from the cold north winds which blew in the winter months. The symbolic importance is drawn from the fact that the theatre was set between the Acropolis – the religious heart of the city – and the sanctuary of Dionysus below. Outside the theatre, further evidence of the prestige given to drama was seen on the street which led from the theatre to the agora (the city's market place) around the north and east sides of the Acropolis. This was known as the Street of the Tripods, because bronze tripods were set up there by festival victors as a monument to their victory.

PRESCRIBED SOURCE

Theatre of Dionysus

Location: Athens

Date: in use from the second half of the sixth century BC

Significance: the main theatre of ancient Athens, which was located above a sanctuary to Dionysus at the south-eastern foot of the Acropolis

FIGURE 1.4 
The remains of the Theatre of Dionysus today date from the Roman era.

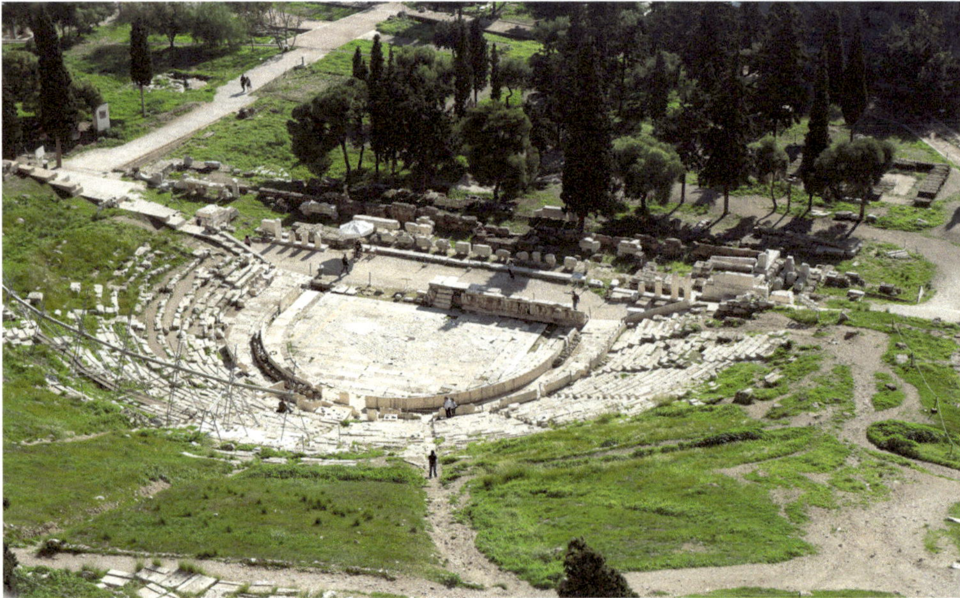

The theatron

The **theatron** (which meant 'watching area' and gives us our word 'theatre') was the area where the audience sat. It was normally built on a hillside, as it was in Athens, and this allowed a steep viewing area and so made the setting clearly visible to all spectators, regardless of their distance from the action.

In the Lycurgan theatre, the theatron was slightly more than semi-circular in shape, and we know from well-preserved theatres such as Epidaurus that this design created outstanding acoustics. The theatre had a horizontal aisle half-way up which helped facilitate access for spectators. The theatron at this time was divided into thirteen wedges, and it seems that ten of these were set aside for the ten Athenian tribes; the other three were for non-Athenians, and perhaps also women and slaves. The front row of the theatron was occupied by officials and dignitaries. This row was called the **prohedria** ('the seats at the front'), and in the theatre of Dionysus its central seat was reserved for the priest of Dionysus.

It is less clear how the seating was arranged during the fifth century or what the theatre's capacity was at that time – the lowest estimates suggest 6,000 although some scholars would argue for many more. Whichever the number, this was still a much larger audience than we would find at a modern theatre. Spectators sat on wooden benches which probably faced straight down, and ancient sources indicate that there was a prohedria, with a seat in the middle for the priest of Dionysus. The most famous such source comes in *Frogs*, when the character Dionysus addresses the priest directly in a moment of fright:

> Priest save me – I'll get you a drink after the show.

> Aristophanes, *Frogs*, 297

theatron the seating area in a Greek theatre

prohedria the front row seating in the theatron reserved for VIPs

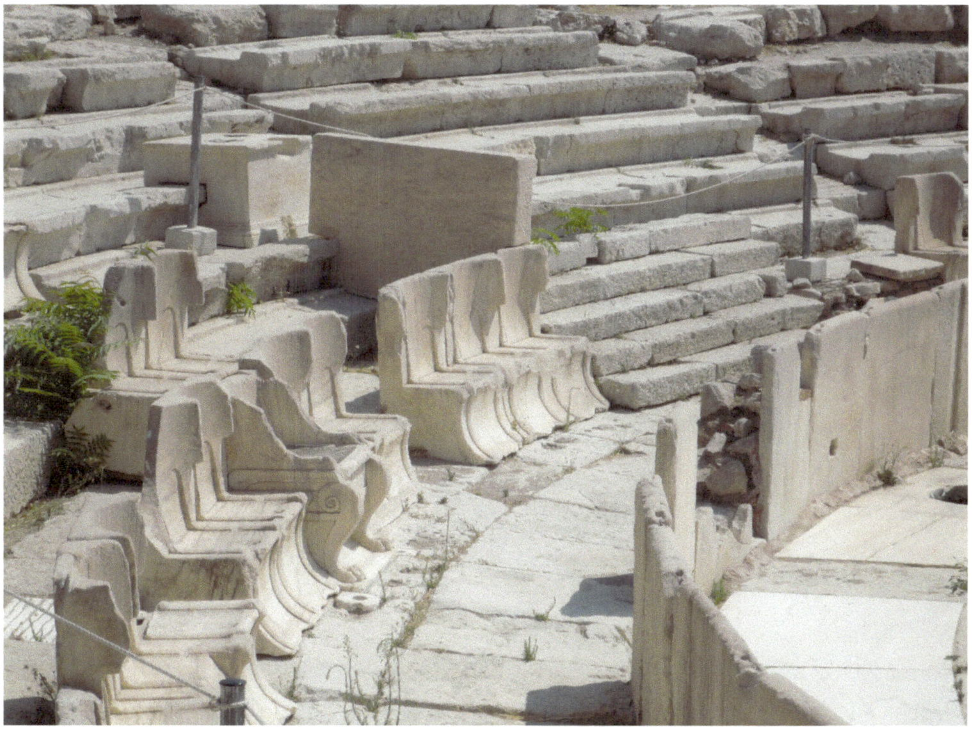

FIGURE 1.5
The central seat of the prohedria from the Roman-era Theatre of Dionysus is still in place today.

The orchēstra

orchēstra the 'dancing-area' below the theatron where the chorus performed

eisodos (or parodos) the entry way into the orchēstra from each side of the theatre

Orchēstra means 'dancing-area' in Greek. Situated at the front of the theatron, in the Lycurgan theatre it was a circular area, about twenty metres in diameter, with the seats wrapped around its front half. The orchēstra was where the chorus of the play (see p. 30) performed – they were never seen on the stage. One consequence of this was that the chorus were located between the actors and the spectators and this fits with their role of mediating the action for the spectators. Somewhere in or near the orchēstra may have been an altar to Dionysus (many theatres had such altars) – if so, it was a reminder that the god was watching over his festival. On each side of the orchēstra, pathways led in from off-stage; each pathway was called an **eisodos**, meaning 'way-on' (it is sometimes also referred to as a **parodos**) and acted as an entrance for the chorus (and also for spectators).

There has been much debate as to the shape of the orchēstra during the fifth century. There is no consensus, but many scholars argue that it was probably not circular, but instead more rectangular or trapezoidal. One argument in their favour is the shape of a number of small deme theatres dating to the early fifth century or earlier which have been excavated; the best preserved of these is the theatre at Thorikos, a deme about twenty miles south-east of Athens.

Thorikos was exactly the sort of local deme which would have seen dramatic performances at the Rural Dionysia. Its theatre has survived remarkably well, and dates to the time at which Athenian drama was in its early development. The capacity is estimated at a little over 3,000, which makes it large for a deme theatre. As you can see from Figure 1.8, its theatron was largely straight-facing, although with curved seating at either end. The orchēstra is more rectangular than circular, and a temple and altar are at either ends of the performance area. Presumably this shape allowed for good acoustics. Another interesting feature is that there is no trace of any permanent building behind the

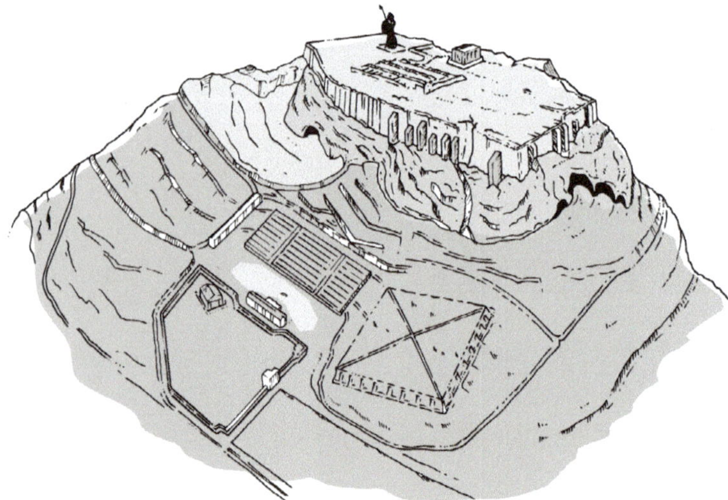

FIGURE 1.6
An artist's impression of the Theatre of Dionysus as it might have looked in the fifth century.

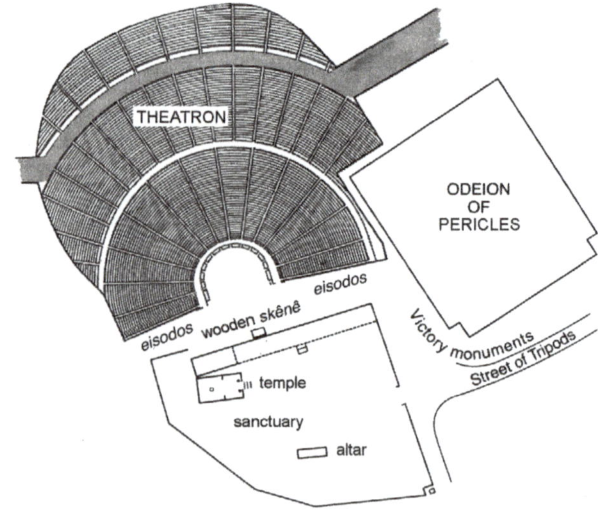

FIGURE 1.7
A plan of the Theatre of Dionysus in the late fourth century.

acting area – such a building became a feature of the theatre of Dionysus in Athens at some point in the fifth century, although it may not have been permanent in the early years of the century.

The skēnē

Behind the orchēstra in the Theatre of Dionysus was a low wooden stage where the main actors performed (there is some debate about when this was introduced; it probably didn't exist when the theatre was first built). At the back of the stage was a building called the **skēnē**, a word which originally meant something like 'tent' or 'booth'. In the early fifth century it may indeed simply have been a tent where actors left the stage to change; by the middle of the century, however, it had come to describe a large wooden hut with a double-door onto the stage (some theatres also had two smaller side-doors). The word 'scenery' is derived from skēnē, since the building provided a backdrop to the action.

> **skēnē** the wooden hut used as a backdrop and for actors to change

The actors used the skēnē as a changing room, so costumes and props were stored there. Inside, a ladder led to a trap-door in the roof, which could be used as a third acting area (it was often where gods appeared). There may have been painting or decoration on the front wall of the skēnē to give more character to the setting. However, this would not have been tailored scene-painting as we would understand it today, since plays with different settings quickly followed on from one another (for example, in 431 Euripides presented *Medea*, set in front of the royal palace in Corinth, and *Philoctetes*, set by a cave on the island of Lemnos). The scene painting may have been on portable panels which could be changed between plays.

The only Attic vase (i.e. a vase made in Attica) which shows a stage is shown in Figure. 1.10, and this is the only painting we have in Greek art which depicts a theatre audience. The drawing contains some reconstructed features since the vase is damaged and missing many of its finer details. The comic actor on the stage seems to be Perseus: he carries a sickle, with which he has cut off the head of Medusa – this is in the bag slung over his left arm. He seems to be dancing, or perhaps pretending to fly as Perseus does in the myth. The lines around his right wrist and feet mark the ends of his body-suit, the part of the comic costume indicating human flesh, and so in this scene he is 'stage-naked'. He does not seem to have a mask, but his costume-phallus is visible tied up between his legs (for the costume-phallus see p. 42).

The artist has dispensed with the orchēstra and brought the two audience members to the foot of the stage. In one sense, they are intended to represent the whole audience. Both are wreathed; one is clearly older and bearded, the other is younger but it is unclear if it is a beardless young man or a woman – the image on the vase is badly damaged. They are sitting on elegant wooden chairs called klismoi: such chairs formed the model for the seating in the prohedria in the Lycurgan theatre, and so it is often thought that these two figures are seen sitting in the front row. There have been a number of ideas as to who they represent, including: two judges; the priest of Dionysus and another priest; Dionysus and his consort Ariadne; or perhaps even the chorēgos and the playwright.

> **EXPLORE FURTHER**
> The first time that we can be sure that the roof of the skēnē was used as an acting area is in Aeschylus' tragedy *Agamemnon*, presented in 458. Read ll. 1–39 of the play – how has the playwright made use of this acting space at the start of the play?

FIGURE 1.8 
An artist's impression of the deme theatre at Thorikos.

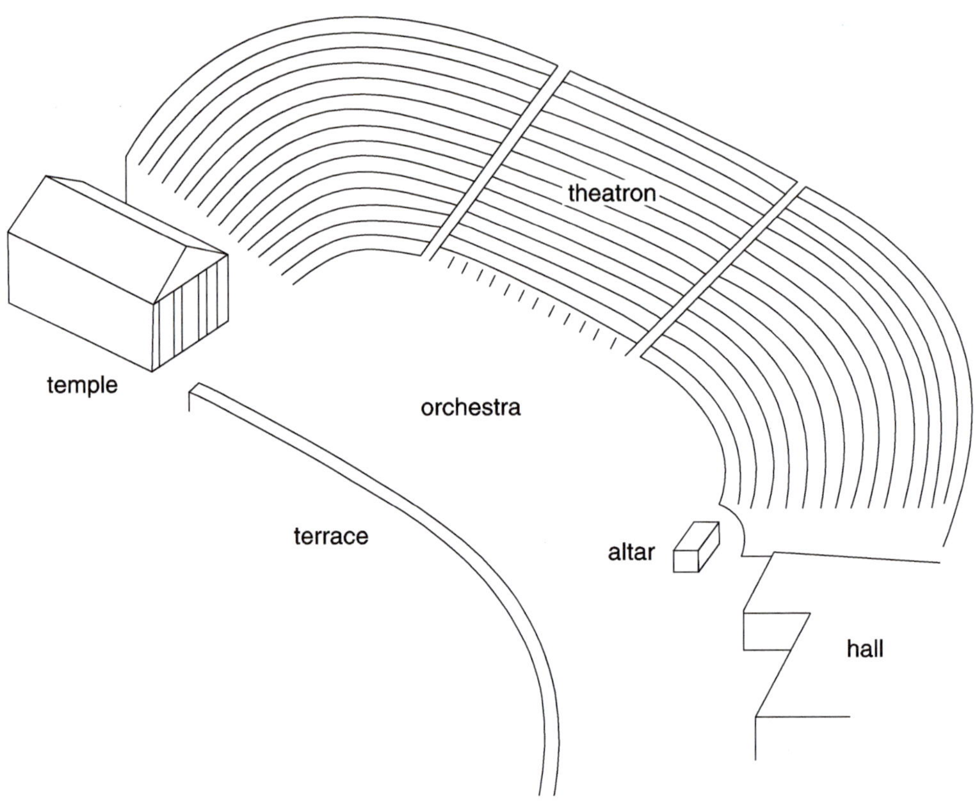

Theatre of Thorikos

Location: Thorikos, a deme (village) on the south-east coast of Attica

Date: in use from the late sixth or early fifth century BC

Significance: a regional theatre of Attica which has a different layout from the circular acting area of the Theatre of Dionysus

FIGURE 1.9 
The remains of the deme theatre at Thorikos today.

EXPLORE FURTHER 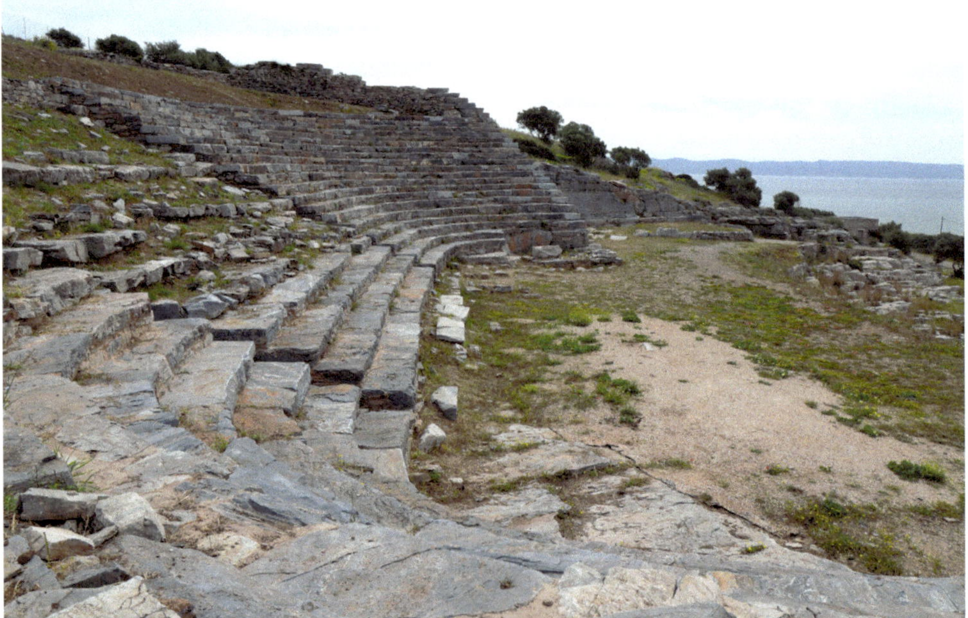
The archaeological site of Thorikos has been excavated by the Belgian School at Athens. You can find out more about their work at: http://www.ebsa.info/pages/

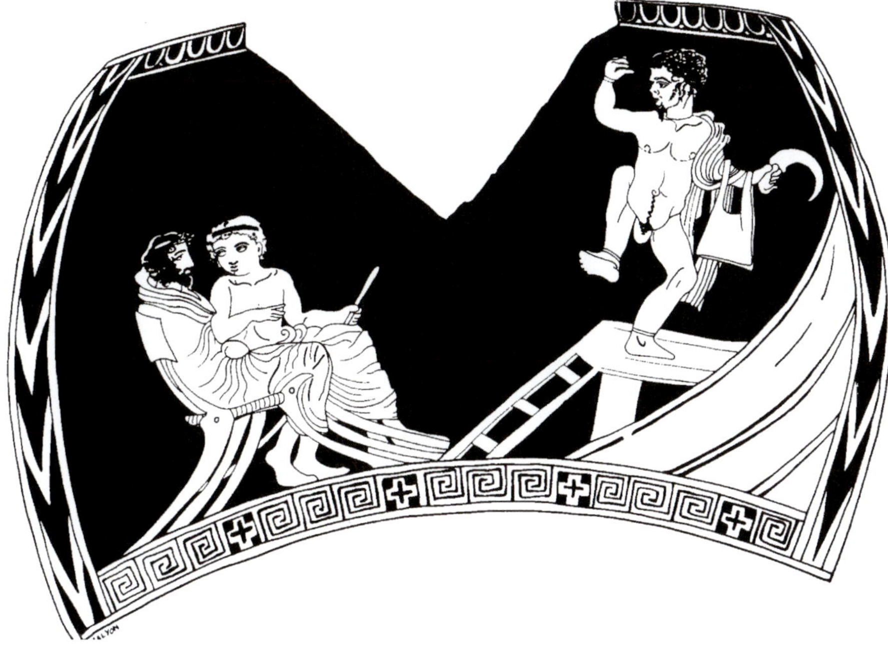

FIGURE 1.10 PS
This line drawing is an artist's impression of the badly damaged scene on the so-called Perseus Dance Vase.

Red-figure vase fragment: single actor possibly playing Perseus and two audience members/judges

Object: Attic red-figure chous (wine-jug)

Artist: unknown

Location: Vlastos Collection, Athens

Date: *c.* 420 BC

Significance: the only Attic vase to show a stage, and the only ancient Greek painting to portray a theatre audience

The wheel platform and crane

As theatre-goers today, we take for granted a number of special effects which help us to imagine the scene before us – a play will normally be supported by features such as sophisticated lighting, amplified sound and an intricate set. This enables us to 'suspend our disbelief' and to believe more readily in the action on stage. The Greek theatre, by contrast, had no such advantages. It relied instead on daylight, outstanding acoustics and the ability of the spectators to play along with the dramatic illusion. Oliver Taplin has therefore described the Greek theatre as 'the theatre of the mind' – a helpful phrase which emphasises that an ancient spectator had to make a much greater leap of imagination than we do today. Often, playwrights tried to help this process by giving the audience information about the setting, particularly at the start of a play.

However, there were two devices commonly used to provide special effects. One was a **wheel platform** (in Greek it was called the ekkyklēma, literally meaning 'something wheeled out'), which was probably simply a wooden platform on wheels brought out onto the stage through the main door. It was used to portray a scene that had happened indoors – in tragedy it often presented the body of a character who had died off-stage. The following **scholion** gives a sense of this (a scholion is a comment by an ancient commentator inserted in the margin of an ancient manuscript):

> It would show things which appear to be happening indoors, e.g., in a house, to those outside as well (I mean the spectators).

Scholion to Aristophanes' Acharnians l. 408

Some believe that the wheel platform may have been produced differently, since sources also speak of it revolving. By this system, the main door revolved around on a circular piece of floor beneath it, revealing an indoor scene.

wheel platform a wooden platform on wheels brought on stage which showed a scene that had happened off-stage

scholion a comment inserted into a manuscript by an ancient commentator

FIGURE 1.11
An artist's impression of three acting levels of the Athenian stage, along with the wheel platform and crane.

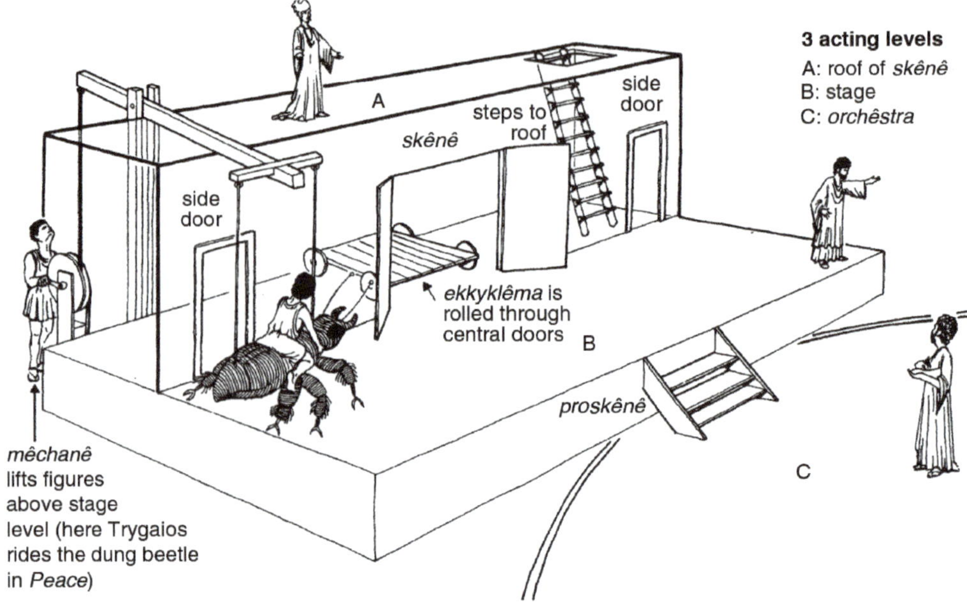

crane a device which raised an actor above the level of the skēnē building

The second device was a **crane** (in Greek, mēchanē, literally 'machine'). This was positioned behind the skēnē and used to hoist characters into the air above the roof. In tragedy, a god might be elevated to make an appearance at the end of a play to sort out human affairs. From this we still use the Latin phrase deus ex machina ('a god from the machine') to describe the intervention of an unexpected piece of good luck to resolve a difficult situation.

We get an amusing insight into the use of the crane in Aristophanes' comedy *Peace*, where the crane itself becomes a source of humour. The play's hero is an Athenian farmer, Trygaios, who flies to heaven on the back of a giant dung-beetle to rescue the goddess Peace and bring her back to war-torn Greece. As Trygaios rides on the crane (which is decorated to look like a dung-beetle), the actor breaks the dramatic illusion and speaks directly to the crane operator:

> He-e-elp! No, I mean it, this is serious! Here, you down there, the crane-handler, do
> for heaven's sake be a bit more careful! I've already got breezes in my stomach, and
> if you don't watch out I'll be giving the beetle the meal!

Aristophanes, Peace 173–6

The meal he is suggesting, of course, is the contents of his bowels!

The first certain use of the crane in tragedy comes in Euripides' *Medea*, presented in 431. The play ends with Medea escaping punishment for killing her own children by being carried off in a chariot supplied by her grandfather, the sun god. She had committed this terrible crime because the children's father, Jason, had divorced her so he could marry the daughter of the king of Corinth. The final scene involves a dialogue between Medea, who takes the place of the gods on the crane, and Jason, who remains helpless and distraught on the stage.

The vase in Figure 1.12 is dated to a few decades after this, and its painting seems to have been inspired by the play's final scene. The focus is on Medea, who flies above the

Study Question
Read ll. 1–12 (1–10) of Euripides' *Bacchae*. What information does the playwright give to the spectators so that they can visualise the scene more clearly?

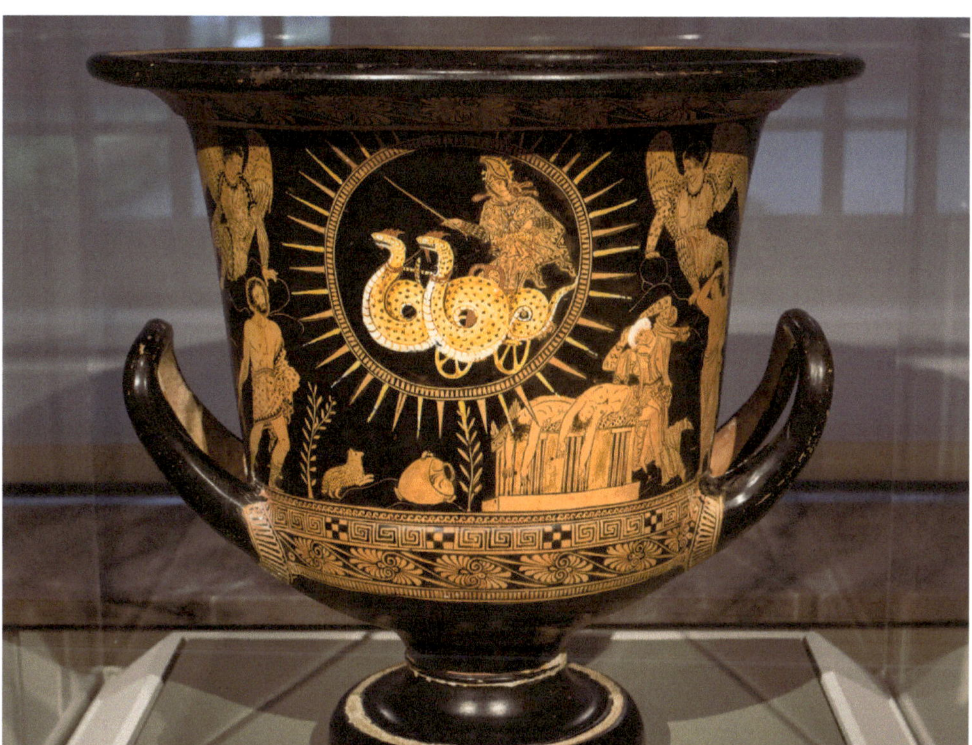

FIGURE 1.12
Medea's escape.

PRESCRIBED SOURCE

Red-figure calyx krater depicting Medea's escape

Object: calyx krater (mixing-bowl)

Artist: attributed to the Policoro Painter

Location: Cleveland Museum of Art

Date: *c.* 400 BC

Significance: a painted scene of Medea's escape which seems to portray the use of the crane and the wheel platform

human scene on a chariot drawn by dragons which is circled by a figure of the sun. On either side, two hideous winged female creatures, perhaps Furies, look down on the scene, where the murdered sons are slumped on what seems to be the wheel platform decked out to look like an altar. To the far right their tutor raises his hands in mourning, while their nurse, identifiable as an old woman by her white hair, does the same. Jason is on the left, bare-chested like a hero – in contrast to the conventions of tragic costume. The artist has heightened the intensity of the scene by having Jason and Medea lock eyes with one another.

What is perhaps most interesting about this vase is that it differs from Euripides' play in some important details. There are no Furies or dragons in the play, while Medea takes her sons with her so that she can deprive Jason of the chance to bury them. We might speculate as to the reason for these differences: perhaps this was the artist's own developed interpretation of Euripides' play, or perhaps he knew a different version of the myth, or even another version of the play. Whichever was the case, the vase reminds us that we should not assume that painted scenes of the Athenian stage are a fully accurate representation of what took place there.

THE REPRESENTATION OF ATHENIAN THEATRE IN VISUAL AND MATERIAL CULTURE

One area which has lent evidence to a number of aspects of Athenian drama is the pictorial record on vases. Athens became a major centre of production of these in the late sixth century (initially the vases were 'black figure' – black figures on a red background; in the fifth century they developed into 'red figure', which reversed the colouring).

EXPLORE FURTHER

Towards the end of his career Euripides wrote a clever scene in which all four spaces of the theatre are used – orchēstra, stage, skēnē roof and crane. Read *Orestes* lines 1549–1693, and try to work out who is speaking from which area of the theatre.

FIGURE 1.13
The so-called
Würzburg Telephus
Vase.

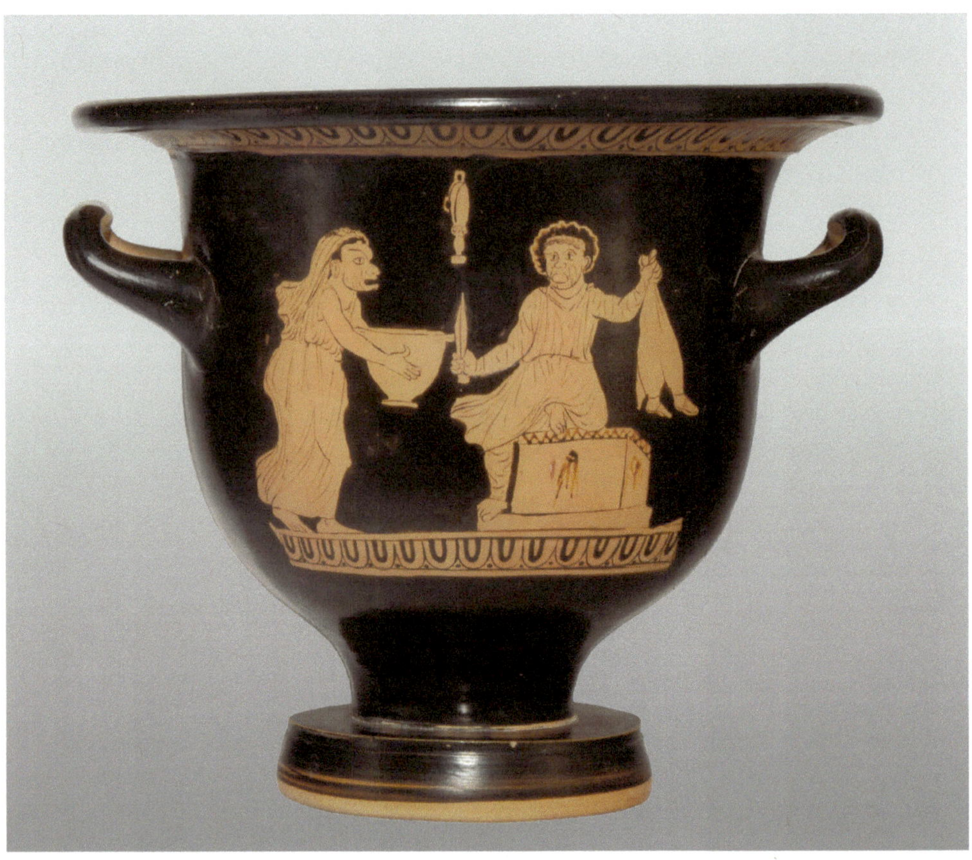

During the years that tragedy was at its zenith (*c.* 500–406), only two paintings have survived which could be interpreted to show a tragic play in performance (one of these is the Basel Vase discussed on p. 30). In addition, there are a number of vase paintings which seem to have been inspired by the performance of a tragedy, among them the Medea Vase discussed above. However, as that example illustrates, we should not assume that such paintings present an accurate representation of what happened on stage. Beyond this, we have a group of vases dated to about 400 which clearly show actors who are in costume but off-stage – the most famous is the Pronomos Vase discussed on pp. 33–5. These give us the best evidence for what masks and costumes looked like.

From *c.* 400, there was a decline in the production of Athenian pottery. However, from this time on a number of vases depicting the comic theatre have survived from the Greek cities of southern Italy, and particularly from the region of Apulia (modern Puglia). The south of Italy and Sicily was later known by the Romans as Magna Graecia ('Great Greece'), owing to the large number of Greek settlements which had been founded there before the sixth century BC. The vases found there indicate that the works of Athenian playwrights were well known in this region and were re-performed there. Some of them give us significant details of comic plays in performance, including staging and costume.

Figure. 1.13 is an example of a vase produced in Apulia. Scholars agree that it shows a scene from Aristophanes' comedy *Women at the Thesmophoria*, which was presented in 411, and so the vase bears witness to the knowledge of Athenian comedy in Magna Graecia. Indeed, for the painting on the vase to be understood properly, *Women at the Thesmophoria* must have been re-performed in at least one southern Italian theatre. This is not all: the play's plot is based on lampooning the tragedies of Euripides, suggesting that his plays were also well known in this region.

The painted scene seems to correspond closely to ll. 730–53 of the play, which is set at the all-women Athenian festival of the Thesmophoria. The plot centres on a meeting they hold to discuss what to do about Euripides, since he presents them so negatively in his plays. Euripides (who appears as a character in the play) persuades an older male relative to dress up as a woman and infiltrate the meeting to speak up for him. However, the women are informed that there is a spy in their midst and the relative's identity is revealed.

At this point in the action (ll. 730–53), the relative snatches the 'baby' of one of the women as a hostage, and runs to the altar, where he picks up a knife and threatens to kill it. In fact, the joke is that the 'baby' is really a disguised wineskin – one aspect of the play's humour is that the women spend the three days of the festival getting drunk. The woman fears that she will lose her wine if the wineskin bursts, and so rushes up with a bowl to catch it. The whole scene is a parody of a scene from a lost tragedy of Euripides, *Telephus*, from which the vase takes its name.

It is interesting to compare the vase painting with these lines from the play. There is a clear correspondence, not least in the details of the figure at the altar's costume. In the play, there is an elaborate dressing scene (ll. 210–79) in which the relative is shaved, dressed as a woman and given a woman's headband; the last is clearly visible in the painting. Most male figures on southern Italian comic vases are shown bearded, and so it is notable that this figure is clean-shaven. Furthermore, in the dressing scene the relative checks himself in a mirror, and in the painting a mirror is suspended above the centre of the scene.

TOPIC REVIEW

These questions should draw on your knowledge of the whole topic, so think carefully about the different things you have learned (check the Topic Overview on p. 4).

1. What similarities and what differences can you find between the three Athenian festivals of Dionysus and a modern arts festival of your choice?
2. In what ways could an Athenian citizen be involved in the City Dionysia festival?
3. How different would it have been to watch a play in an ancient theatre space compared to a modern theatre space?
4. To what extent can the visual and material record give us evidence for the performance of ancient Greek theatre?

Further Reading

Csapo, E. and W.J. Slater, *The Context of Ancient Drama* (Ann Arbor: University of Michigan Press, 1995).

Easterling, P.E. (ed.), *The Cambridge Companion to Greek Tragedy* (Cambridge: Cambridge University Press, 1997), Part 1.

Storey, I.C. and A. Allan, *A Guide to Ancient Greek Drama* (Chichester: John Wiley & Sons, 2014), Chapter 1.

Taplin, O., *The Stagecraft of Aeschylus: The Dramatic Use of Exits and Entrances in Greek Tragedy* (Oxford: Clarendon Press, 1977).

Wiles, D., *Greek Theatre Performance: An Introduction* (Cambridge: Cambridge University Press, 2000).

PRACTICE QUESTIONS

Source A: A pot showing the escape of Medea from a Greek tragedy, *c.* 400 BC

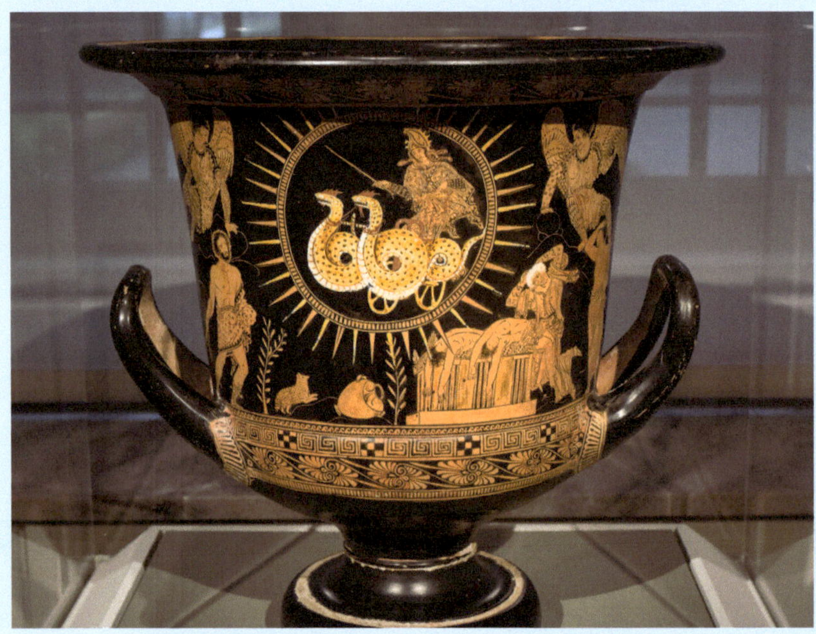

AS Level

1. This is thought to represent a scene from which play? Who was the play's author? [2]
2. Explain what Source A suggests about the staging of Greek tragedy. Make four points and support each point with reference to Source A. [8]

A Level

1. This is thought to represent a scene from which play? Who was the play's author? [2]
2. Evaluate how useful this pot is as a source of information about the staging of Greek tragedy. [10]

1.2 The Nature of Tragedy

TOPIC OVERVIEW

- the origins of tragedy and how it developed during the fifth century BC, including its relationship to satyr-plays
- the contributions of Aeschylus, Sophocles and Euripides
- use of actors and the chorus
- use of masks, costumes and props
- common themes of tragedy
- the relationship between the cultural context and subject matter of the plays
- Aristotle's theories about tragedy, including peripeteia (reversal of fortune), hamartia (tragic mistake), catharsis (purging of emotions)

Literary techniques, structure, and dramatic conventions

- styles and techniques of the different playwrights

The following prescribed sources are covered in this topic:

- Sophocles, *Oedipus the King*
- Euripides, *Bacchae*
- red-figure column krater in mannerist style, Basel Dancers
- volute krater by the Pronomos Painter, depicting a team of actors celebrating with costumes, masks, aulos player, playwright and Dionysus
- pelike by Phiale Painter depicting tragic actors dressing

Don't forget that you will be given credit in the exam if you study extra sources and make relevant use of them in your answers.

This topic examines Athenian tragedy of the fifth century BC, including how it developed, what we know about the playwrights whose work has survived, what the common features of tragedy were, and how Aristotle later came to define a good tragedy.

THE ORIGINS OF TRAGEDY

The origins of tragedy – and indeed of drama more generally – are shrouded in mystery. From the late seventh century, there are a number of vase paintings which are suggestive of links to drama, but we have no surviving dramatic text before Aeschylus' *Persians* of 472. One source gives 534 as the date when tragedy was first performed at the City Dionysia, though we have very little information about the genre at that time or how it developed during the intervening decades. When we examine this issue, therefore, we need to be aware of the limitations before us; there are a variety of sources – the texts themselves, the comments and analysis of later Greek writers, inscriptions relating to dramatic performances, the physical remains of the theatres themselves and the depiction of theatrical scenes – but often they can only give us clues rather than a certain picture.

The most influential surviving ancient text on the development of drama is a treatise, *Poetics*, by the polymath and philosopher **Aristotle**. This dates to about 330 and is our first surviving work of literary criticism – it is examined in more detail on pp. 36–8. The work focuses on analysing the genres of epic and tragedy (a second treatise on comedy has not survived). However, it is hard to know how reliable Aristotle is as a source for events which happened up to two centuries earlier. Indeed, scholars are even unsure if the *Poetics* was meant to be published or was simply a set of lecture notes. For example, Csapo and Slater give the following caution about a central passage in the work (1449a2–25):

> This is one of the most important passages about ancient drama, but it is very obviously a set of ill-written lecture notes not intended for publication. Perhaps more alarming is the thought that some of the sentences could be later additions by someone else.
>
> *The Context of Ancient Drama*, Eric Csapo and William J. Slater (University of Michigan Press, 1995), p. 99.

It is likely that by Aristotle's day, the Athenians had created their own understanding of the 'history' of drama and so his treatise should be seen as part of this understanding, which is outlined in the following paragraphs.

According to ancient sources, the birth of drama at Athens took place during the second half of the sixth century, when the city was ruled by the tyrant Peisistratus and his sons (the word 'tyrant' did not necessarily have a negative connotation at that time). They are credited with instigating a number of artistic, architectural and engineering innovations, one of which was the City Dionysia. The festival was probably first held in the middle of the century, soon after Athens had incorporated Eleutherae, a town near the border with the region of Boeotia, into its territory. Eleutherae was the home of a cult to Dionysus, and it appears that Peisistratus chose this moment to turn a rural festival into a grand civic event based in the city of Athens itself. It is worth reflecting that a festival to Dionysus, the god of wine and revelry as well as drama, was no doubt a popular choice with the Athenian people whose support the tyrant needed to maintain.

The dithyramb

Central to the worship of Dionysus was a choral dance known as the dithyramb. The historian Herodotus reports that this was invented in Corinth in the late seventh century by the song-writer Arion, and that it was performed in honour of Dionysus. What is meant by the term 'choral dance'? It was clearly an event at which people sang and danced at the same time – indeed, the Greek word 'choros' refers to both singing and dancing (the two meanings have survived in English: a choir sings, while a choreographer arranges dance movements).

Dancing has been central to many societies, and in ancient Greece people danced in choruses at weddings, funerals, athletic events, military parades and religious festivals. In sixth-century Athens, dithyrambic performances became a central feature of the new City Dionysia, and we know that during the fifth century there were dithyrambic competitions at which each of the city's ten tribes entered two choruses – one of fifty men and one of fifty boys. Each chorus had a chorēgos, just as the plays did, and so they no doubt required much planning and rehearsing.

It seems that drama developed out of the dithyramb: ancient sources report that in the second half of the sixth century, an Athenian named **Thespis** set himself apart from his chorus. Dressed in a mask and costume, he impersonated different characters from the dithyramb's subject-matter and took part in dialogues with the chorus. This seems to have been the first important step to drama as we know it – Thespis had moved away from merely singing about mythological stories to acting them out; today his name lives on in the word 'thespian'. Choral dance was to remain fundamental to Athenian plays throughout the fifth century.

However, we should remain sceptical about the identity and role of Thespis. The ancients liked to find an 'inventor' for any important literary genre, and there may not have been a single individual who invented tragedy in this manner. But whatever the process by which actors were introduced, it was an essential step in differentiating tragedy from choral song.

According to the sources, this new genre of 'drama' soon had its own competition at the City Dionysia: the first recorded contest was in 534, when Thespis was its winner. Records state that he was awarded the prize of a goat, which may explain the origin of the word 'tragedy': it appears that at the earliest plays a goat – tragos in Greek – was either awarded as a prize or sacrificed in honour of Dionysus. The Greek word tragōdia was therefore a joining of tragos and ōdē, 'song', so that it meant something like 'the song of the goatsingers'. However, we have almost no idea about the nature of the first tragic plays in the time of Thespis.

Satyr-plays

The City Dionysia was reorganised in about 501, when a different type of play was first presented. This was the **satyr-play** and, as we have seen, at the City Dionysia of the fifth century a tragic playwright had to present a satyr-play after his three tragedies. Satyr-plays seem to have been light-hearted parodies of tragedy – one Athenian commentator

FIGURE 1.14
A satyr prepares wine.
Notice the phallus and the
bushy tail.

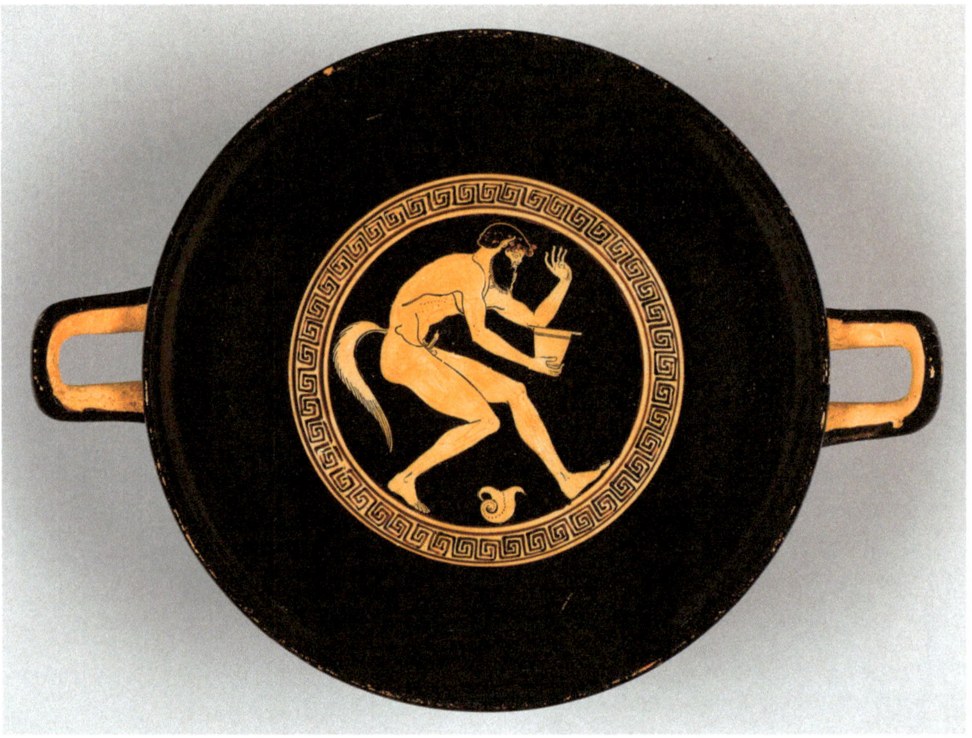

satyr a mythological
creature who was a
follower of Dionysus. In
art, satyrs are depicted as
half-human and half-animal

writing *c*. 300 BC described the genre as 'tragedy playing around'. However, since just one satyr-play has survived in its entirety (*Cyclops* by Euripides), it is unclear how such plays related to tragedy; they may have offered the audience a release after they had sat through three intense tragic dramas. It is important to remember that the prize for best tragic playwright involved judging all four plays of each playwright, and so the satyr-play was more than simply an afterthought.

Satyr-plays take their name from the fact that the choruses of these plays were made up of actors playing satyrs. A **satyr** was a mythological woodland creature, half-human, half-animal: they were followers of Dionysus, and seem to represent the basic human appetites for food, drink and sex. In myth, they usually accompany the god, drinking, dancing and revelling; artists portray them with bushy tails, snub noses, pointed ears and, most notably, large phalluses. Satyrs might be thought to symbolise the release Dionysus can offer his followers through pleasure and also point to the god's association with nature, wild animals and fertility.

Unlike tragedies, satyr-plays remained closely related to Dionysus – the god seems to have been a common character and his worship was at the heart of the action.

PLAYWRIGHTS

The variety of roles undertaken by the playwrights was extraordinary. Not only did they write every line in verse, they also composed the music; some playwrights, such as

Aeschylus, also trained and choreographed the chorus as well as acting in the play them-selves. Fifth-century Athens saw a remarkable flourishing of tragedy. In the following century, the works of three great tragedians – **Aeschylus**, **Sophocles** and **Euripides** – were marked out as classics, so that their texts were preserved and the plays re-performed, and it is these three whose plays have survived into the modern era. However, we know the names of as many as fifty tragic playwrights of the fifth century and some, such as Phrynichus, were clearly held in high regard. We have little information about tragedy in the fourth century, but there is no reason to think there were not other talented play-wrights during that period.

Aeschylus (*c.* 525–456)

Aristotle tells us that Aeschylus introduced a second actor onto the stage, a radical devel-opment from the one-actor tradition that predated him. However, this might be another example of the tendency among ancient critics to find an 'inventor' for every important change. Introducing actors could not have been done at the whim of one playwright but must have required a vote from the public, since it would have involved a greater finan-cial contribution from the state. However, Aristotle may reflect a truth that tragedy developed significantly during Aeschylus' career and that he played an important role in shaping it into the form we now understand. Whether it was Aeschylus' own innovation or not, introducing a second actor was crucial to the development of drama as we under-stand it, since it opened the possibility for dialogue between two individuals. Later in Aeschylus' career, he used a third actor (an innovation the ancients attributed to Sophocles – see below).

Although Aeschylus wrote about eighty plays, only six survive (he is sometimes also credited with a seventh, *Prometheus Bound*, but scholars have doubted whether it was written by him). All date to the last fourteen years of his career. His most famous works are the three plays which belong to the *Oresteia*, a trilogy presented in 458 (individually, the plays are *Agamemnon*, *Choephoroi* and *Eumenides*); this recounts the curse on the house of Atreus and the introduction of justice to Athens. The use of connec-ted groups of three or four plays (trilogies or tetralogies) seems to have been a speciality of Aeschylus' style, and there is no evidence that it was common in his day. It allowed him to develop themes and imagery to a greater level of sophistication, as he can trace them across the plays. This complexity comes at a price, however, and in *Frogs* Aristophanes mocks Aeschylus for writing tedious dramas, full of long silences and verbose speeches. It is certainly true that his language is dense, and this makes his dramas challenging to study. The role of the chorus is still fundamental: he makes greater use of it than the other two playwrights (this ranges from 34% of the total lines in *Eumenides* and 55% in *Suppliant Women*, compared to an average of 17% in Sophocles and 15% in Euripides).

Aristophanes portrays Aeschylus as an anti-intellectual to create a humorous contrast with the radical Euripides. However, we should not forget that Aeschylus lived through a time of great change, when Athens grew from being a relatively unimportant city-state to being the leader of a powerful empire, and attracted artists and thinkers from across

KEY INDIVIDUALS

Aeschylus

Dates: *c.* 525–456

Athenian tragic playwright

Known as the 'father of tragedy', Aeschylus may have written as many as ninety plays, but only six have survived, along with one play whose authorship is disputed

Sophocles

Dates: *c.* 496–406

Athenian tragic playwright

Sophocles wrote over one hundred plays, but only seven have survived

Euripides

Dates: *c.* 480–406

Athenian tragic playwright

Euripides may have written as many as one hundred plays, of which eighteen have survived

FIGURE 1.15
Aeschylus.

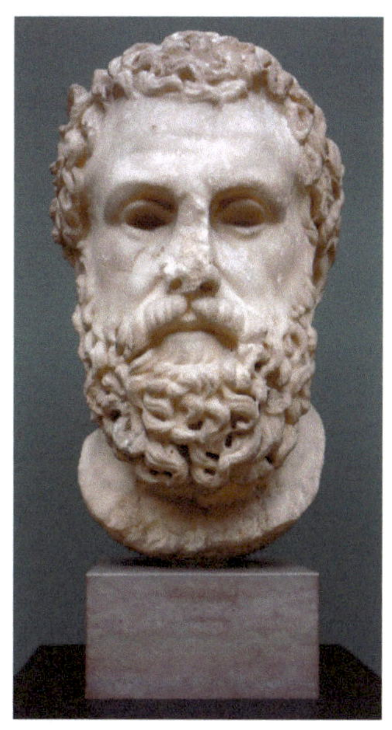

FIGURE 1.16
Sophocles.

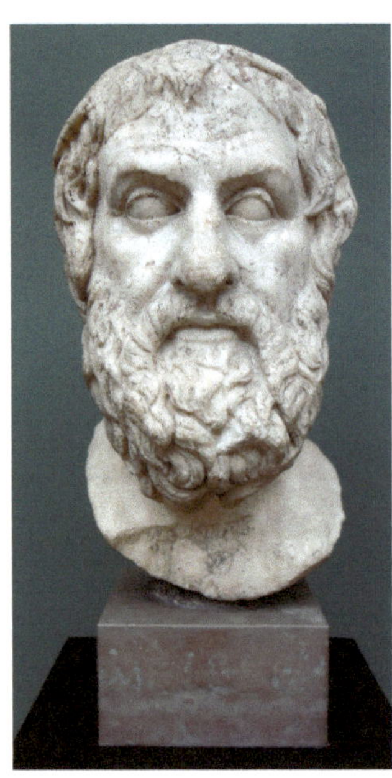

Oedipus the King

Author: Sophocles

Date: *c.* 429 BC

Genre: tragedy

Plot: a summary is downloadable from the website 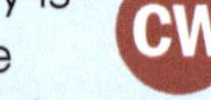

Read it here: translation by Robert Fagles, in *The Three Theban Plays* (Penguin 2008)

Note that this translation uses a different set of line numbers from the original Greek text; in this chapter, both sets of line numbers will be given for quotations, with the original Greek line numbers written first.

the Greek world. The most important events of Aeschylus' lifetime were the Persian Wars of 499–479 and his earliest surviving play, *Persians*, relates the events surrounding the defeat of the Persians at Salamis in 480. He probably fought in this battle himself, and had certainly fought at Marathon ten years earlier. Indeed, Aeschylus' epitaph records his service at Marathon and makes no mention of his career as a playwright. The epitaph also tells us that he died in Sicily, where he had apparently moved to put on his plays – so indicating that Athenian tragedy was known in the Greek west by the middle of the fifth century.

Sophocles (*c.* 496–406)

Sophocles is credited with introducing many innovations to tragedy. We are told that he introduced the third actor, increased the number of chorus members from twelve to fifteen, and made the set more atmospheric through enhancing the look of the skēnē. Unlike Aeschylus, he preferred to offer a series of unconnected plays. He also reduced the role of the chorus compared to Aeschylus.

Sophocles was very successful, winning at least eighteen contests and never coming third. Although he is believed to have written more than 120 plays, only seven survive, the most famous of which are his Theban plays, *Antigone*, *Oedipus the King* and *Oedipus at Colonos*. Though they concerned the same myth, they did not form a trilogy, and were performed years apart. He was a pre-eminent political figure in Athens, serving as a general alongside Pericles in 441, and is said to have played an important role in welcoming the new religious cult of the healing god Asclepius into Athens.

Sophocles is a master of stagecraft, and his skilled handling of structure and plot makes the plays particularly appealing to modern tastes. For example, in contrast to the prologues of Euripides, where a character typically narrates the 'story so far', Sophocles conveys this information subtly. In *Oedipus the King*, the 'back story' is introduced at different points in the play. Rather than beginning with a monologue by Oedipus telling us everything that has happened to him, the play opens with a dialogue between Oedipus and the Priest, which allows the important facts to be established in a way that seems natural and which also reveals Oedipus' personality.

Euripides (*c.* 480–406)

Euripides seems to have been more popular after his death than during his lifetime (he won just five victories, one of which was after his death, when *Bacchae* was produced). Eighteen of his plays have survived (he is sometimes credited with a nineteenth), although he is said to have written ninety-two in all. In *Frogs*, Aristophanes presents him as an unconventional playwright who liked to shock his audiences, and it is true that Euripides enjoyed innovating with myths and characters (for example, the previous versions of the Medea myth probably did not end with Medea killing her children). However, being allowed to present a play at the Dionysia was a mark of esteem, and since Euripides was regularly selected for this, we should not overstate the degree to which he was radical or unpopular.

An accident of history means that far more of Euripides' plays survive than those of Aeschylus and Sophocles. For the other two playwrights, we have only a sample of plays selected by ancient scholars for their excellence, whereas for Euripides as well as ten plays selected by scholars we have a further nine which survived by chance. This means that in the case of Euripides we have access to a group of plays selected randomly, and this gives us an insight into how diverse tragedy was. Several of these non-select plays are 'escape tragedies': plays with upbeat endings that focus on romance, mistaken identity and reunions. Euripides' *Iphigenia Among the Taurians, Ion* and *Helen* are plays of this type. Others such as *Children of Heracles* or *Suppliant Women* have a pro-Athenian stance, describing occasions when Athens saved the day.

Euripides' style is distinctive in a number of ways. His plays are more self-conscious in style. His gods appear on stage more than the other playwrights, and the characters challenge their behaviour (as, for example, at the end of *Bacchae*). Similarly, we find references to contemporary and philosophical themes.

ACTORS AND THE CHORUS

There were two distinct groups of performers in the Athenian theatre – the professional actors who played the leading roles and the amateur chorus members who were chosen from the citizen body. All the actors were male citizens, though they might have played goddesses, women, foreigners or slaves, and this did not prevent playwrights from creating a compelling range of characters.

Actors

In any tragedy, no more than three actors with speaking parts were allowed on stage at any one time (although minor characters such as children could also appear and were sometimes given a line or two). Moreover, these three actors played all the leading roles, something a playwright had to bear in mind when writing his script. Plays usually contained eight to ten different parts, and so an actor could be required to play four or even five characters. There must have been rushed moments as actors changed mask and costume inside the skēnē. For example, in Sophocles' *Oedipus the King*, the same actor was required to play the following four roles:

- the elderly **Priest** of Zeus
- **Jocasta**, Oedipus' mother and wife
- the **Shepherd** who found Oedipus as a baby
- a **Messenger** who reports Jocasta's suicide and Oedipus' self-blinding

Actors also had to be good singers, perhaps in a variety of different character roles; thus, playwrights probably wrote parts with certain actors in mind, aware of their particular vocal talents.

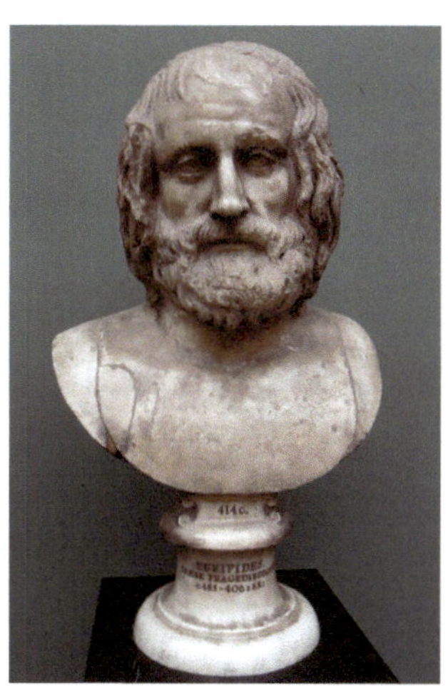
FIGURE 1.17
Euripides.

Bacchae

Author: Euripides

Date: 405 BC

Genre: tragedy

Plot: a summary is downloadable from the website 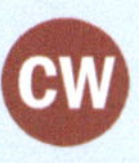

Read it here: translation by David Franklin, *Cambridge Translations from Greek Drama* (CUP 2000)

Note that this translation uses a different set of line numbers from the original Greek text; in this chapter, both sets of line numbers will be given for quotations, with the original Greek line numbers written first.

The chorus

A chorus was made up of fifteen ordinary citizens (or twelve in the early days of tragedy), something which illustrates the democratic spirit of the City Dionysia. Indeed, if the dithyrambic contests are factored in, then more than 1,000 Athenians would have competed in a chorus during the festival. We do not know how chorus members were chosen, but the competitive nature of the festival must have required a chorēgos to find the best available singers and dancers that he could: a chorēgos for tragedy selected chorus members to act in all four of the plays he was financing. Once selected, chorus members would no doubt train hard over the following months, learning and rehearsing all the words, music and dance steps, often while wearing heavy masks and costumes. Training was taken so seriously by the city that chorus members were apparently spared military service during the rehearsal period.

Each chorus had a leader who spoke individual lines in dialogue with the actors (for example commenting on what has happened or responding to a character's questions); that aside, chorus members sang and danced in unison. They were accompanied by a musician who played an **aulos**, a reed instrument similar to an oboe (the musician was called an **aulētēs**). We have little information about the music or dances, and can only guess how a choral ode may have looked or sounded. However, as we can see on the Basel Dancers Vase, the dancing probably involved the whole body, with movement of the arms and swirling of the body. They may have divided into formations of three by five (or three by four in the early years).

The vase in Figure 1.18 is thought to represent a tragic chorus in action and, if so, it is notable that it dates to the early years of the fifth century, when tragedy was still a new art-form. Three pairs of young men dance towards an altar in a choreographed rectangular formation; indecipherable letters (not visible on Figure 1.18) come out of their mouths, indicating that they are also singing. The very similar details on their faces – the hair, extended chins and gaping mouths – are perhaps the painter's way of indicating that they are wearing masks. They appear to be wearing military costumes, although on their heads are diadems rather than helmets as might be expected. They also go barefoot, which seems to have been the norm for choruses.

The altar is decked out with branches and ribbons, and a figure seems to rise from it or stand behind it. This is generally thought to be an actor playing a ghost rising from a tomb (in which case the altar represents the tomb), as happens in Aeschylus' *Persians* of 472 (and so dated after this vase). However, another interpretation is that the figure represents an icon of Dionysus which has been placed on the altar to witness the performance.

The role of the chorus

The chorus served various purposes in a play, some of which are suggested below:

- **actor**. The chorus was usually part of the action, often portraying local townsfolk: in *Oedipus the King* they are elderly citizens of Thebes. In other plays, the chorus is more detached from the locality: in *Bacchae*, they are Asian followers of Dionysus

---

aulos a double-reed musical instrument similar to an oboe

aulētēs the word for an aulos-player; each chorus was accompanied by one

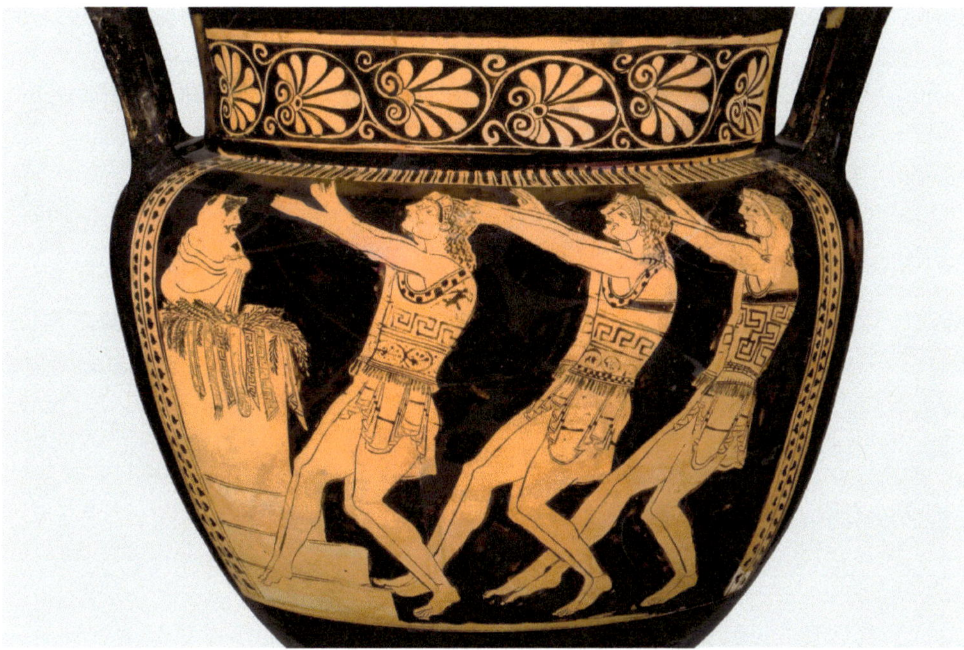

FIGURE 1.18
The Basel Dancers
Vase.

PRESCRIBED SOURCE

Red-figure column krater in mannerist style, Basel Dancers Vase

Object: red-figure column krater (mixing-bowl)

Artist: unknown; Mannerist style

Location: Antiken Museum, Basel

Date: *c.* 500–490 BC

Significance: a painting which seems to show a tragic chorus in action

- **scene-setting**. Choral songs sometimes gave the audience important background information: the opening chorus of *Agamemnon* relates the sacrifice of Iphigenia, which is crucial to understanding why Clytaemnestra wants to take revenge on her husband
- **commentator**. The chorus often stepped back from the actors and offered a commentary or moral opinion on the events of the play. For example, in *Oedipus the King*, the chorus compare Oedipus' downfall to the fragility of human happiness in general
- **wider context**. The chorus put the events of the play into a broader context by connecting them to other myths or through their moralising commentary. This helps to bridge the gap between the world of the play and that of the audience, explaining what the ramifications are of the issues explored on stage
- **background mood**. The chorus also offered a background setting to the action, acting much like the soundtrack of a film does today. In this way, it could build suspense before an act of violence, or lament after a moment of tragedy. For example, in *Oedipus the King* the chorus sing a joyous ode of optimism just before Oedipus' identity is revealed. This increases the irony and emotional tension in this scene
- **scene-break**. The most practical role of the chorus was to create a break between scenes, acting almost as a stage curtain can today. This allowed the actors to leave the stage and change costume if necessary

Study Question
In which ways could watching a Greek tragedy be compared to watching an opera or a musical today?

The music

The chorus reflects how central music was to a Greek play, and watching a tragedy is perhaps most naturally compared to watching an opera or a musical today – indeed, choral odes with their song and dance invite ready comparison with grand opera choruses. However, the main actors often sang during plays as well. This allowed playwrights to heighten emotional intensity, and one ancient commentator called Aristoxenus observed that speech began to sound like song 'when we become emotional'. For example, in *Bacchae*, Agave moves from song during her madness to speech as she begins to recover her sanity (1168–215; 997–1054). By contrast, the emotionally repressed Pentheus sings not a single line during the play.

There were two contexts in which an actor might sing during a play. One was a solo, called a **monody**, which a character often sang at moments of great distress or intensity – such a song could be compared to an operatic solo. The second, called a **kommos**, was a sung dialogue between an actor and the chorus at moments of heightened emotion in the play. In our set tragedies, there is a kommos in *Bacchae* at ll. 1168–201 (997–1043) when Agave describes killing her prey, while *Oedipus the King* has one at ll. 1297–368 (Fagles 1433–98) when the blinded Oedipus appears on stage.

monody a solo song by an actor, often sung at moments of great distress

kommos a formal song at moments of heightened emotion involving dialogue between an actor and the chorus

MASKS, COSTUMES AND PROPS

Study Question
In the absence of facial expression, how important do you think it was for actors to use physicality and tone of voice to express themselves instead?

ACTIVITY
Read ll. 453–9 (362–6) of *Bacchae*, which describe the looks of the god Dionysus. Based on this information, draw or create your own impression of what this mask might have looked like.

chitōn a full-length robe, often ornately decorated

himation a cloak reaching down to the knees

Today, facial expression is a vital part of acting and it is hard for us to imagine a play without it; the concept of actors wearing masks thus seems very alien. Yet the ancient theatre space had no artificial lighting, while many of the spectators were a significant distance from the stage. Facial expression was therefore largely redundant, and in this context the masks added to the performance. They were slightly larger than life-size to make them more visible, and tragic masks were typically painted with the solemn expressions of tragic characters. They were made of linen, cork or wood and had openings for eyeholes and the mouth, while there was often some hair attached at the top to act as a wig.

The use of masks provided some practical benefits which made them indispensable to the play. Since a play was performed by just three actors, masks allowed them to take on a range of roles. Occasionally two different actors would have been needed to play the same character – in Sophocles' *Oedipus at Colonos*, the role of Theseus could not have been played by one actor throughout. Moreover, a change of mask for a character during a play could add a great deal to the action; a famous example comes when Oedipus arrives back on stage after blinding himself in *Oedipus the King* – in the original production he must have worn a new, blood-spattered mask with darkened eye holes to reflect his blinding of himself off-stage.

In the absence of stage-lighting, masks and costumes were also an important way for the playwright to give the audience information. A distinct mask and costume would have made it easier for the audience to identify characters as soon as they arrived: gods, old men, kings, queens, paupers and slaves would all have been instantly recognisable by their garb.

The costumes of tragic actors were based on the two main items of Greek clothing: the **chitōn**, a full-length robe, over which a shorter cloak was often worn, and a **himation**, which reached down to the knees. However, in contrast to everyday clothing, the

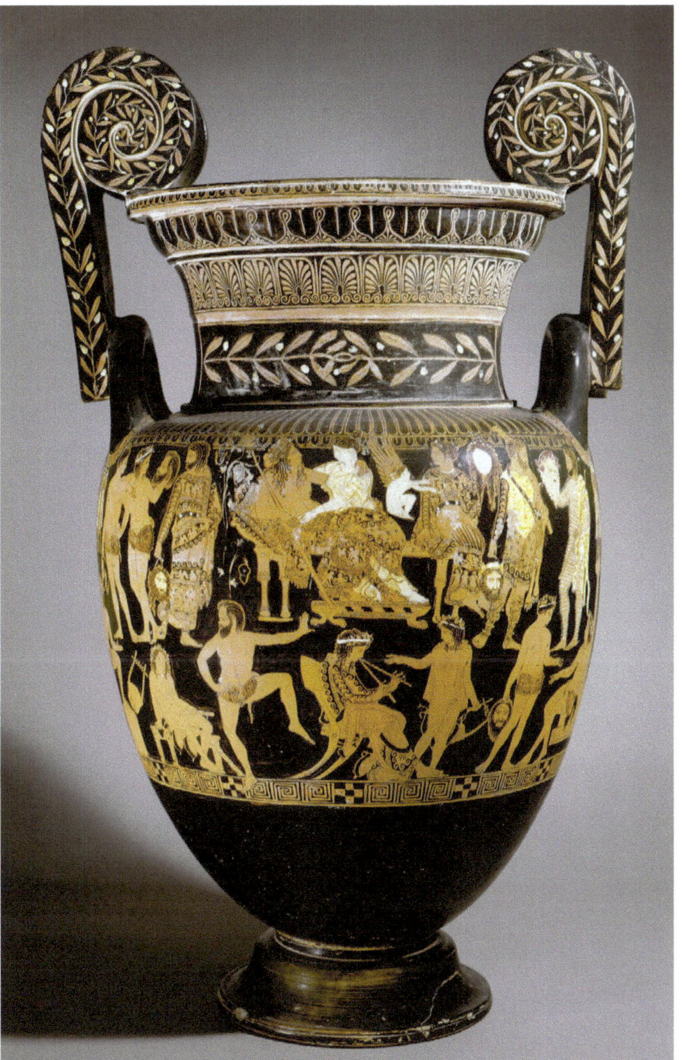

FIGURE 1.19 
The team of actors on the Pronomos Vase.

PRESCRIBED SOURCE

Volute krater by the Pronomos Painter, depicting a team of actors celebrating with costumes, masks, aulos player, playwright and Dionysus

Object: volute krater (mixing-bowl)

Artist: the Pronomos Painter

Location: Museo Nazionale Archeologico, Naples

Date: *c.* 410 BC

Significance: a southern Italian vase painting depicting actors preparing for a satyr-play

evidence from vase paintings suggests that tragic costumes were more closely fitted, had sleeves and were often ornate and colourful, with a rich patchwork of different patterns. Tragic costumes therefore reflected the grand and heroic characters of the genre. Some roles required specific costumes: paupers were dressed in plainer robes, black was reserved for mourners, soldiers wore armour and barbarians wore trousers. On their feet actors wore soft leather boots, **kothornoi**, which reached up to the thigh.

kothornoi soft leather boots which reached up to the thigh

The Athenian theatre did not naturally lend itself to the use of many props, since so many of the spectators were sitting far from the acting area. However, larger props could have great power – in *Bacchae*, Agave appears on stage at l. 1167 (997) holding the severed head of her son, which remains in full view as she begins to realise what she has done; a prop of some sort must have been used during this scene – quite probably the mask used for the character of Pentheus.

The Pronomos Vase (Figures 1.19 and 1.20) is the most famous vase to depict an ancient theatrical scene. It shows a team of tragic actors and chorus members off-stage

FIGURE 1.20
A scene on the Pronomos Vase, showing actors holding their masks.

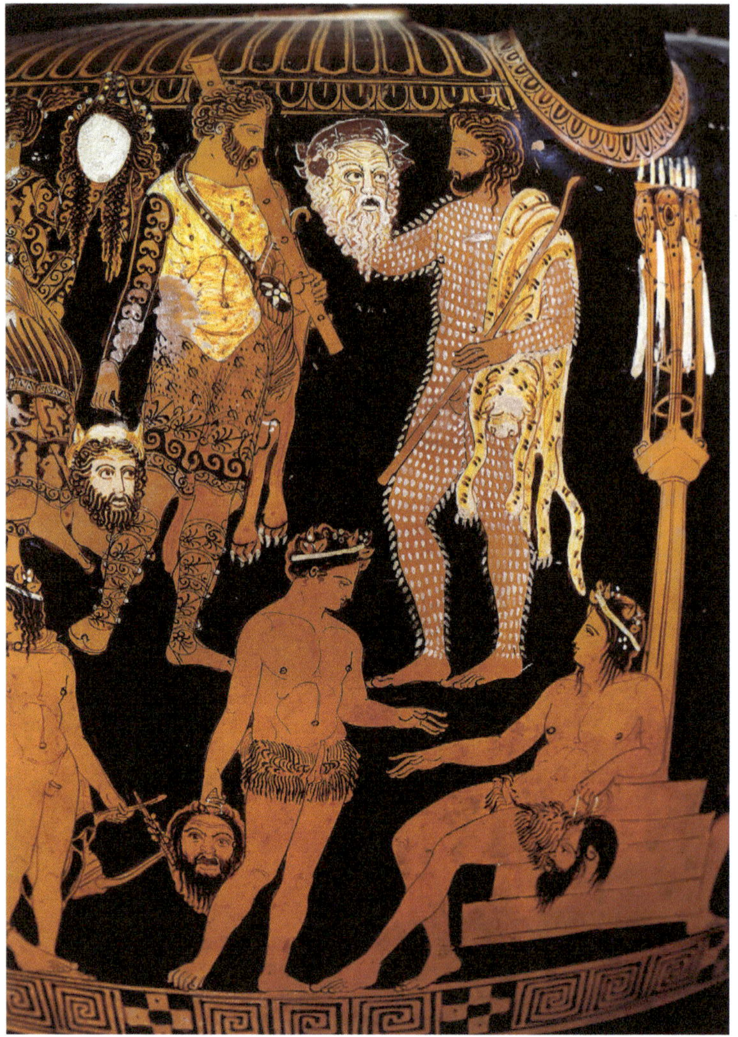

but in costume for a satyr-play. Many of the actors have their real-life names inscribed beside them, and scholars have named the vase after Pronomos, the aulos-player at the centre of the scene. This Pronomos is also known from literary sources – he was from Thebes, and one of the most famous musicians of the late fifth century. Above him on the vase is Dionysus, who seems to be sitting with his consort Ariadne; further along the bench is another female figure carrying a female mask; she may be a personification of the genre of the satyr-play. Two down from Pronomos on the left is Demetrios, who seems to be the playwright as he holds a scroll. The vase also shows some chorus members dressed as satyrs.

The vase offers us good evidence for the type of masks and costumes used in Athens at the end of the fifth century. It shows that the tragic mask at this period was quite plain and not heavily stylised. As Taplin has commented, 'It looks as though the "neutrality" of the mask was ready to take its "expression" from the tragedy rather than imposing a certain tone upon it.' By contrast, the costumes show great decoration and intricate design, with patterns and figures of people and animals. Also visible are the tightly fitting

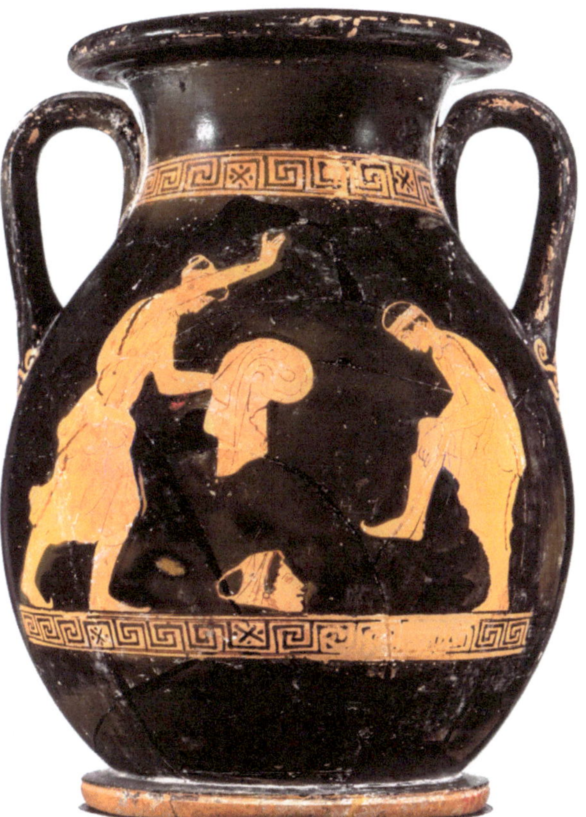

PRESCRIBED SOURCE

Pelike by Phiale Painter depicting tragic actors dressing

Object: red-figure pelike (storage jar)

Artist: Phiale Painter

Location: Museum of Fine Arts, Boston

Date: *c.* 450 BC

Significance: a painting which shows tragic actors getting into costume

sleeves – these hid the age and gender of the actor, and so allowed him to change roles during the play more convincingly.

On the vase in Figure 1.21 we can see two tragic actors or chorus members getting into costume. Both are dressing up as women; the actor on the left is already in full costume, including his mask which is indicated by the gaping mouth. The actor on the right puts on one of his high boots, while his life-like mask lies on the floor beside him. The boots used by tragic actors had thin soft soles and turned up toes that allowed them to move around easily.

THEMES AND CULTURAL CONTEXT

By the early fifth century, Greek tragedy had come to focus on life's deepest questions, and in particular on the nature of suffering: in particular, why do people suffer and to what extent can they control their own destiny? A related theme was the nature of heroism in the face of suffering. Tragedy rarely gave easy answers to such fundamental questions of human life. Indeed, many plays leave the intense pain of their protagonists unresolved – *Oedipus the King* is one good example. In such cases, the audience was invited to suffer with the tragic hero (the Greek verb 'to suffer with' was 'sympathein', from which we derive 'sympathy'). Some tragedies do end on a happier note, with much of the pain resolved. For example, in Aeschylus' *Eumenides* a potential catastrophe is avoided, while in some of Euripides' escape tragedies the movement during the play is from chaos to a more settled situation. However, in such plays the audience still watches a hero who has to engage with great suffering. For example, Euripides' *Helen* shows Helen reunited with Menelaus and the happy couple defeating a dastardly Egyptian king and escaping to Greece. Yet the play still depicts Helen's loneliness and fear, and her grief at knowing her reputation has been unfairly sullied.

Tragic playwrights tended to set their plays in the world of myth, although there were exceptions to this rule. A famous one was presented in 493, when Phrynichus presented *The Fall of Miletus* which depicted the destruction of a Greek city in Asia Minor by the Persians in the previous year. Athens had close ties to Miletus, and the historian Herodotus reports that the audience reacted with great distress to this play. Perhaps this encouraged playwrights to avoid depicting historical events since of our thirty-two surviving tragedies only one – Aeschylus' *Persians* – depicts an historical event (and *Persians* had a very different feel to *The Fall of Miletus*, since it portrays the suffering of the Persian royal family in the aftermath of their defeat by the Greeks). All the other plays were set in the world of Greek mythology, meaning that the audience usually knew the outline of the plot in advance and the interest focused on how the playwright had chosen to interpret it. Different playwrights often wrote plays based on the same myth; for example, we have a play about Electra from each of the three great tragedians.

The world of myth allowed the playwrights to challenge their audience – through the safer distance of the heroic past – with difficult issues. Most commonly, tragedy engaged with themes such as relationships within the family, between the sexes, between mortals and immortals, between the individual and the polis; and the conduct of the polis in its home and foreign affairs. The mythological setting did not prevent playwrights from making their plays relevant to contemporary society. For example, Aeschylus' *Eumenides* seeks to explain the origins of the Athenian legal system just after it had undergone a major and controversial set of reforms. Moreover, if Sophocles' *Oedipus the King* was presented in the early 420s (as many scholars believe it was), then its opening must have reminded the Athenian audience of the horrific plague which had struck their city in 430. Meanwhile, some of Euripides' plays, such as the *Trojan Women* and *Andromache*, posed powerful questions about the nature and ethics of war at a time when Athens was engaged in a brutal conflict with Sparta.

ARISTOTLE ON TRAGEDY

Aristotle's analysis of tragedy in his *Poetics* is very famous, but any study of it should begin with a strong word of caution: *Poetics* was written about a century after many of the tragic plays known to us, and we have no way of knowing if Aristotle's ideas were shared by fifth-century Athenians. All too often, his commentary has been assumed by modern readers to reflect the 'standard' Greek view of tragedy, but there is simply no evidence that this was actually the case. Moreover, at times it is unclear exactly what Aristotle means to say in his text – scholars still debate important aspects of it today.

Definition

Aristotle famously begins his analysis of tragedy with the following definition:

> Tragedy is the representation of a serious and complete set of events, having a certain magnitude, with embellished language used distinctly in the various parts of the play; the representation being accomplished by people performing and not by narration, and through fear and pity achieving the catharsis of such emotions.
>
> Aristotle, *Poetics* 1449b

The 'embellished language' refers to the fact that actors spoke in verse and that the choral songs and monodies were sung; the reference to acting rather than narrative sets tragedy apart from epic poetry (which is also a focus of *Poetics*). The next phrase indicates that Aristotle expects a tragic audience to experience fear and pity, but more controversial is the reference to a **catharsis** of these emotions. The word 'catharsis' is Greek (it means something like 'cleansing') and is the exact word used in the text here, but its meaning has been widely debated by scholars. It could be that Aristotle feels that a tragedy allows spectators to be cleansed of any unwanted excess of fear and pity, or it could suggest that fear and pity are unhealthy emotions which need to be released, and a tragedy helps people do that.

> **catharsis** a word meaning 'cleansing' or 'purification' – Aristotle hoped that watching a tragedy would give spectators a catharsis from their fear and pity

The tragic hero

Aristotle is clear about the sort of person a tragic hero should be. He should not be morally perfect, but nor should he be despicable. Instead, he claims:

> What is left lies in between these: the situation will involve a person who is not outstanding in either virtue or just behaviour, who falls into bad fortune through not vice or wickedness, but through some mistake [*hamartia*], one of those who enjoys great reputation and prosperity.
>
> Aristotle, *Poetics* 1453a

By this definition, the tragic hero must be someone of high status who makes a serious mistake. The Greek word for mistake, **hamartia**, is only used on this occasion in *Poetics*, and has been the source of much misinterpretation, with the erroneous translation 'character flaw' applied to it. A hamartia need not imply that a hero has a specific character flaw (though heroes often do have significant flaws), but that he or she makes a mistake which has terrible consequences.

> **hamartia** a word which meant 'mistake' – in a tragedy, such a mistake led to a disastrous outcome

The plot

Aristotle argues that the best tragic play has a single plotline which is complex. The plot should have three key elements: suffering, recognition and 'reversal'. The notion of suffering speaks for itself, while recognition typically involves a secret coming to light,

> **peripeteia** a terrible reversal of fortune in a tragedy

so that characters move from ignorance to understanding. 'Reversal' is a translation of the Greek word **peripeteia**, which literally means 'a turning right about'; a peripeteia occurs when a situation seems to develop in one direction, then suddenly 'reverses' to another. One of the examples Aristotle gives for this comes from *Oedipus the King*: when Oedipus hears of the death of Polybus, the news seems good until he learns that he was adopted, and so it proves to be disastrous.

EXPLORE FURTHER

Aristotle's *Poetics* is a relatively short text – read it yourself to find out more about his theory of tragedy.

S & C Find out about the technique of 'drama therapy' which is used today. Are there any ways in which the ideas of Aristotle about tragedy foreshadow this technique?

TOPIC REVIEW

These questions should draw on your knowledge of the whole topic, so think carefully about the different things you have learned (check the Topic Overview on p. 23).

1. How believable do you find the traditional Athenian view of tragedy's development?
2. How different do the three playwrights seem to you? What would be most useful to know more of about them?
3. How different would it have been to watch actors perform in the Athenian theatre compared to today?
4. Choose a tragedy from any era with which you are familiar (e.g. a Shakespeare play, a modern film). How applicable to it do you find Aristotle's ideas about tragedy?

Further Reading

Aristotle, *Poetics*.

Easterling, P.E. (ed.), *The Cambridge Companion to Greek Tragedy* (Cambridge: Cambridge University Press, 1979), Part 2.

Gregory, J., *A Companion to Greek Tragedy* (Oxford: Blackwell, 2005).

Landels, J., *Music in Ancient Greece and Rome* (Abingdon: Routledge, 1998), Chapter 1.

Sommerstein, A., *Greek Drama and Dramatists* (London: Routledge, 2002).

Storey, I.C. and A. Allan, *A Guide to Ancient Greek Drama* (Chichester: John Wiley & Sons, 2014), Chapters 2 and 3.

Swift, L., *Greek Tragedy* (London: Bloomsbury, 2016).

Source A: Greek vase showing a troupe of actors, *c.* 410 BC

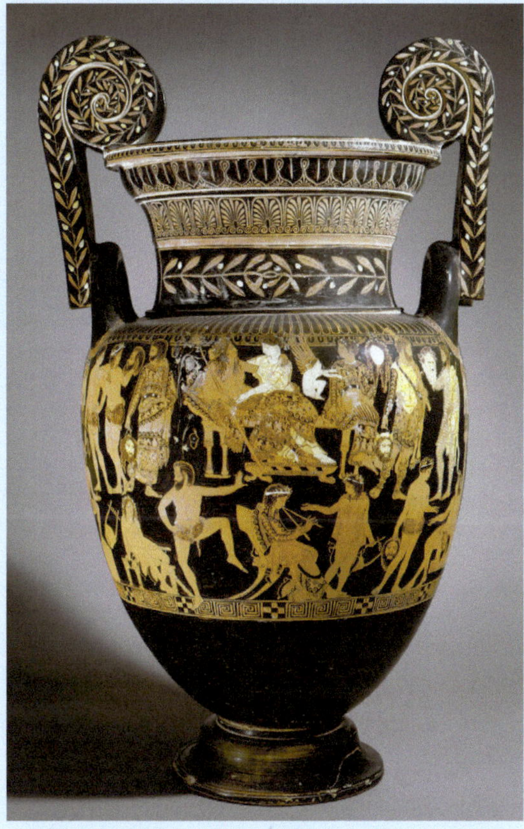

AS Level

1. Which character is this vase named after? What is his role in the cast of characters? [2]
2. How much can we learn about the performance of Greek tragedy from vase paintings? You may use Source A as a starting point, and your own knowledge. [16]

A Level

1. Which character is this vase named after? This character was a real person – give two details known about his life. [3]
2. 'We can only learn a very limited amount about the performance of Greek tragedy from visual sources.' Using Source A as a starting point, explain how far you agree with this statement and justify your response. [20]

1.3 The Nature of (old) Comedy

This topic examines Athenian comedy of the fifth century, including how it developed, what we know about Aristophanes, the only comic playwright of whom we have complete plays, and what the common features of comedy were.

THE ORIGINS AND DEVELOPMENT OF COMEDY

As with tragedy and satyr-plays, comedy seems to have emerged out of the worship of Dionysus. A key element in festivals of Dionysus was the **kōmos**, or 'revel', during which men came out into the streets of the city, drinking, singing and dancing in honour of the god: indeed, the kōmos is a good example of how Dionysus was a god who could relieve people of their daily troubles through wine. In *Bacchae*, Tiresias explains this aspect of the god to a Pentheus:

> . . . he discovered and gave to mortals a drink, the juice of the grape. It puts an end to the pain of suffering humans, when they are filled with the stream of the vine, and it gives sleep to forget the troubles of the day; there is no other cure for pain.

Euripides, *Bacchae*, 279–83 (225–8)

Another key element of the kōmos was the icon of the human phallus: during their song and dance, revellers held aloft leather phalluses as a way of giving thanks to Dionysus. He was commonly associated with the life force, so that the phallus was a symbol of his power and ability to bring new life. Human fertility was a key concern in ancient Greece (as it has been in all pre-industrial societies), since human life was precarious, particularly when it involved pregnancy and childbirth. It is generally agreed that comedy emerged from the songs and dances of the kōmos: in Greek, kōmōidia, from which we derive 'comedy', literally meant 'the song of the kōmos'. As we shall see, the phallus remained a prominent symbol in Greek comedies, where it was worn as part of the costume.

The first recorded entry for a comedy at the City Dionysia was in 486, but we know little about comedy in the early decades of the fifth century. Indeed, our detailed knowledge of fifth-century comedy really only concerns one playwright, **Aristophanes**, who lived between *c.* 450 and 386; his first recorded comic play was presented in 427. We do have references to other comic playwrights, as well as fragments from their plays. For example, Cratinus was active between *c.* 454 and 423 and we know the titles of twenty-four of his plays. Eupolis, a friend of Aristophanes, is often also thought of as his main rival. He was writing between 429 and 411 and we know of the titles of fifteen of his plays; he was very successful, winning three times at the City Dionysia and four times at the Lenaia.

Other playwrights such as these were treated with equal importance to Aristophanes by scholars in the great library of Alexandria during the third and second centuries BC. However, for reasons that remain unclear, only the plays of Aristophanes were preserved into late Antiquity – and in this case, only one copy of eleven of his plays, although he wrote around forty in all.

Since Aristophanes began his career in the early 420s, he was writing at the same time as both Sophocles and Euripides for about twenty years. Although only eleven of his plays have survived intact, we have fragments of many others. The majority were written during the years of the Peloponnesian War (431–404) fought between Athens and Sparta, as well as their respective allies, and these years were a time of particularly lively political life in Athens. As we shall see, his plays were often intensely satirical, making fun of public life and public figures; although he was writing to entertain, his work offers an insight into the political issues of the day.

KEY INDIVIDUAL

Aristophanes

Dates: *c.* 450–386

Athenian comic playwright.

Known as the father of comedy, Aristophanes wrote forty plays, eleven of which have survived

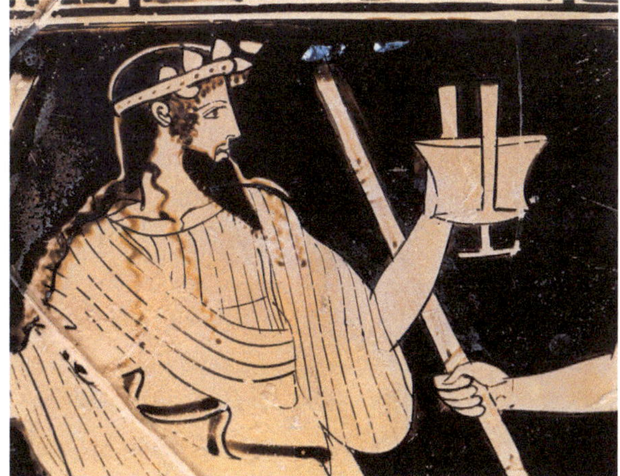

FIGURE 1.22
Dionysus holds up a wine cup.

During the fourth century, comedy changed a great deal in nature, not least since the importance of the chorus was reduced significantly. By the 320s, a new form of comedy had emerged which was far less political than the plays of the fifth century; this is conventionally referred to today as 'New Comedy', and so the plays of the fifth century are therefore often referred to as 'Old Comedy'.

ACTORS AND THE CHORUS

Although comedy had the same distinction between leading actors and chorus as tragedy, there were important differences between the two genres when it came to acting. For a start, it is likely that comedy allowed a fourth leading actor to appear on stage (although some scholars dispute this). Second, a comic chorus consisted of twenty-four members rather than the twelve or fifteen of tragedy; moreover, in some plays a chorus was divided into two semi-choruses of twelve, each of which supported a different side of the argument in the play. Another key difference was that comic actors sometimes broke the dramatic illusion by acknowledging the presence of the spectators and at times even addressing them directly (especially during the parabasis, which is discussed on pp. 52–3).

Costumes and masks

Perhaps the most noticeable difference between the two was their respective costumes and masks. Those of comedy were designed to make the actors look ridiculous and build up the element of farce. A comic actor wore a short tunic, a cloak reaching just below the waist, and tights. The whole costume was thickly padded, especially around the midriff and backside, which made an actor seem shorter and rounder than he actually was. It also enabled him to fall and roll around, since comedy often contained physical humour and slapstick – there were times when a comic actor would have behaved more like a circus clown does today. Another key element was the oversized leather phallus, which may well have been attached by a string to the tunic so that an actor could simulate an erection. The phallus could be a source of humour: in *Wasps*, the old man Philocleon offers his to the music-girl as a hand-rope for her to pull herself up onto the stage.

Sometimes costumes must have been especially colourful or ridiculous, and plays with titles such as *Birds*, *Clouds*, *Frogs* and *Wasps* suggest that costume designers were given entertaining challenges – in the case of *Birds*, the text makes clear that the chorus consisted of twenty-four different types of bird.

Comic masks were also different from those of tragedy. Facial features were grossly exaggerated and mouths often ridiculously large. Some plays satirised public figures (most notably the politician Cleon, the philosopher Socrates and the playwright Euripides) and the masks of these characters must have parodied their real looks: the real Socrates, who was present to watch himself portrayed in *Clouds*, is said to have got to his feet during the performance so that the audience could compare the likeness to his stage character.

The vase in Figure 1.23 was painted in the south of Italy and shows what seems to be a scene from a comedy. Four figures are on a low stage; to the left, a figure has emerged

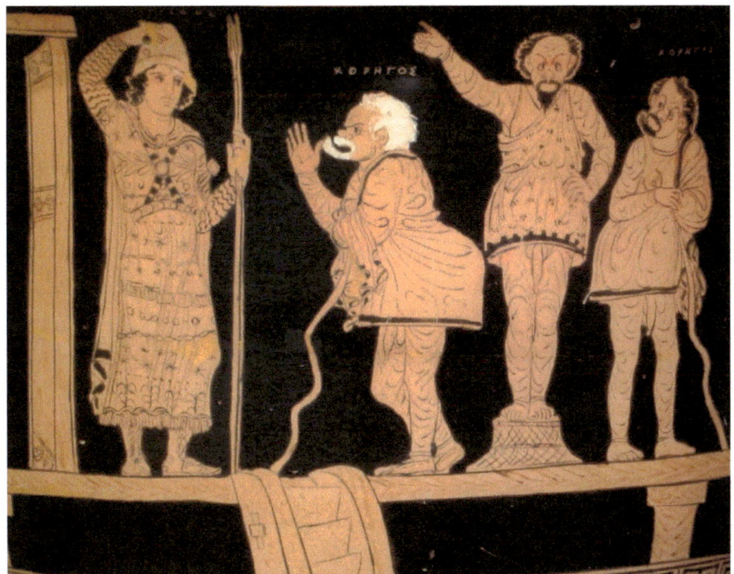

FIGURE 1.23
The Choregos Vase.

from the door of the skēnē; the name above his head says 'Aegisthus', a major character in the myth of Agamemnon and Clytaemnestra. He is clearly dressed as a tragic actor, with his ornate and stylised clothing, laced kothornoi and serious expression. The other three figures to his right are comic actors with grotesque masks; the middle one is standing on a wool basket and pointing; his name is Pyrrhias. Either side of him, the two figures both carry the label 'chorēgos' above. It is clear that one figure is much older than the other.

It is uncertain what is happening in this scene. One theory is that it depicts a comic competition between Aegisthus and Pyrrhias, who represent the genres of tragedy and comedy respectively. The chorēgoi would therefore be part of the chorus, which was perhaps divided into two, with one semi-chorus of older characters supporting tragedy and the other of younger characters supporting comedy. However, this solution only works if the painter has used artistic licence to place the two chorus members on stage. Whatever the correct interpretation, this vase is useful since it allows a direct comparison between the costumes of tragic and comic actors.

The black-figure vase in Figure 1.24 shows an aulētēs on the left playing his aulos – this motif is commonly used by painters to indicate a theatrical or choral scene. Dancing

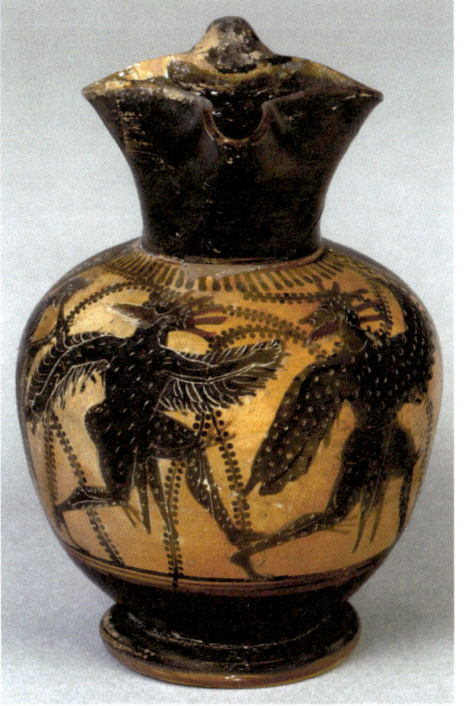

FIGURE 1.24
Two chorus members dressed as birds.

to the tune are two bearded figures dressed as birds, with purple crests on their heads and feathers attached to their knees. They both have dappled skins, with tails hanging down behind, and wings clearly visible on their arms. The vine branches in the background are suggestive of Dionysus.

This is not the only scene of an animal chorus in Greek art. It is significant that this vase dates to the early fifth century, and it shows that such choruses were well known then. Indeed, it may even give some indications as to the origins of comedy. Later in the century, Aristophanes famously presented some comedies with animal choruses, including *Birds*, which was first performed in 414. This vase indicates that the idea of animal choruses – and bird choruses in particular – predates Aristophanes by many decades at least.

HUMOUR AND COMIC TECHNIQUES

The costumes and masks alone illustrate how different comedy was from tragedy in nature. There were other marked differences, not least that where tragedy had carefully developed plots, those of comedy were far looser. A helpful contrast is made by Ian Storey and Arlene Allan:

> Farce or fantasy might be more appropriate descriptions of what Aristophanes created. Old comedy depends not on a complicated plot of intrigue or a subtle interaction between characters, but on the working out of a great idea, the more bizarre the better. Imagine a fantastic idea, wind it up and let it run, watch the splendidly 'logical' conclusions unfold, and let the whole thing end in a riotous final scene.
>
> *A Guide to Ancient Greek Drama,* Ian J. Storey and A. Allan
> (Oxford: Blackwell, 2006), p. 174

In *Frogs*, the great idea is that Dionysus can travel to the underworld to bring back one of Athens' great playwrights; in *Birds* it is that two Athenians can create a utopian society in the sky; in *Women at the Thesmophoria* it is that a man can infiltrate an all-women festival to defend Euripides. All these plays, and others, also have a conflict as a central feature and the final point made in the quotation above is therefore important: unlike tragedies, comedies usually finished with a happy ending, often involving a banquet or wedding.

A further difference between the two genres was the context: while tragedy was typically set in the world of myth, comedy included characters from everyday Athenian life, either public figures or character stereotypes. Consequently, the audience were not usually familiar with a comic storyline in advance, and comic prologues were longer so that they could introduce the plot and main characters.

The scene on Figure 1.25 from an unknown comedy is thought to show a parody of the myth of the centaur Cheiron healed by Apollo, and it illustrates the role that farce and slapstick played. On the left is a theatre set: steps lead up to a stage backed by a doorway with an overhanging porch – this is believed to represent the entrance to the temple of Apollo at Delphi. At the top of the steps up to the stage is a comic actor – the writing above indicates that he is playing the part of Xanthias ('blondie'), a common name for a slave in Greek comedy. He helps someone below him up onto the stage, and this character is identified on the pot as Cheiron, famous in Greek myth as a wise centaur who was a great teacher and healer.

In the myth, Cheiron was terribly wounded by the arrows of Heracles, and this is perhaps a feature of the plot in this play. Behind him in the image is another actor pushing him up the steps – in fact, this actor is playing the 'rear' of the centaur (a centaur had the body of a horse and the neck and head of a man), in much the same way as we might see an actor today playing the back of a pantomime horse. To the right is a young man, quite possibly the hero Achilles, who was tutored by Cheiron; at the top right, a separate scene shows two nymphs conversing, and their presence perhaps reflects the fact that Cheiron bathed in a stream sacred to a group of nymphs after his wounding.

Since this painting clearly depicts a scene from a comedy, it provides a good insight into comic costume. Xanthias is wearing a short bordered tunic over the top of an undergarment with sleeves, and tights in a one-piece suit; his phallus is clearly visible and his midriff heavily padded. His mask is indicated by the snub nose and large mouth. Cheiron's costume is similar, but his mask has different features: white hair, shaggier eyebrows, and eyes closed to indicate blindness. His age is shown by his use of a staff to walk. The actor who plays his rear is presented similarly. The costumes of the other three characters seem more sober, but the nymphs are shown to be wearing masks by their protruding lips and open, gaping mouths.

A further source of humour is often found in the language used by Aristophanes. On the one hand, he could be crude and even obscene, using the Greek equivalents of English four-letter words to describe sex, bodily functions and for his characters to abuse each other. This was in marked contrast to the formal language of tragedy and satyr-plays (this was one significant difference between comedies and satyr-plays). On the other hand, Aristophanes also composed beautiful monodies and choral lyrics. Moreover, he was very inventive, often making up new words for the purpose of the play. One notable example comes in *Clouds*, a play which makes fun of the new learning of Greek intellectuals, some of whom are described in Greek as follows (transliterated with an English translation below):

Thouriomanteis, iatrotechnas, sphragidonuchargokometas,
kuklion te choron asmatokamptas, andras meteorphenekas

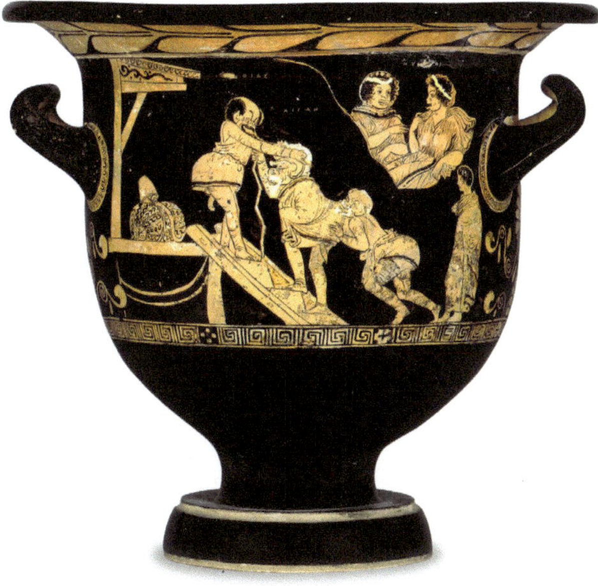

FIGURE 1.25
The Cheiron Vase.

PRESCRIBED SOURCE

Bell krater by McDaniel Painter, Cheiron Vase

Object: red-figure bell krater (mixing-bowl)

Artist: the McDaniel Painter

Location: British Museum, London

Date: *c*. 380–370 BC

Significance: a southern Italian vase painting depicting a scene from a comedy

Thourian-prophets, medical-experts, long-haired-layabouts-with-onyx-signet-rings,
song-twisters for the dithyrambic-chorus, meteorological quacks

Aristophanes, *Clouds* 332–3

Another example of Aristophanes' linguistic inventiveness has survived into modern
English. When the two leading characters in *Birds* think about a name for the utopian city
they propose to establish in the sky, they come up with 'Nephelococcygia', which gives
us the term 'Cloud-Cuckoo Land'.

THEMES AND THE CULTURAL CONTEXT

Aristophanes' plays centred on public life at Athens and made fun of contemporary politics
and public figures. A modern reader of an Aristophanes play therefore needs to be familiar
with the various references to key characters and events of the day. It is worth reflecting
that, even if we were to watch a satirical television show from as recently as the 1990s, we
would need to find out about the current affairs of the time to understand the humour.

The politics of the day often take centre stage. One entire play, *Knights*, focuses
on satirising the leading politician Cleon as a demagogue who manipulates the citizen-
body of Athens. The theme of the war with Sparta is never far from the surface of
many plays: in *Acharnians*, for example, the lead character Dicaeopolis makes his
own private peace with the Spartans after failing to convince the Athenian assembly to do
the same. Perhaps the most famous 'war play' is *Lysistrata*, in which the heroine, an
Athenian woman, gathers a group of women from various Greek cities who swear to hold
a sex-strike until their husbands agree to stop the war. While this play no doubt raised
many laughs, it had a poignant political backdrop: it was written just after Athens and her
allies had lost a huge number of young men in an ill-fated expedition to Sicily – and so
the idea of women surviving without men must have been painfully close to reality.

MODERN SCHOLARSHIP

The political nature of Old Comedy – and its appetite for exaggeration and farce –
is emphasised in the following quotation from one scholar:

> It is not really surprising that no modern form of comedy . . . should come
> anywhere near to reproducing the inimitable cocktail that was an Aristophanic
> play. For if we were to translate its content, tone, style and atmosphere into
> recent or contemporary terms, it was something like . . . broad farce, comic
> opera, circus, pantomime, variety, revue, music hall, television and movie
> satire, the political cartoon, the political journal, the literary review, and the
> party pamphlet – all shaken and stirred into one very heady brew.
>
> Paul Cartledge, *Aristophanes and his Theatre of the Absurd*
> (London: Bloomsbury 1991), pp. 73ff.

As *Knights* and *Acharnians* illustrate, plays often focus on the workings of the democracy. In *Wasps*, Aristophanes makes fun of jury-service, presenting it as a system which is in thrall to conservative elderly citizens, while in *Birds* the main characters are so fed up of life at Athens that they head off to found their own ideal city in the sky. Other areas of public life were also mocked – in *Clouds*, when the playwright makes fun of the new learning in Athens at that time, the main character lampooned is the great thinker Socrates – Plato records that when he was put on trial in 399, he complained that he had been misrepresented by Aristophanes in the play which had first been performed in 423.

Aristophanes also enjoyed parodying poets such as Homer and Pindar, and even more so tragic playwrights – most notably Euripides, who is made fun of in five plays that we know of, and appears as a character in three. Aristophanes enjoyed mocking the grandeur of tragedy. He also enjoyed depicting gods as cowardly and ridiculous, as opposed to powerful and awesome; the most famous example is Dionysus in *Frogs*, who is more cowardly than the slave Xanthias.

> **MODERN PARALLEL**
>
> The idea of women going on a sex-strike may seem far-fetched, but in fact there are some examples of this happening in the modern era in countries as far afield as Colombia, Turkey, Italy and Poland.

MODERN SCHOLARSHIP

One of the most debated issues surrounding the plays of Aristophanes was whether he was simply writing to entertain or whether he had a more serious political purpose. It is notable that at *Frogs* 391–2, the chorus claim that comic playwrights aim to say much that is humorous and much that is serious. Read the following to explore this topic further:

Halliwell, F.S., 'Comedy and publicity in the society of the polis', in A.H. Sommerstein et al. (eds), *Tragedy, Comedy and the Polis* (Levante editori: Bari, 1993), 321–40.

Henderson, J., 'The demos and comic competition', in J.J. Winkler and F.I. Zeitlin, *Nothing to do with Dionysos?* (Princeton: Princeton University Press, 1992). Also in *Oxford Readings in Aristophanes*, 65–97.

TOPIC REVIEW

These questions should draw on your knowledge of the whole topic, so think carefully about the different things you have learned (check the Topic Overview on p. 40).

1. How believable do you find the traditional Athenian view of comedy's development?
2. How different would it have been to watch a comedy rather than a tragedy in Athens?
3. How do the types and sources of humour in an Athenian comedy compare with modern comedy and satire?
4. How much evidence do the three prescribed sources in this topic give for ancient comedy?

Further Reading

Cartledge, P., *Aristophanes and His Theatre of the Absurd* (London: Bloomsbury, 1990).
MacDowell, D.M., *Aristophanes and Athens: An Introduction to the Plays* (Oxford: Oxford University Press, 1995).
Revermann, M. (ed.), *The Cambridge Companion to Greek Comedy* (New York: Cambridge University Press, 2014).
Storey, I.C. and A. Allan, *A Guide to Ancient Greek Drama* (Chichester: John Wiley & Sons, 2014), Chapter 4.

PRACTICE QUESTIONS

Source A: Greek vase showing actors from an unknown comedy, *c.* **380–370** BC

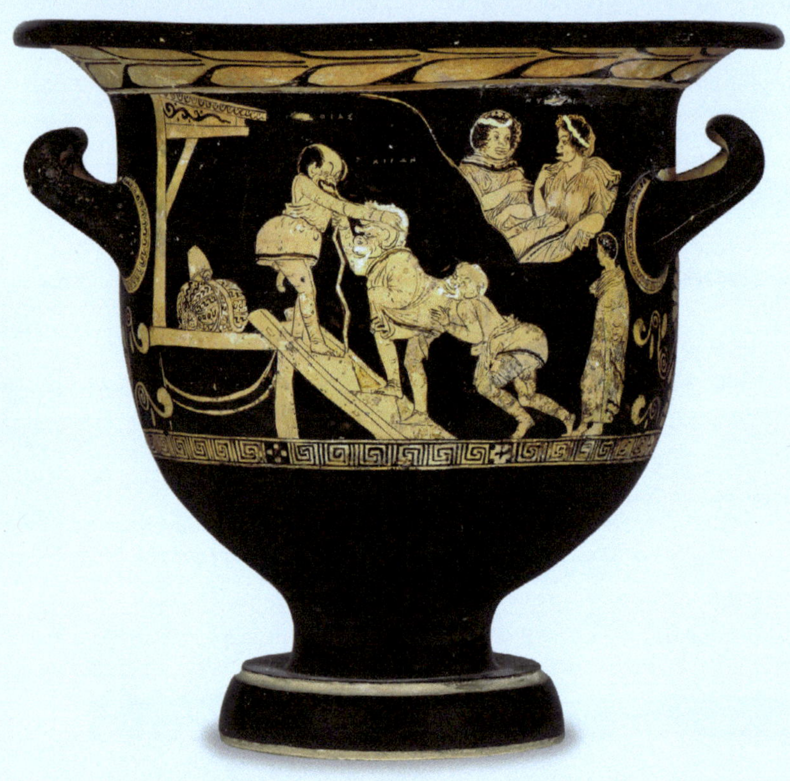

AS Level

1. Identify two characters depicted in this image. [2]
2. To what extent did Greek comedy depend on physical humour? You may use Source A as a starting point, and your own knowledge. [16]

A Level

1. Identify two characters depicted in this image. [2]
2. 'Physicality was an essential element of Athenian comedy.' Using Source A as a starting point, explain how far you agree with this statement and justify your response. [20]

1.4 Literary Techniques, Structure of the Plays, Dramatic Conventions

This topic examines the conventions of Greek tragedy and comedy, with reference to the three set plays. It begins with an overview of how Greek plays are structured, and then examines their language and style, including questions of characterisation. The styles and techniques of the different playwrights have been covered on pp. 26–9.

PLOT STRUCTURE

Before looking at the set plays, let us begin with the building blocks from which a Greek play is constructed. The basic structure of an ancient drama consists of alternating **episodes** (spoken dialogue between actors) and **choral odes** (songs with dancing performed by the chorus). These divide a play into sections comparable to modern scenes.

episodes scenes of dialogue between actors

choral odes songs performed by the chorus

prologue the opening of the play which sets the scene

parodos the first ode which the chorus perform while coming into the theatre

stasimon the name for a choral ode after the parodos

exodos the final section of the play

- an ancient play usually opens with a **prologue**, which sets the scene for the audience. This may take the form of a monologue addressed to the audience, or may be a dialogue between two characters. 'Prologue' is a Greek term, and derives from pro (before) and logos (story or word)
- the chorus then enter and perform their entry-song, known as the **parodos**
- after this, a tragedy continues with alternating episodes and choral odes. In tragedy, the odes after the parodos are known as **stasima** (singular: **stasimon**). Stasimon means 'standing song', because the chorus remain in the orchēstra (though they would be dancing during these odes), as opposed to entering while singing
- the final episode after the last choral ode is often known as the **exodos** ('exit'). The play normally ends with a short comment by the chorus, summing up the action or giving a general moral

In comedy, the structure is less set, but we usually have a series of episodes (short scenes with dialogues). These are punctuated by choral interludes, but there is not necessarily a choral ode between each one. A comedy also contains a parabasis, where the chorus address the audience directly, and an agōn (formal debate): see below.

PLOT DEVICES

A Greek audience would have anticipated certain formal features. However, just because these plot devices occur in most plays does not mean that they lack imagination, and an examination of the set plays reveals how the playwrights adapted them to suit their purposes.

Messenger speeches

Important events in tragedy usually occur off-stage and are reported by a messenger. Violence is rarely portrayed on-stage, and so it is in the messenger speech that the audience learns of the fates of the characters. The messenger speech is one of the most common features of a tragedy, and some plays, including *Bacchae*, have more than one. It is easy for modern readers, accustomed to being dazzled with special effects, to assume that it is dull only to hear about events. In fact, the messenger speech gives audiences a chance to let their imaginations run wild with grisly detail. By not directly portraying violence, the tragedians forced their audience to imagine the horrors for themselves. The power of imagination can do more than any stage gore, especially when we recall that ancient special effects were relatively limited.

Bacchism cult worship of Dionysus, who was also known by the name Bacchus

bacchants female followers of Dionysus

The messenger speeches of *Bacchae* demonstrate how effective this can be. The first messenger speech gives Euripides the opportunity to describe Bacchic worship as observed by a neutral bystander. His speech highlights the beauty of **Bacchism**, as the women make water, milk and wine come gushing from the earth (704–11; 593–8). Yet later in the same speech, the messenger gives a grisly description of the violence that the **bacchants** resort to when threatened, since they attack the herdsmen's cattle and rip them to shreds (740–2; 619–20):

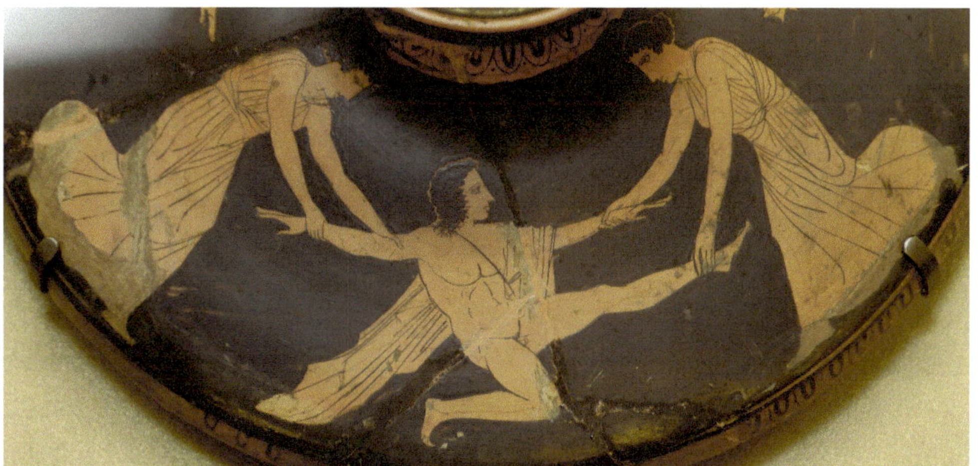

FIGURE 1.26
An Attic red-figure vase from the mid-fifth century depicting Pentheus torn apart by Agave and Ino.

> You could see ribs and a cloven hoof being hurled up and down. Parts hung dripping from the fir trees, smeared with blood.

This sense of harmony turning to violence foreshadows what will happen when Pentheus spies on the bacchants, and the second messenger speech lets us share his experience of watching them in secret, only to be horrified by what happens. Euripides exalts in creating a horror show as he describes the bacchants ripping Pentheus to pieces and playing ball with his dismembered body (1134–6; 965–7):

> 
>
> One of them was carrying a forearm, one a foot with a sandal still on it; his ribs were laid bare by the tearing, and all the women, bloody-handed, were playing catch with the flesh of Pentheus.

The details of the body parts force us to confront how appalling Pentheus' fate is. The shoe on the foot reminds us that this was only recently a living person, while the ball-game creates a terrifying contrast between the bacchants' childish joy and what they are actually doing. Similarly, the messenger speech in *Oedipus the King* contains a harrowing description of events inside the palace after Jocasta and Oedipus have learned the truth (1237–85; 1365–421). The speech describes Jocasta's anguished lament, Oedipus' anger, the discovery of Jocasta's corpse, and the horrific sight of Oedipus using the pins from her robes to blind himself. However, messenger speeches are not simply excuses to indulge in gory detail, they also draw a moral about what we can learn from such terrible events. For example, in *Oedipus the King,* the Messenger tells the chorus that 'The pains we inflict upon ourselves hurt most of all!' (1230–1; 1360–1), and ends his speech by contrasting Oedipus and Jocasta's former happiness with their downfall (1283–5; 1416–21).

The agōn

An **agōn** is a formal debate, and we find these in both tragedy and comedy. The term agōn means a competition, often an athletic contest, and gives us the English word 'agony', from the pain that athletes will go to in order to win. The agōn allows the playwright to

agōn a formal debate in which the playwright can showcase opposing arguments

stichomythia a dialogue in which two characters speak alternate lines of verse. This makes exchanges punchy, and is particularly appropriate for an agōn. From the Greek steicho ('to march in a line' – hence stichos means a line of verse) and mythos ('word' or 'utterance')

showcase opposing arguments. Oratory was important in Greek education, and in Athens all citizens would have had the opportunity to hear public speaking in the Assembly or the law courts. It is therefore not surprising that dramatic agōnes let the playwrights show off their skills as rhetoricians, as well as reflecting the techniques of real-life debaters. Dramatic agōnes often follow a formal pattern, where each speaker sets out his or her argument, and after both speeches are over, the debate continues in **stichomythia** (brief exchanges).

In real life, the purpose of a debate is to reach a conclusion, for example to persuade the Assembly to vote for war, or to convince a jury to convict. In tragedy, however, agōn scenes usually fail to persuade and end with both sides more polarised than before. In *Oedipus the King*, there are two agōnes, one between Oedipus and Tiresias (300–462; 340–526), and the second between Oedipus and Creon (513–630; 573–705). Oedipus initially tries to persuade Tiresias, but when met with resistance he resorts to threats, while Tiresias refuses to engage with Oedipus and attacks him for his ignorance. The scene between Oedipus and Creon resembles a legal trial, with Oedipus taking on the role of prosecutor and cross-questioning Creon. Creon defends himself using several popular rhetorical tricks. For example, he uses the so-called 'argument from probability', where he asks Oedipus whether it is likely that he would have plotted against Oedipus given the advantages he already enjoys (583–91; 652–63). Similarly, he trots out well-known arguments, such as the idea that being a king means living in fear (584–6; 654–5). Unlike a real law court, however, Oedipus is both prosecutor and judge, and so Creon's rhetorical fireworks fall on deaf ears. He is saved by the intervention of Jocasta and the Chorus, rather than by his own persuasive powers.

The agōn offers an opportunity for the playwright to incorporate themes of contemporary interest. The agōn between Pentheus and Tiresias in *Bacchae*, for example, highlights the role of religion in society. Pentheus mocks the story that Dionysus was sewn in Zeus' thigh as an unborn baby, arguing that this is not possible (242–5; 198–200). Tiresias responds by trying to rationalise the story. Whether or not the old myths about the gods should be taken literally or understood as metaphors was a topic of debate among contemporary intellectuals. It relates to the wider question of what the true nature of the gods is. These questions are important to a play like *Bacchae*, where the characters and audience must try to make sense of how Dionysus behaves.

Comic agōnes often drive the action and may influence how events turn out. In *Frogs* the agōn between Aeschylus and Euripides forms the centrepiece of the play, as its role is to decide which playwright Dionysus will take out of Hades. In fact, the agōn proves inconclusive, as Dionysus cannot reach a decision. However, it lays the groundwork for Aeschylus' victory, by presenting him as the weightier playwright and the bastion of traditional morality. The agōn allows Aristophanes to give a brilliant caricature of their styles, as well as contrasting their moral stance.

parabasis a section of a comedy in which the chorus addresses the audience directly, speaking in the voice of the playwright

Parabasis

The comic agōn is often accompanied by the **parabasis**, a feature we find only in comedy. Here the chorus addresses the audience directly, speaking in the voice of the playwright. Parabasis means 'stepping aside', and refers to how the chorus came forward to speak to the audience.

The opening of the parabasis from *Frogs* makes this transition clear (674–7):

Come, Muse! Come to our sacred dances!
Come to bring delight to our songs!
See there where the great clutter of the wise millions sit.

The topic of the parabasis need not relate to the topic of the play it is in, and it usually deals with current affairs, though may refer to the playwright's own life and career. It is often lengthy, and usually involves both choral and spoken sections. A comedy may contain more than one parabasis.

In *Frogs*, the parabasis (674–737) consists of two sung sections, which alternate with speeches. Its theme is that Athens needs to return to old ways and reject the politicians who are leading the city astray. The idea of 'old ways good, new ways bad' is a common theme in comedy, and is today still a reliable way to generate laughter and a feeling of warm nostalgia. It would have been particularly poignant for the audience of *Frogs*, since the play was performed shortly before Athens' final defeat in the Peloponnesian War. The parabasis also contains specific political advice, namely that those citizens who had lost their rights because they were involved in an attempt to overthrow the democracy in 411 BC should have their status restored.

LANGUAGE AND LITERARY TECHNIQUES

Tragedy

The language of tragedy is very stylised, and is grand and poetic to suit the plays' serious themes. Though modern translations often present the plays as prose, they were in fact written as poetry, and follow a strict metre. This is why scholars often refer to the playwrights as 'tragic poets'. Tragedy is divided into two categories, **iambus** or **iambics** (spoken sections) and **lyric** (sung sections, especially choral odes). The language of iambus is more naturalistic than that of lyric, and closer to normal speech, but it would be a mistake to think that ordinary Greeks would have spoken like tragic characters. Iambus follows a metrical pattern based on alternating long and short syllables which create a rhythm that goes 'ti tum ti tum' (for example, try reading out loud the line from Shakespeare's sonnet 'Shall I compare thee to a summer's day?', which creates a similar effect and so gives a feel for how these sections sounded, though the rules of English metre are based on different principles to those of Greek).

The metre of lyric is much more complicated, and the tragedians brought together rhythms from a vast range of earlier poetic forms. Its language is more poetic than that of iambus, and makes greater use of imagery and metaphor. Lyric song is not 'logical' – rather than telling a narrative, it tends to leap between ideas and gives a series of snapshots. Whereas iambus is spoken, lyric is sung, and the aulos-player who accompanied tragedy would have given a musical and rhythmic accompaniment (see p. 30). The characters of tragedy normally speak in iambus, and the chorus normally sing in lyric, but the distinction is not absolute. When the chorus-leader joins in the action to offer brief comments,

> **iambus** (adjective: **iambic**) the spoken sections of a play, also referred to as *iambics*. Iambic metre is fairly close to the pattern of real speech, and the full name of the metre used in tragedy is *iambic trimeter*
>
> **lyric** the sung sections of a play. Choral odes are always composed in lyric, and accompanied by dancing, but the characters sometimes also sing in lyric at particularly emotional moments

those passages are spoken iambics, while as you have seen (pp. 31–2), characters sometimes sing in lyric, usually in moments of great emotional intensity.

Tragic language makes rich use of imagery, and a particular type of imagery (e.g. seafaring, animals, fire) may be used to explore a play's symbolism. Often such imagery runs through the play and helps the audience interpret the significance of particular moments or shapes their response to a character.

Another common device is **tragic irony** (also referred to as **dramatic irony**). Since the audience would have been familiar with the myths, they knew what fates awaited the characters. It is easy to assume that this made it impossible for a tragedian to create any suspense. In fact, however, the playwrights played on this awareness to make the audience pity the characters and generate tension as we see them walking to their doom.

Tragic irony is a favourite technique of Sophocles, and is used in *Oedipus the King* to create a masterpiece of suspense. It is crucial that the audience knows Oedipus' identity throughout. We see him persisting in his quest for the truth, though we know it will bring about his ruin, and we see the scenes where he speaks affectionately to Jocasta with horror, since we know that this is a sexual relationship between mother and son. When Oedipus and the chorus express excitement about uncovering the truth of Oedipus' birth, we know that their hope will soon turn to revulsion, and this makes us feel greater pity for the characters.

Similarly, in *Bacchae*, Euripides uses tragic irony to bring out Pentheus' folly as he rejects Dionysus and ignores the warnings given by the god himself. The audience knows Dionysus' true identity, and this creates tension as we watch the confrontation between Pentheus and Dionysus. We appreciate the contrast between Dionysus' mild persona and the violence he is capable of. When Dionysus submits to punishment at Pentheus' hands, we know that this is just a trick to test the limits of the king's arrogance, and that the further Pentheus goes, the worse it will be for him.

The vase shown in Figure 1.27 depicts the moment in *Oedipus the King* where Jocasta realises the truth but Oedipus is still ignorant. Jocasta, depicted on the right, raises her right hand to her chin and her left hand to her cheek. These are standard gestures in Greek

> **tragic irony** where the playwright contrasts the characters' limited knowledge with the audience's broader understanding

---

EXAM TIP: LITERARY ANALYSIS

In *Oedipus the King*, Sophocles makes repeated use of imagery of sight and blindness. This is emphasised by the paradox that the blind Tiresias sees the truth, while Oedipus is intellectually blind. At the start of the play, Oedipus has sight but no insight, while Tiresias lacks sight but has a great deal of insight. Oedipus in his ignorance taunts Tiresias for his blindness (370–5; 422–8). Yet when he finally understands the truth about his past, he responds by destroying his sight. Oedipus explains that he cannot bear to see the world in the knowledge of what he has done (1369–90; 1499–523), while the chorus wish that they had never seen him (1216–22; 1344–50). While sight and blindness seem like absolutes, in fact human knowledge is fallible and we never have a full understanding of the world, just as Oedipus cannot enjoy physical and intellectual sight at the same time.

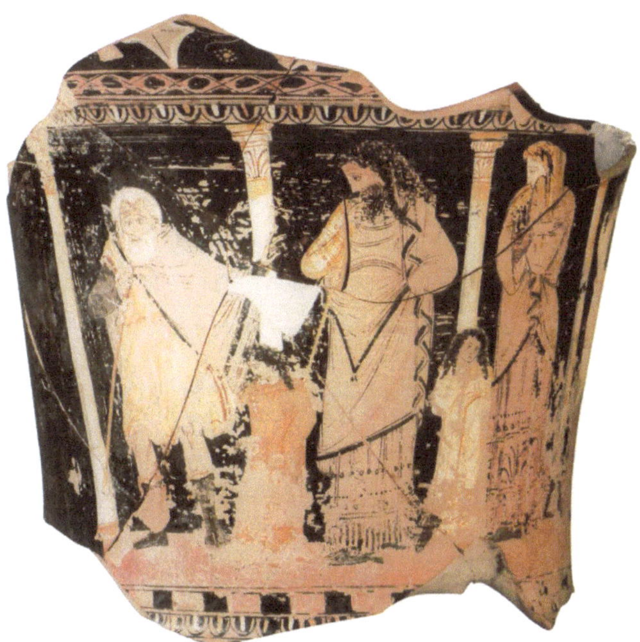

FIGURE 1.27
Jocasta and Oedipus, as depicted by the
Capodarso Painter.

art to indicate grief and worry. Oedipus, in the middle, appears puzzled, as he is stroking his beard, while the Messenger (left) answers his questions. We can tell that it represents a scene in Sophocles' play from the columns behind the characters, which represent the skēnē, and from the positioning of the characters, who stand as though they are in a play rather than as though the scene were occurring realistically. Thus, the Messenger uses theatrical gestures and faces the front, as though talking to the audience. This scene is the climax of the tragic irony that runs through the play, and it was presumably chosen by the artist because of its dramatic power. At the front of the vase are Oedipus' daughters, Antigone and Ismene. While the girls appear in Sophocles' play, there is nothing to suggest they were present in this scene. As with other images of the Greek theatre, we should be careful of taking the artist's depiction as a literal representation of a performance, since he was free to add details to make the image more moving.

Comedy

Though the language of comedy may be more down-to-earth than that of tragedy, it still bore little relation to how ordinary Greeks spoke. It, too, is written in poetic metre and divided into spoken and choral sections. However, the topics of comedy are more everyday than that of tragedy, and this is reflected by the language used. Whereas tragedy steers away from anything to do with the body, comedy uses it to generate humour, and likes to joke about eating, drinking, sex, violence and excreting. Obscene language is common, as are words for particular types of food and drink that we may not find elsewhere in Greek. Comedy enjoys playing with language and sound, and we find jokes making fun of accents or speech defects, or trying to imitate the sound of animals, as in the 'brekekekex koax koax' of the Frog chorus. However, comedy includes high-flown passages, especially in the choruses. This fine language may generate humour by contrasting with more vulgar content.

CHARACTERISATION

When dealing with ancient drama, we should not expect the same type of psychologically-driven characterisation as we find in the works of a modern author. Tragic figures often seem embodiments of a character-type (for example, arrogant king, vengeful woman) rather than an individual personality, while comedy also trades in 'stock figures'. This has made scholars cautious about speaking of 'character' in tragedy, and how far we can read these texts psychologically is a topic of debate.

Nevertheless, Aristotle put character (ethos) second only to plot in his analysis of tragedy, and much of tragedy's power derives from the conflict caused by its heroes' characters. When we speak of tragic characterisation, we need to be careful to avoid anachronism. The concept of psycho-analysis and understanding how personality is shaped only developed in the twentieth century. In its original context, tragedy shows little interest in analysing why someone behaves in a particular way or what has made them who they are. The texts do not invite us to question why Oedipus is an angry person, or what childhood experiences might have made Pentheus so distrustful of women, for example, and to ask these questions would reveal a very modern set of preoccupations. However, this does not mean that the plays tell us nothing about human character. The overarching patterns that we see in tragic heroes are described at pp. 72–5.

The characters of tragedy are generally consistent, in that their behaviour makes sense on its own terms and fits with how they behave throughout the play. The characters of comedy are less so, and we often get the impression that a character says or does something to suit the humour of the moment rather than because it is 'true' to how that person might behave. Comedy deals in stereotypes, whether to confirm or overturn them. For example, Xanthias overturns the stereotype that slaves are inferior to free men, but in the scene where he gossips with Pluto's slave (738–55), they confirm stereotypes of how slaves would behave badly if they could get away with it. Dionysus overturns the expectations that the audience might normally hold about a god, since far from being mysterious and powerful, he behaves like a buffoon. For further discussion of Xanthias' and Dionysus' characters, see pp. 81–2.

The chorus

In both *Oedipus the King* and *Bacchae,* we have choruses with strong views on what happens on-stage. In *Oedipus,* the chorus are deeply loyal to Oedipus. They reject Tiresias' revelation that Oedipus is the killer of Laius, and stand by Oedipus, since he saved the city from the Sphinx. The chorus' affection for Oedipus to some extent allows them to influence the action. For example, it is their intervention that saves Creon. Conversely, in *Bacchae* the chorus is hostile to Pentheus and rejoice in his death. It is important to remember that the playwright has free choice over the characterisation of his chorus. It is interesting to imagine how *Oedipus the King* would be different if Sophocles had chosen a chorus of slaves loyal to Laius who regarded Oedipus as an interloper, or how we would respond to Pentheus if the chorus was elderly citizens of Thebes terrified by the new cult.

When analysing what contribution the chorus makes to a particular play, it is important not to neglect the odes. Though we tend to think of choral odes as an add-on to the main action, choral song long predated tragedy and comedy (see p. 25). When choruses performed in Greek life (for example at religious festivals, civic occasions, weddings, funerals), part of their function was to help the community make sense of these emotionally-charged occasions. The choral odes within a drama play a similar role. They are designed to shape our understanding of the broader issues at stake, and repay careful study.

ACTIVITY

What impression might the chorus of frogs have made on the audience? How could Aristophanes make a chorus of this type entertaining? Consider costume, dance and other types of movement, and sound. You could try drawing your own design for the costumes and masks. Alternatively, try choreographing a dance of the frogs. How will you capture the feeling of dancing like frogs?

EXAM TIP: LITERARY ANALYSIS

A good example of an ode which appears difficult but rewards our efforts is the second *stasimon* of *Oedipus the King* (863–910; 954–97). The ode takes place after Oedipus has told Jocasta his story and Jocasta tells him how the oracle sent to her and Laius never came true. The failure of the gods to fulfil their prophecies worries the traditionally-minded chorus, and the ode sets out their beliefs. They pray that the gods will look kindly on those who obey their laws and punish wrongdoers.

The connection to the play is made explicit at the end of the ode, when the chorus comment that 'They are dying, the old oracles sent to Laius, now our masters strike them off the rolls' (906–7; 994–5). This has prompted a religious crisis, as if the gods fail to honour their oracles and to punish wrongdoers, there is no point in worshipping them (895–910; 985–97). Indeed, it will turn out that the gods have not forgotten their oracles, and the killing of Laius will be punished.

Yet the ode raises moral questions, since the situation is less clear-cut than the chorus envisage. In the ode, the chorus divide the world into wicked and virtuous men, and it is hard to argue that the gods should not punish a deliberate wrongdoer. However, life is more complicated than this: Oedipus is the killer but he is not the evildoer that the chorus imagine. The chorus' stance therefore highlights the dilemma at the heart of the play: how should we deal with situations where someone commits a terrible wrong unknowingly. As the audience listens to the ode, they can question the chorus' confidence that there are simple answers.

Choral odes can at first sight appear to consist of general moralising with little connection to what is going on on-stage. However, the odes are not just decorative filler, and each is tailored to the point in the play where it comes. Even where the ode appears to wander off on a tangent, there is usually a reference to what has led the chorus' thoughts in that direction, even if the audience has to think for themselves to make the connection.

The choruses of *Oedipus the King* and *Bacchae* are emotionally involved in the action. Comic choruses are often more detached, and may represent groupings who are fantastical and whose purpose is to amuse through spectacle. The chorus of frogs reflect a long tradition of animal-choruses (see pp. 43–4). Their relevance to the details of the play is limited; rather their role is to create an entertaining scene involving word-play, sound effects, amusing costumes and humorous conflict.

However, the odes of *Frogs* are also fine pieces of poetry, designed to impress the audience in their own right. For example, the song that precedes the tragedy competition (814–29) echoes the language of Homeric epic, pitting Aeschylus and Euripides as fierce warriors about to fight to the death.

TOPIC REVIEW

These questions should draw on your knowledge of the whole topic, so think carefully about the different things you have learned (check the Topic Overview on p. 49).

1. What similarities and differences can you find in how a Greek play was structured, and how a modern play with which you are familiar is structured?
2. What typical features would an audience member expect when going to see a play, and what function did these achieve?
3. Do you find the characters of Greek drama realistic? How does this compare with the characters in modern dramatic forms you are used to?
4. What is distinctive about the language and style of tragedy? How is this different from comedy?

Further Reading

Easterling, P.E., 'Constructing Character in Greek Tragedy', in C. Pelling (ed.), *Characterization and Individuality in Greek Literature* (Oxford: Clarendon Press, 1990), 83–99.

Robson, J., *Aristophanes: An Introduction* (London: Bloomsbury, 2009).

Rutherford, R.B., *Greek Tragic Style: Form, Language and Interpretation* (Cambridge: Cambridge University Press, 2012).

Silk, M.S., *Aristophanes and the Definition of Comedy* (Oxford: Oxford University Press, 2002).

PRACTICE QUESTIONS

Source A: *Bacchae* 689–711 (*Cambridge Translations from Greek Drama:* 583–98)

MESSENGER: When she heard the lowing of the horned cattle, your mother stood up in the middle of the bacchants, and gave the ritual cry, to stir their bodies from sleep. They brushed off deep sleep from their eyes and leaped up, a marvel of decency and grace to behold, women young and old and still unmarried. First they let their hair down to their shoulders, and pulled up their fawnskins if they had undone the knots which fastened them, and they girdled the dappled skins with snakes that licked their cheeks. Some of them held a fawn in their arms, or the wild cubs of wolves, and they gave them white milk, those who had recently given birth and whose breasts were swollen, having left their babies behind. On their heads they put garlands of ivy and oak and flowering bryony. One took up a thyrsus and struck it against a rock, and from the rock a dewy spring of water leaped out. Another struck her staff against the ground, and for her the god sent up a spring of wine. Those who felt a desire for the white drink scraped the ground with their fingertips, and found gushes of milk, and from the ivied thyrsi dripped sweet streams of honey.

AS Level

1. What is a thyrsus? [1]
2. Why is Pentheus' mother on the mountainside? [2]
3. How do the tragic playwrights make messenger speeches engaging for their audiences? You may use Source A as a starting point, and your own knowledge. [16]

A Level

1. What is a thyrsus? [1]
2. Why is Pentheus' mother on the mountainside? [2]
3. 'One of the main functions of messenger speeches was to allow the tragedians to show off their skill as narrators'. Using Source A as a starting point, explain how far you agree with this statement and support your argument with evidence. [20]

1.5 Social, Political and Religious Themes in Tragedy

With reference to *Oedipus the King* and *Bacchae*:

- ancient religious concepts, beliefs and practices, including:
  - the role of the gods
  - fate and free will
  - prophecy and prophets
  - religious rituals and acts
- importance of the polis (city), including:
  - position and role of men, women and slaves in society
  - political ideas and ideals
- importance of family relationships
- tragic heroism, including:
  - the nature of heroes and heroism
  - justice and revenge
- possible interpretation of these themes and motifs by both ancient and modern audiences
- the representation of such themes and motifs in the visual/material record

The following prescribed sources are covered in this topic:

- Sophocles, *Oedipus the King*
- Euripides, *Bacchae*
- Aristophanes, *Frogs*
- red-figure 'maenad' stamnos by Dinos Painter
- the death of Pentheus, red-figure kylix attributed to Douris, *c.* 480 BC

Don't forget that you will be given credit in the exam if you study extra sources and make relevant use of them in your answers.

This topic will discuss tragedy's handling of social, political and religious themes. First, it will explore how tragedy portrays religious belief and practice. Next, it will examine the relationship between individuals and society, and how tragedy reflects political ideas. Third, it will discuss the depiction of the family, before finishing with an examination of the tragic hero.

ANCIENT RELIGIOUS CONCEPTS, BELIEFS AND PRACTICES

Religion was a central part of Greek life, and since the gods' favour to a city was believed to be essential to its prosperity, the Greek world lacked any division between religious and political authority. As we have seen, tragedy itself was performed as part of a religious festival, and portrayed the gods whom the audience worshipped in their daily lives. It does not just reflect what the Athenians believed, but provided space for them to consider theological issues. How tragedy handled religious matters, therefore, would have had a significant impact on how religion was perceived in Athenian public life.

The role of the gods

From a modern perspective, the most striking feature of tragic theology is the uncaring attitude the gods display. Most modern religions posit a loving deity, and the idea of vengeful or personally-motivated gods seems shocking. Indeed, readers of tragedy since antiquity have found the plays' theology troubling. In Plato's *Republic*, Socrates finds its portrayal of the gods so troubling as to ban it (along with Homer and other unsuitable types of poetry) from the ideal city (5.377d–391e).

However, it is a fundamental belief in Greek religion that the gods were as, if not more, concerned with their honour as human beings are, and this explains their need for worship. In tragedy, the failure of heroes to honour the gods (or a particular god) is often responsible for their downfall. This is clear in *Bacchae*, where Dionysus announces at the start of the play that he will punish Thebes for refusing to worship him. Pentheus is warned repeatedly about the dangers of dishonouring a god, for example by Tiresias near the start of the play (321; 256–7). He adds to his folly as he refuses to acknowledge Dionysus' divinity and attempts to humiliate him (493–518; 404–33). This disregard for divine power could not be tolerated, and a Greek audience would not expect Dionysus to be merciful when treated with contempt.

The punishments meted out by the Greek gods are not limited to the wrongdoer. Thus in *Oedipus the King,* the whole city is afflicted by plague as a punishment for harbouring the killer of Laius, while in *Bacchae* all the women of Thebes are driven mad by Dionysus because his mother's sisters denied that she was impregnated by Zeus. Cadmus suffers greatly as a result of his grandson's actions, although he has never rejected Dionysus. At the end of the play, when Cadmus suggests that Dionysus' punishment was excessive, the god replies 'yes, for I am a god, and I was insulted by you' (1347; 1171). In other words, just as the gods' power surpasses that of human beings, so does their anger, and they will punish transgressions against them with disproportionate violence. Scholars have long debated whether plays such as *Bacchae* represent a criticism of traditional views of the gods, and to what extent we should see tragedy as upholding or as questioning this form of theology.

The gods put little emphasis on whether a human has transgressed intentionally. This issue lies at the heart of *Oedipus the King,* where Oedipus has committed terrible crimes in ignorance. We learn at the start of the play that the gods wish the killer of Laius to be

MODERN SCHOLARSHIP

Since Aristophanes' portrayal in *Frogs*, Euripides has often been described as a writer who undermined traditional belief in the gods. Many scholars have accepted this depiction, and have read Euripides' plays as espousing unorthodox or even atheistic ideas. However, others have argued against this. In exploring these ideas, Euripides is drawing on debates among Athenian intellectuals about religion. The group of thinkers who espoused these views are often known as the ***sophists***.

Read Mary Lefkowitz's article '"Impiety" and "Atheism" in Euripides' Dramas', in *Classical Quarterly* 39 (1989): 70–82. What arguments does she make? Do you find them convincing?

sophists a group of influential philosophers in fifth-century Athens, whose interests included religion, ethics, rhetoric and science

S & C Read E.R. Dodds' article 'On Misunderstanding the *Oedipus Rex*', in *Greece and Rome* 13 (1966): 37–49. How useful do you find his approach to understanding *Oedipus the King*?

Study Question
What sort of things nowadays do we believe determine the sort of person we are or the type of life we lead? How different are these from ancient views about divine intervention?

punished, and the characters assume that he is a wicked man who has acted out of viciousness. When Oedipus' identity is unveiled, no one doubts that he must be punished, yet his ignorance makes his fate horrifying. Sophocles highlights the gulf between our instinctive feeling that our intentions make a difference, and the traditional divine focus on actions. The terrifying power of the play derives from our understanding that any of us might act in ignorance, and yet, as the modern philosopher Bernard Williams put it, 'in the story of one's life there is an authority exercised by what one has done, and not merely by what one has intentionally done' (*Shame and Necessity*, p. 74). To use a modern analogy, if a driver fails to notice a child crossing the road and kills them, the fact that they did not mean to do so would not mean that they bear no responsibility or do not have to live with the consequences.

Fate and free will

In the case of Oedipus, we may wonder to what extent his actions make any difference, since he is fated from before his birth to kill his father and marry his mother. An important principle in tragic religion is double determination, that is, the idea that any action is simultaneously capable of two explanations: one on the human level, the other on the divine level. Divine influence does not diminish the human characters' responsibility for their actions. While the concept of divine intervention may be hard for moderns to relate to, we are familiar enough with the idea that someone must bear responsibility for their actions and yet has their life shaped by forces greater than them. We do not find it hard to understand a statement like 'it was inevitable that he would turn to a life of crime, since he was brought up in such terrible circumstances', nor do we tend to feel that such a person should be let off the hook when they do commit a crime.

On a human level, Oedipus' fate seems particularly unfair since he takes steps to avoid it. Having been told by the oracle at Delphi that he will kill his father and believing that he is the son of the Corinthian king, he goes to Thebes, thereby abandoning his position as heir to the throne of Corinth. On this level, we might say that Oedipus has no free will, since he tries to prevent the oracle coming true. On the other hand, we also see how

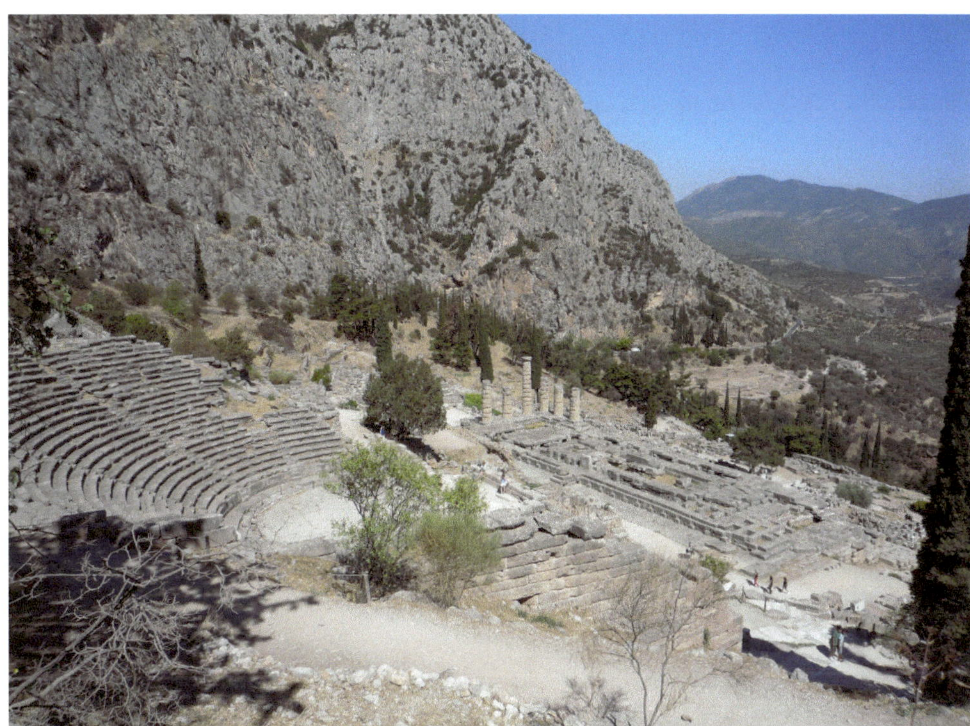

FIGURE 1.28
A view down to the remains of the temple of Apollo at Delphi today.

Oedipus made the choices that led him to kill his father and marry his mother. His response to being provoked by Laius' rude behaviour at the crossroads was to kill him and his entourage in a fit of anger (807–13). We see Oedipus' tendency to lose his temper when he does not get his way in his rudeness to Tiresias, aggression with Creon, and his threats to torture the old shepherd.

However, it is Oedipus' intelligence and dynamism that lead him to his doom as much as his anger, since it is by defeating the Sphinx that he became king of Thebes and married Jocasta. We also see these characteristics in his dogged pursuit of the truth. Thus, Oedipus is a victim of his fate, but it is also his own actions that brought it to pass. When asked by the chorus which of the gods led him to blind himself, he names Apollo and himself (1327–32; 1467–71), and emphasises that both divine influence and human will acted together. Similarly, in *Bacchae*, we see how Pentheus seals his fate by ignoring the warnings he is given.

Prophecy and prophets

While most Greeks probably believed in prophecy, they were also aware that it could be unreliable, and that humans could make mistakes in interpreting the god's message. The difficulty of using prophecy is apparent in *Oedipus the King*, where Oedipus' fate is foretold by two oracles, one given to his parents, and the other to him. The prophecy given to Laius and Jocasta comes out of the blue (711–14; 748–8), while the one for Oedipus (788–93; 869–75) answers a question he did not ask (unlike in real life, where oracles would answer particular questions). We are not told why the gods inflicted this fate on Oedipus, and it is unclear whether the prophecy is couched as a warning that could be avoided ('do not have a child, or he will kill you') or simply a prediction. Jocasta questions the truth of this oracle, saying that it came from the servants of Apollo rather than the god himself (711–12; 785–6): mortals cannot tell which prophesies are truly inspired by a god.

The trustworthiness of prophets is explored through the figure of Tiresias. In both plays, the audience recognise that Tiresias provides wise advice, but the characters discover this too late. Oedipus and Pentheus accuse Tiresias of making money out of prophesying a certain way: Pentheus claims that Tiresias will make money from the new cult (*Bacchae* 257; 207–8), while Oedipus believes that he has been bribed by Creon (380–9; 432–42). The kings may be wrong, but their fears reflect anxiety about religious authorities abusing their power. Equally, the conflict with Tiresias reflects a clash between political and religious forms of authority, and Oedipus and Pentheus overstep the mark by insulting a prophet.

Religious rituals and acts

Greek religion focused on action rather than belief. The gods, it was believed, cared that humans paid them proper honour rather than that they were fervent believers. For this reason, it is significant that Pentheus does not just fail to acknowledge Dionysus' divinity, but seeks to prevent his worship.

What was involved in worshipping Dionysus is one of the central questions of *Bacchae*. The chorus describe Dionysiac ritual in their odes, and they emphasise the joyful nature of their worship, and the importance of dance, music and wine. We are also told of the activities of the Theban bacchants on the mountainside, whose wild practices lead to Pentheus' death.

maenads an alternative name for the bacchants. 'Maenad' means 'frenzied one', because of the madness associated with Dionysus

The worship of Dionysus by **maenads** was practised in real-life in ancient Greece, but we know little about what was involved and it is unlikely that it was as exotic as the maenadic rituals described in *Bacchae* (for example, perhaps real maenads simply handled or cut up raw meat, as a homage to the myth that the first bacchants tore animals apart with their bare hands). Pentheus maintains that the rituals are pretexts for women to indulge in drunkenness and extra-marital sex. The first Messenger corrects him, and gives us an insight into the true nature of Dionysiac ritual (677–774; 575–643). It is tempting at first glance to conclude that Pentheus is entirely misguided in seeing Dionysiac religion as a threat, but when we analyse what the Messenger says, the situation is perhaps more nuanced. The women have left their homes and babies, and have become animal-like in their behaviour. When threatened, they cause destruction to agricultural life and communities, two core elements of human civilisation (737–54; 617–28). Dionysiac worship, while beautiful, is presented as in opposition with normal life, and the challenge facing the audience is how a society can incorporate Dionysus' rituals without losing what makes ordered living possible.

thyrsus a ritual staff made of a fennel stalk carried by followers of Dionysus

The vase in Figure 1.29 shows an artist's impression of Dionysiac worship. The women are dancing around a statue of Dionysus, which is fastened to a pillar and decorated with ivy. Some maenads carry a **thyrsus** (a ritual staff), another plays a tambourine, while one ladles wine from a drinking vessel (the same shape as the vase itself) into a cup. There are several ways in which the rituals resemble those described in *Bacchae*, for example the thyrsus, which is carried by Dionysus himself (and seized by Pentheus at

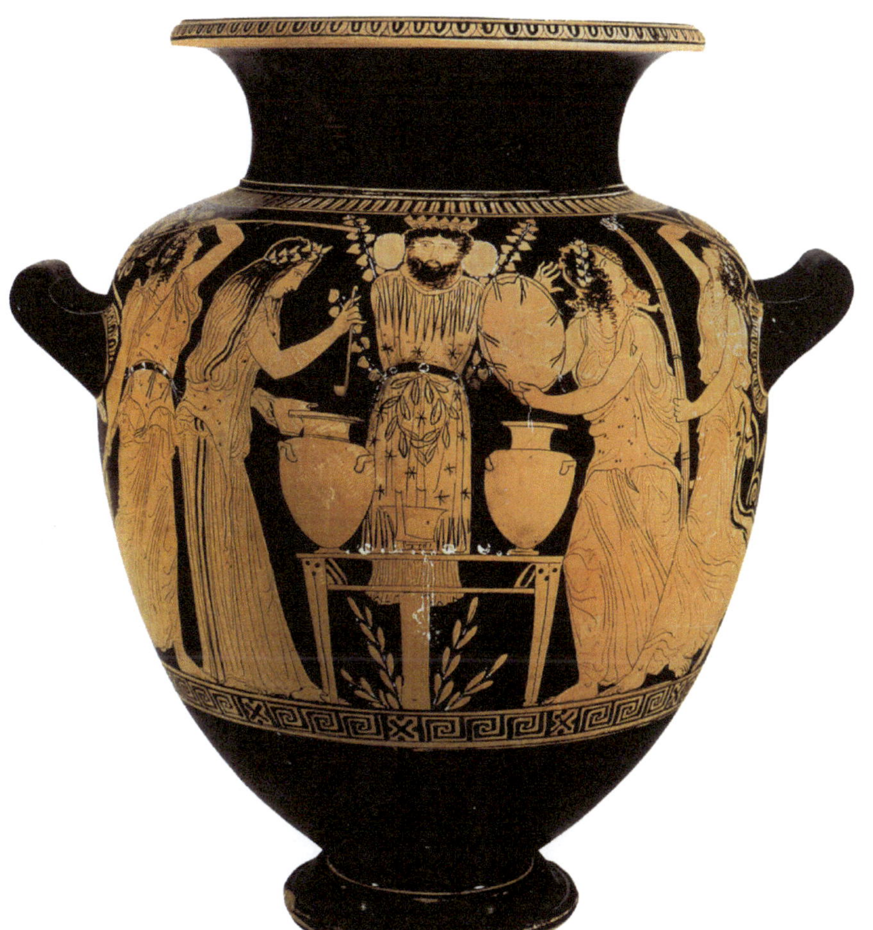

FIGURE 1.29
The Dinos Painter's
'maenad' stamnos.

PRESCRIBED SOURCE

Red-figure 'maenad' stamnos by Dinos Painter

Object: red-figure stamnos (wine vessel)

Artist: the Dinos Painter

Location: Museo Nazionale Archeologico, Naples

Date: late fifth century BC

Significance: a portrayal of Dionysiac ritual

496; 407), and the tambourine, whose association with Dionysus is described by the chorus at 120–34 (104–14). Some of the maenads toss their heads in religious ecstasy, losing all inhibitions in their dance. The woman pouring the wine has let her hair fall over her shoulders (as do the Theban bacchants at 695; 587), another detail that shows the relaxation of normal boundaries, since loose hair was not usually appropriate for an adult woman. The presence of the drinking vessel reminds us that Dionysus' function of god of wine is central to his rituals. Though drinking parties play little role in the Bacchism described in Thebes (for example, the Messenger reassures Pentheus that the women are not drunk at 686–7; 581–2), the choral odes of *Bacchae* often refer to the importance of wine to the rites (e.g. 382–5; 304–7).

Oedipus the King brings out another religious belief, that of pollution. This too relates to a historical idea, that certain actions could cause one to become polluted. Someone in a state of pollution was unacceptable to the gods, and required religious purification. In real life, a Greek would often need purification from minor pollutions from activities such as childbirth or death. Tragedy, however, focuses on more drastic forms of pollution, in particular that caused by homicide. Oedipus is not only polluted himself, but brings a pollution upon the whole city, and he cannot be purified of his guilt but must be driven from the community.

IMPORTANCE OF THE POLIS (CITY)

In Greek thought, human ability to live in a community was one of the most important things that distinguished them from animals. When Aristotle argued that 'man is a political animal' (*Politics* 1.1253a), he meant not that human beings are naturally interested in politics, but that they are designed to live in a polis. It is therefore not surprising that tragedy is interested in how people should live together and how we should handle the conflicts that arise. The polis is made up of individuals, and so a central question explored by tragedy is how the different members of a society should behave. Since tragedy depicts a world where the normal sources of stability are challenged, social roles are tested or distorted.

The position of men and women

The position of men and women, their responsibilities to each other, and what happens when these go wrong are common themes in Greek tragedy. Out of the thirty-two surviving tragedies, only Sophocles' *Philoctetes* has no female characters, and the tragedians frequently select myths for their plays which involve gender conflict.

Bacchae depicts a breakdown in these social codes, since the women of Thebes have abandoned their duties to their families to worship Dionysus. Whereas the ideal for respectable Greek women was to live their lives inside the house, away from public view (though it seems unlikely that this was realistic for poorer women, who needed to work), the bacchants have left their homes to live outside. In his opening speech, Dionysus describes the women as sitting on 'bare rock under the green pine trees' (38; 29), highlighting the degree to which they have abandoned their inhibitions.

MODERN SCHOLARSHIP

The relationship of Greek tragedy to the democratic culture that produced it has been hotly debated by scholars. Some have seen tragedy's role as fundamentally subversive. Others have argued that tragedy affirms the core values shared by the Athenian audience, while a third group have tried to detach tragedy from its political contexts altogether.

The following articles represent very different views on this issue. Which of them do you find the most convincing?

'The Great Dionysia and Civic Ideology', in J.J. Winkler and F. Zeitlin, *Nothing to do with Dionysus?* (Princeton: Princeton University Press, 1990), 97–129.
'Listening to Many Voices: Greek Tragedy as Popular Art', W. Allan and A. Kelly, in A. Marmadoro and J. Hill, *The Author's Voice in Classical and Late Antiquity* (Oxford: Oxford University Press, 2013), 77–122.
'The Social Function of Attic Tragedy', J. Griffin (1998), *CQ* 48: 39–61.

Women in fifth-century Athens

Women in fifth-century Athens led limited lives by modern standards, excluded from many aspects of public life. They played no role in politics, and could not participate in the Assembly and law-courts. They could not own property or be citizens, though freeborn Athenian wives could transmit property and citizenship to their sons. Nor did they have any legal status independent of their male kin, and they were treated as perpetual minors, under the guardianship of a male relative. These ideals of obedience and silence are summarised by Pericles in Thucydides' *Histories*: 'great is your glory if you are no worse than your natural character, and greatest is that of the woman who is spoken about by men as little as possible, whether for good or for bad' (2.45.3). The justification that lay behind this extreme control was that women were believed to be intrinsically uncontrolled, less capable than men of mastering their emotional impulses. Thus, the extreme females of tragedy can in one sense be seen as exploring the consequences that ensue when women slip loose from male control.

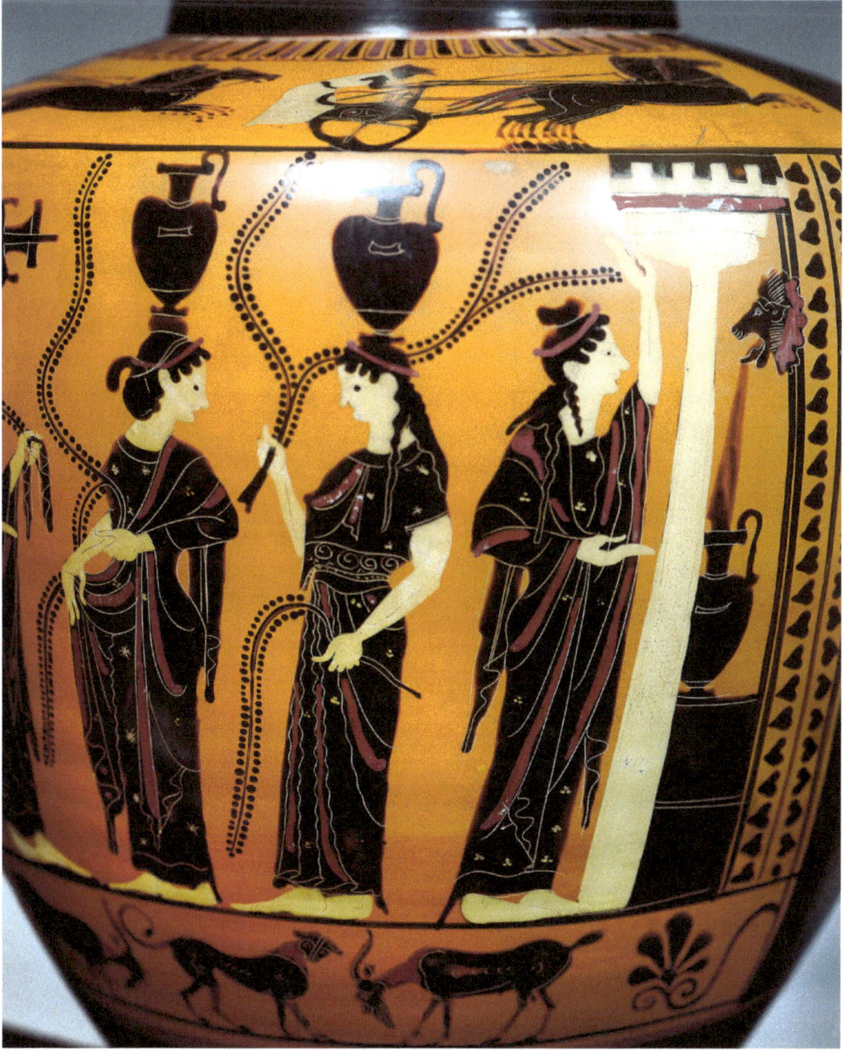

FIGURE 1.30
A sixth-century Attic black-figure vase showing women drawing water from a fountain.

> **Study Question**
>
> When it comes to gender relations, to what extent does Euripides uphold the values of his day in *Bacchae,* and to what extent does he question or subvert them?

This is emphasised in the first Messenger speech. While the Messenger describes the miracles they perform, we also see the negative consequences of women abandoning their position. For example, some of the bacchants are nursing wild animals, in an attempt to replace the babies they have left (699–702; 589–92). The image of them holding wolves or deer to their breast is eerie, and makes the audience think of the baby left behind. The idea that Bacchism can threaten family life is made explicit when the women snatch children from the homes of the villagers (754; 628). Whereas women are meant to protect children, the influence of Dionysus causes the maenads to disrupt families, including their own.

Thus while at first glance we might take Pentheus' distrust of Bacchism as ignorant, on closer analysis we might feel that his worries have some foundation. While Pentheus is wrong to think that the women are having sex, their actions do have an impact on their married lives. The maenadism of *Bacchae* relies on the breaking down of norms that society is founded on. Equally, we could interpret *Bacchae* as an exploration of the tensions in a patriarchal system. One could see Pentheus' fate as a warning either of what can happen if women are not properly controlled, or of the dangers of excessively suppressing them.

Oedipus the King presents a more positive depiction of gender relations, since Oedipus and Jocasta's marriage is presented as one of mutual respect. Indeed, Oedipus states that he has a higher opinion of Jocasta than of the chorus of elders (700; 770–1), overturning any assumption that the Greeks always thought women were inferior to men. For her part, Jocasta is concerned for her husband's wellbeing. The couple listen attentively to each other and speak with affection, and Creon even comments that Oedipus gives Jocasta an equal share in his power (579; 647). This depiction of a supportive marriage echoes Homer's *Odyssey*, where Odysseus tells the princess Nausicaa of the importance of like-mindedness in creating a perfect marriage:

> Nothing is better or stronger than when two people, like-minded in their thoughts,
> keep a house as husband and wife.

Odyssey 6.182–4

Odysseus himself is married to the intelligent Penelope, and this relationship offers a model of a successful marriage where the woman's role is admired. We should not fall into the trap of thinking that the Greeks had only negative things to say about strong women. However, in the case of *Oedipus the King*, the audience's knowledge of Oedipus' identity means that this depiction of a harmonious couple is tainted by horror, since we know that they are really mother and son. Oedipus' happy marriage, like his prosperous career, makes his fall from grace even more pitiful, as he discovers that his whole life has been based on lies. It is a deliberate stroke of irony that the happiest marriage in Greek tragedy is the one that never should have been allowed.

Slaves

Slaves feature regularly in Greek tragedy, usually as minor characters (for example, messengers), though in some plays their roles can be significant. We find little reflection

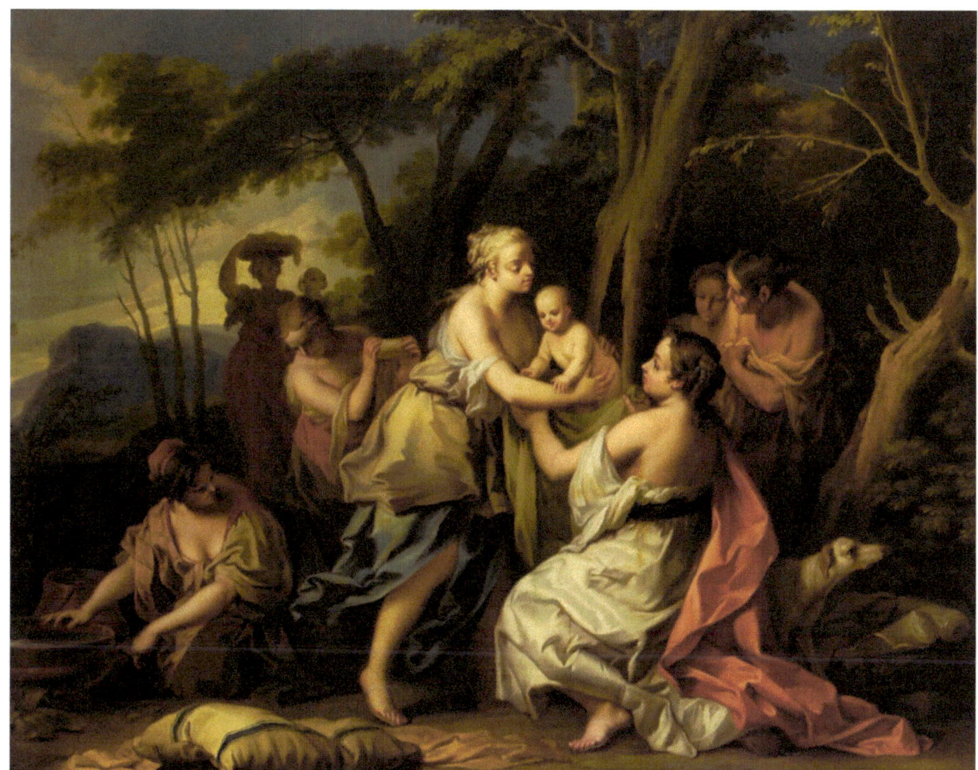

The finding of Oedipus, as imagined by a seventeenth-century French painter.

on the morality of slavery, but the way slave-characters are presented may give us insight into the values of the audience.

Slaves in tragedy tend to be loyal to their masters, and we find no suggestion that they might resent their position. The second Messenger in *Bacchae*, for example, says that he feels sorrow for the Theban royal house, even though he is only a slave (1027–8; 883–5). Similarly, the Messenger in *Oedipus the King* brought his master, the king of Corinth, the infant Oedipus, out of consideration for his childlessness (1022–4; 1118–23).

Nevertheless, tragedy does reveal some of the hardships of a slave's life. For example, Oedipus threatens to torture the shepherd when he refuses to answer his questions (1152–4; 1266–9). While Oedipus behaves harshly, the speed with which he resorts to violence is undoubtedly more shocking to us than to an ancient audience, who would see slaves as the property of their masters. We see the humiliation of slavery when Oedipus assumes Jocasta's distress at learning the story of his birth is because she thinks he was the child of a slave (1062–85; 1164–94). To Oedipus, it is unsurprising that Jocasta should be horrified at the idea of being married to someone of slavish descent, and he therefore brushes off her pleas.

Political ideas and ideals

Tragedy is set in a time when cities were ruled by kings. To some extent, the audience would have accepted this as a fact about earlier times, but the tragedians also use their kings to comment on contemporary beliefs about the dangers of tyranny. In a fifth-century Athenian context, government by a single ruler (or to use the Greek term, a

S & C

Tyranny in sixth-century Athens

Democracy in Athens dates back to 508/7 BC, when the politician Cleisthenes implemented reforms that paved the way for a democratic system. Between 546 and 510, Athens had been ruled by a family of tyrants known as the Peisistratids (first Peisistratus, and then his two sons, Hippias and Hipparchus). Peisistratus came to power on a wave of popular support, but under his son Hippias the regime became oppressive and was eventually overthrown. Fifth-century Athenians remained anxious that a charismatic politician could retrace Peisistratus' footsteps and install himself as a tyrant.

tyrannos a tyrant or king. By the time of tragedy, *tyrannos* could have negative connotations similar to those of the English word 'tyrant' (though the word in tragedy is not always used negatively).

Study Question
Read the scene between Oedipus and Tiresias (300–462; 340–526). To what extent do you think Oedipus shows justified concern for his citizens, and to what extent is he behaving tyrannically?

hybris a range of behaviours from outrageous or excessive conduct through to physical or sexual assault

tyrannos or tyrant) was a troubling prospect, associated with the bad old days and with the Persians, who had invaded Greece in the previous generation. It is no coincidence that the kings of tragedy are often touchy, over-emotional, and dangerously quick to anger, since these are all negative stereotypes that Athenians associated with tyrants.

In *Oedipus the King*, we find an ambiguous presentation of kingship. Oedipus is certainly not the popular image of a wicked tyrant. He rules with the consent of his citizens, who express their respect and fondness for him. The chorus speak of the loyalty they feel for the king who saved them from the Sphinx, while the Priest of Zeus describes him as the 'first of men' (33–4; 41). For his part, Oedipus is a benevolent ruler who cares about his citizens' wellbeing. He expresses his sorrow at the plight of Thebes, addressing his citizens as 'my children' (58; 69). His unwavering determination to discover Laius' murderer is driven by his commitment to saving his people, and the reason he becomes angry with Tiresias is because he believes him to be withholding information that will benefit Thebes (322–3, 330–1, 339–40; 366–8, 376–7, 386–7).

On the other hand, when Oedipus is thwarted, we see some of the stereotypes the Greeks associated with tyrants: he is quick to anger, takes things personally, uses his power arbitrarily, and is paranoid about his position. In the second scene with Creon, we see how a single ruler acts as an impediment to justice, since Creon is forced to defend himself to a judge who is also his prosecutor (513–678; 573–750). Creon has no chance of a fair trial, since Oedipus has already decided he is guilty, and is resolved to have him killed (623; 698).

In *Bacchae* we see a more negative portrayal of how power can corrupt, as Pentheus believes himself to be the only source of legitimate authority in Thebes. Pentheus is paranoid that Bacchism represents a threat to the political stability of Thebes. His power leads him to act with insolence, believing that there are no checks on how he may behave. For example, when he is defied by Tiresias, he orders his servants to destroy his prophetic seat and costume (346–50; 275–8). Similarly, he tries to humiliate Dionysus by cutting his sacred locks and removing his thyrsus (493–6; 404–7), as well as imprisoning him and threatening him with stoning. This type of **hybris** (insolence or arrogance) was a feature the Greeks associated with tyrants, as we are reminded in the chorus of *Oedipus,* who sing that 'pride [hybris] breeds the tyrant' (873; 963). In older scholarship, you may come across the view that hybris always refers to overstepping the boundary between gods and mortals, but this is outdated, and the term is much broader than purely referring to religious matters.

THE IMPORTANCE OF FAMILY RELATIONSHIPS

As we have seen, tragedy is interested in the different components that make up a stable society, and how these can unravel. Since the primary unit of society is the family (or **oikos**), it is not surprising that tragedy is filled with dysfunctional families, where husbands and wives show hostility to each other, and the parent–child relationship is one that brings danger instead of protection.

Both set plays feature distorted family relationships. In *Oedipus the King*, we have a child whose parents try to kill him at birth, and who grows up to kill rather than respect his father, and to marry his mother. Oedipus describes the breakdown of the family that this transgression has brought about (1403–8):

> Marriages! O marriage, you gave me birth,
> and once you brought me into the world
> you brought my sperm rising back, springing to light
> fathers, brothers, sons – one murderous breed –
> brides, wives, mothers. The blackest things
> a man can do, I have done them all.

The image of different family members inside the same womb reflects how Oedipus' behaviour has contaminated his family. This is also brought out in his assumption that his daughters will not find husbands (1501–2; 1643–5). Marriage was the ultimate goal for any Greek woman, and part of a father's responsibility to his daughters was to make them suitable matches. Rather than providing for his children, Oedipus fears that he has doomed them to a miserable life.

Bacchae too depicts killing within the family, since Pentheus is killed by his mother Agave. In both plays, these horrifying events occur without the full understanding of the family-members involved. Thus while Oedipus is well aware that he killed a man, it has never occurred to him that it could be his father, while Agave is bewitched by Dionysus and believes she has killed a lion. The Messenger's description of Pentheus touching his mother's cheek and trying to make her recognise him (1117–19; 952–4) makes the gruesome description of how she tears him limb from limb still more horrific.

The vase shown in Figure 1.32 depicts the moment where Pentheus is torn apart by his mother and aunt. The artist has depicted the dismemberment in grisly detail. Pentheus' torso has already been ripped from his lower limbs, and we can see a bone and internal organs protruding from what is left of his abdomen. The two women are preparing to rip his arms from the shoulder sockets, and to tear off his head. A satyr oversees events, and his presence reminds us that this is all occurring under Dionysus' watch. The panther-skins that the two central women wear are also emblems of the god, as well as showing the maenads' power over wild animals.

The vase predates Euripides' *Bacchae* by some seventy-five years, and so reminds us that Euripides was only one among various artists to be inspired by this myth. The fate of Pentheus captured the imagination of storytellers for generations, and it is by chance that we today regard *Bacchae* as the authoritative version.

oikos literally 'house', this term is used to describe a household or family unit

Study Question
Read the lines where Agave enters with Pentheus' head and is brought back to her senses by Cadmus (1168–300; 997–1130). How might the actors bring out the horror of this scene?

FIGURE 1.32

The death of Pentheus. (Douris Painter red-figure cup showing the death of Pentheus (exterior) and a maenad (interior), c. 480 BC. Terracotta, H. 5 in. (12.7 cm), Diam. 11½ in. (29.2 cm), AP 2000.02, Kimbell Art Museum, Fort Worth, Texas.)

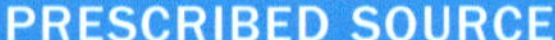

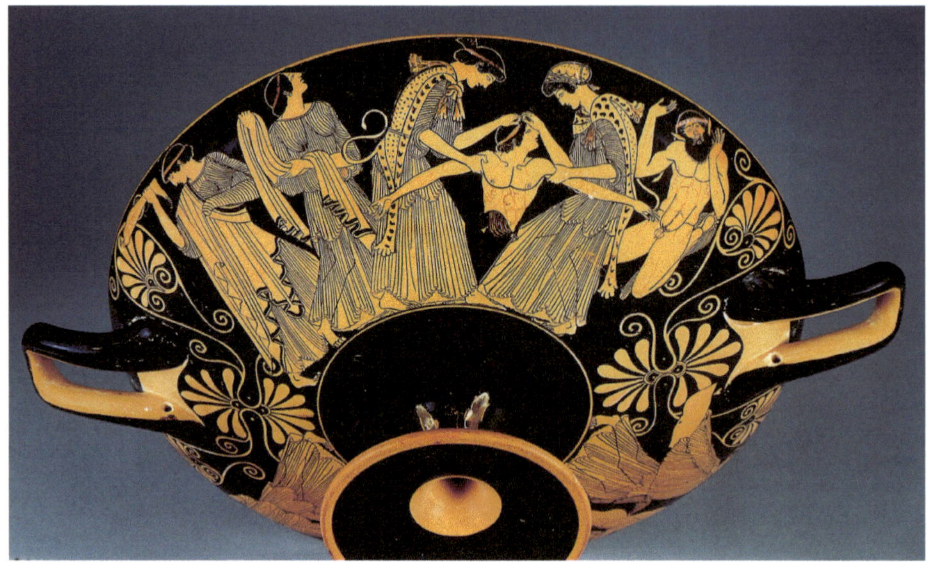

Like Oedipus, Pentheus' mistakes destroy his family, since he is the sole heir to the Theban royal house, as Cadmus laments at 1304–5 (1135–7). Ensuring the safe continuance of one's family line was a central part of male identity, and a man who did not produce legitimate heirs had failed in his duty to his forefathers. Thus, Cadmus' fate is a particularly harsh one, since he lives to see his family destroyed, while Pentheus in turn has failed in his responsibility to his family.

TRAGIC HEROISM

When people speak of a tragic hero, they are usually influenced by Aristotle's analysis of tragedy in his *Poetics,* which you have already encountered on pp. 36–8. As you have seen, Aristotle has firm views on what makes someone a tragic hero: he must not be exceptionally good or wicked, but must fall as a result of a mistake (hamartia). This analysis has been powerful in shaping modern responses, and Aristotle was the first of many attempts to define what is typical about the tragic hero.

It is certainly true that tragic heroes' ruin results from their own behaviour. For example, Oedipus has made choices that led him to kill his father and marry his mother, and during the play he insists on finding out the truth, despite being warned that it will destroy him. Similarly, Pentheus refuses to recognise Dionysus' divinity, despite the warnings of his grandfather, the prophet Tiresias, and the god himself. Seeing someone make mistakes that bring them to destruction is more powerful than watching bad luck happen to an innocent victim, and Aristotle's theory highlights this. However, the risk of trying to isolate a single hamartia in any given play is that it can distract us from the essential issues at stake, and we must not let it become a 'one-size-fits-all' solution to interpreting tragedy.

Oedipus the King is a good example. Oedipus certainly made mistakes (he killed his father and married his mother). He also has character flaws, notably his angry temper, and this is relevant to his killing of his father. But it would be hard to claim that anger

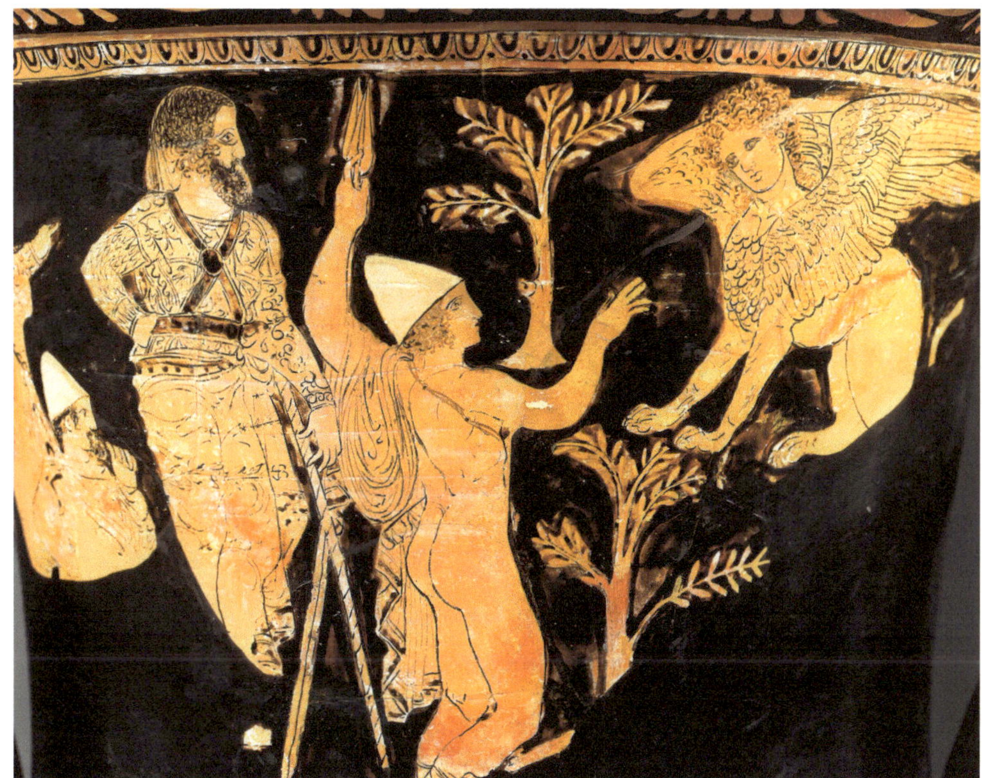

FIGURE 1.33
Oedipus answers the riddle of the Sphinx.

was the single factor that caused his downfall, since one could equally well attribute it to his intelligence, which allowed him to defeat the Sphinx and so marry his mother. Oedipus also committed a hamartia in the intellectual sense, in that he was ignorant of his true identity. However, Oedipus' original mistakes are in the past, and the focus of the play is not on what he did wrong, but on his discovery of his identity and his reaction to it. Much of the play's power derives from the terrifying fact that the gods make good people suffer for no obvious reason, and this refutes any simple answer to what Oedipus did wrong and why.

In the twentieth century, another influential analysis of what defines a tragic hero was that of the classicist Bernard Knox, who applied Aristotle's ideas to the plays of Sophocles and tried to come up with a comprehensive model in his book *The Heroic Temper*. Knox defined the tragic hero as someone who makes a decision rooted in his personal nature (**physis**), and maintains it to the point of self-destruction. Knox saw the crucial feature of the hero as his inability to yield: he is faced with opposition but 'remains true to himself'. Thus, for example, Oedipus will not give up his quest to discover the killer of Laius, despite encountering resistance from all the other characters.

> **physis** personal nature, something you are born with, not taught or changed by circumstances

With both Aristotle and Knox, it is important not to be tempted by the simplicity of a one-size-fits-all approach to understanding Greek tragedy. Tempting as it may be to want a single 'answer' to how to understand the tragic hero, heroism comes in different forms. This is surely something to celebrate rather than be daunted by, since it would be disappointing if the works of the tragedians could be reduced to a formula. While Oedipus and Pentheus have similarities (they are both stubborn and short-tempered, for example), they are also very different in other respects: for example, their age, personality, their standing with other characters in the play, and the route by which they suffer their downfall, and so even looking at the two set plays gives us an insight into the diversity of heroism within tragedy.

However, the fact that there is no simple model for the tragic hero does not mean that we cannot identify typical features, and as long as we avoid the tendency to oversimplify, Aristotle and Knox both offer good starting points. Knox's view of the tragic hero presents the hero's inflexibility in a positive light, and his refusal to yield becomes a badge of honour. Knox is right that we find heroes attractive. Aristotle may claim that a hero must not be pre-eminent for virtue, but heroes in tragedy are often pre-eminent in their capacity for particular virtues, in particular bravery, strength, tenacity and loyalty, and it is because we admire them that we care about their fate. It is hard not to be impressed by Oedipus' dedication to finding out the truth about what happened to Laius, for example. However, the hero's faults are as significant as his admirable qualities, and here Aristotle's focus on the imperfections of the hero becomes relevant.

It is important to be careful about the connotations carried by the English word 'hero', which are strongly positive. Today we call someone a 'hero' when they carry out an exceptionally good and selfless deed (a soldier who risks his life to save a comrade, for example, or a passer-by who pulls a child out of a river). In the Greek world, however, heroes are not necessarily good as much as larger than life, and the traits that they embody are held to excess. Heroes are proud, egotistical, violent and cruel, as well as powerful and charismatic.

The hero's tendency to excess gives the playwright scope to explore the benefits and drawbacks of particular character traits. In *Bacchae*, for example, Pentheus becomes fixated on the idea that Dionysiac cult is dangerous, and will go to any lengths to prevent it taking root in Thebes. His obsession with the idea that the bacchants are indulging in promiscuity brings about his death because of his prurient desire to spy on them. Often the hero's character traits are not inherently bad, but become problematic when pushed to an extreme. For example, Oedipus' persistence is admirable, but his single-mindedness turns him into an unpleasant bully as he threatens Tiresias (334–446; 380–507) and Creon (532–630; 594–705), and suggests torturing the old shepherd (1152–4; 1266–9). Similarly, Pentheus' excessive pursuit of the bacchants in the name of protecting Thebes leads him to imprison the women of his own city and dishonour its prophet.

Heroes not only bring about their downfall but also cause difficulties to those around them. This is clear at the end of *Bacchae*, where Cadmus laments the effect that Pentheus' death will have on him: as an old man he no longer has any relatives to protect him and will end his life dishonoured (1305–15; 1135–42). Oedipus too causes Jocasta's death and leaves his young children to face destitution.

The question of how to reconcile a powerful individual with the needs of his community long precedes Greek tragedy. Homer's *Iliad* explores similar ideas, as it depicts how the greatest Greek hero, Achilles, pushes his desire for honour too far and so becomes alienated from his companions. However, these questions took on a particular resonance in democratic Athens, a society which emphasised that one should act for the common good. Yet aristocratic families remained powerful in the democracy: they formed the majority of generals and speakers in the assembly, and it was they who paid for public benefits, for example funding tragedy as chorēgoi. Heroes therefore appeal to an Athenian audience because they embody these tensions and represent the aristocrats of their own day, but are safely enclosed in a mythological world.

The Greeks expected their poetry to be instructive, and heroes can act as moral paradigms, illustrating the best and worst aspects of human nature. Yet the heroes are rooted in the world of myth, and embody a different set of values to those held by contemporary Athenians. While they might well sympathise with their suffering and admire their power, they would also fear their excess, and were perhaps relieved that such people no longer existed. The glamour of the heroes coupled with their terrible suffering makes them irresistible fodder to the tragedians, and part of the success of Greek tragedy is its ability to depict the different aspects of the heroes on stage, their admirable strength and intellect, combined with their disastrous errors.

Justice and revenge

To an ordinary Greek, the founding principle of justice was that one should help one's friends and harm one's enemies. Thus the idea that justice is a form of reciprocity, and hence of revenge, is deeply rooted in Greek culture. Aristotle takes the view, for example, that the desire for revenge is not only natural, but admirable (*Rhetoric* 1367a24):

> To take vengeance on one's enemies is nobler than to come to terms with them; for to retaliate is just, and what is just is noble; and a real man does not allow himself to be beaten.

However, we should not assume that the Greeks saw no problems with revenge, since a common theme in tragedy is the difficulties that it can cause. Since a wrong act incurs a reciprocal act of retaliation, unchecked vengeance can quickly spiral out of control. Oedipus' killing of Laius, for example, reveals the dangers of a moral code that invites one to retaliate against injustice without thought for the consequences (800–13; 884–98):

> Making my way toward this triple crossroad
> I began to see a herald, then a brace of colts
> drawing a wagon, and mounted on the bench … a man,
> just as you've described him, coming face-to-face,
> and the one in the lead and the old man himself
> were about to thrust me off the road – brute force –
> and the one shouldering me aside, the driver,
> I strike him in anger! – and the old man watching me
> coming up along his wheels – he brings down
> his prod, two prongs straight at my head!
> I paid him back with interest!
> Short work, by god – with one blow of the staff
> in this right hand I knock him out of his high seat,
> roll him out of the wagon, sprawling headlong –
> I killed them all – every mother's son!

Laius commits the first injustice by trying to push Oedipus off the road, and Oedipus retaliates by hitting his driver. Laius then hits Oedipus over the head with the goad used to whip the horses, and Oedipus returns a blow which kills him. At each stage, the act of retaliation takes the violence to a new level. Because neither party can let go of their desire for revenge, a disagreement over who has right of way ends up as a bloodbath.

The dangers of reciprocity are what distinguishes human vengeance from that of the gods, since the gods can respond as harshly as they please to any slight, without fear for how the injured party or their relatives may respond. This idea is made explicit at the end of *Bacchae,* when Cadmus acknowledges that Dionysus has been wronged, but criticises him for going too far in his punishment (1344–9; 1167–74):

PS

> Cadmus: Dionysus, we beg you – we have done wrong!
> Dionysus: You are late in recognising me; when you should have seen me, you did not.
> Cadmus: We have come to understand that, but you punish too severely!
> Dionysus: Yes, for I am a god, and I was insulted by you.
> Cadmus: It is not right that the gods should resembe mortals in their passions.
> Dionysus: My father Zeus agreed to this long ago.

Dionysus' defence of his actions is that this is the moral order decreed by Zeus: the justice of the gods is harsher than that of mortals. However, Cadmus questions this *status quo*, arguing that gods should aspire to higher ethical standards than mortals. Questioning the justice of the gods is typical of Euripides, and we find similar scenes in other plays. In making these issues explicit, Euripides is drawing a connection with contemporary debates among intellectuals about what justice means, and whether it is something derived from human society or imposed upon us by the gods.

The principle that motivates Dionysus' concept of justice is that the wrongdoer must suffer. Whether this punishment is proportionate to the crime is less important than that Pentheus is punished for his failure to respect the god. This basic principle that the 'doer suffers' is found throughout Greek tragedy, and is perhaps the cornerstone of tragedy's conception of justice. This cycle of crime and punishment may be harsh, but it is also predictable, and people who commit wrong acts must do so in the knowledge that they and those around them will be punished. However, this does not mean that the audience has to accept it unquestioningly, and tragedy often depicts the painful results of this system.

S & C Read the ending of Euripides' play *Heracles* (1255–428). What arguments are made on both sides about the nature of the gods? How does it compare to *Bacchae?*

In real life, retaliation was not the appropriate way to respond to an unjust act, however tempting it might be. Then as now, an organised system of justice existed to arbitrate disputes. The close relationship between justice and vengeance that existed in the Greek mind is shown by the fact that the Greek word 'timōria' can mean both 'vengeance' and 'the punishment decided by the court'. Thus the city exacted vengeance on behalf of the individual, but by depersonalising the system, a judgement could be a final verdict rather than causing a chain of violence.

Fifth-century Athenians were proud of their legal system, which formed an important part of the democracy, and tragedy often shows the superiority of a legal process to vendetta violence. Tragedy is set in a pre-legal age, where formal law courts often do not yet exist and the king can take justice into his own hands. Unsurprisingly, this system frequently has disastrous consequences.

We see its drawbacks in the scene between Oedipus and Creon. As the king, Oedipus is entitled to decide whether Creon is guilty and how he should be punished. However, Oedipus is personally involved in the situation, and is unable to act dispassionately. Creon is only saved because Oedipus is persuaded by Jocasta and the chorus, who are better positioned to convince him. This highlights the random nature of personalised justice, whereby a person's fate depends on the whim of someone more powerful.

Study Question
Does Pentheus deserve his fate? Do you think that a modern audience's response to this question would be different to an ancient audience's?

TOPIC REVIEW

These questions should draw on your knowledge of the whole topic, so think carefully about the different things you have learned (check the Topic Overview on p. 60).

1. Do you think the gods behave justly in Greek tragedy?
2. How political do you think the tragedies you have read are?
3. To what extent do you think Sophocles and Euripides uphold traditional beliefs about women, and to what extent do you think they undermine them?
4. How would you define the tragic hero? Do you feel that the theories you have read help you?

Further Reading

Foley, H., *Female Acts in Greek Tragedy* (Princeton: Princeton University Press, 2001).

Garvie, A., *The Plays of Sophocles* (London: Bloomsbury Academic, 2016), Chapter 4.

Knox, B.M.W., *The Heroic Temper* (Berkeley: University of California Press, 1964).

Mills, S., *Euripides: Bacchae* (London: Bloomsbury Academic, 2006).

Morwood, J., *The Plays of Euripides* (London; Bloomsbury Academic, 2016), Chapter 17.

Parker, R., 'Gods Cruel and Kind', in C. Pelling (ed.), *Greek Tragedy and the Historian* (Oxford: Clarendon Press, 1997), 147–60.

Stuttard, D., *Looking at Bacchae* (London: Bloomsbury Academic, 2016).

PRACTICE QUESTIONS

Source A: *Oedipus the King* 1–13 (1–15)

O my children, the new blood of ancient Thebes,
why are you here? Huddling at my altar,
praying before me, your branches wound in wool.
Our city reeks with the smoke of burning incense,
rings with cries for the Healer and wailing for the dead.
I thought it wrong, my children, to hear the truth
from others, messengers. Here I am myself—
you all know me, the world knows my fame:

I am Oedipus.
                          Helping a Priest to his feet.
                Speak up, old man. Your years,
your dignity – you should speak for the others.
Why here and kneeling, what preys upon you so?
Some sudden fear? Some strong desire?
You can trust me. I am ready to help,
I'll do anything. I would be blind to misery
not to pity my people kneeling at my feet.

AS Level

1. What is the crisis that Oedipus is referring to here? [1]
2. How does Oedipus come across as a ruler in this passage? Make *four* points and support each
   point with Source A [8]

A Level

1. What is the crisis that Oedipus is referring to here? [1]
2. Evaluate what we learn from Source A about the representation of kingship in Greek tragedy? [10]

1.6 Social and Political Themes in Comedy

This topic will investigate how *Frogs* engages with social and political themes relevant to its audience. First it will discuss how Aristophanes depicts tragedy and the tragedians. Next it will explore what the play reveals about religious belief, and end with a discussion of how the play relates to the social values of its day and to contemporary politics.

THE REPRESENTATION AND SATIRE OF TRAGEDY

Comedy's interest in tragedy reveals how central tragedy was to Athenian cultural life. Some of Aristophanes' other plays include parody of tragedy, for example his *Women at the Thesmophoria* presents the women of Athens secretly plotting against Euripides. However, it is in *Frogs* that tragedy receives its most sustained treatment, since the plot is dominated by the personalities of the individual tragedians and the idea that tragic poetry can save Athens.

Frogs begins with Dionysus deciding to go to Hades to recover a tragic playwright for personal reasons: he tells Heracles that he is pining for the work of Euripides, since the tragedians left in Athens are inferior (64–103), At the end of the play, however, when unable to determine which playwright is better, Dionysus reveals that there is another factor that will influence his decision (1418–19):

I came down for a poet.
Why? So that the city could be saved and put on plays.

Tragedy is not just for enjoyment, but has a civic function. The right playwright will save Athens from the crisis that is engulfing her. Dionysus expands upon this by asking both tragedians for political advice. This reflects the ancient idea that poetry of all kinds should fulfil a didactic function (from the Greek word 'didasko' meaning 'I teach'): its aim was to offer moral guidance and make them better citizens. Tragedy's special place in Athenian culture gave it particular influence, and this forms a central theme of the agōn between Aeschylus and Euripides. Thus Euripides states that a tragedian should be admired 'because we make people in our cities better' 1010), while Aeschylus comments 'Children have teachers to instruct them, young men have poets' (1055). However, while the playwrights agree on the educational importance of tragedy, they argue about how this mission should be fulfilled. Aeschylus claims that Euripides has corrupted Athenian morals by presenting wicked deeds on stage, and argues that a tragedian should conceal bad behaviour, not encourage it by presenting it on stage (1053–4). Half a century later we find the same argument used by Plato in his *Republic*, who criticises all the tragedians (including Aeschylus) for promoting immoral behaviour.

Aristophanes also satirises the tragedians as individuals. As we have already seen (pp. 27–9), his presentation needs to be viewed with scepticism, especially since the personalities of Aeschylus and Euripides are derived from stereotypes about their work. Yet we also find references to well-known characteristics about contemporary tragedians, who were celebrities of their day and so attracted interest and gossip. For example, Aristophanes refers in passing to Sophocles' genial personality (82), and refers to Sophocles' son Iophon, another tragic playwright, with the snide suggestion that he had help from his father in writing his best works (77).

The focus on Aeschylus and Euripides also demonstrates how the formation of the canon of the three great tragedians was already well underway in Aristophanes' lifetime (Sophocles probably died shortly before *Frogs* was first performed, and so too late to be fully incorporated into the script). Dionysus makes it clear that these are the only playwrights worth considering truly great. Nevertheless, jokes about other playwrights such as Xenocles, Agathon and Pythangelus reminds us that tragedy continued after the death of Sophocles. Aristophanes' insistence in *Frogs* that no playwrights other than Aeschylus, Sophocles and Euripides wrote anything of merit itself probably played a role in the exclusive focus on these playwrights, and the loss of the works by others.

Frogs also includes a sustained and sophisticated parody of the style of the individual tragedians. This assumes a high level of knowledge on the part of Aristophanes'

A good example of how Aristophanes satirises the tragedians' style is his parody of the style of Euripidean **monody** (1330–63). As we have seen, tragic characters often sing **monodies** in moments of emotional turmoil, and this tendency is particularly marked in Euripides. Here, however, the singer is a poor woman who has a bad dream and then discovers that her neighbour Glyke has stolen her cockerel. The gap between the mundane subject matter and the high-flown language creates humour. For example, the singer calls out 'Ah, house-mates, behold the signs: My cockerel has been stolen. Glyce's taken him, off and away!' (1342–3). We might expect the horrible sight in this tragedy to be a dreadful murder, but all we have is a missing bird. Similarly, the singer's response to this loss, calling upon the gods to avenge her and weeping excessively over her loss, is humorously over the top. The song picks up on Euripides' boast that he brought everyday affairs on stage (959) and takes it to absurd lengths. The monody also parodies detailed aspects of Euripides' style, for example his tendency to repeat words for emotional effect (here satirised in phrases such as 'And left me grief, grief, tears, tears from my eyes pouring forth, pouring forth in my misery', 1353–5).

audience: indeed the chorus encourage Aeschylus and Euripides not to worry that the audience will not follow (1108–14):

> If what alarms you is the ignorance
> of the audience, the fear they may not see
> The subtlety of your arguments, don't panic.
> It's not like that any more. They've all seen combat:
> They've got the book and grasped the finer points.

Of course this is designed to flatter the audience, as we can see from the passage that follows where they are said to be physically well-endowed as well as intellectually capable, and we should not take it as evidence that every audience member had a personal library. However, there must have been enough who could appreciate the subtler allusions that it was worth Aristophanes' while to put them in. Those who had seen some of their plays would still get the gist of the humour even if they missed the finer points, and would not feel excluded by what they did not notice. Even those with little knowledge could find humour in the contrast between the fine words of the playwrights and Dionysus' naive interjections.

EXPLORE FURTHER

Read *Orestes* 1368–1502, a monody sung by a lowborn character. Can you find similarities with Aristophanes' parody of Euripidean monody at *Frogs* 1330–63?

ANCIENT RELIGIOUS CONCEPTS

The role of the gods

Far from being supremely powerful and all-knowing, the Dionysus of comedy is a buffoon. Mocking the gods in the context of comedy was not considered blasphemous by the Athenians, and Dionysus in particular was fair game. As we have seen with reference to *Bacchae*, Dionysus in myth was presented as a new god who had to fight to establish himself on the same level as the other Olympians. While *Bacchae* presents this as a deadly serious struggle, comedy uses Dionysus' unusual status to make him the target of mockery. The fact that he is also the god of wine, and of liberation from inhibitions, gives comedy leeway to present him as wild and humorous.

We know of other comedies where Dionysus tries to do something serious but instead becomes the butt of the humour. Twenty-five years before *Frogs*, the playwright Cratinus had produced a comedy called *Dionysalexandros* (*Dionysus as Paris*) where Dionysus tried to take on the role of Paris but botched it (in myth, Paris judged a beauty contest between three goddesses and chose Aphrodite because she promised him the love of the most beautiful woman in the world). Other comedies depicted Dionysus trying and failing to become a soldier or an athlete. Thus Aristophanes' portrayal draws on a tradition of finding humour at the god's expense. The fact that this was a comedy gave the playwrights licence to make jokes that might in other circumstances be considered inappropriate. That it was performed at a festival in honour of Dionysus himself only adds to the humour.

In *Frogs*, Aristophanes overturns traditional attributes of Dionysus. A striking example is the contest in which Dionysus and Xanthias are beaten to establish who is really the god, which draws on the belief that gods could feel no pain. However, Dionysus in fact feels the pain just as much as his slave, and has to try to conceal it. Similarly, he is forced to row himself to Hades and does not even know how to do this properly, since he takes Charon's instruction 'at your oar' literally, and does not realise he is meant to row (197–9). He is a coward, and having boasted that he is looking forward to taking on monsters in the underworld (285–311) is terrified when he thinks he will actually meet one (285–311). Whereas in *Bacchae* Dionysus is beautiful, in *Frogs* he is out of shape (200). However, Dionysus is not unlikeable, and like many heroes of comedy, he represents a kind of 'everyman' figure, whom the audience can sympathise with as well as laugh at.

Nevertheless, Dionysus reflects the traditional idea of the gods as saviours, since it emerges that he wishes to bring back the playwright most likely to save Athens. Towards the end of the play, Dionysus becomes less of a figure of fun, and is able to make a decision between the playwrights and so ensure the city's salvation. The torchlit procession which ends the play creates a mood of holiness, reminiscent of real-life rituals.

Death and the afterlife

In many ways, *Frogs* depicts the traditional poetic view of the afterlife, which can be traced back to the epic poetry of Homer. This portrays the dead as ghosts with their old personalities and memories. Hades itself is a place neither of blessings nor punishment, but the dead would much prefer to be restored to life. In *Frogs* the dead appear to live in Hades in much the same way as they lived in the world above, and the playwrights behave as they did in life, though both Aeschylus and Euripides are keen to return to the world above. The myth of Charon the ferryman is also traditional (though not found in Homer), and Aristophanes alludes to other myths about the underworld, for example the story that Heracles travelled to Hades to capture the guard dog Cerberus. However, in the spirit of comedy, many of these elements are gently parodied: thus the bleak waters of the underworld are filled with singing frogs, Pluto is a genial host, and Heracles is vilified as a common dog-thief.

By travelling down to Hades while alive, Dionysus repeats a folkloric story-pattern of the hero who travels into the realm of death to fulfil a quest. Heracles had to travel to Hades as the last of his twelve labours, while Odysseus had to consult the dead to find his way home. Dionysus' motivation at first appears more trivial than those of these heroes, since at the start of the play he compares his desire for Euripides to lust for pea soup or sex (58–69). However, as the true nature of his quest is revealed to be the redemption of Athens, his depiction as a hero becomes less absurd; as in the myths of Heracles and Odysseus, it is only by breaching the gulf between death and life that salvation can be achieved.

The chorus represent another strand in Greek beliefs about the afterlife, since they consist of initiates into the **Eleusinian Mysteries**, one of the most important cults in the Greek world, and one open to everyone, male or female, free or slave. This was a set of rites which celebrated the myth of Demeter's separation from and reunion with her daughter Persephone. The details of what initiation into the Mysteries involved was secret, and it was a serious offence to reveal the details. Making fun of the Mysteries was also considered deeply shocking, and so Aristophanes needed to handle the subject with delicacy to avoid upsetting his audience.

The chorus in *Frogs* reveal no secret information about the initiation process but they do draw on real aspects of the Mysteries, for example, their prayer to Demeter (383–93) or their invocation of the god Iacchus (316–52). Iacchus was the god carried in procession from Athens to Eleusis when the Mysteries were celebrated, and this procession would have been public. Similarly, the chorus' joy in their worship and the beautiful meadow in which they live reflect the belief that initiation into the Mysteries led to rewards in the afterlife. This privileged status is also suggested by the smell of roast pork

> **Eleusinian Mysteries** an important religious cult in honour of Demeter and her daughter Persephone. Anyone who wished could be initiated into the cult at the annual rites in September

EXPLORE FURTHER

The story of Demeter and Persephone is told in the *Homeric Hymn to Demeter*, an early poem associated with the goddess. Persephone was abducted by Hades (an alternative name for the god who in *Frogs* is called Pluto), and in her grief, her mother Demeter stopped the earth's fertility. Fearing that humanity would be destroyed, Zeus arranged for Persephone to return to earth, but Hades tricked her into eating pomegranate seeds, which compelled her to return to the underworld for part of the year. Persephone was believed to spend the winter in Hades, but could return to the upper world in spring. The story of Demeter and Persephone is therefore associated with death and rebirth, a theme echoed in the Mysteries.

The poem also tells how during Demeter's wanderings, the goddess travelled to Eleusis, where, disguised as an old woman, she became nursemaid to the king's son. Demeter tried to make the baby immortal by holding him in the fire, but was interrupted by his mother. She revealed her true identity, and ordered a cult to be established in her honour at Eleusis. Thus the poem explains the origins of the Mysteries.

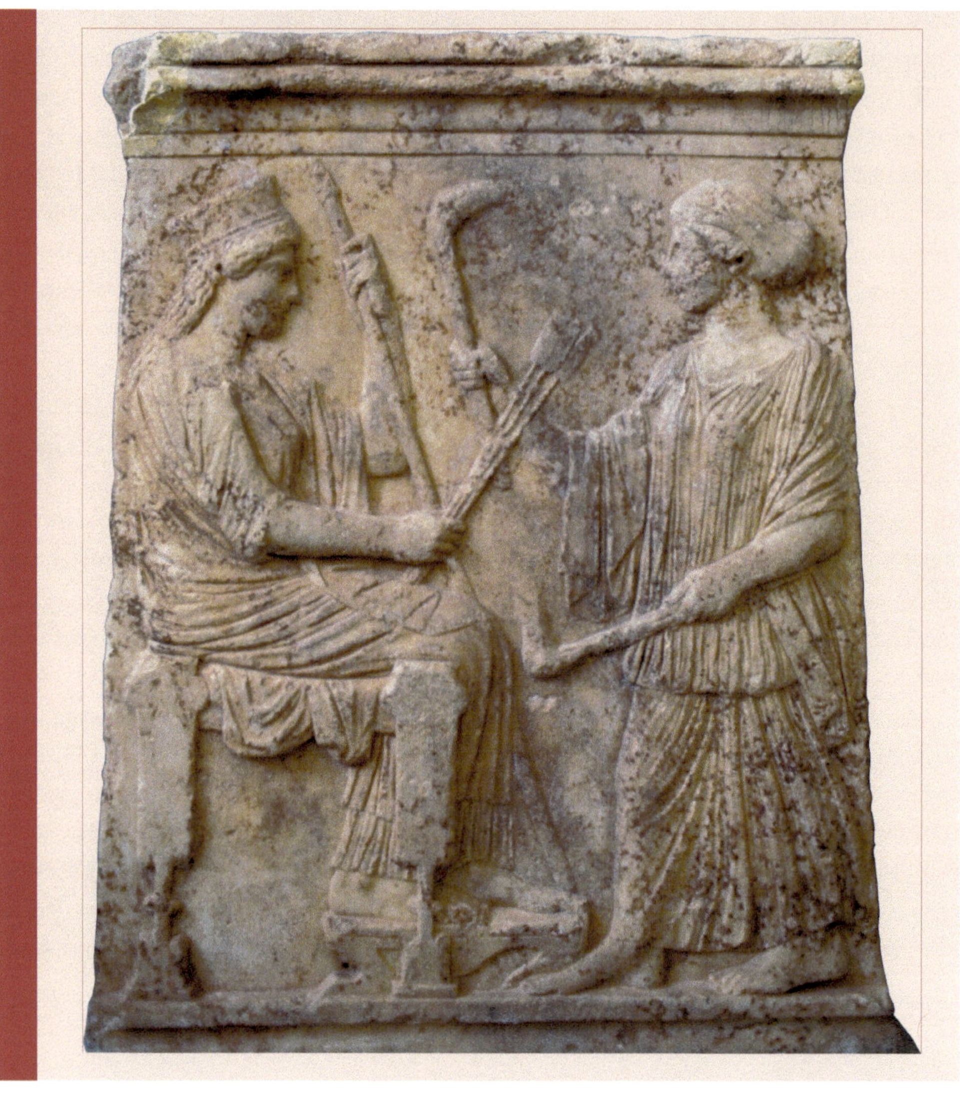

which Xanthias comments on (338): sacrificing suckling pigs to Demeter was part of the rituals, and the initiates continue their feasting in the underworld.

The founding myth of the Mysteries is death followed by rebirth, and this echoes the wider pattern of the play, where Dionysus travels to the underworld and resurrects a dead playwright. Just as the rebirth of Persephone saved the earth from starvation, the rebirth of a tragedian will save Athens from disaster. Thus by choosing a chorus of initiates, Aristophanes not only links his chorus to the themes of the play but offers his audience a sense of hope.

THE IMPORTANCE OF THE POLIS (CITY)

The preoccupations of contemporary Athenians are central to comedy's themes. The jokes are aimed at social as well as political matters, and relationships within the family are also a source of humour. Thus comedy explores daily life in the polis and pokes fun at all of its members, regardless of their social status.

Position and role of men, women and slaves

While there are few female characters in *Frogs*, women's position in society is still of interest to the play. This is foregrounded in the debate between the tragedians, where Aeschylus accuses Euripides of damaging Athenian society by depicting wicked women (1049–51):

> Euripides: And what harm did my Stheneboeas ever do to the city, you old fool?
> Aeschylus: You persuaded noble ladies, wives of noble husbands, to drink hemlock
>   because they were ashamed of your Bellerophon.

This refers to Euripides' lost play *Stheneboea*, in which the title character attempts to seduce Bellerophon, her husband's guest, and when rejected, falsely accuses him of raping her. Aeschylus argues that this portrayal of women brings shame on the whole female sex, going as far to claim that it is causing an epidemic of suicide among upper-class Athenian women. The idea that women are killing themselves because of tragedy is no doubt a comic invention, but it does highlight the gap between dramatic depictions of women and the submissive role they are meant to adopt in everyday life. Adultery was a matter of serious concern to Athenian men, since it dishonoured them and threatened the legitimate succession of their family line, and so adulterous wives feature regularly in both tragedy and comedy. In *Frogs*, Dionysus claims that Euripides' own wife was adulterous (1047–8), turning the playwright into a laughing-stock who is unable to avoid the same fate that befell his characters.

Frogs also generates humour from the boundary between slaves and citizens. The relationship between Xanthias and Dionysus is marked by competition and banter. In fact, Xanthias overturns the stereotype that slaves are inherently inferior to free men (let alone gods!), and repeatedly outwits Dionysus, particularly in the scene where they attempt to enter Pluto's house. Far from being able to command his slave's obedience, Dionysus has to cajole him to persuade him to swap costumes, 579–82). Equally, Xanthias speaks to his master with outright insolence, for example describing him as a 'fool' (480) and a coward (486). Xanthias outwits Dionysus by accepting the role of Heracles, but when put in a tight spot, offering his 'slave' to torture as compensation (612–17). When both are beaten, the slave turns out to be the equal of the god in his ability to withstand pain, and (as he later boasts to Pluto's slave) he gets away with his insubordinate behaviour (741–3).

The presentation of a slave as more intelligent and resilient than a god is part of how comedy inverts real life structures, and we should not take it as a call for abolition of slavery. Just as a conventional Athenian would find it amusing to see a god presented as a buffoon, so too he would find humour in the topsy-turvy setup that presents a slave as better than his master.

Nevertheless, the play refers several times to the recent decision to free the slaves who had fought for Athens in the battle of Arginusae, and Xanthias regrets that he was not involved (33–4; 192). This decision is praised by the playwright in the parabasis, where it is described as 'about the only sensible thing you've done!' (695–6). The overturning of the boundary between slaves and free men is thus paralleled by recent events in Athenian history, and the audience is reminded that in real life too, slaves can be courageous, and that Athenian society depends upon them.

Nevertheless, the dialogue with Pluto's slave presents a more troubling stereotype (to an Athenian audience) of slaves gossiping and wishing their masters harm. The relative powerlessness of the slaves is clear: all they can do in response to being beaten is to curse their masters behind their backs (745–8). Yet the two slaves immediately bond over their position and swear allegiance to one another (754–5). Far from being loyal to their masters, they joke about how they like to eavesdrop on private conversations and pass them on (750–2). Since most Athenian households would have had slaves, and they would have observed private moments, this must have touched a nerve with the audience.

Political ideas and ideals

Frogs was produced at a dark time in Athenian history and the play cannot avoid reflecting the looming crisis. Athens was running out of manpower and money, and her defeat by the Peloponnesians seemed increasingly likely. Ancient cities defeated in war often suffered gruesome fates, and the Athenians themselves had inflicted dreadful punishments on the cities they had conquered. Athens risked total destruction: the exile, death, or imprisonment of the male population and the enslavement of the women and children, and the audience of *Frogs* must have been aware of the danger that they were in.

It is perhaps not surprising that in this time of crisis Aristophanes looks back with nostalgia to the days of Athenian greatness. The idea of returning to a better time underpins the debate between the tragedians, and Aeschylus repeatedly claims that his poetry is filled with the values that made Athens powerful. For example, he compares the Athenians in his day to the current generation (1013–17):

Now look at the sort of characters he got from me.
Weren't they noble and tall – not the shirkers and layabouts, the
cheats and villains you see today, but men who breathed spears
and javelins, with snowy-plumed crests, helmets, greaves and
hearts encased in seven layers of ox-hide?

Aeschylus likens the Athenians of the early fifth century to epic warriors: the language and equipment here is that of the Homeric battlefield. Shortly after this passage, he refers to the moral lessons he imparted in his play *Persians*, which commemorated the Greek defeat of the Persian invasion (1026–7). In the contemporary conflict, the Persians had joined in the fight on the side of the Spartans, and this was causing difficulties for the Athenian war effort. Aeschylus' words remind the audience of a time when Greeks were united, and when the Athenians were victorious over a mighty power.

This nostalgia takes on political form in the parabasis, where the chorus set out their complaints. They compare politicians to coins, contrasting the old coinage to the currency that Athenians now have to rely on. Athenian coinage was indeed regarded as pure, and was traditionally made of silver from the local mine at Laurium. However, the Spartan occupation of Attica had made access to the silver mines difficult, and the city was facing a currency crisis. Athenians were forced to use low-quality bronze coins for internal purchases (referred to in line 725), so that the remaining silver coins could be used for imports. The degraded coinage must have been a humiliating reminder of Athens' declining status whenever an Athenian did his shopping.

Aristophanes draws an analogy with the politicians of the current age, and complains that many of them come from foreign stock (730–3). The target of Aristophanes' abuse is the politician Cleophon (674–86), who is presented as a liar, demagogue and foreigner. Conversely, he complains that the city is ignoring virtuous men brought up with a traditional education: Raised to wrestle and dance and sing (these men we chuck aside) (729). Much of Aristophanes' political humour takes the form of general complaints rather than specific opposition. However, the parabasis does contain a piece of detailed advice: those citizens who had been stripped of their rights for supporting the oligarchic coup of 411 should have their status restored (688–92). This advice must have been controversial, as it could be seen as support for traitors who opposed democracy. However it was in fact followed later that year, after Athens lost the final battle of the Peloponnesian War.

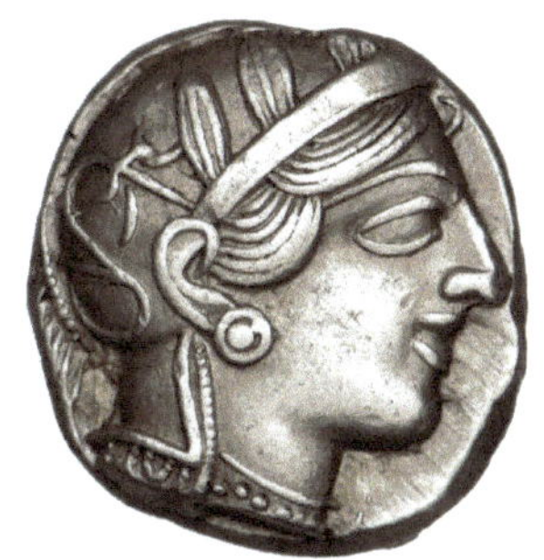

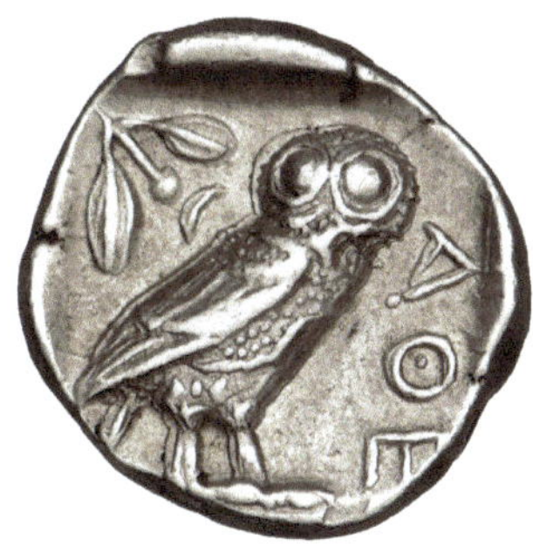

FIGURE 1.35
An Athenian silver coin showing Athena on one side and her symbol, the owl, on the other.

TOPIC REVIEW

These questions should draw on your knowledge of the whole topic, so think carefully about the different things you have learned (check the Topic Overview on p. 79).

1. How does Aristophanes present tragedy? From your own reading of tragedy, how accurate do you think his parody is?
2. Is Dionysus in *Frogs* simply a figure of fun? Does he tell us anything about how the Athenians viewed their gods?
3. What picture of the underworld do we find in *Frogs*?
4. What sort of stereotypes do we find in *Frogs* about the roles people from different social positions should adopt?

Further Reading

Bowie, A., *Aristophanes: Myth, Ritual and Comedy* (Cambridge: Cambridge University Press, 1996), Chapter 10.
Dover, K., *Aristophanic Comedy* (Berkeley and Los Angeles: University of California Press, 1974), Chapter 15.
Konstan, D., *Greek Comedy and Ideology* (Oxford: Oxford University Press, 1995), Chapter 4.
MacDowell, D., *Aristophanes and Athens* (Oxford: Oxford University Press, 1995), Chapter 12.

PRACTICE QUESTIONS

Source A: *Frogs* 21–34

Dionysus: This is the limit. It's what comes of spoiling him. Here am I, Dionysus, son of Flagon, and I am the one walking and doing all the hard work. I let him ride so that he won't get worn out by carrying the burden.

Xanthias: And aren't I the one carrying it?

Dionysus: How can you be carrying it, when you are the burden?

Xanthias: I'm carrying all this.

Dionysus: And how are you bearing it?

Xanthias: Very badly.

Dionysus: Now this burden you're bearing – isn't the donkey carrying it?

Xanthias: Definitely not. I've got it, I'm the one bearing it – not the donkey, goddamit.

Dionysus: But how can you be doing the carrying, when you are actually being carried by something else?

Xanthias: I don't know. But my shoulder's feeling the pressure.

Dionysus: Since you say the donkey's no help to you, swap over. You pick the donkey up and carry him instead.

Xanthias: Ah, woe is me, poor wretch! Why didn't I fight in that sea-battle! Then I could tell you to bugger off.

AS Level

1. What happened to the slaves involved in the battle of Arginusae? [2]
2. How is the relationship between Dionysus and Xanthias characterised in this passage? Make four points and support each point with Source A. [8]

A Level

1. What is the relevance of the battle of Arginusae mentioned by Xanthias? [2]
2. What impression of the master–slave relationship does Source A give us? [10]

What to Expect in the AS Exam for Greek Theatre

This chapter aims to show you the types of questions you are likely to get in the written examination. It offers some advice on how to answer the questions and will help you avoid common errors.

THE EXAMINATION

This component of the AS Classical Civilisation examination is designed to test your knowledge, understanding and evaluation of Greek theatre. The examination is worth 65 marks and lasts 1 hour and 30 minutes. This represents 50% of the total marks for the AS Level.

There are two Assessment Objectives in your AS Level, and questions will be designed to test these areas. These Assessment Objectives are outlined in the table below, together with the total number of marks available for each on the paper:

	Assessment Objective	Marks
AO1	Demonstrate knowledge and understanding of: • literature and visual/material culture • how sources and ideas reflect, and influence, their cultural contexts • possible interpretations of sources, perspectives and ideas by different audiences and individuals.	32
AO2	Critically analyse, interpret and evaluate literature and visual/material culture, using evidence to make substantiated judgements and produce coherent and reasoned arguments.	33

Exam structure and question types

The exam is divided into two sections, Section A and Section B.

There are four question types in this exam:

- two sets of short answer questions (four marks in total each)
- 8-mark stimulus questions
- 16-mark shorter essay
- 25-mark essay

Try to plan your time well. The shorter essay question and the essay question together make up 41 of the 65 marks available, and so you should aim to spend the majority of your time on these two questions.

Section A has the following format:

There will be a prescribed visual/material source on the paper. This will be called 'Source A'.

- You will be asked the first set of short answer questions, worth 1 or 2 marks each. Of the 4 marks available, 3 will test AO1, 1 will test AO2
- You will then be asked an 8-mark stimulus question on Source A

There will also be a textual source, which will be a passage from one of your prescribed plays. This will be called 'Source B'. The questions follow the same format as above (in fact, the textual source could come before the visual/material source or after it):

- You will be asked the second set of short answer questions, worth 1 or 2 marks each. Of the 4 marks available, 3 will test AO1, 1 will test AO2
- You will then be asked an 8-mark stimulus question on Source B.

The final question in Section A will be the 16-mark shorter essay question.

- You may be asked to use one or both of Sources A and B as a starting point for your answer, as well as your own knowledge

Section B has the following format:

- You will be given a choice of two essays, of which you should **only do one**. This is worth 25 marks.

Section A

Short answer questions and visual/material stimulus question

Let us look at an example. You could be shown the following prescribed visual/material source.

Source A: the Basel Dancers Vase.

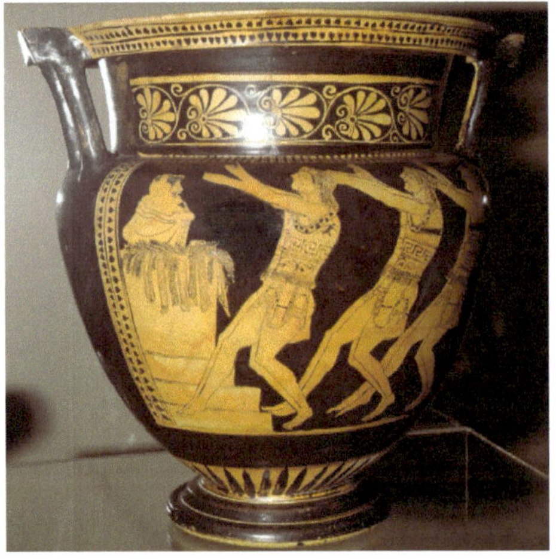

An example of an AO1 **short answer question** would be:

Question: What type of pot is shown in this source and what is the name of this type of vase painting? [2]

Answer: It is a (column) krater [1], and this type of vase painting is called red figure [1].

Both these marks are AO1 since they require you to show knowledge and understanding, but there is no analysis or evaluation required.

By contrast, an example of an AO2 question would be:

Question: Why might this vase be problematic as a source about Greek tragedy? [1]

Answer: You could make any one of the following points: the vase dates to the beginning of the fifth century, when we know very little about Greek tragedy and so it may not reflect the performance of later tragedies which we do know about [1]; even if this does represent a scene from a tragedy, we don't know if it is supposed to represent a 'typical' performance of a tragedy or not [1], that we don't know who the person on the left is and what structure he is sitting on, so it is hard to know whether this represents a tragic performance or not [1].

The answer above is AO2 because you are being asked to critically analyse the image on the vase so as to give your own evaluation of the question.

You will then be asked a **stimulus question** worth 8 marks. Of those 8 marks, 4 are available for AO1 and 4 for AO2. AO1 marks are awarded for the selection of material from the source, AO2 marks for the interpretation, analysis or evaluation of this material.

Therefore, for the Basel Dancers Vase, you might be asked a question such as this:

Question: Explain what this source suggests about the nature of the tragic Chorus. Make four points and support each point with reference to the source. [8]

One example of **one** point that you might make is as follows:

Answer: The fact that they are portrayed with their arms raised identically [1] suggests that they are dancing in formation [1].

In this answer, the key point of interpretation is that the figures are dancing in formation (AO2), and the evidence for this is that they have their arms raised up identically (AO1). Remember that you have to make four interpretations of this nature. Answers will be marked point by point, rather than with a marking grid (as per the following two question types – see below). The four interpretations that you are asked to make are AO2, while the evidence you find to support them is AO1.

Short-answer questions and textual-stimulus question

Exactly the same principle applies for the questions based on the textual source. For example, look at the passage below from Aristophanes' *Frogs*, lines 250–78.

Source B: Frogs 250–78.

DIONYSUS + FROGS	Bre-ke-ke-kex, co-ax, co-ax.	
DIONYSUS	I'm borrowing your refrain.	
FROGS	That will cause us horrible pain.	
DIONYSUS	Not as much as I will hurt if this rowing makes me pop!	
DIONYSUS + FROGS	Bre-ke-ke-kex, co-ax, co-ax.	5
DIONYSUS	Wail away – see if I care.	
FROGS:	Indeed, we will croak	
	All day,	
	As long as our throats can take it.	
DIONYSUS + FROGS	Bre-ke-ke-kex, co-ax, co-ax.	10
DIONYSUS	You won't win at this.	
FROGS	You're not going to beat us – no way!	
DIONYSUS	And you'll never beat me.	
	Not ever! For I will *co-ax*	
	All day, if I must.	15
	'Till I get the better of your	
	Co-ax.	
	BRE-KE-KE-KEX, CO-AX, CO-AX.	
	There. I knew I'd stop that *co-ax* in the end.	
CHARON	Stop, stop. Bring her alongside with the oars.	20
	Give me the fare and get out.	
DIONYSUS	Here you are, two obols.	
	Xanthias! Where are you, Xanthias? Hey, Xanthias!	
XANTHIAS	Ho, there!	
DIONYSUS	Come here.	25
XANTHIAS	Hello, master.	
DIONYSUS	What's that over there?	
XANTHIAS	Darkness and filth.	
DIONYSUS	I suppose you saw the father-killers and oath-breakers	30
	he told us about?	
XANTHIAS	Didn't you?	
DIONYSUS	Oh yes, by Poseidon, I certainly did, and I can still see	
	them now. Ok, what do we do next?	
XANTHIAS	We'd best keep moving, because this is the place	35
	where Hercules said the wild beasts are.	
DIONYSUS	He'll be sorry. He was just bragging to make me afraid,	
	knowing what a good fighter I am. Pure envy. He's so	
	conceited.	

Trans. J. Affleck and C. Letchford

As an example of an AO1 question, you could be asked:

Question: Who did Dionysus intend to collect and bring back to Athens from the Underworld? [1]

Answer: Euripides [1].

As an example of an AO2 question, you could be asked:

Question: Why might the original audience have found this an engaging plot for a comedy? [1]

Answer: You could give one of a number of interpretations to this question. For example, you could say that Euripides was a popular tragedian who had only recently died and so the audience would enjoy a play with him as a central character [1]; or you could say more generally that the audience might have enjoyed a comedy which poked fun at the traditionally serious genre of tragedy [1]; or you could say that Athens was politically in a terrible situation in their war with Sparta, and a plot involving a journey to the underworld to meet their greatest playwrights would offer them an escape from the grimness of their plight [1].

As an example of a stimulus question, you could be asked:

Question: Explain what impression Aristophanes gives us of Dionysus in this passage. Make four points and support your answer with reference to the passage. [8]

One example of **one** point that you might make is as follows:

Answer: Dionysus is presented as a ridiculous character [1] since in l.2 he admits that he is copying the bizarre non-human noises which the frogs are making [1].

Here, the analysis that Dionysus is seen to be ridiculous is AO2, while the evidence which supports this from the passage is AO1. When you refer to the passage, try if possible either to give line references or quote directly the relevant words or lines.

Shorter essay question

The final question in Section A may ask you to bring together the two sources, as well as asking you to demonstrate your wider knowledge of the Greek Theatre topic. There are 16 marks available, 8 for AO1 and 8 for AO2. This question has its own tailored marking grid which you can view on the OCR website.

An example of such a question might be as follows:

Question: In which type of play was the Chorus more important: tragedy or comedy? You may use Sources A and B as a starting point, and your response shows your own knowledge.

When you **plan** your answer to this question, it might be a good idea to write down some key points of factual evidence which you are going to use for AO1. Some examples might be:

- the passage from *Frogs* shows how central the chorus was to the humour of the play
- in both the set tragedies the chorus express strong views on what is happening. For example, in *Oedipus the King* the chorus are very loyal to Oedipus, whereas in *Bacchae* the chorus are devotees of Dionysus who are horrified by Pentheus

- comic choruses had twenty-four actors, tragic choruses had twelve or fifteen
- the Basel Dancers Vase suggests that tragic choral dances were solemn and beautiful
- the Basel Dancers Vase and the Pronomos Vase suggests that the choruses for tragedies and satyr-plays wore ornate and majestic costumes
- we have little evidence for what sort of costumes comic choruses wore
- comic choruses broke the dramatic illusion so that the chorus leader could deliver the parabasis, which did not exist in tragedy
- choruses in both comedy and tragedy allowed for scene breaks so that actors could change off-stage

You should also try to write down some key points of evaluation, analysis or interpretation in your plan which you are going to use for AO2. Remember you can give both sides of the argument. You might think that there are some ways in which the comic chorus is more important, and others in which the tragic chorus is more important. You could put forward each of these, and then draw an overall conclusion one way or another. Some examples might be:

The tragic chorus was more important because:

- the moral reflections in choral odes can make the audience think deeply about the issues of life and suffering raised in the play
- the tragic chorus can draw connections between these broader issues and what is happening on-stage, and so encourage the audience to see the relevance of what happens to the characters.
- the tragic chorus comments on the action and provides an insight into the characters' motives and actions, in a way which is less common in comedy
- The evidence on vases suggests that the tragic chorus was visually and aesthetically very impressive, and so a key part of the performance

The comic chorus was more important because:

- the comic chorus makes the audience laugh, which is the main aim in a comedy
- the comic chorus gives the playwright the opportunity to show how creative he is by making up an exotic grouping with outlandish costumes
- the comic chorus gives background information to the plot, which was more important in comedy when plots were not based on well-known myths
- a comic chorus engages with the audience more directly, often breaking the dramatic illusion and speaking directly to the spectators
- the parabasis allows the playwright to put forward a message of social or political importance in contemporary Athens through the mouth of the chorus leader

Try to ensure that you give your essay a clear structure. Perhaps draw up a plan paragraph by paragraph or argument by argument. While it is a good idea to have a brief introduction and conclusion to the essay, try not to make these too long. Your introduction should simply briefly outline the key issues, and perhaps the line you are going to take, while the conclusion should be short and simply summarise the key points you have made to conclude your argument.

Section B

Essay question

In Section B, you will be given a choice of two essays. **You should only do one essay and you will not be given any extra credit for doing both of them!** The essay is out of 25 marks, with ten marks for AO1 and fifteen marks for AO2 (this question also has its own tailored marking grid, which you can download from the OCR website). However, this does not mean that you should be aiming to give evidence and evaluation in exactly that ratio. You should just aim to write the best essay you can, where you back up your arguments with evidence from your studies. What you should avoid doing, however, is over-narrating: telling the examiner what happens in the play rather than analysing it according to the question.

The first thing you need to do then is to decide which question to choose. Make sure that you read both questions carefully and think about what is being asked. It is common for candidates to read the question as they want it to be, rather than as it is. For example, consider the following question:

Evaluate the importance of the search for the murderer of Laius in Sophocles' *Oedipus the King*. [25]

It is asking you to evaluate how important you think is the theme of the search for Laius' murderer in the play. A key word here is 'evaluate'. You should weigh up the importance of this plotline against other plotlines and themes, such as Jocasta's discovery of the truth of her marriage, or whether Oedipus was simply an instrument of fate.

However, notice that it would be very easy to misread this question slightly. A learner may previously have written a practice essay such as: 'How does the search for the murderer of Laius create suspense in Sophocles' *Oedipus the King*?' If so, it would be very tempting to reproduce many of the arguments made in that essay. Be very careful not to do this. You must answer the question in front of you, which in this case is about the importance of this plotline to the play as a whole.

Therefore, when you make your choice about which essay to attempt, ensure that you have read each question carefully and are very sure about what each one is asking for. It may be that you think that you could answer both. This is a good problem to have! However, try to make a clear decision one way or another and then stick with it. The skills required for this question are the same as those for the shorter essay question, but you have the chance to go into more depth. Make sure you create a good plan which allows you to put forward a well-structured essay.

What to Expect in the A Level Exam for Greek Theatre

This chapter aims to show you the types of questions you are likely to get in the written examination. It offers some advice on how to answer the questions and will help you avoid common errors.

THE EXAMINATION

This component of the A Level Classical Civilisation examination is designed to test your knowledge, understanding and evaluation of Greek theatre. The examination is worth 75 marks and lasts 1 hour and 45 minutes. This represents 30% of the total marks for the A Level.

There are two Assessment Objectives in your A Level, and questions will be designed to test these areas. These Assessment Objectives are outline in the table below, together with the total number of marks available for each on the paper:

	Assessment Objective	Marks
AO1	Demonstrate knowledge and understanding of: • literature and visual/material culture • how sources and ideas reflect, and influence, their cultural contexts • possible interpretations of sources, perspectives and ideas by different audiences and individuals.	35
AO2	Critically analyse, interpret and evaluate literature and visual/material culture, using evidence to make substantiated judgements and produce coherent and reasoned arguments.	40

Exam structure and question types

The exam is divided into two sections, Section A and Section B.

There are four question types in this exam:

- a number of short answer questions (5 marks in total)
- 10-mark stimulus questions
- 20-mark shorter essay
- 30-mark essay

Try to plan your time well. The shorter essay question and the essay question together make up 50 of the 75 marks available, and so you should aim to spend the majority of your time on these two questions.

Section A has the following format:

There will be a prescribed visual/material source on the paper. This will be called 'Source A'.

- one or more short answer questions relating to the source (worth 2 or 3 marks in total). These questions will test AO1 only
- you will then be asked a 10-mark stimulus question on this Source A

There will also be a textual source, which will be a passage from one of your prescribed plays (in fact, the textual source could come before the visual/material source or after it). This will be called 'Source B'. The questions follow the same format as above:

- one or more short answer questions relating to the source (worth 2 or 3 marks in total, adding up to 5 marks when combined with the earlier short answer questions). These questions will also test AO1 only
- you will then be asked a 10-mark stimulus question on Source B

The final question in Section A will be the 20-mark shorter essay question

- you may be asked to use both Sources A and B as a starting point for your answer, as well as your own knowledge

Section B has the following format:

- You will be given a choice of two essays, of which you should **only do one**. This is worth 30 marks.

Section A

Short answer questions and visual/material stimulus question

For example, you could be shown the following prescribed visual/material source.

Source A: the Basel Dancers Vase.

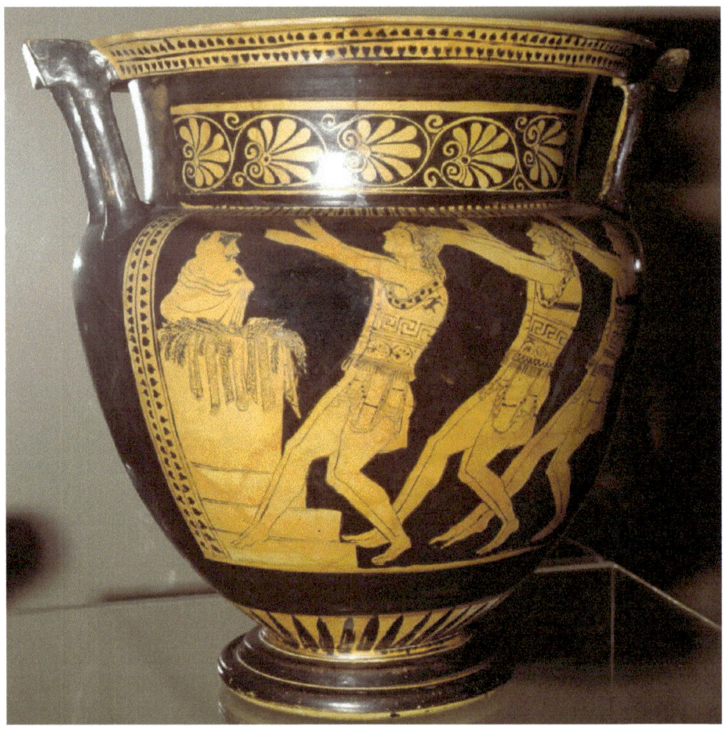

Short answer question

An example of a short answer question would be:

Question: There are two common ideas about what the structure on the left of this image is. Identify one of these. [1]
Answer: One of: an altar [1]; a tomb [1].

This question is AO1 since it requires you to show knowledge and understanding, but there is no analysis or evaluation required.

Stimulus question

After the short answer questions, you will be asked a 10-mark stimulus question. Of the 10 marks available, 5 are for AO1 and 5 for AO2. AO1 marks are awarded for the selection of material from the source, AO2 marks for the interpretation, analysis or evaluation of this material. These questions are marked according to a marking grid which you can view on the OCR website.

For example, for the Basel Dancers Vase, you might be asked a question such as this:

Question: Evaluate how useful this pot is as a source of information about the chorus in Greek tragedy. [10]
Answer: A key word here is 'evaluate'. You need to think about how far the pot can give us accurate information about the chorus in a Greek tragedy. As the marking grid indicates, you should aim make a range of points which give clear and thoughtful analysis and are backed up with good supporting evidence from the source. Here are examples of two points you could make (you do not need to separate them in your answers):

Point 1: The fact that the figures on the vase are portrayed with their arms raised identically suggests that they are dancing in formation and gives us evidence that a tragic chorus was carefully choreographed.

Point 2: This is a static image, and so does not really capture the movement of the dancers, meaning that we cannot really know what the choral dance looked like throughout the length of a choral ode.

Notice that in each case, evidence from the image leads to a point of analysis. Try to make your arguments as clear and distinct as possible, and always back them up with evidence from the source. In addition, notice that together the two points would then help you to evaluate the question further. The first point suggests that we can learn something about the chorus from the evidence on the vase, while the second point explains the limits of this evidence. This then starts to build towards a clear and well-reasoned evaluation.

Short-answer questions and textual-stimulus question

As an example of a literary source, look at the passage below from Aristophanes' *Frogs*, line 250–78.

Source B: *Frogs* 250–78.

DIONYSUS + FROGS	Bre-ke-ke-kex, co-ax, co-ax.	
DIONYSUS	I'm borrowing your refrain.	
FROGS	That will cause us horrible pain.	
DIONYSUS	Not as much as I will hurt if this rowing makes me pop!	
DIONYSUS + FROGS	Bre-ke-ke-kex, co-ax, co-ax.	5
DIONYSUS	Wail away – see if I care.	
FROGS:	Indeed, we will croak	
	All day,	
	As long as our throats can take it.	
DIONYSUS + FROGS	Bre-ke-ke-kex, co-ax, co-ax.	10
DIONYSUS	You won't win at this.	
FROGS	You're not going to beat us – no way!	
DIONYSUS	And you'll never beat me.	
	Not ever! For I will *co-ax*	
	All day, if I must.	15
	'Till I get the better of your	
	Co-ax.	
	BRE-KE-KE-KEX, CO-AX, CO-AX.	
	There. I knew I'd stop that *co-ax* in the end.	
CHARON	Stop, stop. Bring her alongside with the oars.	20
	Give me the fare and get out.	
DIONYSUS	Here you are, two obols.	
	Xanthias! Where are you, Xanthias? Hey, Xanthias!	

XANTHIAS	Ho, there!	
DIONYSUS	Come here.	25
XANTHIAS	Hello, master.	
DIONYSUS	What's that over there?	
XANTHIAS	Darkness and filth.	
DIONYSUS	I suppose you saw the father-killers and oath-breakers	30
	he told us about?	
XANTHIAS	Didn't you?	
DIONYSUS	Oh yes, by Poseidon, I certainly did, and I can still see	
	them now. Ok, what do we do next?	
XANTHIAS	We'd best keep moving, because this is the place	35
	where Hercules said the wild beasts are.	
DIONYSUS	He'll be sorry. He was just bragging to make me	
	afraid, knowing what a good fighter I am. Pure envy.	
	He's so conceited.	

Trans: J. Affleck and C. Letchford

Short answer question

An example of a short answer question would be:

Question: Describe why Dionysus travelled down to the Underworld in *Frogs*. [2]

Answer: You could make any two points from: Dionysus has gone down to the Underworld to fetch Euripides [1] back from the dead [1] to bring him back to Athens [1] because all the great tragedians have died [1].

Once again, no analysis is required here, you simply need to show two pieces of knowledge and understanding (AO1).

Stimulus question

As an example of a textual 10-mark stimulus question, you might be asked a question such as this based on the passage given from *Frogs*:

Question: Explain how Aristophanes makes this passage an effective piece of comic drama. [10]

Notice that in this instance you are not being asked to evaluate but to explain. You should aim to make a range of points, using evidence from the passage. If possible, refer closely to the passage, either by referencing line numbers, or by quoting directly. One example of one point that you might make is as follows:

Answer: The reference to stopping the boat with oars in ll. 20–1 shows that the characters must have been acting out rowing while talking, and this would have required either a model boat or some extravagant acting which would have amused the audience.

Once again, the point contains evidence from the source (in this case the passage), which enables a point of analysis to be made.

Shorter essay question

The final question in Section A may ask you to bring together the two sources, as well as asking you to demonstrate your wider knowledge of the Greek Theatre topic. There are 20 marks available, 10 for AO1 and 10 for AO2. This question has its own tailored marking grid which you can view on the OCR website.

An example of such a question might be as follows:

Question: The impact of the chorus in Greek theatre depended more on how it looked and what it did than on what it said. Explain how far you agree with this statement and justify your response. You may use Sources A and B as a starting point.

When you **plan** your answer to this question, it might be a good idea to write down some key points of factual evidence which you are going to use for AO1. You could start by noting the evidence from the two sources on the paper. The Basel Dancers Vase gives no evidence for what the chorus said, but it probably offers evidence for how the chorus looked and what it did. The opposite is largely the case for the *Frogs* passage – it has plenty of evidence for what the chorus said, but less so for how it looked and what it did (however, the text does allow scope for some guesswork here). You might then list other examples and pieces of evidence from your wider studies. One important example could be the Pronomos Vase, which shows the costumes of a chorus of a satyr-play. You could also, of course, think about the contributions made by the choruses in your three set plays, and the extent to which the texts illustrate not just what they said, but also what they did and what they looked like.

Think about some of the key words and phrases in the question. The word 'impact' asks you to imagine the experience of a spectator in the theatre of Dionysus. The phrases 'depended more' and 'Explain how far you agree with this statement' give you plenty of flexibility to examine both sides of the argument, and to agree to some extent but not fully. For example, you are not being asked to examine whether the words of the chorus made little or no impact, but whether their impact was less in comparison to the impact of a chorus' actions and appearance. Likewise, you are not being asked to agree or disagree with the statement, but to explain 'how far' you agree. You really do have the opportunity to give exactly your own opinion on this question! There is no 'right' or 'wrong' answer to a question such as this – you simply need to back up your opinions with strong evidence from your studies.

Section B

Essay question

In Section B, you will be given a choice of two essays. **You should only do one essay and you will not be given any credit for trying to do both of them!** The essay is out of 30 marks, with ten marks for AO1 and twenty marks for AO2 (this question also has its own tailored marking grid, which you can download from the OCR website). However, this does not mean that you should be aiming to give evidence and evaluation in exactly that ratio. A good essay is likely to have more evaluation than evidence in any case, and so you should just aim to write the best essay you can, where you back up your arguments with evidence from your studies. What you should avoid doing, however, is over-narrating: telling the examiner what happens in the play rather than analysing it according to the question.

The first thing you need to do is to decide which question to choose. Make sure that you read both questions carefully and think about what is being asked. It is a common mistake for candidates to read the question as they want it to be, rather than as it is. For example, consider the following question:

'The most important aspect of Sophocles' *Oedipus the King* is the question of who killed Laius.' Discuss how true you think this statement is, and justify your response. [30]

You should weigh up the importance of this aspect of the play against other important aspects, such as what the play has to say about the nature of the gods, or whether Oedipus was simply an instrument of fate. However, notice that it would be possible to misread this question. A learner may previously have written a practice essay such as: 'How does the search for the murderer of Laius create suspense in Sophocles' *Oedipus the King*?' If so, it would be very tempting to reproduce many of the arguments made in that essay. Be very careful not to do this. You must answer the question in front of you, which in this case is about whether this aspect of the play is the most important one. Therefore, when you make your choice about which essay to attempt, ensure that you have read each question carefully and are very sure about what each one is asking for. It may be that you think that you could answer both. This is a good problem to have! Make a clear decision one way or another and then stick with it.

Try to ensure that you give your essay a clear structure. Perhaps draw up a plan paragraph by paragraph or argument by argument. While it is a good idea to have a brief introduction and conclusion to the essay, try not to make these too long. Your introduction should simply briefly outline the key issues, and perhaps the line you are going to take, while the conclusion should be short and simply summarise the key points you have made to conclude your argument. To score good marks in AO1, make sure you choose a range of factual evidence from at least two of your authors. To score good marks on AO2, make sure you examine the issue and weigh up your arguments carefully. You will want to make a variety of points, and again you may find that there are arguments on both sides.

Modern scholarship

In this essay question, you are required to show knowledge of secondary sources, scholars and academic works in your answer. This requirement of the exam is supported in the textbooks by 'Modern Scholarship' boxes. The OCR rubric says that 'Learners are expected to make use of scholarly views, academic approaches and sources to support their argument'. It is essential that you build in such material in order to do well on this question. How should you do this?

First of all, you of course need to read more widely about the topic. In this book, you have been given suggestions for articles and books to read on a variety of topics relating to the Greek theatre. Try to follow up as many as possible, and take notes about some of the key arguments that scholars make. It is especially interesting when two authors disagree with each other on a topic, such as whether or not women could attend the theatre. When referring to the view of a scholar, you need not quote them directly, although if you are able to remember a few words that they have written accurately, then that will be very impressive. However, it may be that you refer to a general argument that they put forward in a book, an article or a chapter. However, you will not be expected to quote the name of a book or give a chapter reference. For example, you might cite Taplin's view quoted on page 34.

Let us take an example relating to the question above. One of your books for recommended reading is *The Plays of Sophocles* by A.F. Garvie (2nd edition, Bloomsbury Academic, 2016). On p. 42, he writes: 'The subject of the play itself is not Oedipus' crimes, but his discovery that he has committed them, and his reaction to that discovery. Much of its appeal for modern readers may derive from its resemblance in some respects to a detective-novel.' This might well be a quotation or a view worth putting forward in your essay, particularly since it implies that a modern readership may have a different response to the play from an ancient readership. There was no such thing as a detective-novel in ancient times, and so the quotation speaks to the fact that Greek tragedy can appeal to modern readers in ways unanticipated by the playwright. You may wish to reflect more on this view in your essay. You do not necessarily need to quote the details of where you read the ideas, it will be enough to mention the scholar's name and explain what they say.

Above all make your use of secondary sources relevant to the question you are answering. To use a secondary source well you should think carefully about why it is supporting your argument or showing a different argument, and make it clear why you are including it. You might want to agree or disagree with the scholarly view, in which case you will need to explain why you do so. You may not remember everything about the secondary source you have read, but if you ensure the examiner understands what you are using and why, this will strengthen your argument. Using secondary sources in this way gives you a skill that is crucial at university level in many different subjects because engaging with what other people have thought about a particular topic enriches your own understanding.

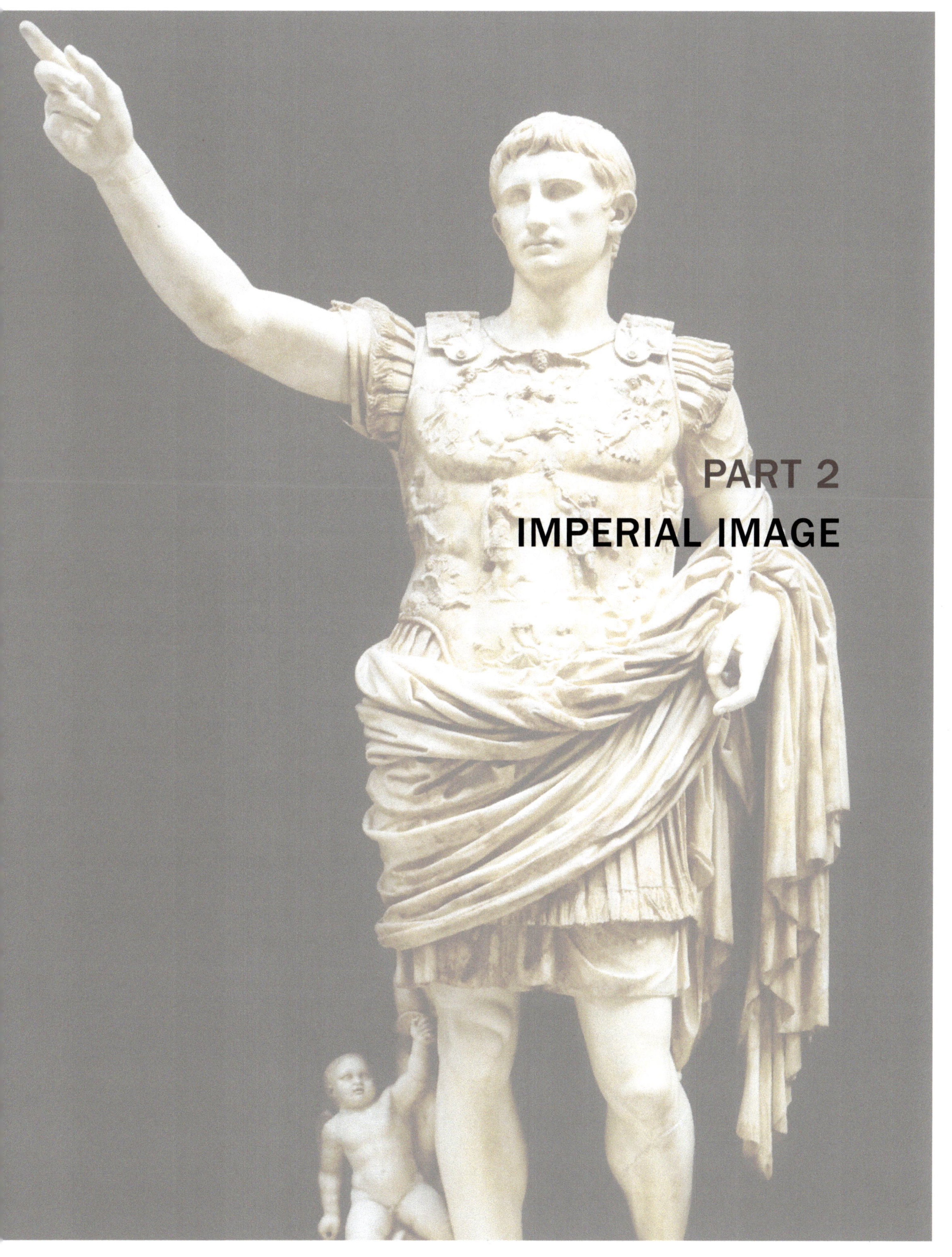
PART 2
IMPERIAL IMAGE

Introduction to Imperial Image

The focus of this component is the image which Augustus projected to the Roman world.

Augustus' political career spanned half a century and he was largely responsible for transforming Rome from a more or less democratic Republic into a Principate. His remarkable rise to prominence and his unprecedented reign as the leading man in Rome were made possible by his careful manipulation of public opinion. In this component you will study the main events of his life and times in order to be able to analyse and interpret some of the propaganda material that survives from this period to the present day. In terms of literary sources, you will be working with a range of different types of poetry, inscriptions and biography. You will also have the chance to engage with a range of stunning works of art and architecture, as well as coinage from the period that Augustan Romans would have used in their everyday lives.

This textbook is organised chronologically. This will enable you to appreciate how Augustus' public image changed over time, in response to current events and shifting values. The exam specification, however, is organised by theme. This is to enable you to appreciate the different strands of Augustus' personal brand and see how each shifted and changed throughout his lifetime and beyond. To help you keep track of these different themes, this book includes an icon code. Each theme has its own icon, and these appear next to prescribed sources where that theme is relevant. It is important to note that these icons are only intended as a guide and are not exhaustive. Strong candidates will interpret the sources, using what they have learned about Augustan society, and will reach their own conclusions about their significance.

The icons are as follows:

 Divi Filius – Anything which stressed Augustus' link to Julius Caesar and the Divine Julius

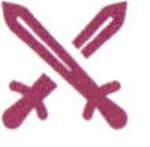 Imperator – The idea of Augustus as a strong, capable military commander whose wars were just and beneficial to Rome

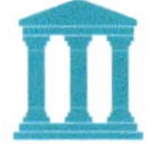 Augustus – Augustus the religious leader

 Culture Hero – The notion that Augustus was responsible for bringing about a new Golden Age of peace and prosperity in the Roman Empire

 Pater Patriae – Augustus as a father figure for all Romans, giving him the authority to direct their moral behaviour

In your exam you will be expected to comment on how your sources convey aspects of Augustus' 'personal brand' to the people of Rome and the Empire, and to evaluate how effective this communication was. Focus, therefore, on what the sources convey and how they convey it to their intended audiences. As the component is not intended to be a historical investigation into the life and times of Augustus, you will not need to evaluate the reliability or accuracy of sources. However, you will need knowledge of historical events to contextualise your understanding of Augustus' propaganda needs at any given point in his reign. The information in this book provides this narrative history so that you will be able to comment on your sources' context and on how Augustus' audience may have responded to a particular source.

To help you to understand this approach, consider the example of Suetonius' *Life of Augustus*, selections from which are a prescribed source for this component. Suetonius' work is one of our most complete accounts of the events from Augustus' life and times, and ancient historians often use it as the basis for historical investigations, considering the reliability of his account and questioning his methodology to help them uncover the truth of what happened in this period. While this can be a rewarding and intellectually stimulating exercise, this approach would not be suitable for this component. Rather, you will be expected to analyse the *Life of Augustus* as a literary text and to analyse its content rather than to comment on its historical accuracy or usefulness.

General bibliography

Bradley, P. (2012). *Ancient Rome Using Evidence* (Cambridge: Cambridge University Press).

Clark, M.D.H. (2010). *Augustus, First Roman Emperor: Power, Propaganda and the Politics of Survival* (Liverpool: Bristol Phoenix Press).

Cooley, M.G.L. (2013). *Lactor 17: The Age of Augustus* (London: The London Association of Classical Teachers).

Galinsky, K. (1996). *Augustan Culture: An Interpretive Introduction* (Princeton: Princeton University Press).

Goldsworthy, A. (2014). *Augustus: From Revolutionary to Emperor* (London: Weidenfeld & Nicolson).

Wallace-Hadrill, A. (1993). *Augustan Rome* (London: Bloomsbury).

Zanker, P. (2014). *The Power of Images in the Age of Augustus* (trans. A. Shapiro) (Ann Arbor: University of Michigan Press).

EXAM OVERVIEW: AS LEVEL	H008/22

Your assessment is a written examination testing AO1 and AO2. It is

50% of the AS Level	1 hr 30 mins	65 marks

32 marks will test AO1: demonstrate knowledge and understanding of:

- literature, visual/material culture and classical thought
- how sources and ideas reflect, and influence, their cultural contexts
- possible interpretations of sources, perspectives and ideas by different audiences and individuals

33 marks will test AO2: critically analyse, interpret and evaluate literature, visual/material culture, and classical thought, using evidence to make substantiated judgements and produce coherent and reasoned arguments

The examination will consist of two sections.

All questions in **Section A** are compulsory. There are three question types:

- short-answer questions
- 8-mark stimulus question using the prescribed sources
- 16-mark essay

Section B has one question type:

- 25-mark essay

There is a choice of one from two essays.

EXAM OVERVIEW: A LEVEL   H408/22

Your assessment is a written examination testing AO1 and AO2. It is

   30% of the A Level   1 hr 45 mins   75 marks

35 marks will test AO1: demonstrate knowledge and understanding of:

- literature, visual/material culture and classical thought
- how sources and ideas reflect, and influence, their cultural contexts
- possible interpretations of sources, perspectives and ideas by different audiences and individuals

40 marks will test AO2: critically analyse, interpret and evaluate literature, visual/material culture, and classical thought, using evidence to make substantiated judgements and produce coherent and reasoned arguments

The examination will consist of two sections.

All questions in **Section A** are compulsory. There are three question types:

- short-answer questions
- 10-mark stimulus question using the prescribed sources
- 20-mark essay

Section B has one question type:

- 30-mark essay

There is a choice of one from two essays. In these essays learners will be expected to make use of secondary sources and academic views to support their argument.

TIMELINE OF EVENTS AND SOURCES

	Political Events	Cultural Events	Prescribed Sources
44 BC	March 15 – assassination of Julius Caesar. May – Octavian arrives in Rome and meets with Antony. Julius Caesar's comet appears during the games in honour of Venus. Interpreted as a sign of Julius Caesar's deification.		
43 BC	The Senate declares war against Antony. April 21 – Octavian fights alongside the consuls Hirtius and Pansa against Antony at the Battle of Mutina. Octavian marches on Rome. August 19 – Octavian becomes consul following the deaths of both Hirtius and Pansa. November 27 – The *Lex Titia* is passed, which legitimised the Second Triumvirate and gave them extraordinary powers. The Second Triumvirate's campaign of proscriptions begins.	The orator Cicero delivers a series of speeches against Antony known as the Philippics. Some of these speeches champion Octavian as an ally of the Republic.	Aureus, obv. bare head of Octavian, rev. head of Julius Caesar with laurel wreath.
42 BC	January 1 – Julius Caesar proclaimed a god. October 23 – Octavian and Antony avenge Julius Caesar's assassins at the Battle of Philippi. The Second Triumvirate sieze land across Italy to give to their war veterans. November 16 – Tiberius is born.	Octavian orders the Temple of Divus Iulius to be built in the Roman Forum. Octavian vows to build a temple to Mars Ultor.	
41 BC	Antony meets Cleopatra at Tarsus. Octavian fights the Perusine War against Mark Antony's brother (Lucius Antonius) and wife (Fulvia).	Propertius writes *Elegies* 1.22, which bemoans the destructive effect of the Perusine War on his hometown.	
40 BC	The Treaty of Brundisium signed between the triumvirs. Octavian given the western Empire to govern, Antony given the Eastern Empire to govern and Lepidus given the African provinces to govern. Octavian orders the deaths of around 300 senators and equites who had allied with Lucius Antonius and Fulvia against him in the Perusine war. Antony marries Octavian's sister, Octavia.		

(Continued)

	Political Events	**Cultural Events**	**Prescribed Sources**
39 BC	The Second Triumvirate make a pact with Sextus Pompeius to end his blockade of Rome's grain supply. October 30 – Julia the Elder born to Octavian and Scribonia. Octavian divorces Scribonia and marries Livia.		
38 BC	Octavian begins a war against Sextus Pompeius.	Virgil publishes his *Eclogues*. The fourth book contains a famous passage which refers to a blessed child/messiah who will bring about a golden age of peace and prosperity.	
37 BC	Antony marries Cleopatra.		
36 BC	Octavian and Agrippa lead an invasion of Sicily against Sextus Pompeius. Lepidus attempts to take over Sicily, but Octavian convinces Lepidus' men to mutiny. Lepidus stripped of his powers as a triumvir.		
35 BC	Octavian campaigns in Dalmatia.		
34 BC	Antony celebrates a triumph in Alexandria known as the 'Donations of Alexandria'.		
33 BC	Octavian takes the consulship for the second time. Antony attempts to declare Cleopatra's son Caesarion (the alleged son of Julius Caesar) as Julius Caesar's official heir.		
32 BC	Octavian seizes Antony's will from the Temple of Vesta and reads it to the Senate. The Senate declares war against Cleopatra, electing Octavian as the leader of the war effort.		Work begins on the Mausoleum of Augustus. *c.* 32–29 – Denarius, obv. bare head of Octavian, rev. Pax standing left holding olive branch and cornucopia.

31 BC	Octavian takes the consulship for the third time. September 2 – The Battle of Actium.		Portrait bust of Livia.
30 BC	Octavian takes the consulship for the fourth time. Octavian invades Egypt. August 1 – Antony's death. August 12 – Cleopatra's death. Octavian orders Caesarion and Antony's eldest son by Cleopatra to be killed. The rest of Antony and Cleopatra's children are taken to Rome and cared for by Octavia.		Horace, *Epode* 9 Augustus and Isis relief, Kalabsha Gate.
29 BC	Octavian takes the consulship for the fifth time. August 13–15 – Octavian celebrates three consecutive triumphs (triple triumph).	Arch of Augustus built to commemorate his triple triumph.	
28 BC	Octavian takes the consulship for the sixth time. Agrippa's second consulship. Octavian carries out an audit of the Senate. Octavian declares that the rights and laws of the Roman people have been restored.	Octavian opens the Temple of Apollo Palatinus, next to his home on the Palatine hill in Rome.	Aureus, obv. head of Octavian, rev. Octavian seated on bench holding scroll.
27 BC	Octavian takes the consulship for the seventh time. Agrippa's third consulship. January 16 – The 'First Settlement', which included: – The Senate confers the name 'Augustus' on Octavian. – Augustus given control over Spain, Gaul, Syria and Egypt, as well as imperium for a period of ten years. – The Senate dedicates the clipeium virtutis to commemorate Augustus' virtues. Augustus on campaign in Gaul.		
26 BC	Augustus takes the consulship for the eighth time.		
25 BC	Augustus takes the consulship for the ninth time. Julia the Elder married to Marcellus (Octavia's son). The Senate votes to close the gates of the Temple of Janus.		
24 BC	Augustus takes the consulship for the tenth time. Augustus returns to Rome from his campaigns in Spain and Gaul.		

(Continued)

	Political Events	**Cultural Events**	**Prescribed Sources**
23 BC	Augustus takes the consulship for the eleventh time. Augustus falls ill and nearly dies. The 'Second Settlement' – Augustus lays down the consulship, to allow other noblemen the chance to hold the highest office in the land. – Augustus awarded tribunician power and maius imperium, two powers which gave him authority and influence, despite not being consul. Marcellus (the son of Octavia) dies.		Propertius, *Elegies* 3.11 Horace, *Odes* 1.37 Horace, *Odes* 3.6 Horace, *Odes* 3.14
22 BC	Rioting breaks out, which prompts the Senate to offer Augustus the dictatorship. He refuses.		
21 BC	Augustus forces Agrippa to divorce his wife and marry Julia the Elder.		
20 BC	Peace negotiated between the Roman and Parthian empires. Augustus travels to Sicily and the eastern Empire. Birth of Gaius.		Prima Porta statue commissioned (bronze original). Propertius, *Elegies* 3.4 Propertius, *Elegies* 3.12
19 BC	Birth of Julia the Younger. Agrippa campaigns in Spain. Augustus' return from the East is celebrated with the dedication of a new altar of Fortuna Redux. The 'Third Settlement' – the Senate votes Augustus consular imperium for life. This also gives him the ability to wear the consul's insignia in public, regardless of whether or not he held the consulship at that time.	The poet Virgil dies.	*c.* 19–18 – Denarius, obv. portrait of Augustus with laurel wreath, rev. eight-rayed comet with tail pointing upward.
18 BC	The first Leges Iuliae (social/morality laws) passed, regulating adultery and marriage, as well as electoral fraud.		
17 BC	Birth of Lucius. Augustus adopts his grandsons, Gaius and Lucius. May 31–June 3 – the Saecular Games are celebrated, heralding the beginning of a new age.		Horace – *Carmen Saeculare*.
16 BC		Actian Games celebrated at Nikopolis.	Propertius, *Elegies* 4.6

15 BC		Virgil's *Aeneid* published.	
14 BC			
13 BC	Tiberius takes the consulship for the first time.		Work on the Ara Pacis begins. Horace, *Odes* 4.15 Horace, *Odes* 4.4
12 BC	Death of Agrippa. Death of Lepidus (or late 13 BC). Augustus elected Pontifex Maximus. Tiberius campaigns (until 11 BC) in Pannonia and Dalmatia.		Denarius, obv. bareheaded portrait of Augustus, rev. sacrificial implements above tripod and patera.
11 BC	Tiberius forced to divorce his wife Vipsania so that he can marry Julia the Elder, Agrippa's widow.		
10 BC			
9 BC		Theatre of Marcellus opens to the public.	Dedication of the Ara Pacis.
8 BC	The sixth month, Sextilis, renamed 'August' in honour of Augustus. Tiberius on campaigns in Germany.	Death of Maecenas.	
7 BC	Tiberius takes the consulship for the second time.		
6 BC			
5 BC	The Senate declares Gaius and Lucius Princeps Iuventutis (first amongst the young).		
4 BC			
3 BC			

(*Continued*)

	Political Events	Cultural Events	Prescribed Sources
2 BC	Augustus takes the consulship for the thirteenth time. Augustus declared pater patriae (father of the state). Julia the Elder sent into exile.		*c.* 2 BC–AD 4 – Aureus, Gaius and Lucius as princeps iuventutis, obv. Augustus head wreathed, rev. Gaius and – Lucius Caesar standing veiled with shields and priestly symbols The Forum of Augustus opened and the Temple of Mars Ultor dedicated.
1 BC			
AD 1	Gaius takes the consulship for the first time.		
AD 2	August 20 – Death of Lucius.		
AD 3			
AD 4	April 23 – Death of Gaius. Augustus adopts Tiberius and Agrippa Postumus.		
AD 5			
AD 6	Agrippa Postumus sent into exile.		
AD 7			
AD 8	Julia the Younger sent into exile.		Ovid's *Metamorphoses* published.
AD 9	The general Varus suffers a catastrophic defeat in Germany, resulting in the massacre of three legions. The Lex Papia Poppaea introduces further regulations on marriage.		
AD 10			
AD 11			
AD 12			
AD 13	Tiberius given maius imperium.		The *Res Gestae* finished and deposited with the Vestal Virgins.
AD 14	August 19 – Death of Augustus.		

2.1 Octavian Comes to Rome, 44–42 BC

It would be impossible to fully understand the life and times of Octavian without first understanding the extraordinary life of his adoptive father, Julius Caesar. What is more, it would be impossible to fully understand how and why Octavian presented himself in the way he did without understanding the legacy left to him by Julius Caesar. It is for these reasons that this companion to the life and image of Octavian will begin years before he was even born.

*Note that Augustus is referred to as Octavian in the specification for periods before he assumed this name in 27 BC.

THE LIFE AND TIMES OF JULIUS CAESAR

Gaius Julius Caesar (100–44 BC) was a Roman politician and general. Born into the ancient Julian clan, he traced his family lineage back to the legendary founders of Rome: Aeneas and his divine mother Venus (the goddess of love) and Romulus and his divine father Mars (the god of war).

Hugely popular with the common people of Rome and with legions of veterans who had served in his army, Julius Caesar became one of the most powerful men in Rome in the first century BC. He was a gifted military general and a skilful public speaker. He advanced quickly up Rome's political ladder, being elected **Pontifex Maximus** in 63 BC and eventually being elected as consul (Rome's highest political office) for the year 59 BC. He was overwhelmingly popular with the urban poor, many of whom were disenfranchised Italian farmers or discharged veterans. He sought to improve their living conditions through initiatives such as his land distribution bill, which gave these impoverished city-dwellers a chance for homes and livelihoods in Italy.

At this stage, Julius Caesar made an informal alliance with two of Rome's leading men: Pompey the Great (a great general) and Crassus (who was exceedingly wealthy). They were known as the First **Triumvirate**. The three men used their combined influence to manage Roman politics. Many saw this as unconstitutional as they were bypassing the traditional, legal routes to political power. Some went so far as to accuse the triumvirs of treason against Rome.

Regardless, the triumvirate continued to work together and were the three most powerful men in the Empire. Eventually, however, the triumvirate turned against itself, with each man vying for sole power. Crassus died in 53 BC while on a military campaign in Parthia, leaving only Julius Caesar and Pompey. Private squabbling turned to outright civil war in 49 BC when Julius Caesar marched his army across the Rubicon river and into the city of Rome. The following year Caesar's forces won a decisive victory at Pharsalus in Greece. Pompey was forced to flee to Egypt, where he was captured by local rulers and beheaded.

Following his victory in the civil war, Julius Caesar was named **dictator** of Rome for a year. In 46 BC he was named dictator for ten years. In 44 BC he was named 'Dictator in Perpetuity', which meant that he would hold absolute power in Rome until his death. In all but name, Julius Caesar was the king of Rome.

While dictator, Julius Caesar began several ambitious architectural projects to improve the city of Rome, including a new civic and religious space called the Forum Iulium. He improved conditions for soldiers in the military, doubling their pay. He was also famous for his clemency – he preferred to pardon those who had fought on Pompey's side rather than to punish them. Clemency (or clementia in Latin) was deemed to be the 'proper' way to handle defeated enemies, and so Julius Caesar was presenting himself as an upstanding Roman by doing this.

On the Ides of March (15 March) 44 BC, Julius Caesar was ambushed by a gang of senators at the Theatre of Pompey. Around sixty men were involved in the conspiracy,

DEBATE

The manner of Julius Caesar's self-presentation is a subject of debate among scholars of this period. Some sources suggest that Julius Caesar styled himself as a king – wearing a crown and a purple toga. Purple was a sign of wealth and power, and an entirely purple toga would have reminded Romans of their first king Romulus, who was supposed to have worn one. Most Romans in the Republican period hated the idea of monarchy. They had exiled their corrupt kings centuries earlier, and many of the laws of the Republic were designed to prevent one man gaining too much power. If Julius Caesar did, in fact, present himself as a king then conservative Romans would surely have been shocked and appalled. The reliability of the sources on this matter are questionable, however. Julius Caesar's opponents certainly claimed that he had worn a crown and purple toga – but how far can their reports be believed?

which was led by two men: Brutus and Cassius. The assassins overpowered the dictator (who was in his sixties at this point), stabbing him a total of twenty-three times. He died at the scene.

OCTAVIAN BECOMES CAESAR

Octavian first entered Rome's political arena in 44 BC, shortly after the assassination of his great-uncle Julius Caesar. Octavian was just eighteen years old.

Octavian had been born into a wealthy but politically insignificant family: the Octavii. This background meant that Octavian was never likely to be a major player in Roman politics, which put a great emphasis on the achievements of one's ancestors. Julius Caesar's will stated that Octavian was his heir and requested that Octavian take his name. Octavian interpreted this as a legal adoption. Roman law did not distinguish between adopted and biological children and so, following Julius Caesar's death, Octavian suddenly had important (even divine) ancestors that would help him to get a good reputation in Rome.

From the moment he arrived in Rome, Octavian abandoned his childhood name of Octavius and called himself Gaius Julius Caesar (although this book and most other modern works continue to refer to him as Octavian for ease). In one move, Octavian associated himself with the most powerful Roman of the past century and disassociated himself from the Octavii, a family of no outstanding prominence.

Octavian fulfils Julius Caesar's promises

In the early years of his political career, Octavian's public image was entirely defined by his relationship with Julius Caesar. He wanted people to see him as the legitimate heir, not only to Julius Caesar's property and name, but also as the legitimate heir to his political power.

KEY INDIVIDUALS

Brutus

Dates: 85–42 BC

One of Julius Caesar's friends and allies, who turned on him and led the plot to assassinate him.

Cassius

Dates: uncertain birth date c. 85–42 BC

Brutus' co-conspirator in the plot to assassinate Julius Caesar.

denarius (pl. denarii) a silver coin with a value enough to pay a soldier's wage for three days and buy enough wheat to bake daily bread for a month

games public events held, usually by magistrates or by rich individuals, to honour a particular god or in celebration of an event. Games were a rare chance for the urban poor to enjoy entertainments such as theatrical plays, chariot racing, circus performances and gladiatorial shows

His first move in Rome was to fulfil a request made in Julius Caesar's will: to give seventy-five **denarii** to each of Rome's poor, the plebeians. Octavian had to borrow money to fulfil this request, but it was well worth it. It won him popularity with the urban poor and solidified his image as Julius Caesar's heir. He also held **games** in honour of Venus that had been promised by Julius Caesar. A combination of cash (which would be used to buy food) and entertainment had been used for years as a quick and easy way to win popularity with the poorer classes. A century later the poet Juvenal coined the phrase 'panem et circenses' (which is Latin for 'bread and games') to describe the tactic. While these games were being held, a comet appeared in the sky over Rome. Octavian claimed (and had a soothsayer confirm) that this was his 'father' Julius Caesar rising to the sky to be made a god. Later sources tell of a variety of such omens that surrounded Octavian's coming to Rome – a fine example of this can be found in Suetonius' *Life of Augustus* 95.

EXPLORE FURTHER: SUETONIUS

One of our best surviving accounts of the history of this period comes from a biographer named Suetonius. His *Life of Augustus* is a biography of Octavian/Augustus, written around a century after Augustus' death. This biography is one in a collection of twelve, collectively referred to as the *Lives of the Twelve Caesars*, which begins with an account of Julius Caesar's life, then Octavian/Augustus', and then the next ten men who would be called Emperor of Rome.

The genre of biography in ancient Rome was seen as being less prestigious than history. Biographers, such as Plutarch, openly admitted to focusing their accounts on events that revealed the character of their subjects, rather than focusing on events that were historically significant. Nevertheless, it seems as though biography was treated seriously, and we have evidence of biographers in the Roman world going to great lengths to research and verify facts.

Suetonius was writing well after Augustus' death. As such, his text can provide a valuable insight into how Augustus' public image changed over time. It is, however, vitally important that you do not confuse his work with the sources that were produced during Octavian/Augustus' lifetime.

You are reminded that, although Suetonius' biography is one of our best and most complete sources for the history of this period, this module is not primarily concerned with establishing historical facts. As with all prescribed sources in this component, you should consider the nature of the image conveyed by the author, rather than whether that image is accurate or reliable.

KEY INDIVIDUAL

Mark Antony

Dates: 83–30 BC

One of Julius Caesar's closest friends and most trusted lieutenants.

Octavian enters the Senate

Unfortunately for Octavian, he was not the only person who wanted to inherit Julius Caesar's power. One of Julius Caesar's former lieutenants, Mark Antony, was positioning himself as the rightful heir. He had delivered a powerful speech at Julius Caesar's funeral attacking the assassins, turning the tide of popular opinion against them. This caused the assassins to flee Rome and also won popular support for himself.

Many senators were afraid that Antony would try to seize power for himself. They saw the young Octavian as the lesser of two evils, thinking that they might be able to control him. Despite the fact that he was only eighteen, a majority of senators voted to induct Octavian into the Senate (the usual minimum age was thirty) and he was sent to help lead an army against Antony's personal army at Mutina. In April 43, Antony's army was defeated and he was forced to retreat. The two consuls for the year, Hirtius and Pansa, had both been part of this campaign and were both killed. This left Octavian in sole command of the Senate's army. This campaign is mentioned in Suetonius' *Life of Augustus* 10–11.

The Senate misplayed their hand at this stage. They tried to curb Octavian's rise to power by refusing to give him honours for the victory. Octavian responded by refusing to pursue Antony. In fact, he marched his army on Rome and demanded that he be given the consulship now that Hirtius and Pansa were dead! The Senate had no army left to defend itself, and so had to bow to Octavian's demands. A show-election was held and Octavian was declared consul in August 43 BC. Augustus himself wrote a brief account of the circumstances surrounding his first consulship in section 1 of the *Res Gestae*. Much of the finer detail of how he gained the position is omitted from the text.

Before his death, Augustus composed an **elogium** for himself, outlining the achievements of his life. This text is referred to as the *Res Gestae* (see pp. 187–92 for an extended discussion of the composition, dissemination and purposes of the *Res Gestae*). As the text was written towards the end of Augustus' life, with instructions to be displayed to the public after his death, it seems likely that the *Res Gestae* was intended to ensure that Augustus was remembered in a particular way.

Much like Suetonius' *Life of Augustus*, the *Res Gestae* should not be used as evidence for Octavian/Augustus' public image during his lifetime. Rather, it should be examined as evidence of how Augustus hoped to be remembered.

elogium (pl. **elogia**) a funerary inscription

Octavian had managed successfully to present himself as the obvious successor to Julius Caesar's power and popularity and then to leverage this into official political power. In just over a year Octavian had gone from being a boy with no history of holding political office, to consul of Rome.

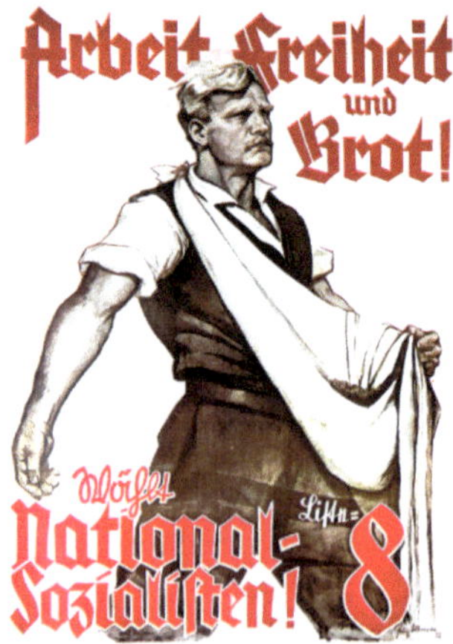

FIGURE 2.1
German propaganda poster from the 1930s.

EXAM TIP: SOURCE SKILLS

Who's the Audience?

Because this module is concerned with *how* Augustus portrayed himself to the public, all prescribed sources have something that they are trying to 'say' to their audience. When you are studying this kind of source, it is important to determine who the intended audience was. This will help you to work out what the message of the source was, and to evaluate how effective it was at conveying the message.

For example, the strapline at the top of this political poster 'Arbeit, Freiheit und Brot' (which translates as 'work, freedom and bread') is simple enough to understand. It promises food and work (and therefore money) to the viewer, if they vote for the Nazi party (mentioned below, National-Sozialisten) in an upcoming election. But without any knowledge of the audience it is difficult to understand why it says this and how effective it was.

The poster was, in fact, published in the early 1930s in Germany, following a period of intense economic depression that left many out of work and unable to feed their families. The Nazi Party was not yet in complete control of Germany, and was trying to attract voters. Armed with this knowledge about the audience, we are able to analyse the poster in far greater detail. We can understand how it was designed to appeal to the audience's concerns and evaluate how effective it might have been at winning support for the Nazi Party from the German people.

PRESCRIBED SOURCE

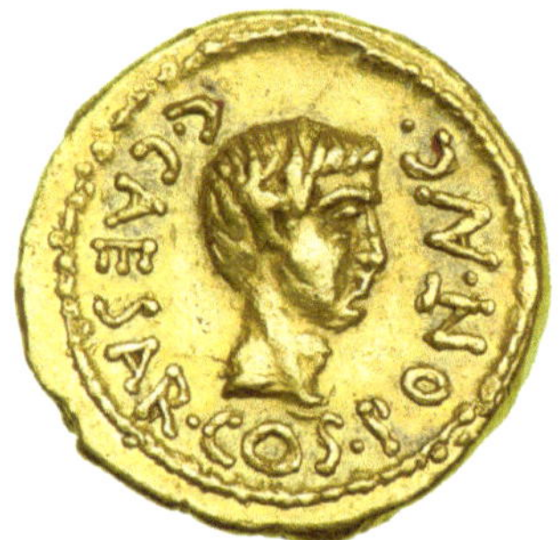

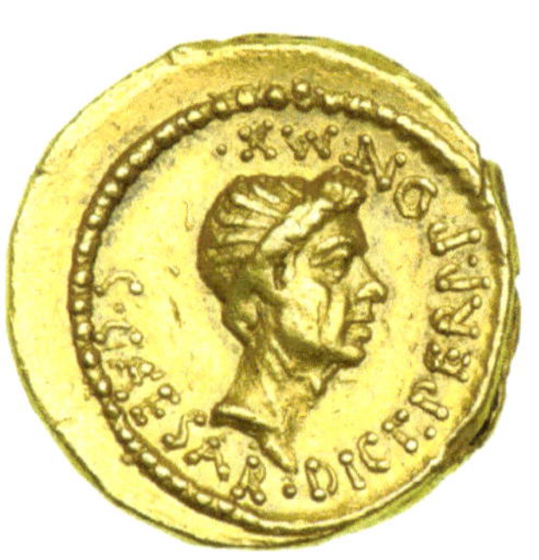

Aureus, obv. bare head of Octavian, rev. head of Julius Caesar with laurel wreath

Date: 43 BC

Coin struck by: unknown

Text reads: C CAESAR COS PONT AUG // C CAESAR DICT PERP PONT MAX

Translation: Gaius Caesar (Octavian), consul, pontifex, augur // Gaius Caesar (Julius), dictator in perpetuity, pontifex maximus

Significance: one of Octavian's earliest attempts at crafting his public image, by linking himself with Julius Caesar

FIGURE 2.2
Aureus of Octavian.

The coin in Figure 2.2, struck in 43 BC just after he was appointed consul, is one of the earliest surviving examples of Octavian's propaganda intended to manage his public image. It shows Octavian alongside his 'father', Julius Caesar. This served to align the young Octavian with Julius Caesar's memory and encourage the viewer to think of Octavian as the heir to Julius Caesar's power. Julius Caesar had been one of the first

Romans to use his own portrait on coins. By following his example, Octavian highlighted the similarities between Julius Caesar and himself.

The text on the coin cleverly highlights similarity and also difference between Octavian and Julius Caesar. Each side follows this model: name, highest government position held, highest religious position held. This parallel encourages the viewer to see Octavian as a new Julius Caesar. The positions on Julius Caesar's side, Dictator in Perpetuity and Pontifex Maximus, were both positions that were held for life. Octavian's side, however, references the consulship – a fairly elected position that lasted for a set amount of time. This difference is crucial. Julius Caesar's assassins viewed Julius Caesar's power as unconstitutional and they saw him as a tyrant. Octavian needed to avoid this image lest he too meet a violent end. This coin stresses the link between Julius Caesar and Octavian, but also suggests differences in their policy and approach to politics that would make Octavian seem less threatening to those in power.

The laurel wreath on Julius Caesar's head is a reference to his military victories. When a Roman general led a particularly successful campaign, they could be awarded a **triumph**. On the day of the triumph, the general would be allowed to wear a laurel wreath as a sign of honour. The Senate voted Julius Caesar the privilege of wearing a wreath at any time, making it a particularly evocative symbol for him.

triumph granted by a Senate vote, a special celebration of a successful military campaign in which the conquering general would ride through the streets of Rome on a chariot with his spoils of war paraded behind

EXAM TIP: SOURCE SKILLS

Roman Coins

All classes of Romans used coins to buy and sell goods and services. This means that they were an excellent tool for sending messages to the populace, as a great many people would see them. Scholars believe that the Romans paid closer attention to what was on their money than we do today. Whereas we are bombarded with thousands of new images a day, new pictures were rare in ancient Rome. If a new coin came into circulation, it is likely that people paid attention to it simply because it was something new.

Coins commonly included a mix of writing and images. Not all Romans could read, so the writing would have been understood by the educated. Images were more likely to be understood by the majority of the people. However, without being able to read the accompanying text, illiterate people were more likely to misinterpret the symbols.

THE SECOND TRIUMVIRATE

Still resentful of the Senate's attempts to stand in his way, Octavian formed an alliance with Mark Antony and another politician named Lepidus in 43 BC. This alliance became known as the Second Triumvirate. Unlike the First Triumvirate, which had been an informal alliance, the Second Triumvirate was ratified by a law which gave the three men extraordinary powers for a five-year period.

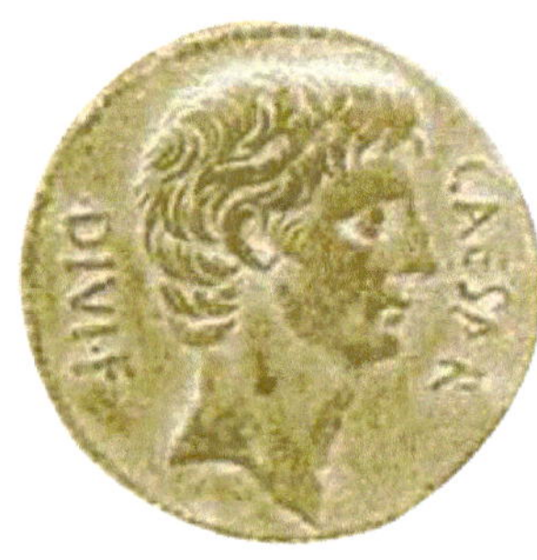

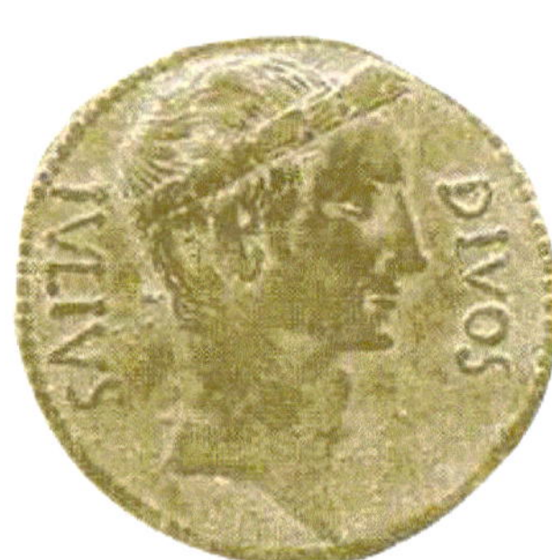

FIGURE 2.3
Aureus of Octavian.

The Second Triumvirate solidified their power by setting out proscriptions, which named individual senators as public enemies. Once proscribed, a person's property was confiscated and they could be legally killed. This allowed the Second Triumvirate to eliminate their political opponents and also to fill their own pockets with the proceeds of the sale of confiscated goods. They used these funds to pay their personal armies. The proscriptions were public and everyone knew that Octavian was in part responsible. Historians disagree on how many were proscribed in this period, but a conservative estimate suggests at least 100, but perhaps as many as 300, senators were killed out of a total of 900. Octavian must have seemed to be ruthless and power hungry – at least to the politically savvy upper classes. It is unclear how much the poorer classes knew about the proscriptions and thus what they might have thought about Octavian.

DIVI FILIUS: THE SON OF A GOD

From 42 BC Octavian's self-presentation took on a new and important dimension. In this year, the Senate declared Julius Caesar a god, a move which allowed Octavian to call himself 'divi filius'. This title, which literally translates as 'son of a god' was used as part of his official name and Octavian began to incorporate 'divi filius' into his coins as a way of communicating his semi-divine status to the people of Rome. Figure 2.3 is an example of Octavian's coinage, which identifies Julius Caesar as a god ('DIVOS IULIUS' meaning 'the divine Julius') and Octavian himself as divi filius.

Many Romans liked to claim that they were distant descendants of the gods, but Octavian's claim to be the son of a god gave him an aura of importance and authority that few mortals could rival. Indeed, now he was on a par with such legendary heroes as Aeneas and Hercules, who were themselves demigods.

OCTAVIAN AVENGES HIS FATHER

mos maiorum 'The ways of our ancestors': an unwritten code of behaviour and values, looking to the ancestors as role models

The Romans had an unwritten code of 'proper behaviour' referred to as the **mos maiorum**, which put great importance on duty. As both Octavian and Antony were presenting themselves as heirs to Julius Caesar, it was important that they be seen to avenge his murder, otherwise, they could be accused of failing in their duty to the dead man (now a god). And so in 42 BC the triumvirs launched a military campaign against Julius Caesar's assassins, who were led by Brutus and Cassius. Later that year, the triumvirs won a decisive victory at the Battle of Philippi, forcing Brutus and Cassius to commit suicide. Octavian promised to dedicate a temple to Mars Ultor in thanks for the victory (the god of war – 'ultor' means 'the avenger'). He fulfilled this promise in 2 BC when the Forum of Augustus was unveiled (see pp. 175–6).

Octavian and Antony had fulfilled their duty to Julius Caesar and removed any political opposition in one fell swoop. The men of the Second Triumvirate were now the most powerful men in Rome.

ACTIVITY

The unwritten code of the mos maiorum influenced the behaviour of upper-class Roman men. Research the following concepts which, for many Romans, formed the basis of the mos maiorum. For each, give a one-sentence definition: pietas, fides, gravitas and constantia.

Design a 'Mr Men' character who personifies each concept, then write a short story where the 'Mos Maiorum Men' work together to try to solve a problem.

TOPIC REVIEW

These questions should draw on your knowledge of the whole topic, so think carefully about the different things you have learned (check the Topic Overview on p. 115).

1. What were the political obstacles facing Octavian when he first came to Rome following Julius Caesar's assassination?
2. Why was Octavian's association with Julius Caesar so important to his early public image?
3. What was a triumph and why was it important?
4. How did the proscriptions help Octavian to solidify his power?
5. How would you characterise Octavian's relationship with Mark Antony throughout this period?

Further Reading

Bradley, P., *Ancient Rome Using Evidence* (Cambridge: Cambridge University Press, 1990), 394–405

Clark, D.H., *Augustus, First Roman Emperor: Power, Propaganda and the Politics of Survival* (Liverpool: Bristol Phoenix Press, 2010), Chapter 3.

Galinsky, K., *Augustan Culture* (Princeton: Princeton University Press, 1996), Chapter 2.

PRACTICE QUESTIONS

Source A: Gold coin (aureus), 43 BC

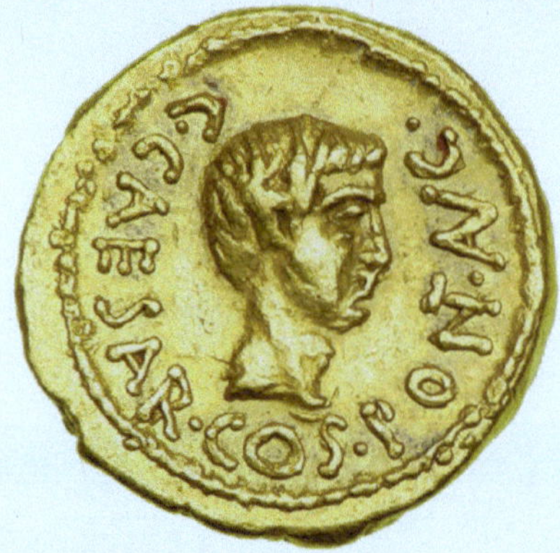 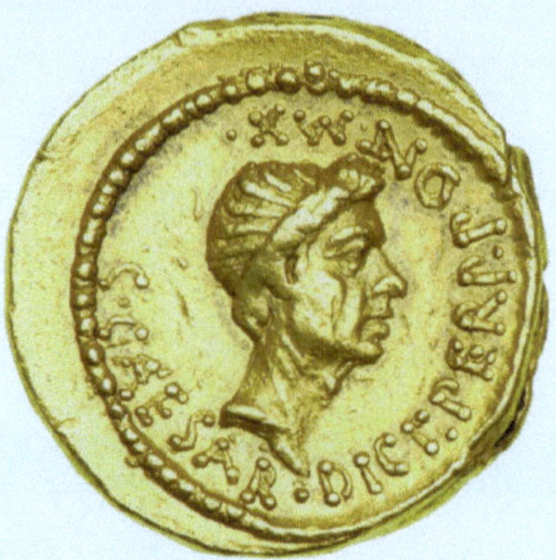

Inscriptions on coins:

C CAESAR COS PONT AUG – Gaius Caesar (Octavian), consul, pontifex, augur

C CAESAR DICT PERP PONT MAX – Gaius Caesar (Julius), dictator in perpetuity, pontifex maximus

AS Level

1 a. What is the significance of the laurel wreath in Roman culture? [1]
    b. Why is Octavian not depicted wearing this? [1]
2. How does this coin create an image of Octavian as the legitimate heir to Julius Caesar's power? Make four points and support each point with reference to the coin. [8]

A Level

1 a. The pontifex maximus was the chief priest in Rome. Once elected to this position, how long did one hold it for? [1]
    b. Outline how dictators were chosen in Rome and what powers this position conferred. [2]
2. How similar do Octavian and Julius Caesar seem based on their depiction on this coin? [10]

2.2 Power Struggle, 42–30 BC

*Note that Augustus is referred to as Octavian in the specification for periods before he assumed this name in 27 BC.

Having removed all obstacles to their power, the Second Triumvirate were firmly in command of the Roman Empire. Following their defeat of Caesar's assassins, the triumvirs drew up an agreement, known as the Treaty of Brundisium, which gave each man a portion of the Empire to govern. Octavian was to control the western provinces, Antony took the eastern provinces and Lepidus governed the African provinces.

IMPERATOR OCTAVIAN

KEY INDIVIDUAL

Agrippa

Dates: 63–12 BC

Octavian's right-hand man, his best friend and his most trusted advisor in military concerns. Agrippa was the general in charge of almost all of Octavian's wars.

At this time, the son of Pompey the Great, known as Sextus Pompeius, had taken control of Sicily for himself and was using this stronghold to blockade Rome's trade routes. This made it very difficult to get grain into the city, and by 39 BC almost caused a famine. It was clear that Sextus Pompeius would have to be dealt with forcibly. Octavian worked with Agrippa (his friend and gifted military leader) to plan a naval campaign against Sextus Pompeius.

In 38 BC Octavian added 'Imperator' to his title, which meant 'commander'. This name strengthened Octavian's link to Julius Caesar, who had also been called Imperator, and encouraged the idea that Octavian was a great military leader. At this stage, Octavian had not had a particularly illustrious career as a general.

By July of 36 BC, Agrippa had gathered and trained an impressive fleet. He led the fleet in an invasion of Sicily, totally destroying Sextus Pompeius' navy.

See section 25 of the *Res Gestae* for how Augustus later referred to this campaign – it is interesting to note that Sextus Pompeius is not mentioned by name, nor is there any indication that he was a Roman citizen and thus the conflict could have been reasonably called a civil war. Octavian celebrated this campaign as a great personal victory. He erected a rostral column, decorated with the prows of defeated ships and topped with a golden statue of himself.

THE TRIUMVIRATE FALLS APART

Having taken power for themselves and eliminated all outside threats, the Second Triumvirate began to turn on each other. In 36 BC, Octavian bribed some of Lepidus' legions to turn on him, effectively ending Lepidus' political career. Lepidus was exiled to his country estate in Italy until his death in 13/12 BC.

Lepidus' unceremonious exit from the political scene left Octavian and Antony as the foremost men in Roman politics. The years that followed were characterised by increasingly intense competition between the two that would ultimately lead to civil war in 32 BC.

Each man knew that his political future hinged on his ability to win over the hearts and minds of the Roman people, the Senate and the army. This gave rise to an all-out propaganda battle, with each faction selling the benefits of their leader and presenting their own vision for the future of Rome.

OCTAVIAN AS BENEFACTOR OF THE PEOPLE OF ROME

Although the elite senatorial class held almost all positions of official political power, they were a small minority of the total population of Rome. Far more numerous were the urban poor. Octavian, like Julius Caesar before him, realised that the support of the urban poor could be a very powerful asset, and so Octavian, again like Julius Caesar, positioned himself as the generous benefactor of the Roman people and of the city itself.

One of Octavian's key strategies for winning public support in Rome was to have his followers make gifts to the people and to the city itself. In 42 BC, Octavian started work on a new temple in honour of his father, known as the Temple of the Deified Julius Caesar, in the Roman Forum. In 34 BC, one of Octavian's allies, a general called Statilius Taurus, commissioned a new stone amphitheatre that would be used to hold gladiatorial and animal games. Octavian's right-hand-man, Agrippa, also oversaw a programme of urban renewal, repairing dilapidated streets and sewer systems, as well as a range of public buildings. All of these projects were highly visible and all of them were designed to improve the quality of life of the Roman people. Octavian's message was clear: I care about and am investing in the future of the city of Rome.

Octavian's followers also made one-off gifts to the people. A notable example was Agrippa throwing tokens (which could be exchanged for money or clothing) to crowds at the theatre. He also arranged for free admission to the public baths and gifts of salt and oil to be made to the urban poor.

OCTAVIAN AS APOLLO'S FAVOURITE

One of the most striking features of the propaganda campaigns of both Octavian and Antony was that each man chose a particular god as his patron. Antony chose to align himself with Dionysus, the god of wine and theatre, and the conqueror of the East. Octavian's chosen patron was Apollo, a god whose spheres of influence included the sun, prophecy, archery, music, medicine and civilisation itself. Apollo also stood for discipline, moderation and morality.

The personalities and powers of these gods would have been well known to all Romans. They featured in many popular myths and were worshipped in a variety of public festivals. As such they were very useful cultural touchstones for an ambitious politician who wanted to convey their own 'personal brand'. All Octavian needed to do to convey the idea that he was a force for civilisation was to publish his own image alongside one of Apollo's symbols. All Antony needed to do to convey the idea that he would end war and bring celebrations and plenty was to publish his own image alongside one of Dionysus' symbols. A prime example of this is Figure 2.5. The obverse depicts Antony with his wife Octavia, and the reverse a depiction of Dionysus stood on a cista mystica ('secret casket'), holding a cantharus and thyrsus (both symbols of Dionysus). These images, presented alongside each other, encourage the viewer to make a mental association between Antony and Dionysus, and to view them in the same light.

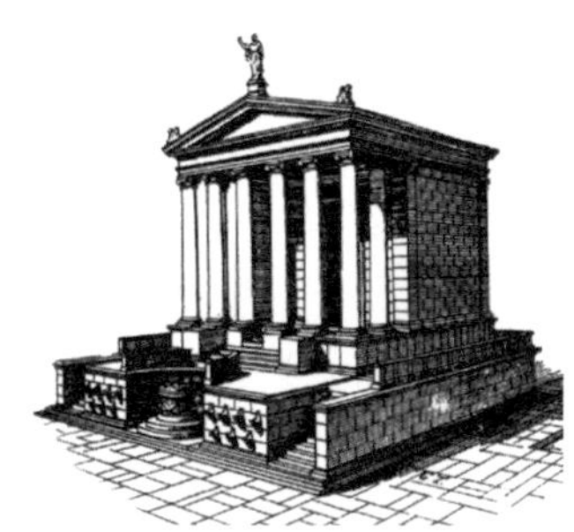

FIGURE 2.4
Unfortunately, the Temple of the Deified Julius Caesar has not survived. This illustration is a reconstruction based on the work of archaeologist Christian Hülsen.

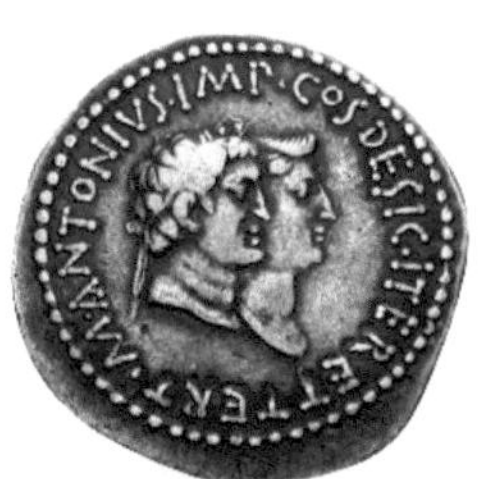

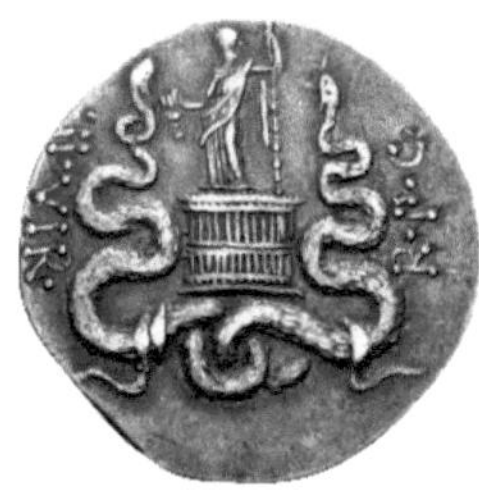

FIGURE 2.5
Cistophorus of Antony.

Comarketing

The strategy of presenting two distinct things alongside one another for the purpose of impacting the perception of a viewing audience is still in use today by advertisers, who refer to the practice as 'comarketing'. When an audience is presented with a well-known thing alongside a less well-known thing, they tend to transfer what they know about the well-known thing onto the less well-known thing. For example, imagine a print advert for a sports car. Alongside an image of the car prowls a panther. The advertisers hope that the audience will transfer what they know about the big cat (powerful, fast, responsive etc.) onto the car. If successful, the audience starts to think and feel about the car in a particular way, despite the fact that they have never seen it, touched it or driven it themselves and despite the fact they have no specific knowledge about its specification or capabilities.

Symbolic Messages

Messages are not always presented to us in a straightforward way. Artists and writers will often make use of symbolic language or imagery to imply something to their audience. For example, a haunted house at a fairground might not have a sign that says 'This will give you a scary experience!' but the image of an old lopsided house, surrounded by gravestones and covered in spider webs implies that it will be scary inside. The viewer has learned (perhaps by visiting other haunted houses, from watching horror films or by experiencing what happens at Halloween) that these items are connoted with 'scary', so when they see these symbols, the message is conveyed.

Symbolic communication works because the artist/writer makes use of symbols that the intended viewer has encountered before and learned the meaning(s) of.

It is important to bear in mind that the symbols used by ancient Roman artists/writers may have had different connotations or secondary meanings than they do today. As such, your job, as a Classicist, is to find out what the connotations of a particular symbol were in its original context and to factor these in to your interpretation of the sources.

Putting it into Practice

This coin, minted after 27 BC, depicts Augustus on the obverse and an eagle on the reverse.

a) List the connotations that you, a modern viewer, have for eagles.
b) Based on your list, what assumptions would you make about Augustus, who chose to present himself next to an eagle?

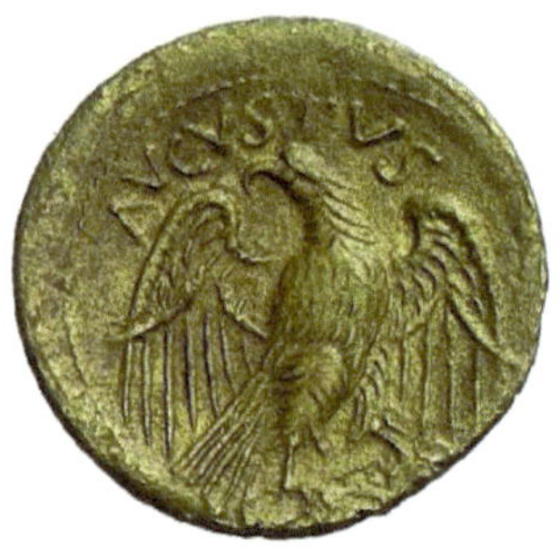

FIGURE 2.6
Quadrans of Augustus.

c) Roman culture associated eagles with: Jupiter (the king of the gods), the idea of fate and Roman military strength (the eagle was depicted on Roman standards). How does this information change the assumptions you made in part b)?

It can be difficult to keep track of ancient connotations and keep them separate from your own modern connotations. You might like to start a glossary of Roman symbols that you can refer to throughout the course. This book will give you the meanings of some symbols, but you will need to research others for yourself. You might find the following resources helpful for this:

The Oxford Classical Dictionary
The *Encyclopaedia Britannica* website: britannica.com

How effective this strategy was is debatable. Certainly, people would have started to associate Antony with Dionysus and Octavian with Apollo, but they might also begin to associate them with something else. Traditionally it was Hellenistic kings, not Roman senators, who had associated themselves with particular gods. Might this strategy have made both of them seem like aspiring monarchs rather than traditional republicans?

MODERN SCHOLARSHIP

At a splendid feast all participants could relive the experience of being liberated from ordinary existence. The life of intense pleasure and indulgence which Mark Antony unabashedly enjoyed in Athens and Alexandria could be viewed as a means to freedom and salvation, to release from suffering, with the promise of a happy future . . . The Alexandrians understood the meaning of those statues that showed Antony as Dionysus . . . When Antony entered Alexandria in the guise of Dionysus triumphant after his victory in Armenia, this was perceived as an appropriate form of celebration. . . . Toward the end, his entire lifestyle was shaped by this role. He celebrated the outbreak of war with dazzling feasts, went out to face Octavian as Dionysus with his thiasos, and even when he knew his cause was lost remained in character, treating life as one great party.

P. Zanker, *The Power of Images in the Age of Augustus*, pp. 46–7 (2014)

Zanker argues that Antony did not only use Dionysus to help shape his public image, but that he began to believe his own hype and to live like a new Dionysus. He claims that this image played well in Alexandria, with Cleopatra's Egyptian subjects, but we must remember that Romans had very different values. To a Roman audience, the East was synonymous with decadence and effeminacy – not admirable qualities for a leading man.

Octavian continued to associate himself with Apollo throughout his life. Indeed, he allowed a rumour to circulate in Rome that he was Apollo's son. The rumour stated that Octavian's mother, Attia, had been visited in the night by Apollo in the form of a snake, and this was how Octavian was conceived. This boosted Octavian's image in three ways: first it strengthened his association with his patron god Apollo, it also made the 'divi filius' seem even more godly by being 'descended' from two divine fathers, and finally it invited people to link Octavian with the great Macedonian king Alexander the Great, whose mother Olympias was said to have conceived her son in the same way.

Suetonius mentions another anecdote – the so-called Feast of the Twelve Gods. In Section 70 of the *Life of Augustus* Suetonius describes how Octavian had, as a young man, given a feast for his friends in which each guest took the role of a major Roman deity. Of course, Octavian dressed as Apollo. This early sign of Octavian's preference for the god may have been part of a wider attempt to encourage the Roman people to view him as Apollo's favourite. If it was, it seems to have backfired. Suetonius, writing a century after Augustus' death, says that the party was the subject of 'scandalous gossip', in part because of the adulterous behaviour of the guests, in part because the lavish feast took place in the midst of a city-wide famine.

MODERN SCHOLARSHIP

The relationship with Apollo would prove to be ideally suited to Octavian himself and to furthering his political image. All these goals and objectives, both during the struggle with Antony and then later in the building of a new order, could be associated with the god. Apollo stood first of all for discipline and morality. . . . Apollo also stood for purification and for punishment of any form of excess. As such he could well represent Italy's position during the civil war with Antony, with the motto 'Italy versus the Orient with its *luxuria*, against Egypt with its animal-headed gods and its decadence'. But after the victory was won, then Apollo took on his role as singer, lyre player, and god of peace and reconciliation. As the prophetic god, with sibyl and sphinx, it was he who proclaimed the long-awaited new age.

P. Zanker, *The Power of Images in the Age of Augustus*, pp. 51–3 (2014)

Here Zanker outlines how Octavian took advantage of Apollo's multifaceted nature in establishing his own public image. Throughout the Triumviral Period, Apollo represented discipline and morality, a clear counterpoint to Antony's Dionysus. After his defeat of Antony, however, this aspect was less relevant and so Octavian's propaganda began to bring other aspects of Apollo to the fore.

Octavian allowed different aspects of Apollo's personality to come to the fore as the political situation changed. For the duration of the power struggle against Antony, Apollo was used as a modest, stoic and sensible counterpoint to the luxury and decadence of Dionysus.

LIVIA AND OCTAVIAN: POWER COUPLE

Although they were excluded from holding political office themselves, Roman women could play an important role in supporting the political careers of their husbands. Often marriages would be made and broken to solidify political alliances and the wives of prominent women would entertain guests in the home, helping to grease the wheels of business and politics. A well-behaved wife with a reputation for duty and chastity could be a real asset. Conversely, a wife who failed to live up to the expected standards of behaviour could ruin the reputation of a budding politician.

Octavian had been married twice in his first four years in Rome, first to Clodia and second to Scribonia. Both marriages were made and broken for political reasons. In 38 BC, Octavian's wife, Scribonia, gave birth to his only child, a girl named Julia. On that very day, barely a year since they married, Octavian divorced Scribonia so that he could marry Livia. Livia came from one of the oldest noble families in Rome – the Claudii. This made her an ideal partner for the ambitious Octavian as he was able to take advantage of her excellent family connections. She had two sons from a previous marriage: Tiberius and Drusus. Livia was famously beautiful and also highly intelligent, both of which reflected well on Octavian. Despite her family's wealth and the prominence of her new husband, Livia fulfilled all the duties expected of a traditional Roman **matrona** – it was reported that she even spun and wove all of Octavian's clothes herself by hand. This gave the right impression that Octavian himself embodied traditional Roman behaviour and values, which gained him popularity with old-fashioned conservatives.

The portrait of Livia in Figure 2.7 lacks any strong emotional expression. This is in line with the Classical style that the Romans inherited from fifth-century Greece, but this portrait is not an unrealistic and idealised version of the real woman. The prominent nose, small mouth and distinctive chin are likely imitations of the real Livia. As such this portrait is absolutely typical of portrait sculptures of the Roman Republic, which depicted their subjects with a high degree of realism. Thus Livia herself is shown as a quintessentially Roman woman – an idea that is reinforced by her hairstyle: a roll of hair on the top of the head, with a small bun at the nape of the neck being a popular style for Roman women in the first century BC.

FIGURE 2.7
Portrait of Livia.

PRESCRIBED SOURCE

Portrait of Livia

Date: *c.* 31 BC

Material: Egyptian basanite

Currently located:
The Louvre,
Paris, France

Significance: depicts
Livia as a typical Roman
matrona, implying
traditional values

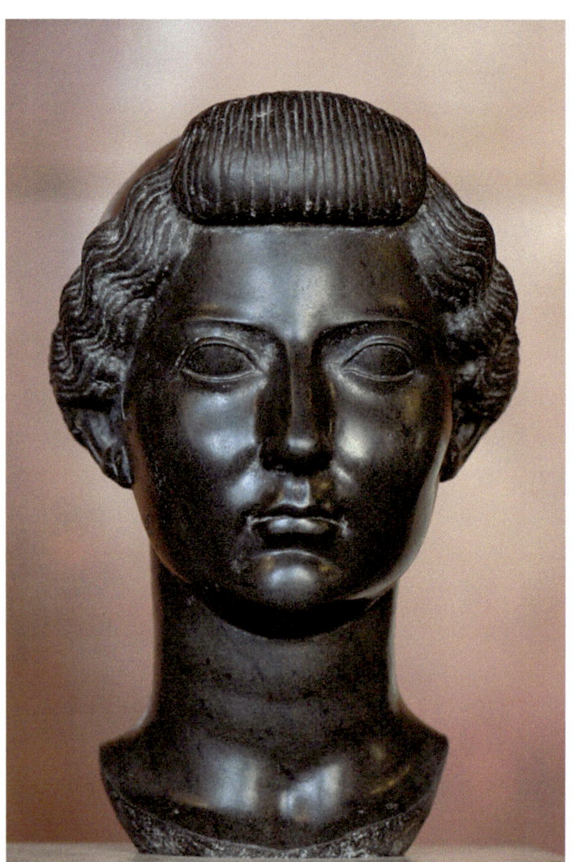

FIGURE 2.8
This idealised bust (left) is
typical of the Classical
Greek style which focused
on depicting perfect human
forms rather than realistic
portraits. The portrait bust
of the Republican politician
Cicero (right) in contrast
emphasises personal
details, such as the large
and asymmetrical nose,
jowls and lines around the
eyes. This is typical of the
Roman style which prized
realism over idealism.

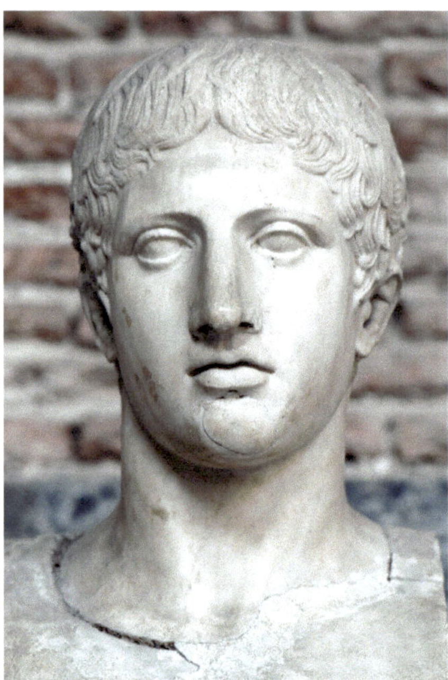

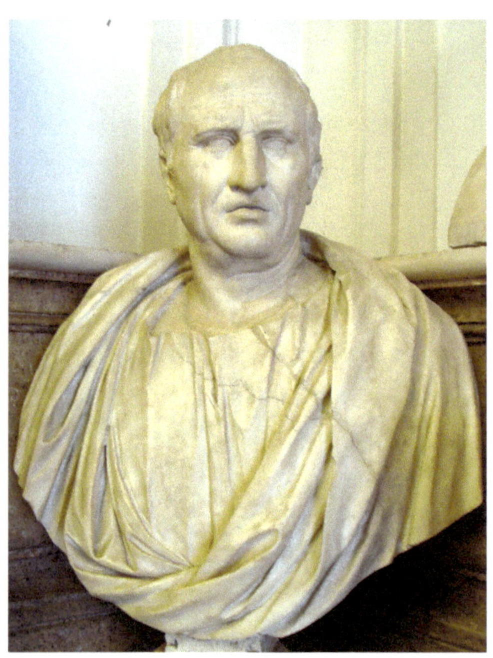

ANTONY MISMANAGES HIS PUBLIC IMAGE

While Octavian was busy setting up a traditional Roman household that would serve his image as a traditional, conservative Roman, his rival Antony was doing quite the opposite. Antony was distracted and often away from Rome, entertaining a love affair with the Ptolemaic queen, Cleopatra. This love affair alienated him even further from Octavian and enabled Octavian and his supporters to smear Antony's image with accusations of anti-Roman behaviour, decadence and effeminacy.

> **S & C** A common 'smear tactic' in Rome was to accuse your opponent of effeminacy (calling their masculinity into question). Roman men were expected to conform to a very narrow idea of masculinity. For more information on Roman masculinity and femininity, explore these resources:
> L.G. McManus, *Performing Masculinity: Control, Manhood and the Rhetoric of Effeminacy*, (2007). Dissertation. Chapter 1: Roman Oratorical Masculinity, 22–48.
> M. McDonnell, *Roman Manliness: 'Virtus' and the Roman Republic* (Cambridge: Cambridge University Press, 1994).

Antony's choice of Cleopatra as a mistress caused a scandal in Rome. Normally, a Roman man would choose a lover of a lower status than himself, possibly a slave or a prostitute or a foreigner. This ensured that any children they had would not be legitimate, would not inherit property, and would not be able to enter the realm of politics as an official heir. In short, they wouldn't be dangerous. Although Cleopatra was a foreigner to Rome, she was also the ruler of a rich and powerful state. She was at least Antony's social equal – if not his better. This was quite unusual, and it also meant that any children would be Egyptian royalty. Indeed, Cleopatra did bear Antony's children in 40 BC – fraternal twins named Alexander Helios and Cleopatra Selene. Another son followed in 36 BC, Ptolemy Philadelphus. These children were a dangerous prospect indeed, should they ever come to Rome and stake a claim to power.

Antony was not Cleopatra's first Roman lover. She had been Julius Caesar's mistress, and borne him a child named Caesarion. Octavian and his supporters were surely keen to downplay this problematic aspect of Julius Caesar's past. Certainly, the association is not mentioned by any of Octavian's client artists or writers.

In 36 BC Antony moved to Alexandria to live with Cleopatra full-time. He married her despite the fact that he was still married to Octavia. Roman values tolerated infidelity, but did not allow bigamy. Octavian's supporters claimed that Antony had been bewitched by Cleopatra, robbed of his senses and his masculinity by a dangerous eastern witch. Antony's behaviour played right into this story. He minted coins that depicted himself alongside Cleopatra – Octavian's supporters pointed out that it was unfit for a foreign woman to appear on a coin as though she were an important Roman. Antony spent his time in Alexandria enjoying sumptuous feasts and lavish entertainment – Octavian's supporters claimed that Cleopatra had corrupted Antony's traditional Roman austerity with her eastern taste for luxury.

> **KEY INDIVIDUAL**
>
> **Cleopatra**
>
> **Dates:** 69–30 BC
>
> Cleopatra VII Philopator was ruler of Egypt from 51 to 30 BC.

FIGURE 2.9
Denarius of Mark Antony. The obverse shows Cleopatra, the reverse Antony himself.

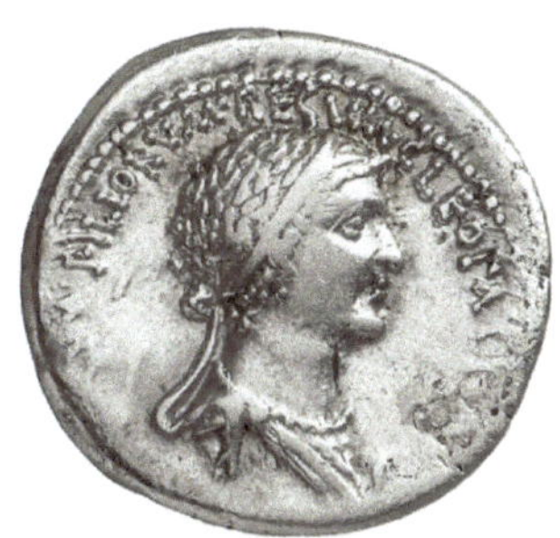

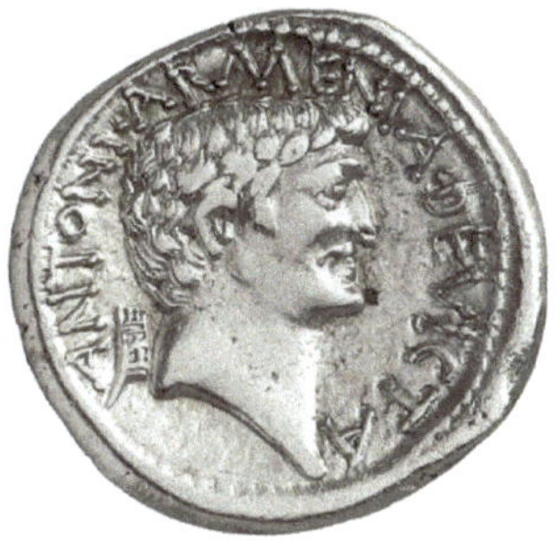

Contrast all of this with Octavian's relationship with Livia. She was from one of the oldest noble Roman families, dressed in Roman fashion and behaved like a traditional Roman matrona. Whether genuine or not, Octavian's relationship with Livia offered a stark counterpoint to Antony's relationship with Cleopatra.

Antony must have known how his actions would have played in the city of Rome. Later sources, writing after Antony's death, have tended to portray him as a love-struck fool. They suggest that he was so distracted by his love for Cleopatra and his party lifestyle, taking the role of a new Dionysus, that he neither understood nor cared what people in Rome thought of him. This interpretation seems a bit far-fetched. Antony had seen first-hand at Julius Caesar's assassination what could happen when public opinion turned sour. It is perhaps more likely that Antony was taking a big-picture perspective. Rome at this time was much more than a single city, it was a great empire of different people and cultures. It could be that Antony's public image in this period was aimed not at the city of Rome, but at the wealthy eastern Empire.

ANTONY'S FATAL MISTAKE: THE DONATIONS OF ALEXANDRIA

In 34 BC, Antony used Cleopatra's money to launch a campaign into Armenia. Aware that his reputation was slipping, he wanted to publicise his victory to the masses. The traditional Roman ceremony for celebrating a military victory was a triumph. Triumphs involved a parade through the streets of Rome, with booty and slaves captured in war being displayed to the gathered masses. A triumph was the ultimate demonstration of Roman military might. Antony did not celebrate a triumph after his victory in Armenia. What happened instead is known as the 'Donations of Alexandria'.

The ceremony followed the same basic model as a triumph, with the victorious general and the spoils of war parading through the streets. But the streets were in Alexandria, not Rome. This was a highly symbolic step and Octavian's supporters were quick to interpret its meaning: Antony wanted to reduce the power of Rome and maybe even make Alexandria the centre of the Empire. Antony also gave away great swathes of Roman-controlled land to Cleopatra and her family. Antony and Cleopatra were dressed as Dionysus/Osiris and as Aphrodite/Isis throughout the ceremony, and as a finale Cleopatra was proclaimed 'Queen of Kings', and her children called kings as well.

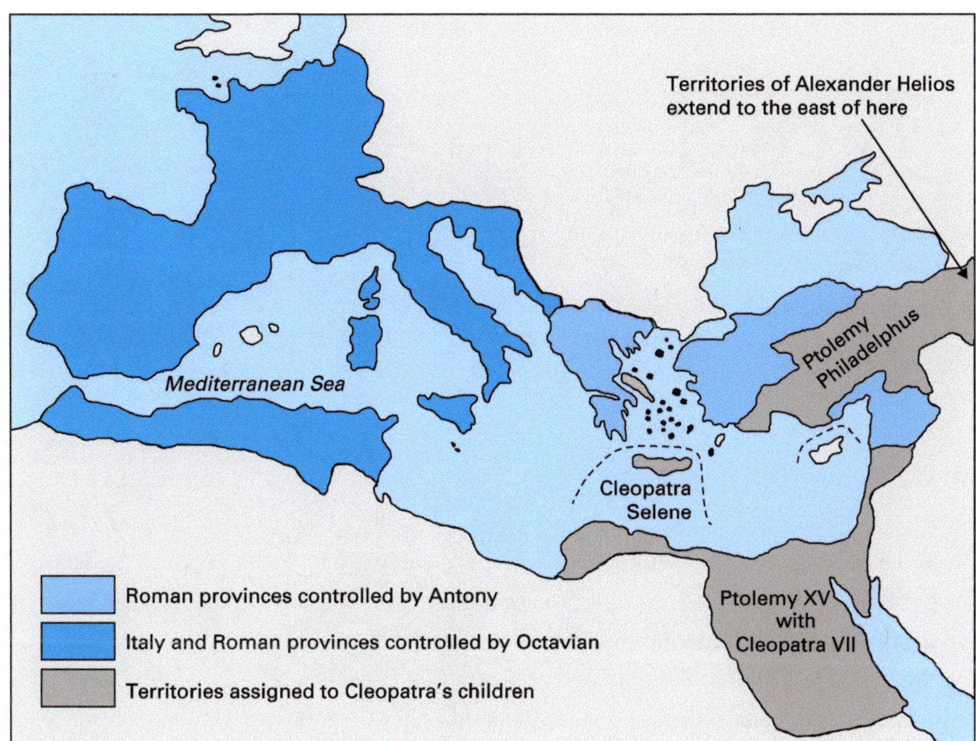

FIGURE 2.10
Map showing the Donations of Alexandria.

OCTAVIAN SEALS ANTONY'S FATE

Octavian's masterstroke against Antony occurred in 32 BC. First he seized Antony's will from the Temple of Vesta, where the Vestal Virgins had been entrusted with keeping it safe. He called a meeting of the Senate and had the will read aloud. The will stated that Antony wanted to be buried alongside Cleopatra in Alexandria. This was seen as the ultimate sign of Antony's disloyalty to Rome and absolute proof of his preference for Egypt. Octavian blamed Cleopatra, not Antony, for the contents of the will. He took advantage of the Senate's anger, convincing them to declare war on Cleopatra and Egypt. This was a political masterstroke from Octavian, as declaring war against Cleopatra meant that his fight with Antony would not be perceived as a civil war (which would surely upset at least some people in Rome) but a campaign against a dangerous foreign power.

By 32 BC, Octavian began work on an enormous building project: a **mausoleum** for himself (prescribed source, see pp. 186–8 for more). Octavian was only thirty years old and although it was common for Romans to build burial monuments for themselves before their deaths, Octavian chose to start building his own monument at this time to coincide with the reading of Antony's will. While he was demonstrating Antony's disloyalty to Rome, he was reinforcing to the Senate and to all of Rome that he was a dedicated Roman and he intended to spend eternity in the city.

mausoleum a building meant to house at least one tomb

Denarius, obv. bare head of Octavian, rev. Pax standing left holding olive branch and cornucopia

Date: 32–29 BC

Coin struck by: unknown Italian mint

Text reads: CAESAR DIVI F

Translation: Caesar (Octavian), son of a god

Significance: commissioned especially to pay his armies and to convey his promise: through war, peace

FIGURE 2.11
Denarius of Octavian. **PS**

OCTAVIAN BRINGS PEACE

From the outset, Octavian presented this war as a campaign to bring peace to the Empire by putting down a dangerous foreign monarch. The coin in Figure 2.11, minted at Octavian's request and used to pay his armies, gives an insight into how Octavian justified his war. The goddess Pax, the personification of peace, stands 'alongside' Octavian, holding symbols which identify her as Pax and also communicate Octavian's promise: through war, peace. Cleopatra was the implied disruptor of peace, as the war was officially being waged against her, but Octavian avoided naming her directly.

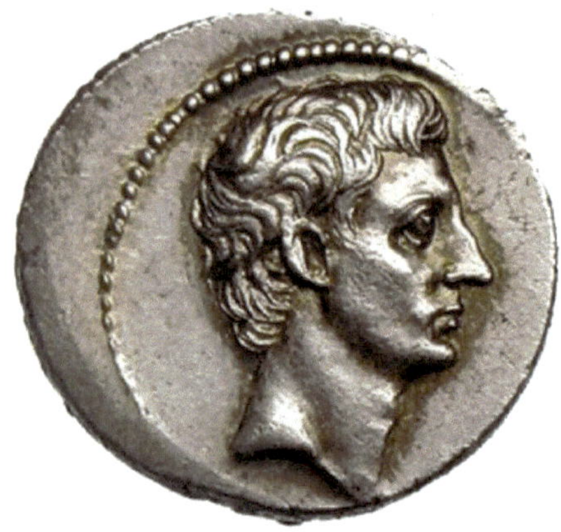
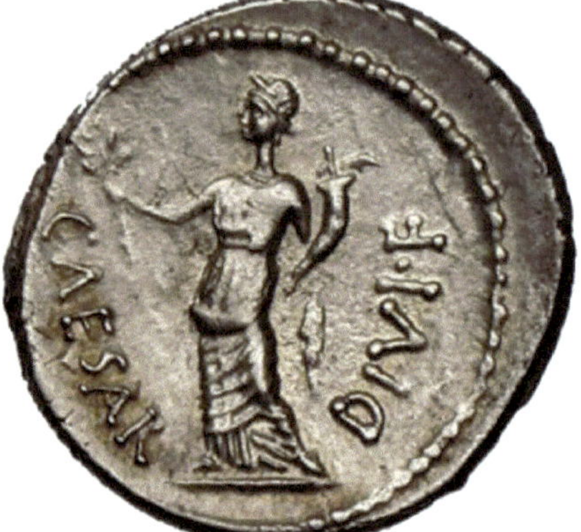

The decisive conflict of the civil war occurred on 2 September 31 BC. Known as the Battle of Actium, it was a naval battle fought just off the coast of Greece. Octavian's official propaganda would hail this battle as one of the grandest, most significant and glorious moments in Roman history.

Octavian, with the help of the gifted general Agrippa, led his forces to a victory over Antony and Cleopatra's navy. Antony and Cleopatra fled to Alexandria and there they awaited Octavian's inevitable advance. The following year Octavian arrived at Alexandria with an army at his back. Seeing no way out of his situation, Antony fell on his sword on 1 August 30 BC. Cleopatra did not follow Antony in suicide straightaway – she first tried to negotiate with Octavian (some sources claim she tried to seduce him). He was not willing to make a deal with her, and he told her that she would be taken back to Rome and paraded through the streets in his triumph. Preferring death to humiliation and a life of imprisonment or servitude, Cleopatra committed suicide on 12 August 30 BC. Having removed the entire Egyptian royal family, Octavian took Egypt as a province for Rome. Although he was never officially named Pharoah, he was depicted in this way within Egypt (see pp. 180–1).

EXPLORE FURTHER

Research the events preceding the Battle of Actium, and what happened in the battle itself. You might like to make a storyboard to help you visualise events. This course asks you to consider a range of interpretations of the Battle of Actium. By learning about what really happened, you will be able to see how certain aspects of the conflict were emphasised and how others were downplayed.

S & C

Read Plutarch's *Life of Antony* for another perspective. Plutarch wrote his biographies in the first century AD, and his work was certainly influenced by Octavian's propaganda campaign. This means that they were not objective history. Indeed, he doesn't pretend that his work is objective. His version of events is interesting, since he tried to draw moral lessons from what happened.

'SPINNING' ACTIUM

The Battle of Actium itself may not have been one of the largest or most tightly-fought battles in history, but it was certainly one of the most significant. The battle marked the end of Octavian's struggle with Antony and ensured that Octavian would be in

KEY INDIVIDUALS

Horace

Dates: 65–8 BC

A poet of the Augustan period who wrote primarily lyric poetry. Maecenas was his patron.

Propertius

Dates: uncertain date of birth *c.* 50–15 BC

A poet of the Augustan period who wrote primarily elegiac (love) poetry. Propertius mostly wrote independently, but Maecenas commissioned some works.

Maecenas

Dates: 68–8 BC

One of Octavian's close advisors, often thought of as his 'culture minister' or even his 'propaganda minister'. Maecenas was responsible for organising Augustus' client network of artists and poets, as well as being a political 'fixer'.

sole control of Rome for as long as he wished. Nobody remained who had enough money, support and experience to challenge him. It is for this reason that Octavian used the Battle of Actium as a recurring theme in works of art and literature. The battle represented a turning point and the beginning of the age of Octavian and his uncontested regime.

But the truth of the battle was problematic. It ended in flight and surrender, not glorious and decisive victory by force of arms. Octavian himself had taken a backseat, letting Agrippa plan and execute his strategy. And most importantly, the battle had been fought between Romans. No matter Octavian's official message and the Senate's decree that the war was against Cleopatra, the Battle of Actium was part of a civil war. In total, it has been estimated that at least 7,000 soldiers died that day, most of them Roman.

The truth didn't tally with Octavian's desired public image, so he recast the events and players of the battle to suit his needs. Octavian's 'official version' of the battle can be cobbled together from various literary sources depicting the battle, including the following poems by Horace and Propertius.

EXAM TIP: SOURCE SKILLS

Analysing Poetry

It can be daunting to be faced with an ancient poem, filled with unfamiliar words and references. There is no right or wrong way to go about analysing ancient poetry, but you might find this step-by-step process helpful:

1. Read through the poem in its entirety once to get the general sense of what the poem is about.
2. Based on your initial reading, note your impressions. What is the poem saying (i.e. do you think it has a message)? Is it telling a story or exploring an idea? Does a particular theme seem to be important?
3. Go back through the poem line by line, looking for particular lines and phrases that link to the impressions you just wrote down. Depending on how you like to make notes, you might use different coloured highlighters and a key, or copy down short quotes.
4. If you haven't done so already, look through the poem for technical language features – you will have already done this as part of your English GCSEs – and consider what effect they produce to the poem. Does the effect contribute to one of your ideas? It might not tie in with one of your existing ideas. It might even contradict an idea you've had. That's OK – poetry can have lots of different meanings all at once.
5. You will now hopefully have a good handle on the poem itself and you can start to make links. Compare the poem with other literary and visual sources you have studied. Consider how the poem fits with events in Rome at the time it was composed. Try to put yourself in the position of the original audience – what do you think they would have thought or felt about the poem?

At any stage in this process, feel free to consult the line-by-line glossaries on the Companion Website which will help you unpick the connotations of unfamiliar words and phrases.

This process should help you to formulate your own ideas that you can back up by referring to the evidence of the poem itself. When writing your own analysis, don't forget to explain how the poem supports your ideas – you must not just let quotes speak for themselves.

Shortly after the conclusion of the Battle of Actium, the poet Horace composed his *Epode* 9. One of the earliest works celebrating Octavian's victory at Actium, Horace addresses the poem to his patron, Maecenas. Horace speaks of Octavian's triumph, soon to be celebrated in Rome and creates a suitable festive atmosphere, mentioning Caecuban wine, a famously fine Italian variety. He goes on to remind the reader of the reason for the recent battle:

A Roman – you'll not credit it, posterity –
Sadly, ups sticks and arms himself,
For a woman's sake

Horace, *Epode* 9, ll. 11–13

The unnamed Roman is surely Antony. Horace's choice not to give his name is typical of literary sources dealing with the theme of the Battle of Actium. Nor does he name Cleopatra, referring to her only as a woman on a 'shameful pavilion'. By focusing on the scandalous actions of Antony and Cleopatra, Horace reminds the reader of why battle was necessary, and by leaving them unnamed he allows the reader to forget the complicated history between Octavian and Antony.

Horace mentions how the army of the Gallic king Amyntas deserted Antony just before the battle, joining Octavian's side instead. This is as much detail as Horace gives about the battle itself, however. He leaves the events of the battle vague and up to his reader's imagination. The poem ends by comparing the victory at Actium with some of Rome's previous military victories, and finishes with another reference to celebrations and fine wine.

Seven years after the publication of *Epode* 9, Horace returned to the theme of the Battle of Actium in another poem, *Ode* 1.37. This poem is addressed directly to the reader, encouraging them to prepare for a feast. Horace's focus in *Ode* 1.37 is not Octavian and his leadership, but Cleopatra. For the majority of the poem, he demonises her, emphasising the danger she posed to Rome and her lack of dignified self-control:

a maddened queen was still plotting
the Capitol's and the empire's ruin,
with her crowd of deeply-corrupted creatures
sick with turpitude, she, violent with hope
of all kinds, and intoxicated

Horace, *Odes* 1.37 ll. 7–11

The next lines contain a problematic simile where Horace compares Cleopatra to a gentle dove fleeing from a sparrow hawk. This serves to emphasise Octavian's superior military strength, but at the same time, it shows Cleopatra as vulnerable and helpless. Such gentility is in stark contrast with her portrayal earlier in the poem. It is possible that Horace chose a dove for this simile because of its association with Venus, the Roman goddess of love. Doves were sacred to Venus, and Horace could be alluding to Cleopatra's doomed love affair with Antony.

The poem ends by addressing the issue of Cleopatra's suicide. Here Horace shows Cleopatra at her most impressive, with 'no sign of womanish fear at the sword' (l.23) and no thought to flee. Suicide was not seen as shameful in ancient Rome. Horace presents a version of Cleopatra who is stoic and in control of her actions and of her fate.

Years after her death, this poem highlights the many sides of Cleopatra. She seems mad and dangerous, but also vulnerable and scared. At the end, she seems noble. Horace presents Cleopatra as a formidable enemy, brought down by the superior force of Octavian, and thus he implicitly praises Octavian for having defeated such a foe.

S & C | Horace

Quintus Horatius Flaccus (Horace for short) is best known for writing poetry under the reign of Augustus. Most of his surviving work is lyric poetry, a genre that would have been performed to music and which usually expressed personal feelings. All of Horace's *Odes* are examples of lyric poetry. He also wrote some satires, epistles and iambic poetry, an aggressive genre that placed blame on a subject and pointed out their faults. Horace's *Epodes* are iambic poetry.

Horace was the client of Maecenas and acted as his assistant. Some of his work praised Octavian and his regime, and so he has been seen by some scholars as nothing but a simpering propagandist. Others have pointed to the quality of his poetry, and to poems which do not directly mention politics, suggesting that he was a master poet who simply did what he had to in order to avoid Octavian's displeasure.

PRESCRIBED SOURCE

Elegies 3.11 – *Woman's Power* 

Author: Propertius

Date: *c*. 23 BC 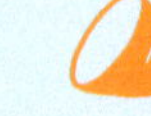

Significance: conveys the power of Cleopatra over Antony and the threat she posed to Rome

Read it here: OCR source book. 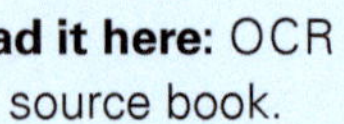 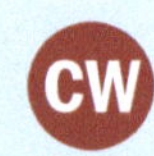

Propertius was a writer of love poetry, known as elegy. In *Elegies* 3.11, published in the same year as Horace's *Odes* 1.37, he explains how he has been enslaved by love for his unnamed lover. He presents himself as powerless against the chains of his love, subject to her power, and compares his present situation to that of mythical heroes who had been ruled by love for powerful women, including Jason, Achilles and Hercules.

He proceeds to tell of how Cleopatra enslaved Antony in the same way:

Cleopatra, who heaped insults on our army, a woman worn out by her own attendants, who demanded the walls of Rome and the Senate bound to her rule, as a reward from her obscene husband

Propertius 3.11, ll. 29–32

Propertius adopts the same approach as Horace, refusing to name Antony. Referring to him as Cleopatra's 'obscene husband' reduces him in status, implying that he was under her control, while reminding the audience that the marriage between Antony and Cleopatra was an obscenity because it was bigamous.

The poem goes on to contrast a threatening Egypt with a glorious Rome. Propertius stresses the danger posed by Cleopatra by introducing iconic symbols of Rome (Jupiter, the Tiber, Roman trumpets and warships) and answering each with an iconic symbol of Egypt (the god Anubis, sistrums and Nile barges). In this way, Cleopatra's assault is made to seem particularly targeted and thus threatening.

Like Horace, Propertius skips over the events of the Battle of Actium itself, limiting his account to a few words:

You fled then to the wandering mouths of frightened Nile

Propertius 3.11, l. 51

This clearly refers to the fact that, during the battle, Cleopatra gave the order for her Egyptian ships to flee.

The poem ends with a reference to Apollo of Actium and an explicit warning to sailors on the Ionian Sea to fear the might of Caesar. Propertius seems to be praising Octavian's victory over Cleopatra, glorifying the battle by stressing Cleopatra's strength.

This interpretation is complicated, however, by the fact that Propertius' poem is framed by the idea of woman's power. He clearly states that he is under the thrall of his lover, which means that he sympathises with Antony. Propertius' work presents Octavian's victory over Cleopatra as glorious, and Octavian is made to seem the saviour of Rome. But it calls into question whether Antony was really to blame.

S & C Propertius

Sextus Propertius was a writer of elegiac poetry. Elegiac poetry was a popular genre in Rome – it dealt with love. Propertius wrote four books of poetry, the *Elegies*, all of which survive to modernity. The central theme in Propertius' poetry is his love for a woman, Cynthia. Cynthia is almost certainly a pseudonym and her identity is unknown. His poetic talent was noticed by Maecenas after the publication of his first book of poems in 25 BC. Although most of his work continued to be on the topic of love, to and about Cynthia, Maecenas did encourage Propertius to write about Augustus and politics on occasion.

Virgil's *Aeneid*

One of the greatest poets of the Augustan age was Virgil. Perhaps his most significant work was an epic poem called the *Aeneid*, which tells the story of the Trojan prince Aeneas (the alleged ancestor of the Julian clan) as he leads a band of refugees away from the destruction of the Trojan War on a quest to found a new city. Aeneas is destined to found a city that will eventually become Rome. On his journey he receives a divinely-crafted set of armour and a shield, which has wrought on its surface pictures of all of Aeneas' descendants and their great feats. In pride of place at the very centre of the shield is a depiction of the Battle of Actium. Read this passage (Virgil's *Aeneid*, Book 8 ll. 626–731) and compare it to the poems prescribed in this section. How similar is it? How is Augustus presented? How are Antony and Cleopatra?

Octavian also made a number of highly visible gestures to commemorate the Battle of Actium and cement the image of himself as a glorious military leader. In 29 BC, the Senate (who by this point were almost entirely under his control) awarded him a triple triumph to celebrate his victories at Actium, the following year in Alexandria, and in Dalmatia. No general had ever been awarded three triumphs together like this before.

EXAM TIP: SOURCE SKILLS

Literature in Rome

Literature played a very different role in ancient Roman society than it does today. In modern Britain, almost everyone is literate, books are readily available and there are more new books published each year than one could reasonably expect to read in a lifetime. In Rome, on the other hand, only those whose family could afford to pay for private tutors would be educated. Books were incredibly expensive to hand-produce and so they were not readily available and new books were published relatively infrequently. So when we consider literature of this period, we must remember that it would usually only have been read and analysed by a privileged few. The masses would have had some access to literature through public performances.

It was common for the wealthy, intellectual elite of Rome to gather for poetry readings or to listen to recitations of literature at dinner parties. In particular, the lyric and elegiac genres were probably sung rather than spoken. We have evidence to suggest that these gatherings would include lively discussion of the literature – much like a modern 'book club'.

Professional writers would usually have a **patron** who would suggest themes for their work, or directly commission particular poems. Maecenas, one of Octavian's closest advisors, was the patron of many of Rome's most prominent poets. Maecenas gave them the support that they needed to become literary celebrities, and they wrote poetry that reinforced Octavian's regime.

patron patronage was a social practice in Rome whereby a rich and powerful individual would offer support to poorer, less influential individuals. The kind of support given was variable. Clients were expected to give political support to their patrons.

Across three consecutive days he paraded through the streets in a chariot. On the day celebrating the victory over Cleopatra, his chariot was followed by the spoils of battle, a statue of Cleopatra on her deathbed and with Cleopatra's surviving children locked in chains. The central and most symbolic act of the triple triumph was the closing of the **Temple of Janus Quirinus**. This act signalled that peace had been restored to Rome. Although the custom was well established, it had fallen out of practice. Octavian revived it to signal that he had fulfilled his promise. Through war, he had brought peace to Rome. A triumphal arch was also built in the Forum to commemorate Octavian's victory, and the Temple of the Deified Julius Caesar was decorated with prows of ships and weapons – a clear reference to Actium. He also founded a new city in Greece at the spot where his army had camped before the battle. He called it 'Nikopolis', which means 'City of Victory' in Greek.

Years later, in his elogium, Augustus told his own version of the Battle of Actium. Section 25 of the *Res Gestae* makes passing reference to the battle, claiming that the 'whole of Italy of its own volition swore allegiance' to him and demanded that he lead them 'in the war that I won at Actium'. What can we make of this brief treatment of such a significant battle? Perhaps Augustus did not wish for the battle to be a major part of his legacy. Perhaps he thought that the story had been told well enough by his poets.

> **Temple of Janus Quirinus** Janus, the double-faced god of transitions and in-betweens, had a temple in Rome whose gates could only ever be closed if there was peace in Rome and throughout the entire Empire. Before Octavian's lifetime the gates had only ever been closed on two occasions in all of Rome's history.

TOPIC REVIEW

These questions should draw on your knowledge of the whole topic, so think carefully about the different things you have learned (check the Topic Overview on p. 125).

1. What were Octavian's most pressing political concerns throughout the Triumviral Period?
2. How did Livia contribute to Octavian's public image during the Triumviral Period?
3. How did Octavian use peace in his propaganda of the Triumviral Period?
4. How important was Octavian's association with Apollo to his ultimate defeat of Antony?
5. Do you think that Octavian succeeded in convincing the Senate to declare war on Antony because he had crafted an attractive image for himself, or because the image Antony put forward was so unattractive?
6. What was the single most effective piece of propaganda that Octavian produced throughout the Triumviral Period? Justify your response.

Further Reading

Bradley, P., *Ancient Rome Using Evidence* (Cambridge: Cambridge University Press, 1990), 408–11.

Clark, D.H., *Augustus, First Roman Emperor. Power, Propaganda and the Politics of Survival* (Liverpool: Bristol Phoenix Press, 2010), Chapter 4: The Battle for the Empire.

Miller, J.F., *Apollo, Augustus and the Poets* (Cambridge: Cambridge University Press, 2009), Chapter 1: Octavian and Apollo.

Zanker, P., *The Power of Images in the Age of Augustus* (trans. A. Shapiro) (Ann Arbor: University of Michigan Press, 2014), Chapter 2: Rival Images: Octavian, Antony and the Struggle for Sole Power.

Source A: Horace, *Odes* 1.37, ll. 7–30

A maddened queen was still plotting
the Capitol's and the empire's ruin,
with her crowd of deeply-corrupted creatures
sick with turpitude, she, violent with hope
of all kinds, and intoxicated
by Fortune's favour. But it calmed her frenzy
that scarcely a single ship escaped the flames,
and Caesar reduced the distracted thoughts, bred
by Mareotic wine, to true fear,
pursuing her close as she fled from Rome,
out to capture that deadly monster, bind her,
as the sparrow-hawk follows the gentle dove
or the swift hunter chases the hare,
over the snowy plains of Thessaly.
But she, intending to perish more nobly,
showed no sign of womanish fear at the sword,
nor did she even attempt to win
with her speedy ships to some hidden shore.
And she dared to gaze at her fallen kingdom
with a calm face, and touch the poisonous asps
with courage, so that she might drink down
their dark venom, to the depths of her heart,
growing fiercer still, and resolving to die:
scorning to be taken by hostile galleys,
and, no ordinary woman, yet queen
no longer, be led along in proud triumph.

Source B: Denarius, 32–29 BC

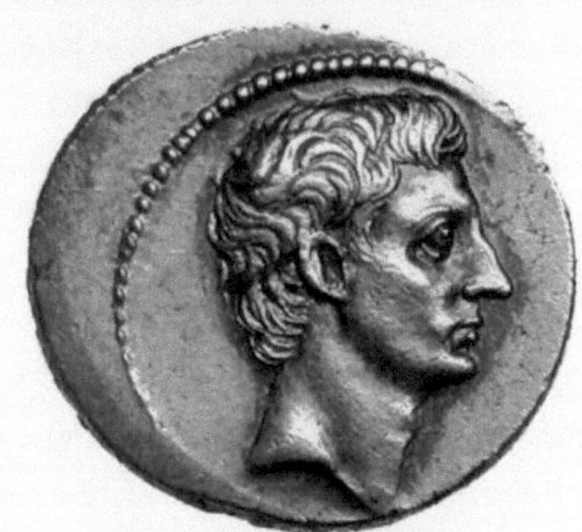

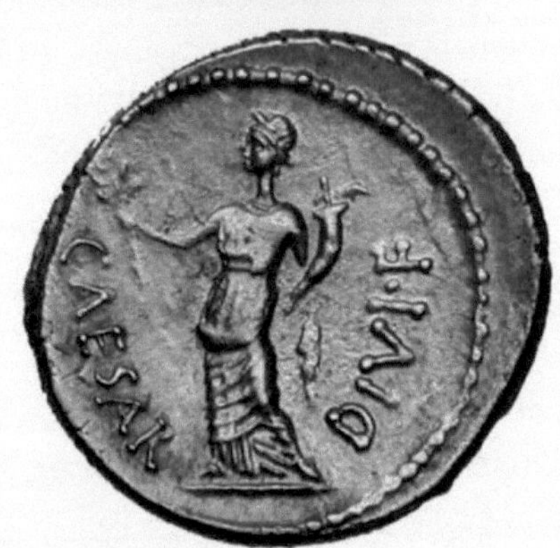

Inscription on coins:

CAESAR DIVI F – Caesar (Octavian), son of a god

AS Level

1 a. In what battle did Octavian defeat Cleopatra? [1]
   b. 'It would have been wrong, before today' – according to the poem, what happened 'today'? [1]
   c. Why did Octavian and the Senate go to war with Cleopatra? [2]
2. Evaluate how effectively Octavian legitimised his wars. Use Source A and Source B above as a starting point, and your own knowledge. [16]

A Level

1. Explain how Horace creates a complex image of Cleopatra throughout this poem. [10]
2. How successfully did Octavian legitimise his civil war against Antony to the people of Rome? Justify your response using Source A and Source B above as a starting point, and your own knowledge. [20]

2.3 Augustus' Reign, 29 BC–AD 14

Divi Filius

- the possible dangers of association with Julius Caesar and how Augustus sought to distance himself from the problematic aspects of Julius Caesar's public image

Imperator

- the presentation of Augustus as a capable military commander whose wars were glorious and impressive
- the reality of the military victories, including the involvement of Agrippa
- the presentation of campaigns at the edges of the Empire as beneficial to Rome, and to individual Romans

'Augustus'

- the idea of Augustus as Rome's religious leader and representations of this role
- Augustus' role in restoring religious observances that had fallen out of practice
- the restoration and building of temples and altars
- the positions Augustus held in Roman civic religion and changes to religious practice in his reign

Culture Hero

- myths of the Saturnian Golden Age and Augustus as a new Saturn or a saviour
- the significance of the Secular Games
- Augustus' improvements to the city of Rome and the quality of life of Roman citizens, including the building programme
- the use of the iconography and language of peace and plenty

Pater Patriae

- the significance of the title pater patriae and Augustus' presentation as a father to the Roman state
- the encouragement of morality and 'proper' behaviour regarding marriage, adultery, childbearing, religion and luxury
- Augustus as a role model for proper Roman male behaviour
- the intended role of the imperial family as role models

The following prescribed sources are covered in this topic:

- Aureus, obv. head of Octavian, rev. Octavian seated on bench holding scroll
- Denarius, obv. bareheaded portrait of Augustus, rev. sacrificial implements above tripod and patera
- Propertius, *Elegies* 4.6
- the Prima Porta statue of Augustus
- Propertius, *Elegies* 3.4
- Propertius, *Elegies* 3.12
- Denarius, obv. portrait of Augustus with oak wreath, rev. eight-rayed comet with tail pointing upward
- Ovid, *Metamorphoses* 15.745–870 (OCR 1–126)
- Horace, *Odes* 3.6
- Horace, *Carmen Saeculare*
- Horace, *Odes* 4.15
- Horace, *Odes* 4.4
- Aureus, Gaius and Lucius as princeps iuventutis, obv. Augustus head wreathed, rev. Gaius and Lucius Caesar standing veiled with shields and priestly symbols
- The Forum of Augustus in Rome
- the Ara Pacis
- Octavian relief from Kalabsha Gate

Don't forget that you will be given credit in the exam if you study extra sources and make relevant use of them in your answers.

At the very beginning of his career, Octavian's most pressing need was to make people aware of him. Before he could have influence, he needed to be noticed. This he achieved quickly, and by the time the Second Triumvirate was formed he was one of the most famous men in all of Rome. In the decade that followed, Octavian's most pressing concern became convincing people that he was preferable to Antony. Whether he succeeded in this respect is up for debate. Even so, after Antony's defeat at Actium and his suicide the following year, Octavian no longer needed to prove that he was preferable to anyone. Nobody remained alive who could realistically challenge Octavian's power and influence. Free from the need to prove himself, Octavian could now settle down to the business of governing Rome.

Octavian never stopped carefully managing his public image. He had seen what could happen when the crowd turned against their leaders. Julius Caesar had been seen, by some, as a tyrant and had been killed because of it. Octavian was determined not to make the same mistakes as Julius Caesar, or to suffer his fate.

Over the course of his forty-one-year dominance Octavian continued to carefully manage his public image, and the image of Rome itself. His continued safety depended on all Romans buying into the idea that Octavian was the best man to lead Rome and the Empire and that they were better off under his leadership. Considering the fact that Rome had been a Republic founded on the idea that one man should not rule alone, this was no mean feat.

AUGUSTUS SAVES THE REPUBLIC

History has remembered Octavian as the man who once and for all ended the Roman Republic and established the **Principate**. In his lifetime, however, Octavian presented the idea that he had saved the Republic from ambitious politicians and destructive civil wars.

During his rise to power, Octavian had been given a number of extraordinary powers by the Senate which went against political tradition. For example, he had been admitted to the Senate and held the consulship too young, he had commanded armies before holding public office, and as a triumvir he had suspended the courts and free elections. Octavian had used these powers to tighten his grip on power, but now they were becoming problematic. Such powers could make him look like a tyrant and a despot.

In 28 BC, Octavian had the Senate elect him as **princeps senatus**. This honour allowed him to speak first in the Senate, which allowed him to direct its actions to an extent. He also continued to hold the constitutional position of consul. Comfortable in the authority that these positions conferred, Octavian officially relinquished all the unconstitutional powers he held in 27 BC. This event is referred to as the First Settlement, which signalled an official end to the crisis period of the civil wars. Perhaps more importantly it signalled that he, unlike Julius Caesar, would not hold absolute power indefinitely.

This moment was commemorated on coins, like the one in Figure 2.12, which hailed Octavian as the saviour of the Republic. It is representative of the change in Octavian's public image after 29 BC. Where his coinage had previously been

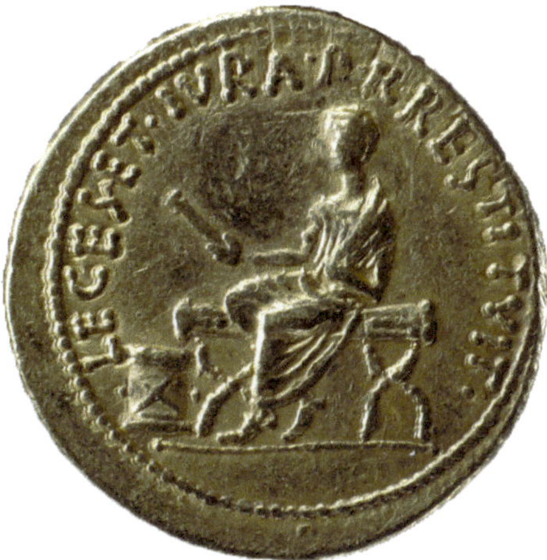

FIGURE 2.12
Aureus of Octavian.

principate government by one man, referred to as the 'Princeps' or 'first person', with many of the structures of a Republican system, such as a Senate and elections, although the power of these is diminished

princeps senatus (often just **princeps**) the first member of the Senate; every five years the censors voted for a member of the Senate for this role; they spoke first in discussions, decided when to summon and dismiss the Senate and set its agenda

Aureus, obv. head of Octavian, rev. Octavian seated on bench holding scroll

Date: 28 BC

Coin struck by: unknown mint

Text reads: IMP CAESAR DIVI F COS VI // LEGES ET IVRA P R RESTITVIT

Translation: Imperator (commander) Caesar, son of a god, consul for the sixth time // He restored to/of the Roman people their laws and rights

Significance: introduces the idea that Octavian was a saviour of the Republic

dominated by militaristic images designed to convey power and martial prowess, this coin suggests Octavian in a different role – that of magistrate and peacetime politician.

The obverse follows his usual pattern, a portrait accompanied with a list of achievements – he is still identified as 'son of a god' and by this stage in his career he had held the consulship six times. He is shown wearing a laurel wreath (just visible in his hair, more obvious from the string trailing behind his head), awarded to him as part of his triple triumph of the previous year. The reverse shows a figure, presumably Octavian himself, seated on a magistrate's chair, holding a scroll with a magistrate's document box at his feet. Combined with the legend, which speaks of restoring laws and rights to/of the Republic and the Roman people. We can be relatively certain that the image shows Octavian as a consul, legally undoing all unconstitutional laws that had been passed during the civil wars.

Thanks to this politically savvy move, Octavian was able to have his cake and eat it too. To the public, he was a hero who had kept his extraordinary powers just long enough to navigate Rome through a period of crisis before returning to his natural role as a member of the Senate. In practice, however, Octavian barely lost any power at all. Through his role as consul he was able to direct the activities of the Senate and throughout his career he often had them vote to give him additional powers. Moreover, his vast personal fortune (amassed during his time as a triumvir) allowed him to influence elections and to act as patron for the great and good of Rome. And while he no longer held control of an army, his veterans were loyal to him and through loyal commanders such as Agrippa he was able to control the military. In the *Life of Augustus* 28, Suetonius discusses the issue of Augustus restoring the Republic. It is clear that Suetonius did not believe Augustus had, in fact, done this.

In response to the return of his powers, the Senate granted Octavian a number of honours. They bestowed upon him the **civic crown**, for having brought an end to civil wars. They also gave him control of the provinces of Spain, Gaul, Egypt and Syria, which in turn gave him control of the grain supply. He was referred to as 'Princeps', which means 'leading man' – an honour that gave no actual power but that implied his role as leader of Rome. The Senate also commissioned a golden shield (known as the Clipeus Virtutis) engraved with his four cardinal virtues (**virtus**, **clementia**, **iustitia** and **pietas**). The shield was displayed prominently in the Senate House. Replicas were made and distributed throughout the Empire and representations of the shield appeared on coins.

Perhaps the most significant honour granted by the Senate was a new name: Augustus. The word Augustus derives from the Latin 'augere' which means 'to increase', 'to enrich' or 'to praise'. The word has a religious connotation as 'augustus' was a title linked to the Lares, Rome's household gods. It also relates to the practice of augury.

This name change, which emphasised religious duty and pietas, sealed Octavian's attempts to rebrand himself. Gone was the ruthless, unconstitutional Octavian. From this point onwards – in theory – began the benevolent rule of Augustus.

civic crown the second highest military honour a Roman could achieve, awarded to a citizen who had saved the lives of other Roman citizens

virtus masculine virtue, including courage, strength and general excellence (derived from the Latin 'vir', 'man')

clementia clemency or mercy

iustitia justice, in particular with regard to the law and courts

pietas duty to the family, to the state and to the gods

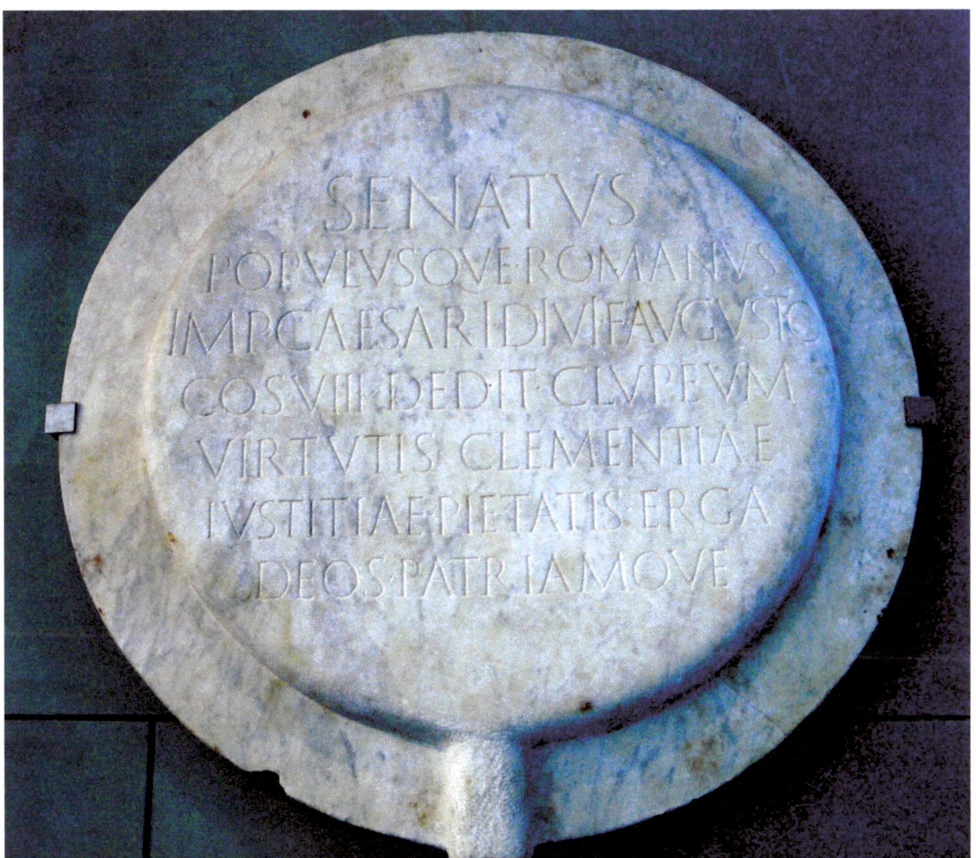

FIGURE 2.13
This marble copy of the Clipeus Virtutis was produced in 26 BC and was found in Arles, France.

One senator had suggested that Octavian be awarded the name 'Romulus', rather than Augustus. Conduct some research on the mythical king Romulus and come up with some ideas as to why Octavian might not have wanted to take this name. One such source you might consider is Livy's *History of Rome* 1.4–16. Livy, a Roman historian, was alive during Augustus' reign and his work catalogues events from the earliest days of the Roman people – including a developed life of Romulus.

AUGUSTUS THE RELIGIOUS LEADER

Roman state religion was a public affair and closely tied to the world of politics. Custom dictated that hundreds of rituals be fulfilled each year by a vast array of priests and priestesses. It was usual for prominent politicians and their families to hold priesthoods, rather than professional clergymen like most modern religions. For example, the triumvir Lepidus had also been elected Pontifex Maximus, the chief priest for life. Augustus' self-imposed role as religious leader was an important part of his 'personal brand'. It made him more appealing to older conservatives who thought that all of Rome's recent troubles had been caused by neglecting the gods. It also strengthened his link with the gods, in particular Apollo and Julius Caesar, encouraging people to think he had a privileged relationship with these deities.

Augustus cultivated the image of a religious leader by being actively involved in religious practice – he was a member of almost every priestly college. He also revived several priestly colleges, such as the Arval Brethren, that had fallen out of observance and individual priesthoods, like the flamen dialis (priest of Jupiter). He reformed traditional religious festivals, such as the Lupercalia (a ritual which was thought to cleanse the city of pollution and encourage fertility).

The denarius of Augustus in Figure 2.14 stresses his role as a religious leader. The tripod (bottom left), simpulum (top left) and patera (bottom right) were used in religious rituals, such as sacrifices. The lituus (top right) was a curved wand used by augurs and was a symbol of that college of priests. Note that, although this coin was struck in 12 BC when Augustus was fifty-one years old to celebrate his election as Pontifex Maximus, he is still depicted as a young man. This is typical of Augustus' official art, which portrayed him as a young, vigorous man until his death in AD 14. There are many possible reasons for this. Apollo was always depicted as a young man, so it is possible that Augustus was encouraging a comparison to the god by 'freezing himself in time'. It could also have been to discourage the idea that he was old and therefore weak. Whatever the reason, because most of Rome and her Empire had never seen Augustus in person, he was able to successfully project a youthful image throughout his life.

Perhaps the most visible sign of his role as religious leader and his campaign to restore Roman religion to its glorious past was his repair of temple buildings. Starting in 28 BC, Augustus oversaw the repair of eighty-two temples throughout the city. A highly symbolic act, his repair of the temple buildings represented a rejuvenation of Rome's religious devotion. He was also responsible for building several new temples, dedicated to such

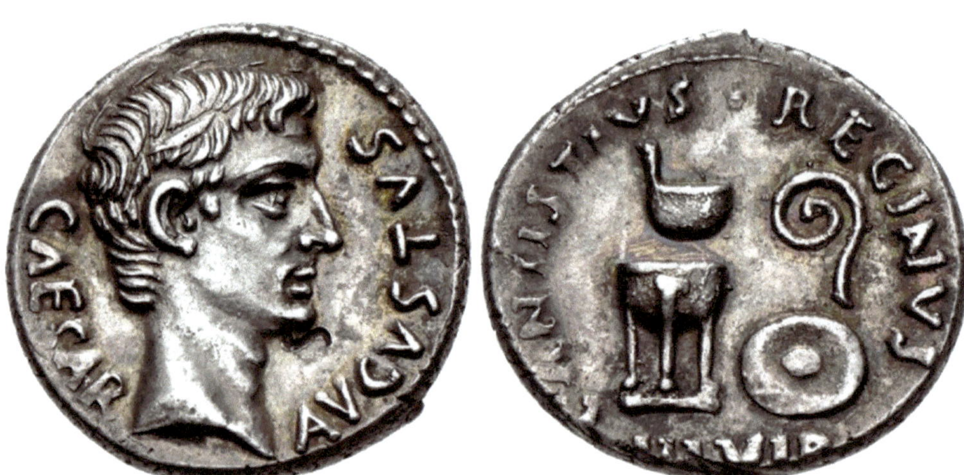

FIGURE 2.14
Denarius of Augustus.

deities as Jupiter Feretrius (the aspect of Jupiter who oversaw the signing of contracts and marriages), Minerva (goddess of wisdom), the Great Mother (an earth/fertility goddess), Mars Ultor (the aspect of Mars who seeks vengeance) and Apollo. The temple of Apollo, opened in 28 BC on the Palatine hill adjacent to Augustus' own home, was particularly significant as it underscored his personal relationship with and devotion to the deity.

The idea of Augustus as a religious and moral leader endured well beyond his own lifetime. Suetonius outlines some of his major accomplishments in this field in sections 29 and 31 of the *Life of Augustus*. Suetonius' writing here gives the impression that Augustus' building programme was both generous and extensive, and that his influence on Roman religion was generally positive.

The Temple of Palatine Apollo is the setting and theme of one of Propertius' later poems, *Elegies* 4.6. Much of Propertius' early work had been on the theme of love, but by this stage in his career he was just as well known for his political poems. This poem praises Augustus. It was probably composed in 16 BC, many years after the opening of the temple itself, to coincide with the celebration of the Actian Games. These games were held in Nikopolis, the city founded after Actium near the site of the battle. In honour of Apollo, they included athletic contests, musical competitions, horse racing and mock sea battles. Inaugurated by Octavian to celebrate his victory over Antony and Cleopatra, they were celebrated every four years. Propertius' poem begins with the Temple of Palatine Apollo, before shifting to the theme of the Battle of Actium itself.

The opening stanza is evocative of a festival day, complete with a ritual sacrifice. The identity of the narrator is unclear – perhaps it is Apollo or even the temple itself. Propertius goes on to invoke Calliope, the muse of epic poetry. This seems an odd choice, since Propertius is not writing epic poetry but elegy (whose muse was Euterpe). Calliope's name elevates the status of his work and the theme of his work to the lofty heights of epic, which was seen to be the highest form of literature in antiquity.

Following this invocation, Propertius moves away from the theme of the Temple of Palatine Apollo, and begins to retell the story of the Battle of Actium. All the might of Rome's gods is invoked here, with Propertius making reference to Quirinus, Jupiter, Nereus and Apollo.

Apollo's awe-inspiring appearance is described through comparisons with myth (31–6) and then the god proceeds to speak directly to Augustus, lavishing praise upon him, and declaring his allegiance:

> O Augustus, world-deliverer, sprung from Alba Longa,
> acknowledged as greater than your Trojan ancestors,
> conquer now by sea: the land is already yours: my bow is on your side,
> and every arrow burdening my quiver favours you.

> Propertius, *Elegies* 4.6.37–40

Propertius is clearly referring to the close personal bond that Augustus suggested he had with Apollo. Propertius' focus here is on the glory of Apollo and how he worked alongside Augustus to secure victory. This version of events is in stark contrast with his previous treatment of the Battle of Actium in *Elegies* 3.11, which focuses on Cleopatra (see pp. 140–1). A similarity between the two poems is the fact that the events of the battle itself are only alluded to, not narrated in any great detail.

Towards the end of the poem, the tone shifts yet again, as the scene moves away from the battlefield and back to the festival atmosphere of the beginning. Apollo is again the inspiration:

> I have sung of war enough: Apollo the victor now demands my lyre, and sheds his weapons for the dance of peace.

> Propertius, *Elegies* 4.6.69–70

Propertius stresses the peace and plenty that have arisen as a result of Augustus' victory in war. He also refers to ritual symbols such as 'white robes', 'gentle grove' and 'roses', underscoring Augustus' role as religious leader.

The poem may not all be straightforward praise of Augustus, however. An interesting reference to Bacchus complicates the atmosphere:

> Let the Muse fire the mind of drunken poets:
> Bacchus you are used to being an inspiration to your Apollo.

> Propertius, *Elegies* 4.6.75–6

S & C A poem celebrating the new Temple of Palatine Apollo was written by Propertius for publication in 26 BC as part of his second book of elegies. Read Propertius, *Elegies* 2.31. How does this poem contribute to Augustus' image as a religious leader?

Bacchus was god of grapes, wine, fertility and madness, the Roman equivalent of the Greek god Dionysus, with whom Antony had so strongly associated (see pp. 127–31). So, this mention of Bacchus could be an intentional reference to Octavian's enemy. But why would Propertius want his audience to think of the defeated Antony at this point in the poem?

It could be that Propertius was being subversive – making a veiled reference to Antony to remind the audience that Augustus' war was a civil conflict and not the foreign war he had made it out to be. Alternatively, Propertius could be indicating that, with Antony defeated, his god is now united with Augustus' patron deity, just as all of Rome had become united. Most likely, the poet was deliberately playing with the ambiguity of these two possible interpretations.

AUGUSTUS SECURES PEACE THROUGHOUT THE EMPIRE

War was a way of life to the Romans of the Republic. Wealthy men were expected to serve as officers in the army, a high percentage of ordinary citizens were conscripted into service. Through war, individuals could win glory and Rome could benefit from the slaves and booty that were taken as prizes of war.

But by the time Augustus had secured power for himself many Romans were tired of war. Decades of civil war and proscriptions had decimated the population, in particular of the noble classes. Wars, which were normally fought in far-off provinces had come too close to the capital and had taken a severe toll. People were ready to enjoy a period of prolonged peace. Augustus perceived this, and made sure that the language and iconography of peace pervaded the literature and art of the time. The peace of Augustus was known as the 'Pax Augusta', and it helped to protect him from assassination or overthrow. The close association of the person of Augustus with the idea of peace meant that anybody challenging his power was also threatening the peace of the Roman world. By so closely associating the absence of war with himself, he subtly reminded the people that to remove him as leader of the state would be to remove the relative security that his peace promised.

The big problem that Augustus faced in communicating this idea was that Rome was not, in fact, at peace. By the time Augustus had secured power for himself, the Roman Empire covered thousands of square miles. Millions of inhabitants of Europe, North Africa and the Near East were under Roman control. The vast majority of Roman territory had been taken by force, won through military campaigning. People at the edges of the Empire would often rise up against the occupying Roman forces to reclaim their independence. In these instances, Roman soldiers would need to fight to pacify the local population. In addition to these reactionary battles, Augustus continued to plan campaigns to expand the Empire into new territory. With every new province captured, Rome enriched herself with plundered booty and taxes, and Augustus won glory for himself as a victorious military leader. So although Augustus' defeat of Antony marked the end of civil wars, it did not mark the end of all wars. The gates of the Temple of Janus Quirinus, symbolically closed during Augustus' triple triumph, did not stay closed for long.

Augustus made sure that poets wrote about his wars at the edges of the Empire in a positive way. In particular, his wars were presented as necessary, either to ensure peace or to redress past injustices. Where art and literature deal with the subject of Augustus' wars, they hardly ever focus on the battles themselves. Instead they focus

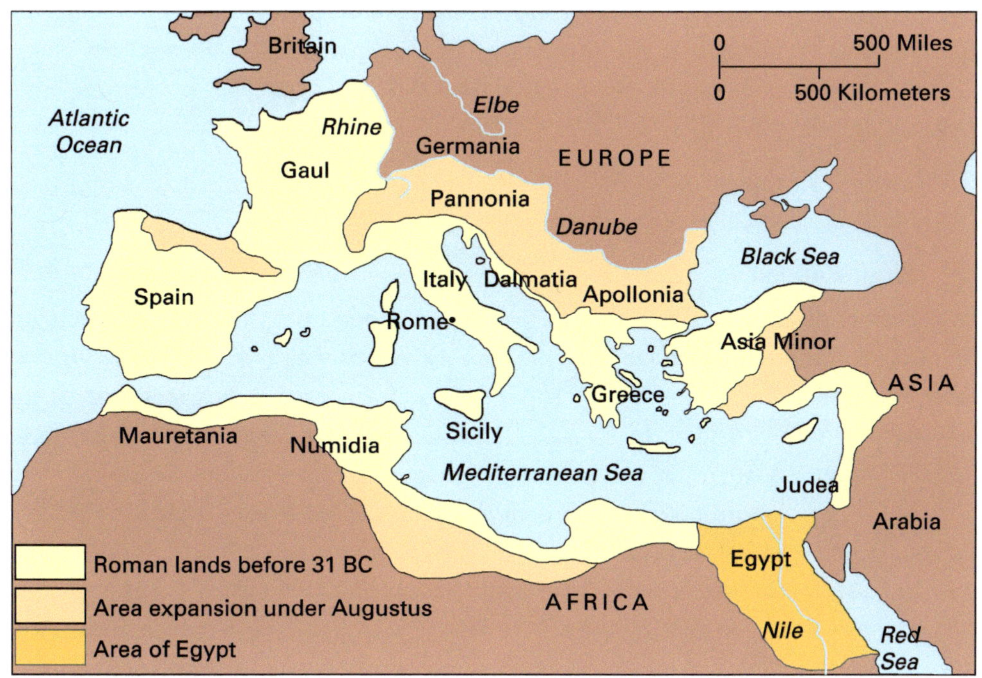

FIGURE 2.15
Map showing the expansion of the Roman Empire during Augustus' reign.

legionary standard a pole bearing an eagle (and thus sometimes referred to as 'eagles'), carried into battle by a legion's standard bearer

Elegies 3.4 

Author: Propertius

Date: 20 BC 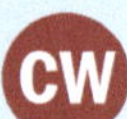

Significance: emphasises the glory and benefits to Rome of Augustus' foreign campaigning

Read it here: OCR source booklet **CW**

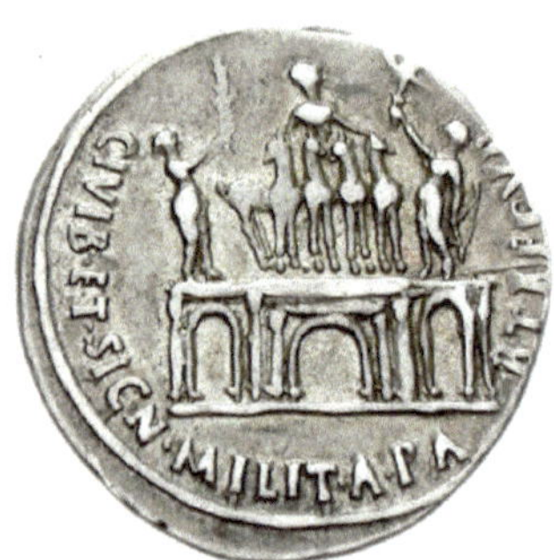

FIGURE 2.16
Denarius of Augustus.

on the noble justifications for the wars and on the great rewards that Rome reaped after the wars were over.

One conflict that received a great deal of attention from Augustan poets was Augustus' threatened campaign against Parthia in 22–19 BC. The Parthian Empire was responsible for one of Rome's most humiliating military defeats. Crassus, member of the First Triumvirate, had led an expedition into Parthian territory north of the Euphrates river in 53 BC. His plan was to lead an army of 50,000 men to the Parthian city of Seleucia, take the city and in doing so conquer the Parthians once and for all. Crassus' poor strategic leadership led his army right into an ambush. He was killed, 40,000 Roman soldiers were slaughtered and his **legionary standards** were captured by the Parthians. The loss of the standards had a dramatic effect on the morale of ordinary Romans. They felt as though their supremacy and their safety were being undermined by the Parthians. Before his assassination, Julius Caesar had been planning a renewed campaign against the Parthians to retrieve the standards. Clearly this was a sore spot for Rome. Augustus sent his stepson Tiberius to negotiate the return of the standards, securing them and establishing friendly relations with the Parthians in 20 BC. Some Romans were unhappy with the fact that the Parthians had not been made to pay for what they had done to Crassus and his legions. Others, no doubt, were happy that there had been no further loss of Roman lives. Augustus presented the return of the standards as proof that Parthia had submitted to Roman control, but in actual fact they did no such thing. Parthia remained an independent state with an empire of its own.

In *Elegies* 3.4, Propertius looks ahead to Augustus' victory over the Parthians, stressing the wealth and material gain from the campaign. He exhorts his readers to join in with the fighting, to win glory and do their duty to Rome:

Men, the rewards are great: far lands prepare triumphs.  **PS**

Propertius, *Elegies* 3.4.3

The patriotic tone of the poem is somewhat undercut in the final lines where it becomes apparent that Propertius has no intention of joining in the battle himself. He looks out from a window alongside his girlfriend watching the triumphal procession, safe from harm:

I'll begin to look, pressing my dear girl's breast,  **PS**
and scan the names of captured cities.

Propertius, *Elegies* 3.4.15–16

Propertius must have been a conflicted poet. On the one hand, the celebrity poets of Augustan Rome were encouraged to write patriotic poems with military themes. On the other, Propertius himself was an elegiac poet whose poetic persona was more pampered playboy than serious soldier. In *Elegies* 3.4 we see the marriage of these two aspects. Propertius supports Augustus' regime, but only engages in it himself to an extent.

Augustus was awarded a triumphal arch in the Forum to commemorate his Parthian expedition. Unfortunately, this no longer survives, but archaeologists have determined that the arch was made of marble and its base would have been 18 × 6 metres. Coins minted at the time, such as the denarius in Figure 2.16, depict the arch and suggest that it included a statue of Augustus in a four-horse chariot, a reference to the triumphal procession.

Another monument to Augustus' Parthian campaign is the so-called Prima Porta Augustus statue. The marble statue which survives today is thought to be a copy of a bronze original statue that was vowed to Augustus by the Senate in 20 BC. The original might have been displayed in a public place, but this copy was found in the private villa of Livia at Prima Porta, hence the name of the statue.

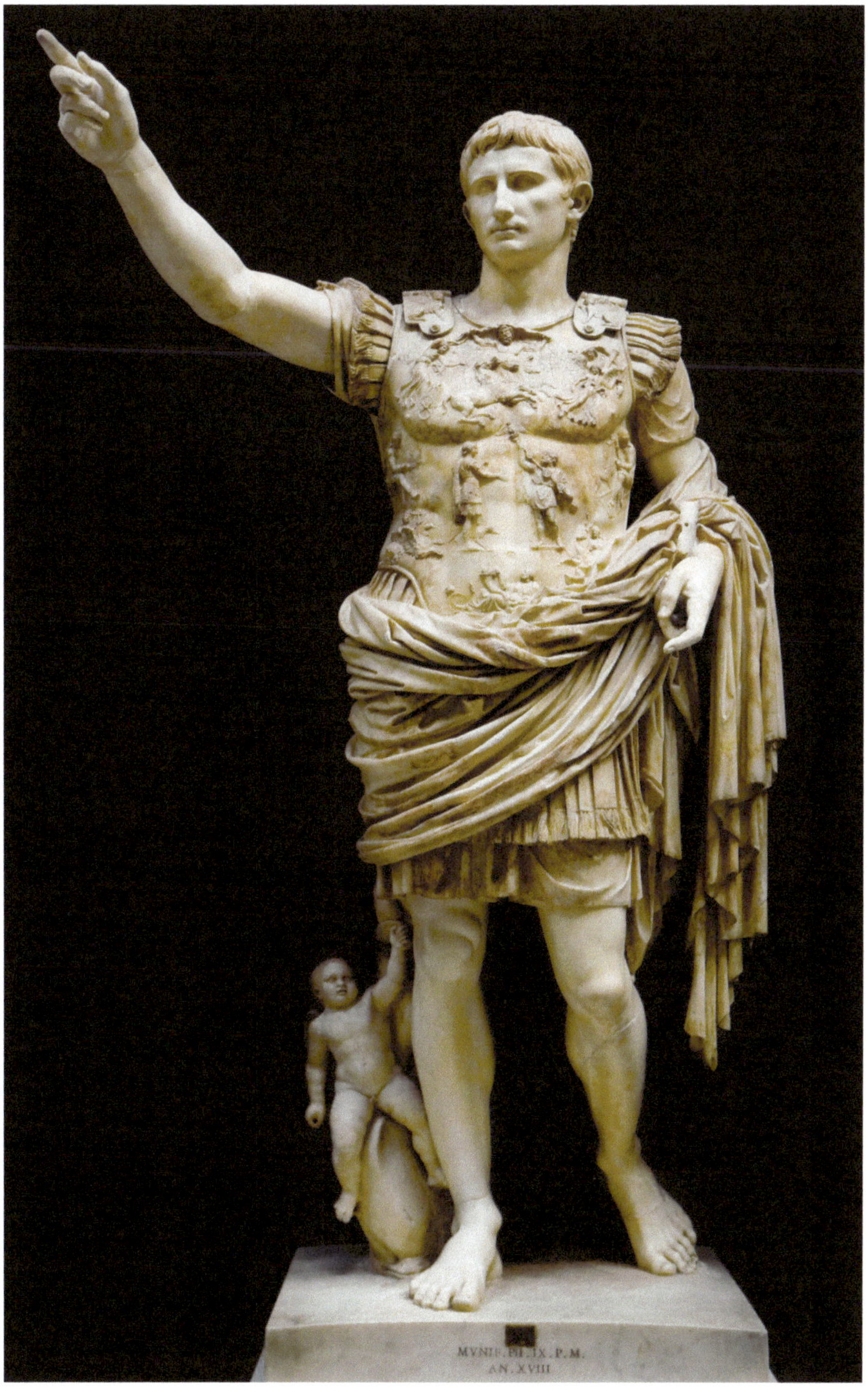

FIGURE 2.17
Prima Porta Augustus.

PRESCRIBED SOURCE

Prima Porta Augustus statue

Date: *c.* 20 BC

Material: marble

Currently located: The Vatican Museums, Rome

Significance: copy of an original statue commissioned to celebrate Augustus' Parthian campaign

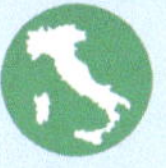

Augustus is depicted as a young, vigorous man in line with his usual portrayal. His athleticism is emphasised not only in the defined musculature of the arms, legs and the shape of the breastplate, but by the pose. The positioning of the feet and weight distribution are a clear visual reference to the Doryphoros (spear carrier – see Figure 2.18) statue type. This statue type was popularised by the fifth-century-BC Greek sculptor Polycleitus, and was widely thought in antiquity to embody physical perfection. The Prima Porta Augustus mimics the pose and thus implies that Augustus, its subject, possessed similar excellence.

MODERN SCHOLARSHIP

The high estimation in which Classical art was held was also due not primarily to aesthetic standards, but rather to ethical ones . . . This led to an increasingly vague definition of aesthetic criteria, which evolved naturally into moral categories. Concepts derived from a work's effects on the viewer, such as *decor*, *auctoritas* or *pondus*, were now used to define formal qualities, which in turn determined the ranking of the Classical masters. At the top of the list stood the art of Phidias and Polyclitus. In the age of Augustan reforms, this system of aesthetic ranking, which had been developed by and for art critics, was borrowed and applied to the selection of specific works for use in an artistic program defined primarily by moral and political objectives.

P. Zanker, *The Power of Images in the Age of Augustus*, 2014, pp. 245–7

Zanker theorises that the art of Augustus' Principate appealed to the style of the Greek Classical period (fifth century BC) because it carried a moral message. He suggests that Augustan Romans viewed the Classical period as one of superior moral behaviour and, by ensuring that the art of his regime looked like Classical masterpieces, Augustus encouraged the idea that his reign was similarly one of moral superiority. Zanker's view is not universally accepted by modern scholars, many of whom point to the variety of artistic styles that were produced during Augustus' reign as evidence against this theory.

Augustus' right hand is raised as though he is addressing a crowd – this is an oratorical pose known as adlocutio. This, combined with his general's cloak, suggests that Imperator Augustus is addressing his troops. Augustus' left arm is positioned to hold a pole. Scholars dispute what he could have been holding. A spear would strengthen the connection to the Doryphoros, but a consul's staff or a recaptured legionary standard are equally plausible.

Next to his right leg is a dolphin being ridden by Cupid, the winged god of love and Venus' son. Such details were often included in marble sculpture because they helped to give stability and safeguard against overbalancing. The choice to use a dolphin and

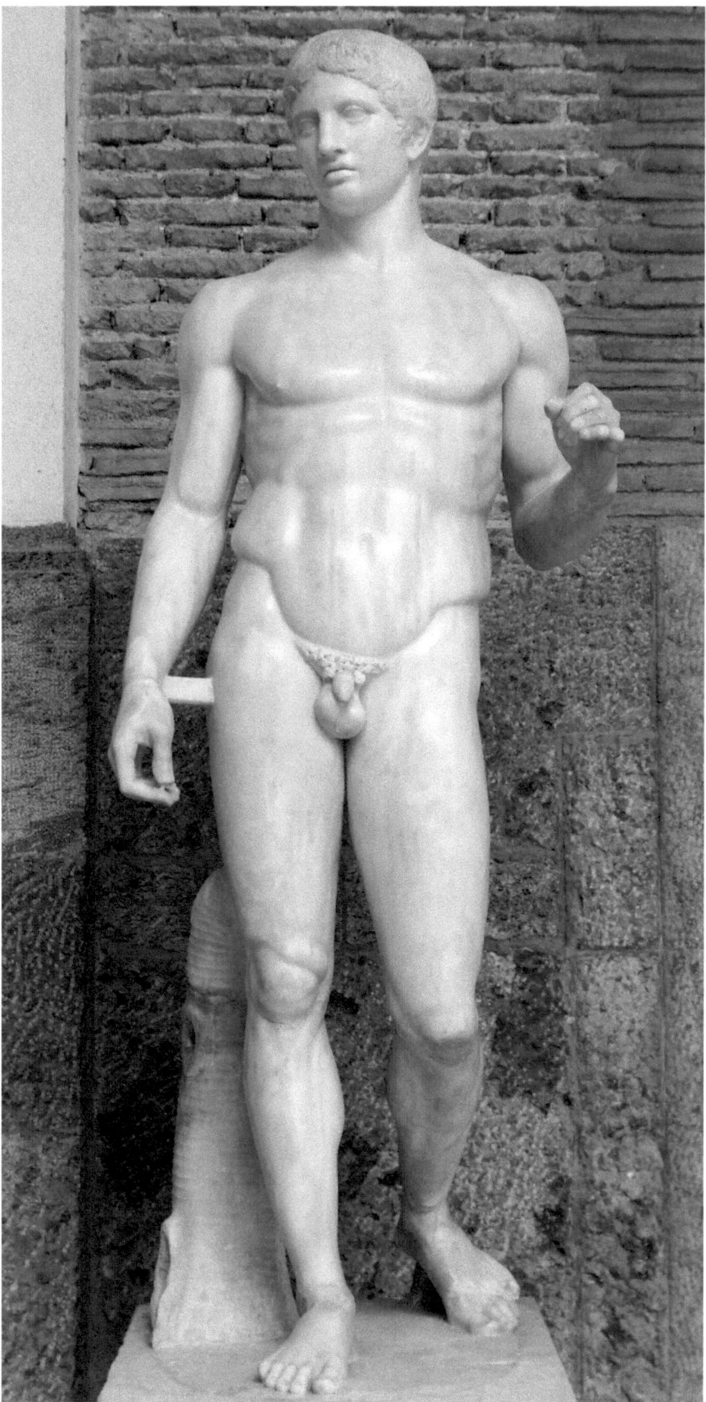

FIGURE 2.18
A Roman copy of the Doryphoros.

Cupid was likely made because of their association with Venus, the mother of Aeneas and ancestor of the Julian clan. Augustus' link with the divine is further suggested by the fact that he is depicted barefoot. Roman sculpture did not usually show mortals barefoot – this was reserved for depictions of gods and heroes. Augustus did not want to be seen encouraging Romans to worship him as a god (unlike some later emperors), but this detail certainly communicates the idea Augustus was more than merely mortal. This

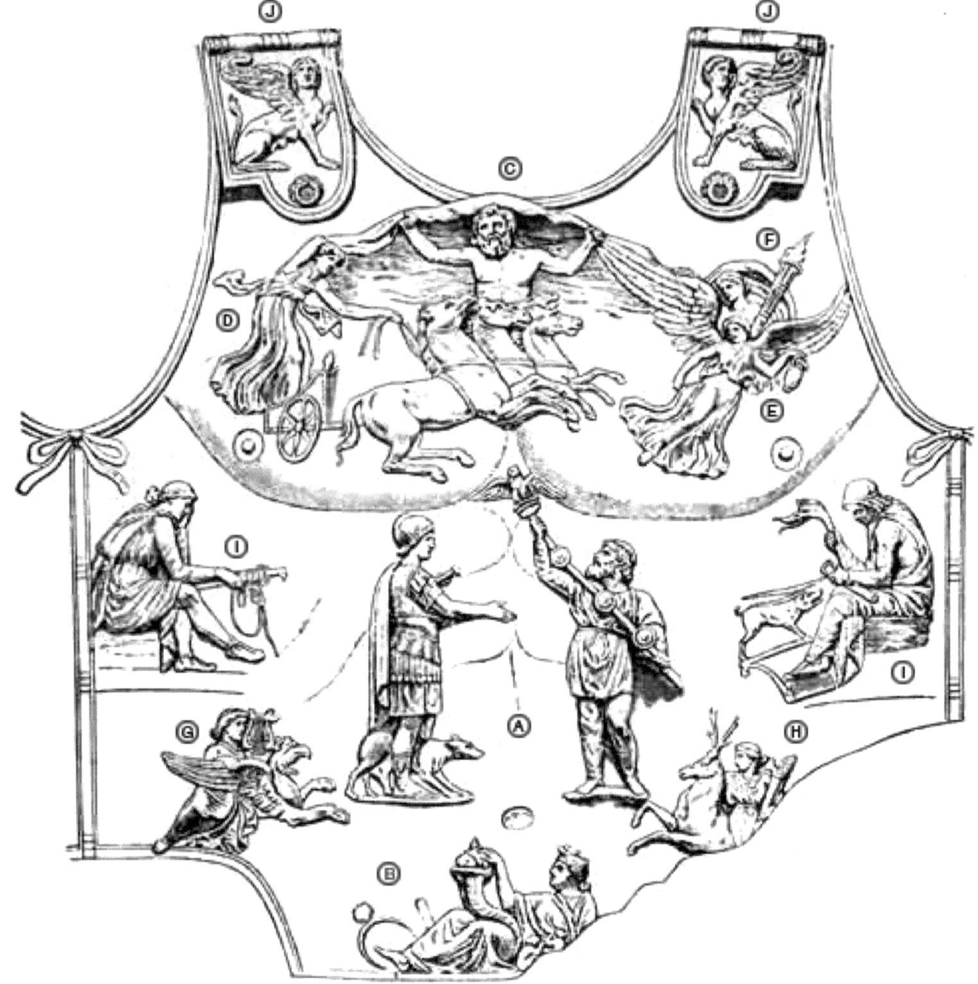

detail could also indicate that this copy of the statue was made after Augustus' death, once he had been declared a god.

The breastplate (see Figure 2.19), covered with relief sculpture, presents an image of peace and reconciliation. The central pair (A) represent the end of war: a Parthian (distinguishable by his beard and trousers underneath a short tunic) hands a Roman legionary standard to another figure who holds out his arms to receive it. The identity of the figure on the left is unknown. Scholars have suggested it represents Tiberius, Augustus' stepson and general on the Parthian campaign. Others have suggested that it is another Roman general or perhaps even Mars Ultor. He wears a Phrygian cap, which hints at Trojan ancestry, a further link to the illustrious past of the Julian clan.

Below this central scene reclines a woman holding a cornucopia (B). This could be the goddess Pax, but more likely it represents a mother earth figure, with the cornucopia referring to the earth's bounty. At the very top is a representation of the heavens (C), with a central figure pulling a cloth that represents the sky. Just beneath this (from left to right) is the sun god Sol in his chariot (D), then the goddess Dawn with a water jar to sprinkle morning dew over the world (E), and at the very right is the moon goddess Luna (F). These personifications of the earth and the sky suggest that the Pax Augusta and the authority of Rome spread across the world.

Augustus' patron god Apollo is depicted at the bottom left of the breastplate riding a griffon (G). Opposite is Apollo's sister Diana, shown riding her favourite animal, a hind (H). The other figures, which cover both flanks, are thought to be personifications of Rome's allies and her conquered provinces (I). Finally, the shoulder straps each feature an inward-facing sphinx (J). This mythical beast was associated with Egypt and so it is possible that these refer to Augustus' defeat of Cleopatra.

The overall impression is of a commanding and self-assured military leader, whose actions have brought peace to the world and are sanctioned by the gods. The Prima Porta Augustus builds on an image already seeded by official coinage, the triumphal arch and the poetry considered so far. However there remained some who questioned the wisdom of going to war at the edges of the Empire. These questions went against the official message, and hint at a counter-culture that wanted Augustus to stop campaigning altogether.

Not all artistic output of the Augustan period was supportive of campaigning at the edges of the Empire. In *Elegies* 3.12, Propertius focuses on the negative impact of foreign wars on those left at home. Galla, the wife of the addressee of the poem Postumus, suffers because her husband is away at war:

> Postumus, how could you leave Galla crying,
> to follow Augustus' brave standard as a soldier?
> Was the glory of Parthia's spoils worth so much to you,
> with Galla repeatedly begging you not to do it?
> If it's permitted may all you greedy ones perish equally,
> and whoever else prefers his weapon to a faithful bride!

Propertius, *Elegies* 3.12.1–6

The image of chaste and faithful Galla, in tears, begging her husband not to leave her to go on campaign aims to arouse the sympathies of the reader. It is difficult to side with Augustus here, as the motivation for the Parthian campaign is shown to be material greed. Where other poems emphasise the positives of foreign wars, *Elegies* 3.12 bluntly reminds the reader that some soldiers never return, imagining Galla fearfully waiting for rumour of his death or the sight of his ashes.

The experience of going on foreign campaign is likened to the journey of the mythical hero Ulysses (the Latin name for Odysseus). Homer's *Odyssey*, a Greek epic poem which tells the story of Odysseus' travels, would have been well known to Propertius' audience. The works of Homer were studied like school texts throughout the Roman world. The interesting question is: does the comparison to Ulysses portray Postumus as a hero? If the answer is yes, then the poem itself could be described as somewhat supportive of Augustus' wars. If the answer is no, then it is damning of them.

PRESCRIBED SOURCE

Elegies **3.12**

Author: Propertius

Date: 20 BC

Significance: provides a dissenting voice which stressed the negative impact of Augustus' foreign campaigning

Read it here: OCR source booklet 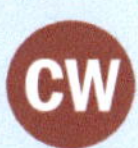

EXPLORE FURTHER

The poetry, art, architecture and artefacts considered in this topic have been solely to do with the Parthain campaign, but this was not the only campaign undertaken by Augustus. For another perspective, research Augustus' campaigns in Gaul from 27–24 BC. Augustus was also away from Rome on campaign in Spain and Gaul from 16–13 BC. Research what happened here and then read Horace's *Odes* 4.5, which entreats Augustus to return to the capital.

PRESCRIBED SOURCE

Denarius, obv. portrait of Augustus with oak wreath, rev. eight-rayed comet with tail pointing upward

Date: *c.* 19–18 BC

Coin struck by: unknown Spanish mint

Text reads: CAESAR AVGVSTVS // DIVVS IULIUS

Translation: Caesar Augustus // The Divine Julius

Significance: stresses the divine status of Julius Caesar

AUGUSTUS ADJUSTS HIS RELATIONSHIP WITH JULIUS CAESAR

As we have seen, in the early years of his political career Augustus (then Octavian) sought to establish a close relationship between himself and Julius Caesar in the minds of his public. This suited his needs well at first, as it gave him much-needed visibility and it enabled him to 'borrow' Julius Caesar's popularity with the urban poor and the army. It had also lent him the aura of a great general, as Julius Caesar had been famous for his military victories. Moreover, it allowed him to curry the favour of the urban poor, who had loved Julius Caesar because of his work to improve their living conditions. Julius Caesar was, however, not an ideal figure. Although he had been loved by many, the way he seized and retained power earned him many enemies in the Senate. In particular, conservative senators thought him a tyrant and a de facto king. This was why they conspired to kill him.

Now that Augustus was in sole command he was ready to distance himself from the memory of Julius Caesar, lest people begin to think of him as a tyrant and de facto king. Unfortunately, Julius Caesar had become such a key part of Augustus' public identity that he wouldn't have been able to divorce himself from Julius Caesar with much success.

Augustus' solution to this problem was ingenious and much more subtle than a crass rejection of Julius Caesar's memory. He shifted the focus of his own propaganda from stressing a relationship with Julius Caesar the man onto a relationship with Julius Caesar the god. As a man, Julius Caesar had done many terrible things and the association could have been a liability for Augustus. As a god, Julius Caesar was beyond reproach. He was separated from his deeds and personality and became, instead, a generic symbol of divinity and of Rome. Of course, Julius Caesar had been thought of as divine since 42 BC, but it wasn't until Augustus' reign began that he stopped depicting Julius Caesar as a man entirely.

Virgil, a poet and client of Maecenas, published a poem called the *Georgics* in 29 BC which listed Julius Caesar among a list of Italian fertility gods. Art and coinage of the period frequently featured an eight-point star with one long point. Figure 2.20 is a typical example of this. The star represented Julius Caesar's comet – the one that appeared shortly after his death during commemorative games. The star was used to symbolise

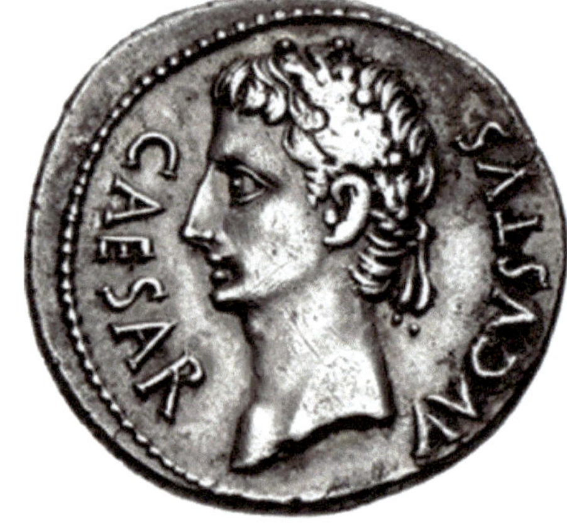
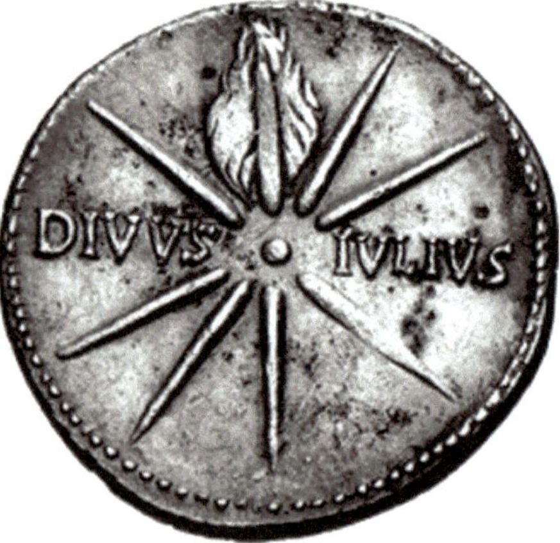

FIGURE 2.20  Denarius of Augustus.

Ovid

Publius Ovidius Naso was one of the most prominent poets in Augustan Rome. He rose to prominence with a series of poems on the theme of love, the *Amores*, and the rather scandalous *Ars Amatoria* which gave readers instruction in the arts of love and seduction. Today Ovid's most well-known and widely-read work is the *Metamorphoses*. He also wrote a collection of poems known as the *Fasti* which gives an account of the Roman year and its annual festivals. Ovid suffered a dramatic fall from grace when, in AD 8, he was exiled by Augustus to the small Greek town of Tomis. We do not know for sure why Augustus chose to exile Ovid. It could have been due to the scandalous nature of his love poetry, which went against Augustus' strict moral agenda. It has even been suggested that Ovid was complicit with Augustus' granddaughter, Julia the Younger's adulteries.

Julius Caesar the god, rather than a portrait, to stress his divinity and encourage people to forget Julius Caesar the mortal man.

Another poet dealt with this theme. Ovid's *Metamorphoses* is a fifteen-book epic poem that deals with the theme of metamorphosis (change). A grand undertaking, Ovid wanted his poem to encompass the stories of the whole universe, and so it begins with creation and, via a large number of myths, ends with a celebration of the most recent metamorphosis at Ovid's time of writing: the deification of Julius Caesar.

This section begins by outlining the reason why Julius Caesar was made a god. Ovid's account of Julius Caesar's achievements is very brief and vague, but this ensures the reader is not reminded of the events of Julius Caesar's dictatorship, nor of his civil wars. Ovid goes on to explain the reason why Julius Caesar was deified:

> There is no greater achievement among Caesar's actions
> than that he stood father to our emperor.

Ovid, Metamorphoses 15.750–1

In these lines, Ovid stresses Julius Caesar's relationship to Augustus, encouraging the reader to focus on this aspect as well. Ovid then lists some of Julius Caesar's military victories in the next lines, but again he stresses that these achievements pale into insignificance when compared with his relationship to Augustus. At the end of the list, Ovid invites his reader to reimagine their own history:

> Therefore, in order for the emperor not to have been born of mortal seed,
> Caesar needed to be made a god.

Ovid, Metamorphoses 15.758–9

Following this explanation, the scene shifts to the home of the gods. Venus, the progenitor of the Julian clan, is frantic as she realises that Julius Caesar is about to be assassinated. She catalogues the pains she has had to suffer, first at the hands of the mortal hero Diomede during the Trojan War, then as her son Aeneas was forced to wander in search of a new city. The assassination of Julius Caesar is elevated to mythological status by association with these events from Roman legend.

PRESCRIBED SOURCE

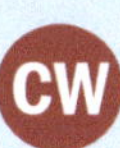

***Metamorphoses*, 15.745–870 (OCR 1–126)**

Author: Ovid

Date: AD 8

Significance: provides a narrative account of the deification of Julius Caesar and the reasons for his promotion to godhood

Read it here: OCR source booklet

Despite Venus' protests, it is clear that the assassination has been fated to occur. Jupiter, king of the gods and voice of fate, reassures Venus that Julius Caesar's time to die has come, but that his son Augustus will avenge him:

> Augustus, as heir to his name, will carry the burden placed upon him alone, and will have us with him, in battle, as the most courageous avenger of his father's murder.
>
> Ovid, *Metamorphoses* 15.819–21

By putting this prophecy (which goes on to detail events in the civil wars) in Jupiter's mouth, Ovid legitimises Octavian's civil wars. Surely he cannot be blamed for spilling Roman blood if the king of the gods said that it must be so? This section also underlines a specific aspect of Augustus' relationship with Julius Caesar: Augustus as his avenger.

Ovid describes Julius Caesar's metamorphosis into a comet (which had become his symbol when one appeared in 44 BC) and ends his account by showing him contemplating Augustus' deeds from on high and judging them superior to his own. Ovid praises Augustus as greater than his father and goes so far as to suggest that he too will become a god:

> I beg that the day be slow to arrive, and beyond our own lifetimes, when Augustus shall rise to heaven, leaving the world he rules, and there, far off, shall listen, with favour, to our prayers!
>
> Ovid, *Metamorphoses* 15.868–70

MODERN SCHOLARSHIP

Ovid, who constructed a mythological epic towards the end of Augustus' reign around the theme of Metamorphosis, of bodies changed from one form to another, understood that despite appearances, transformations are neither instantaneous nor abrupt. His metamorphoses take place gradually, sometimes gruesomely so, and the new shapes are fashioned, element by element, from the old. The beautiful girl Arachne, so skilled at spinning, becomes a spider through the gradual shrinkage of her head and body, and the transmutation of her long slender fingers into the spinning legs of a spider, in her new guise, she keeps weaving as before (*Metamorphoses* 6.140ff.) . . . Augustus' transformation of Rome was a long and gradual process.

A. Wallace-Hadrill, *Augustan Rome*, 1993, p. 10

Wallace-Hadrill suggests a possible reading of Ovid's *Metamorphoses*: that the entire epic is a metaphor for the change in Rome and the change in Augustus himself. Many of the transformations in Ovid's work are slow and seem to be painful – perhaps a criticism of Augustus' attempts to reform the city and its people. Another feature of Ovid's metamorphoses is that there is usually an element of continuity alongside the change – Arachne the girl was an excellent weaver, and so too is the spider she transforms into. Could Ovid be asking his reader to question Augustus' own transformation and inviting us to remember that the ruthless Octavian still lives within the benevolent Augustus?

AUGUSTUS THE FATHER OF THE STATE

In the last century of the Republic, Rome had seen a slip in moral standards, especially among the elite. Traditional ideals of modest living had given way to indulgence and luxury, which in turn had led to an increase in greed and personal ambition. This, in turn, led to a political environment where individual politicians sacrificed the good of the state in a quest for personal advancement and enrichment.

Similarly, some were concerned that conservative sexual morals had seen decline. There had been a perceived increase in adultery among the upper classes. This was seen to be unacceptable for two reasons. Firstly, in a world with no DNA tests the only way to be certain of the paternity of a child was to be sure that its mother had only had sex with one man. As such, married women were forbidden from having sex outside marriage. Secondly, chaste women were believed to have a special potency in religious ceremonies. It seems as though the gods of Rome hated unfaithful women! Roman men were relatively free to seek sexual gratification outside of their marriage, as long as they did not seduce the wife/daughter of another Roman citizen.

Many believed that Rome's troubled history in the last century of the Republic was, at least in part, due to a lapse in moral standards and dwindling respect for the gods.

In *Ode* 3.6, Horace explores an insecurity held by many Romans that the recent civil wars and defeats suffered from foreign enemies were punishment from the gods. Why were the gods so angry with the Romans? Horace provides two reasons, the first of which is:

> Romans, though you're guiltless, you still expiate
> your fathers' sins

> Horace, *Odes* 3.6.1–2

These lines seem to allude to a great misdeed committed by a prior generation. It could even refer to the very founding of Rome, when Romulus (Rome's first king) killed his twin brother Remus. This was the first act of civil conflict in Rome, and some Romans believed that the civil wars that had plagued all of Rome's history were punishment for this act.

Horace proceeds to suggest another reason: the gods are angry because the people have been neglecting their religious duties and hammers his point home with a catalogue of Rome's recent military embarrassments (9–16).

The cause of military failure is attributed to a slip in the moral standards of living Romans. Here Horace shifts his blame from the 'fathers' of previous generations and aims his accusation firmly at his contemporary Romans:

> Our age, fertile in its wickedness, has first
> defiled the marriage bed, our offspring, and homes:
> disaster's stream has flowed from this source
> through the people and the fatherland

> Horace, *Odes* 3.6.17–20

Roman religious belief held that chaste women were particularly loved by the gods and so there were several religious rituals that required that the participants be married and

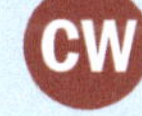

chaste. This was particularly true in times of national emergency. Conversely, the Romans believed that the gods hated infidelity. It is unsurprising, therefore, that Horace links recent military failures with the idea of sexual morals.

Horace harkens back to the Punic Wars, a series of conflicts between Rome and Carthage in the third and second centuries BC. These wars were the closest Rome ever came to being defeated by an enemy power, and so those who fought in them were seen as heroes. Horace praises these men's military success, but also their hard work and obedience to their 'strict mothers'. Thus he links military success (and by implication divine approval) with old-fashioned, clean living.

This poem, then, offers a call to action for the reader. To undo the damage that lax moral standards have done, and to repair Rome's relationship with her gods, the reader must ensure that they behave well. They must look to the example of the heroes of the Punic War and, as mentioned in the opening lines of the poem, they must ensure that the temples are restored.

To address this general feeling of moral decline, Augustus needed to inspire his people to change their ways. He did this encouraging the people of Rome to look upon him as a father figure, with the authority to dictate their behaviour.

He passed laws that regulated the behaviour of citizens. The Leges Iuliae (Julian Laws) were passed in 18–17 BC, some of which encouraged marriage and childrearing. They introduced exclusions for those who chose not to marry. They were not allowed to join in celebrations of public games. These laws also made adultery a crime, with severe punishments for all parties. Traditionally the head of household (paterfamilias) would have been responsible for arranging marriages and for handling any instances of adultery within his family. By introducing and enforcing laws such as these, Augustus was positioning himself as the paterfamilias of all of Rome. Suetonius' account of Augustus' life seems to suggest that he had some trouble implementing these laws. Section 34 of the *Life of Augustus* mentions open rebellion as well as more subtle attempts to circumvent these new laws. Perhaps Suetonius wanted his reader to question whether Augustus was an effective moral reformer and father of the state.

Augustus also encouraged people to look on him as a father figure by the active role he took in state religion (see pp. 149–52). It was the responsibility of the paterfamilias to take part in certain religious festivals and duties on behalf of the family. As discussed previously, Augustus was a member of almost every college of priests and, after Lepidus' death in 12 BC, he held the role or Pontifex Maximus (chief priest). This meant that he would personally take part in a huge amount of public religious rituals on behalf of the people of Rome. In this respect he behaved as a paterfamilias for the entire state. In 2 BC he was given a great honour by the Senate – the title of Pater Patriae, which literally translates as 'father of the fatherland'.

Having established his position at the head of Rome's 'household', he hoped he could change the behaviour of his subjects by setting a strong example of moral behaviour himself and within the imperial family. Anecdotes abound in the writings of ancient authors that tell of the imperial family's upstanding behaviour and of Augustus' efforts to control their behaviour. A prime example of this is in Suetonius' *Life of Augustus* section 59, which details how he cared for his grandchildren and taught them proper

S & C The poet Ovid dedicated a section of his poem the *Fasti* to Augustus as the father of the state. In it he compares Augustus to the legendary founder and first king of Rome, Romulus. Read *Fasti* 2.119–44 and make notes on how Ovid presents Augustus and what are the key differences between him and Romulus.

behaviour. The extent to which we can believe these stories is debatable. We also need to remember that these anecdotes were written after the reign of Augustus. But the fact that they survive to us are testament to the reputation for fine behaviour that the imperial family displayed during Augustus' lifetime.

Another excellent example can be found in the writings of the Younger Seneca. He states that, after the death of her son Drusus, Livia was very upset. However, she put aside her grief the moment she had laid him to rest and rather than indulging herself in excessive mourning, she honoured his memory (in true Roman custom) by displaying his likeness in public and talking about him and his exploits openly and happily (Younger Seneca, *On Consolation*). Regarding Augustus' behaviour, various sources agree that he had very modest tastes. His home on the Palatine hill was not a spectacular palace nor did he appear in public in luxurious clothes. He hoped that, by setting such an example, others would be discouraged from indulging too much in luxury and thus develop excessive greed.

Poetry of the period also frequently included mention of members of the imperial household, invariably engaging in respectable activities.

Horace's *Ode* 3.14 was written to commemorate the return of Augustus from military campaigns in Gaul. It touches on common themes of Augustan poetry: the peace that comes from war, prosperity for the Roman people and the importance of religious observances. It is notable, however, for the way it holds up the women of the imperial household as role models for the audience:

> May his wife rejoice in a matchless husband,
> having sacrificed to true gods, appear now
> with our famous leader's sister, and, all dressed
> in holy ribbons,
> the mothers of virgins and youths, now safe and sound

Horace, Odes 3.14.5–9

Livia is explicitly linked with the practice of Roman religion, as she has been participating in ritual sacrifice. Indeed, her virtue is highlighted even more strongly because she has been sacrificing in the absence of her husband. Clearly Augustus can trust Livia to maintain the affairs of the household and to honour the gods while he is away. Livia and Octavia appear alongside the mothers of Rome. The detail 'dressed/in holy ribbons' implies that the scene is a religious festival, as well as a celebration of Augustus' return. Here the women of the Imperial household are out in public, acting as role models for onlookers.

The imperial family were not perfect role models, however. His only biological daughter, Julia the Elder, was scandalously accused of adultery in 2 BC by Augustus himself. This incident must have been difficult for Augustus in a personal sense, and yet he dealt with it in a way that reinforced his moral agenda. Julia was, in accordance with the Leges Iuliae which criminalised adultery, exiled from Rome. Various of her other lovers were exiled and others were compelled to commit suicide. Augustus' family troubles weren't over yet, as in AD 8 his granddaughter Julia the Younger (daughter of Julia the Elder) was also accused of having an affair with a Roman senator. Just like her mother, Julia the Younger was sent into exile. The high moral standards of Augustus' regime applied to everyone – even his own family. By removing the disobedient Julias

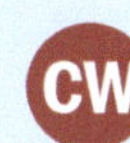

PRESCRIBED SOURCE

Odes **3.14**

Author: Horace

Date: 23 BC

Significance: celebrates Augustus' return from foreign campaigns, mentions Livia and Octavia, women of the Imperial household

Read it here: OCR source booklet

from Rome, Augustus probably wanted to distance himself from their misdeeds and so preserve his own reputation and the reputation of the imperial family. This proved impossible, however, and these stories were retold by Suetonius in his *Life of Augustus*. Section 65 conveys the devastation that Augustus felt, claiming that Augustus himself had said 'Would I had never married, and childless had died'.

THE DAWN OF A NEW GOLDEN AGE

Augustus was eager to influence not only how the Roman people viewed him, but how they viewed themselves. If he could convince them that their lives were significantly better with him as their ruler, then they would be less likely to revolt against him. To this end, he encouraged the idea that his reign was a new 'Golden Age'. By extension, the people of Rome could view themselves as a new 'Golden Race'.

Greek and Roman mythology told of an idyllic Golden Age. The first race of men, the Golden Race lived carefree lives, free from suffering and hard work. They were loved by the gods and spent their days in unending feasts. The earth was fertile and crops came forth without the need for farming. The first surviving example of the myth of the Golden Age was written by the Greek poet Hesiod. Hesiod states that the Golden Age was presided over by the god Cronus (the Greek equivalent of the Roman Saturn) and that it ended when he was deposed by his son Zeus (Jupiter) and a lesser, Silver Age began. The mortals of Augustus' time would have been of the Race of Iron, the fifth race to have been made by the gods, living lives far inferior to the Golden Race. Hesiod's myth of the ages of man is a story of decline. There is no sense that there might ever be a return to the good old days of gold. Augustus, however, provided a new vision of the ages of man that was cyclical. He claimed that a new Golden Age had come to the world and that his Romans were the new Golden Race.

Drawing specifically on the myth of the Saturnian Golden Age made Augustus' position as leader of Rome even more secure. The Saturnian Golden Age ended because Saturn was removed from power by his son Jupiter. The implication was, therefore, that Augustus was the bringer of the Golden Age and it would end if he were ever removed from power.

In 17 BC Augustus announced the start of a new age and marked the occasion with games called the ludi saeculares. So that his declaration would not seem to be overtly political, Augustus claimed that the coming of a new age had been prophesied in the **Sibylline Books**. The new age, then, was ordained by the gods and not by himself. The games involved a three night and day festival in honour of the gods, with many grand sacrifices, and were followed by days of entertainments of all kinds. All Romans were invited and expected to attend, even those who had been banned for their unmarried status under the Leges Iuliae. Hundreds of people took part in the festival, performing various religious rituals. Augustus, of course, took the leading role in the rituals, along with Agrippa. The poet Horace composed a hymn especially for the occasion, and it was sung by a chorus of Roman youths all dressed in white at the Temple of Apollo next to Augustus' home on the Palatine hill, and then again on the Capitol. The symbolism was clear for all to see: these children are Rome's future and the best hope for her continued prosperity.

The *Carmen Saeculare* addresses various gods, praising their greatness and asking for blessings on the Roman people. The deities selected for inclusion each had some connection to Augustus himself or to his regime. For example, his patron god Apollo and Apollo's twin sister Diana feature as the addressees of the hymn (1–4).

As in previous poems, when speaking of Apollo, Horace distinguishes between warlike Apollo and peaceful Apollo, perhaps as a veiled reference to the militaristic and civic 'versions' of Augustus himself:

> Gentle and peaceful Apollo, lay down your arms,
> and listen now to the young lads' supplications.

Horace, Carmen Saeculare 33–4

Venus also features, just as she does in Ovid's *Metamorphoses* 15, in her role as the mother of Aeneas and the progenitor of the Julian clan (49–50). At first the presence of Ilithyia, a relatively minor goddess of childbirth, is less explicable. However, the reason for her inclusion is explained through a clear reference to Augustus' social and moral legislation, the Leges Iuliae. Horace beseeches Ilithyia:

> Goddess, nurture our offspring, bring to fruition
> the Senate's decrees concerning the wedlock
> of women who'll bear us more children,
> the laws of marriage.

Horace, Carmen Saeculare 17–20

The health and vitality of present-day Rome is stressed in the next section, both in terms of military strength and in terms of the strength of her citizens' morals. Horace's *Carmen Saeculare* is clearly intended to be a celebration of Augustus' new age. The language of fertility reminds the audience of the Golden Age of peace and plenty that Augustus brought. References to religious and social reforms simultaneously remind the audience how they are expected to behave in Augustus' new world order.

DEBATE

It is not known whether Augustus 'rigged' the declaration of the new age or not. He was a member of the quindecimviri, the college of priests who were responsible for keeping and interpreting the Sibylline Books, so he could easily have arranged for a convenient prophecy to be made. However, as the books were sacred it would have been blasphemous to intentionally misrepresent their contents to the people of Rome. Augustus certainly had good reason to want the new age to begin when it did – the settlement with the Parthians of 20 BC had secured peace on the eastern frontier of the Empire, and Agrippa's campaigns in Spain in 19 BC on the west. It seemed as though a lasting peace was secured at the edges of the Empire. What's more, the Leges Iuliae introduced in the previous year had already introduced the idea that Augustus' Romans would be morally superior to those who came before. But was Augustus willing to compromise religion for a PR stunt?

PRESCRIBED SOURCE

Carmen Saeculare 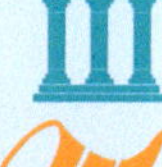

Author: Horace

Date: 17 BC 

Significance: 
composed to be performed during the ludi saeculares.

Read it here: OCR source booklet 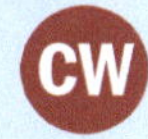

S & C

A desire to return to the Golden Age was already in the air before Augustus rose to power. In 40 BC the poet Virgil published his *Eclogues*. Book 4 of the *Eclogues* contained a famous passage that predicted the coming of a messiah-like child who would bring about a new Golden Age. In the years following Augustus' rise to power, the poem was read as predicting his coming. Still later, in the years after the advent of Christianity, readers have interpreted this passage as predicting the birth of Jesus. Read Virgil's *Eclogues* 4. What does this poem reveal about the thoughts, desires and concerns of Virgil in 40 BC?

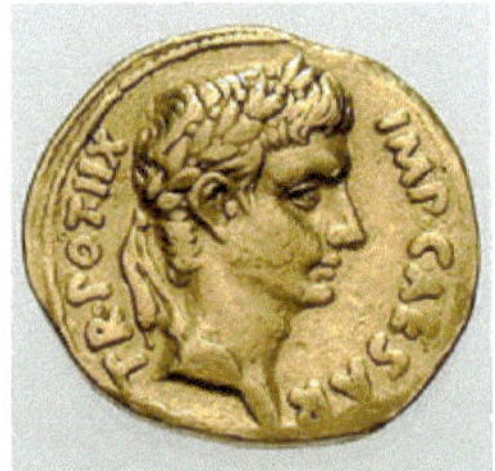
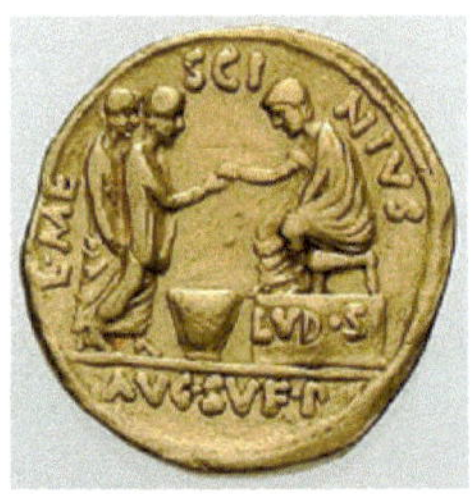

FIGURE 2.21
Aureus of Augustus, minted
16 BC.

PRESCRIBED SOURCE

Odes **4.15**

Author: Horace

Date: 13 BC

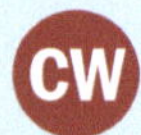

Significance:
communicates the idea that peace and prosperity reign in Rome, thanks to Augustus

Read it here: OCR source booklet

The ludi saeculares declared the official beginning of a new saeculum/age. Augustus encouraged the idea that the new age was golden, continuing to reference this idea throughout his reign. Any mention of Saturn, of lasting peace and prosperity and the imagery and language of abundance would have been understood by Augustus' contemporaries as a reference to the Golden Age. Constant reminders that they were living in a blessed state and that it could only be maintained through moral vigilance, diligent religious observance and continued loyalty to Augustus' regime.

The coin in Figure 2.21 depicts a laureate Augustus on the obverse and three figures on the reverse. This scene is usually interpreted as Augustus himself (seated) distributing suffimenta to the people of Rome before the ludi saeculares (identifiable by LVD.S on the plinth). Suffimenta were gifts of sulphur and other flammable materials that would be used to make torches for the rituals during the festival.

The poets of the Augustan period similarly continued to reinforce the idea that Augustus' reign was a Golden Age. As time went on, they became more confident in thanking Augustus himself, rather than the gods, for the peace and prosperity that the state enjoyed.

Horace's *Odes* 4.15 opens with a self-deprecating apology. Horace tells his reader that he had tried to write military poetry but Apollo (god of music) had stopped him:

Phoebus condemned my verse, when I tried to sing
of war and conquered cities.

Horace, *Odes* 4.15.1–2

Whether this is meant literally or as a reference to Augustus' personal influence on Horace's literary career is unclear.

Horace goes on to explain that, now Crassus' standards have been recovered from the Parthians (see pp. 116, 154) and the gates of Janus' temple have been closed, there is no war to celebrate. Interestingly, Horace links the idea of peace throughout the Empire with the renewed prosperity of Italy (4.15.4–10).

Horace explicitly states that this blessed state of peace and plenty exists because of Augustus' position at the head of the state:

> With Caesar protecting the state, no civil
> disturbance will banish the peace, no violence,
> no anger that forges swords, and makes
> mutual enemies of wretched towns.

Horace, Odes 4.15.17–20

This links closely with the myth of the Saturnian Golden Age, where a charmed state of peace and plenty is brought about by a single ruler. By inviting his readers to make this link, Horace is most likely supporting Augustus' regime by suggesting that, should Augustus be overthrown, the Golden Age would end, just as when Saturn was overthrown by Jupiter.

In the closing lines of the poem, Horace suggests rekindling the old Roman tradition of singing stories of past leaders on festival days. This ties in with Augustus' own drive to restore Roman religious practice to its bygone glory days, and also gives Horace the opportunity to praise Augustus' ancestors:

> we'll sing of Troy,
> Anchises, and the people of Venus

Horace, Odes 4.15.31–2

AUGUSTUS AND HIS 'SONS'

As time went by, Augustus turned his attention from the present to the future. His Principate was stable and it seemed highly unlikely that anyone would attempt to overthrow him (although there were two unsuccessful plots, the first in 2 BC and the second in AD 8). The most pressing issue for him to consider now was: what happens when I die?

The Principate was not a hereditary position. He was not a king, and there was no set plan for what happened and who got to rule when he died. The last time there had been a power vacuum in Rome (on Julius Caesar's death) there had been decades of instability and civil war. Surely Augustus wanted to avoid this, as it would undermine all of the achievements of his reign.

Another reason for wanting to secure the succession of power was to increase the prestige of his family. Thanks to his rise to power and the programmatic glorification of the Julian clan's ancestors, his family was pre-eminent in the Roman world. By ensuring that he was succeeded by a relative, he made sure that this remained the case.

To encourage a smooth transition of power from himself to an heir, Augustus proceeded to groom his younger male relatives for power. He used formal adoption as a way of signalling his intentions to the people and carefully managed the images of his

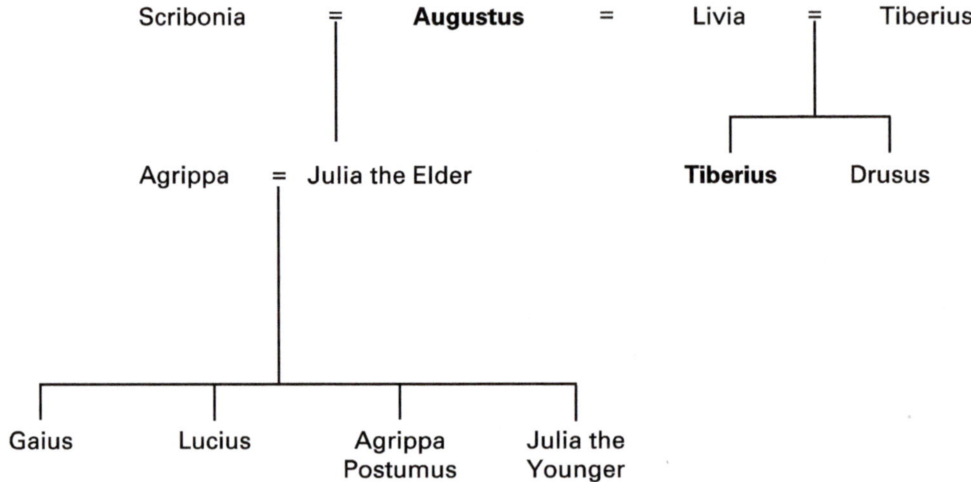

FIGURE 2.22
Family tree showing the relationship between Augustus and his potential heirs.

potential heirs, as he did his own. Bringing heirs to prominence also gave additional opportunities for the imperial family to act as role models for the Roman people and it enhanced Augustus' image as a father figure.

Augustus had only one natural child, Julia the Elder. As women were excluded from Roman politics, she could not act as the heir to his power. She was vital, however, to Augustus' plans for the transmission of his power. Julia had been forced to marry Agrippa, Augustus' best friend, trusted lieutenant and gifted general. The couple had two sons together, Gaius and Lucius, and Julia gave birth to a third son after Agrippa's death who was named Agrippa Postumus, as well as at least one daughter.

In 17 BC, Augustus formally adopted Gaius and Lucius, thereafter called Gaius Caesar and Lucius Caesar. They were the ideal candidates as they were related to Augustus by blood. The fact that they were the sons of Agrippa was also advantageous as Agrippa had a reputation for political and military excellence that was only eclipsed by that of Augustus. Evidently Augustus was proud of the boys and of the way in which he introduced them to public life. He recounts some of this process in the *Res Gestae* Section 14.

The elder of the two, Gaius, was first presented to the public in 13 BC. He took part in the **Troy Game**, which stressed his nobility and also his links with the ancestors of the Julian clan. The origins of this ritual were traced back to Aeneas and the Trojan refugees. It had fallen out of practice for many years until Julius Caesar reinstated them shortly before his death. Lucius was presented in public a couple of years later, to troops stationed by the Rhine (modern Germany) and he also took part in an equestrian pageant.

Gaius and Lucius began to appear on official coinage. Often, as in Figure 2.23, Augustus' portrait would appear on the obverse, with the portraits of the princes on the reverse. This echoed the coinage of Augustus' early career which sought to establish himself as the heir of Julius Caesar.

Figure 2.24 is packed with information both about Augustus and about Gaius and Lucius. It reinforces Augustus' achievements by depicting him wearing a wreath; this may be the civic crown (oak wreath) which would reinforce his identity of being saviour of the Roman people. The inscription reminds the viewer of his most illustrious titles:

Troy Game an ancient ritual that involved young noblemen showing off their horsemanship with a series of complex manoeuvres

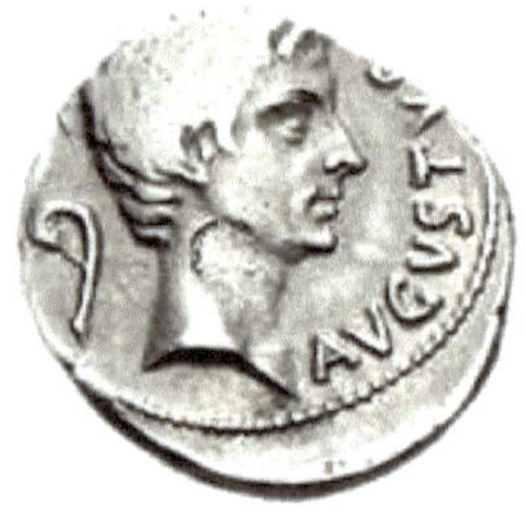

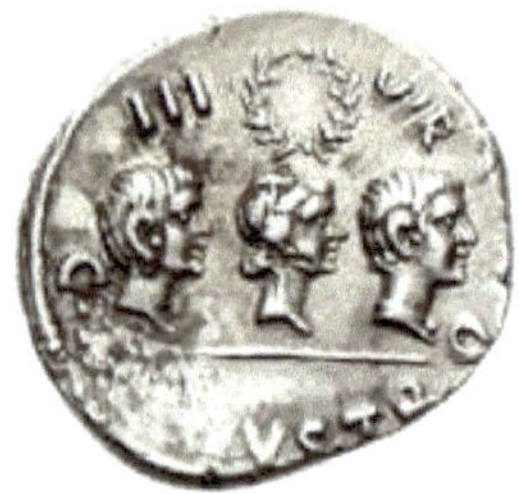

FIGURE 2.23
This coin of 13 BC depicts Augustus on the obverse and Gaius and Lucius, either side of their mother Julia, on the reverse.

divi filius and pater patriae. The princes, on the obverse, are shown with shields and spears. These could be a reference to their military might, or could represent the honorary shields and spears that they were given by the Roman nobles. The **simpulum** and **lituus** refer to priestly colleges that the princes belonged to, and convey their piety as being like Augustus'. The inscription lists their achievements also, although being so young they were few. They had held no official political office, but the Senate had made them consuls designate for future years. The most important titles were 'Augustus' sons', as this was the source of their legitimacy, and 'princeps iuventutis' was an honorific title awarded to Gaius by the Senate which gave no official power but which equated him with Augustus, who was often referred to as princeps.

> **simpulum** a ritual ladle used for pouring libations at sacrifices
>
> **lituus** a crooked wand used in religious rituals by the college of augurs

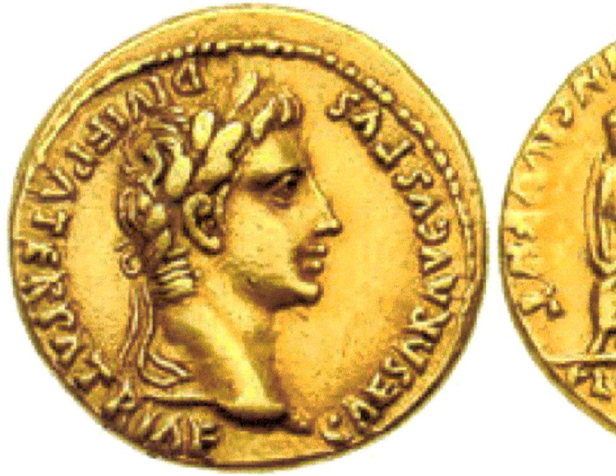
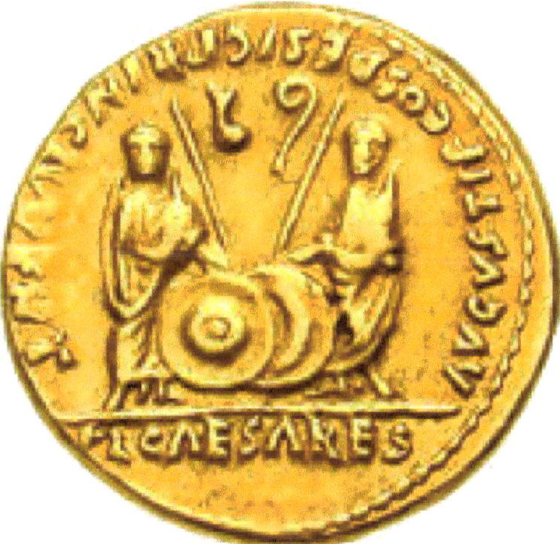

FIGURE 2.24
Aureus of Augustus. **PS**

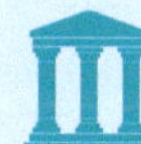

PRESCRIBED SOURCE

Aureus, Gaius and Lucius as princeps iuventutis, obv. Augustus' head wreathed, rev. Gaius and Lucius Caesar standing veiled with shields and priestly symbols

Date: *c.* 2 BC–AD 4

Coin struck by: Lyon mint

Text reads: CAESAR AVGVSTVS DIVI F PATER PATRIAE // AVGVSTI F COS DESIG PRINC IVVENT C L CAESARES

Translation: Caesar Augustus, son of a god, father of the state// Augustus' sons, consuls designate, first among the young, Gaius and Lucius Caesar

Significance: depicts Gaius and Lucius as the obvious successors to Augustus' position

Unfortunately Augustus' work of carefully positioning Gaius and Lucius as his successors would come to naught. Lucius was taken ill in AD 2 while on campaign in Gaul and died. In AD 4 Gaius was killed when on campaign in Armenia.

After the deaths of Gaius and Lucius, Augustus needed to change tactic. He adopted Agrippa Postumus in AD 4, the youngest son of Julia and Agrippa, but it seems as though he was never a strong contender for the succession. He was exiled from Rome in AD 6. Also in AD 4 Augustus adopted Livia's son from her previous marriage, Tiberius. Almost all ancient sources agree that he did this with great reluctance.

Tiberius had never been Augustus' favourite and as such was unlikely to be made his official heir. Rather than pushing him down the political route, Augustus had arranged for Tiberius to become a general in the army alongside his younger brother Drusus. The pair had been sent on several campaigns at the edges of the Empire, including the expedition to Parthia, campaigns in the Alps, the Rhine and Germany. Augustus' commissioned poets to celebrate their virtues and exploits.

In *Odes* 4.4, Horace celebrates the achievements of Tiberius and Drusus against the Germanic tribes living around the Alps in 15–14 BC. It should be remembered, when reading of the achievements of the young generals, that Augustus was the supreme commander in Rome and thus technically responsible for all military victories. By praising the successes of Tiberius and Drusus, he is indirectly glorifying Augustus himself.

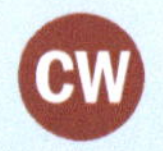

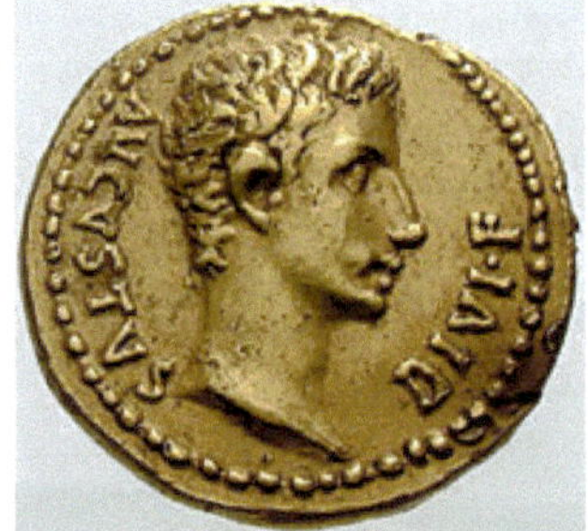

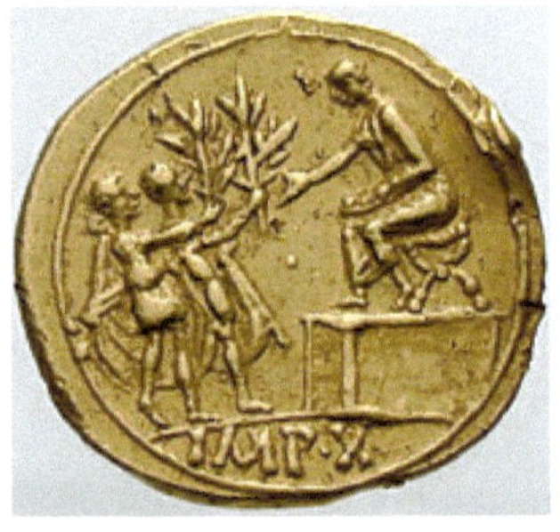

FIGURE 2.25
This coin of *c.* 16 BC, depicts Augustus on the obverse, and a scene on the reverse showing Augustus seated being presented with laurels by victorious Tiberius and Drusus.

Towards the beginning of the poem, a simile compares Drusus to a 'lion-cub newly weaned from fresh milk' (4.4.12). This simile conveys the youth and inexperience of Drusus, but does not suggest that he is an ineffective commander. The lion-cub of Horace's simile is fated to kill a deer, despite its inexperience. Surely Horace intended for the audience to be impressed by the innate power and skill of the lion-cub, and thus of Drusus.

A central theme of the poem is the role education and proper upbringing. When this poem was published, Tiberius and Drusus were Augustus' step-sons. Nevertheless, Horace praises the role Augustus played in shaping the men they had become:

> They came to realise what mind and character
> nurtured, with care, in a fortunate household,
> by Augustus' fatherly feelings
> towards his stepsons, the Neros, could do.

Horace, Odes 4.4.25–8

Drusus is subsequently likened through a simile to a lion. With this innate skill and careful nurturing by Augustus, he is shown to be an impressive young man indeed.

Horace goes on to mention one of the most glorious achievements of Tiberius and Drusus' ancestors: the defeat of the Carthaginian general Hasdrubal by Gaius Claudius Nero in 207 BC during the Punic Wars. This victory was particularly sweet to the Romans, since Hasdrubal was the brother of the infamous Hannibal. Remembered as one of the greatest generals of all time, Hannibal was a source of genuine fear for ordinary Romans during the Punic Wars, so the defeat of his brother ensured Gaius Claudius Drusus' place in the history books.

The final section of the poem takes the form of a speech, put in the mouth of Hannibal himself. He curses the foolishness of the Carthaginians, to pit themselves against the power of Rome and pours such flattery that it seems completely unbelievable. His assertion 'There's nothing that Claudian power can't achieve' (4.4.73–5) hints strongly at what impression Horace was trying to create about Augustus and his stepsons by inventing this unlikely speech.

Tiberius was a hugely successful general, having been victorious in campaigns against Germanic tribes in the Alps, the Rhineland and on the Danube frontier. As discussed above, he also played a key part in retrieving Crassus' standards from the Parthians. Despite the glory this brought him, and the privileges he enjoyed as part of the imperial household, Tiberius went into self-imposed exile to Rhodes in 6 BC. The reason for this

S & C
The Punic Wars were a series of wars fought between Rome and Carthage between 264–146 BC. These conflicts were perhaps the closest the Roman Republic ever came to being conquered by a foreign power. Conduct your own research into the events of the Punic Wars, and into the role Hannibal played. Why do you think he, in particular, continued to inspire fear and unease in Roman audiences, more than a century after his death?

is unknown and the subject of much speculation. Some suggest that Tiberius was resentful of Augustus' preference for Gaius and Lucius. Others say that it was in protest over his arranged marriage to Julia the Elder following Agrippa's death. Whatever the reason for his exile, Tiberius was summoned back to Rome in AD 2 when Lucius died. When Gaius died in AD 4 Augustus adopted Tiberius, making him the heir apparent.

> **EXPLORE FURTHER**
>
> Another possible successor had been Marcus Claudius Marcellus, the son of Augustus' sister Octavia, and thus his nephew. He fell ill and died in 23 BC, when he was only nineteen years old. Before this, however, Augustus had been grooming him for power. Conduct your own research to see how Augustus had introduced him to the world of Roman politics and promoted his image. How similar was this to his promotion of his other protégées in the years that followed? Virgil includes mention of Marcellus in the *Aeneid* Book 6, placing him alongside Rome's greatest heroes. You might like to read Book 6 ll. 856–87 of Virgil's *Aeneid* for his account of Marcellus' life and accomplishments.

FOUND IT OF BRICK AND LEFT IT MARBLE – AUGUSTUS' BUILDING PROGRAMME

One of Augustus' most famous sayings was that he found the city of Rome made of brick, but he left it clothed in marble. This boast was in reference to his extensive building programme. At the beginning of Augustus' reign, the city of Rome was significantly less well developed and with far fewer architectural marvels than other great capitals of the ancient Mediterranean. Indeed, Philip V of Macedon is said to have mocked the humble appearance of the city when he visited in 182 BC. By the end of his reign, he had changed the face of Rome by dilapidated temples (see p. 150) and by building a series of new religious and civic buildings, public amenities and monuments. His use of marble to beautify the city was on an unprecedented scale. Indeed, the building programme was so impressive that, a century later, Suetonius wrote approvingly about it in section 29 of his *Life of Augustus*.

Such highly visible projects contributed to the idea of Augustus as a benefactor to the city and the bringer of a new Golden Age. The quality of the city's public buildings and amenities were improving in a very real way. Particular projects carried additional meanings, depending on the building and the circumstances of its construction. For example, Augustus finished building the Forum of Julius Caesar as well as the Curia of Julius Caesar, both projects which Julius Caesar had started. By finishing these projects Augustus reinforced his relationship with Julius Caesar (now deified), stressing his filial and also his religious pietas.

Augustus tasked Agrippa with organising and funding projects to improve the quality of life of the urban residents. For example, as aedile in 33 BC he was responsible for an overhaul of the city's water supply, restoring aqueducts and commissioning new ones to be built. Agrippa also donated many acres of his own land to public use. He surrounded his villa with theatres, parkland, exercise grounds and baths. All of these were available for public use. He was also responsible for a new temple dedicated to all the gods: the Pantheon. Today, the Pantheon is one of the most impressive and iconic buildings in all of Rome. Agrippa's building was, in fact, added to by a later emperor, and so his Pantheon was far less impressive. But still, the contribution that Agrippa made to the city was significant. But how does all this relate to Augustus and his public image? First, the majority of Romans would have understood that Agrippa's projects were Augustus' projects. They had worked closely together for years and had appeared together in public many times. Agrippa was married to Augustus' daughter Julia. They even appeared together on official coinage. Allowing Agrippa to build structures under his own name in no way detracted from the idea that Augustus was the true benefactor of Rome. Second, by allowing Agrippa to publicise his own name via building projects Augustus was showing other noblemen how they could go about winning fame for themselves. In the Republic, members of the noble families jockeyed for prominence by running for elected office. With Augustus the uncontested leader of the state, opportunities for noblemen to win renown were now more sparse. To prevent resentment among the nobility, Augustus needed to show that he was happy to share the spotlight. Agrippa's building programme helped him to do this.

Agrippa's public works were impressive, and they certainly improved the quality of life of the urban poor, but they were significantly less spectacular than Augustus' own building projects. Augustus restored the Basilica Aemilia and Basilica Julia,

EXAM TIP: SOURCE SKILLS

Reading Architecture and Space

When considering architecture, you will use many of the same skills used when considering artworks. The materials used and symbols included can convey a message to the viewer without using words. But more than this, architects can prompt a visitor to *behave* in a certain way. A church, surrounded by a grassy churchyard and enclosed by a high stone wall, encourages contemplation of a world apart. A shop, with a wide doorway and produce in the window, will entice a visitor to come inside. Similarly, architects can make visitors *feel* a certain way. A narrow street, with high buildings that block out the sun could elicit fear, whereas a wide boulevard, flanked with trees and grand houses could put the visitor at ease. The experience of architecture is participatory. That is, we experience architecture by being in and around it.

When you study – or visit – your architectural sources think about how ancient visitors would have interacted with the buildings and spaces as part of their daily lives, and how this might have impacted their understanding of the architecture itself. This will enable you to assess how effectively the architecture conveys a particular feeling or idea.

multifunctional civic spaces which incorporated law courts and space for businesses/ trade. These were necessary because the population of Rome was increasing to such a degree that the old law courts could not handle the volume of cases being brought! Augustus also expanded the city of Rome by moving its sacred boundary (pomerium). Only one leader had ever done this before him and it must have signified an improvement to the scale and grandeur of the city.

One of the largest and most impressive of Augustus' building projects he named for himself: the Forum of Augustus (see reconstructed diagram in Figure 2.26). Building began in 20 BC and it was completed two decades later in 2 BC. It was the fulfillment of a promise he had made in 42 BC, before the Battle of Philippi, when he vowed to erect a temple to Mars Ultor (Mars the Avenger) if he won the battle. The focal point of the forum was a large temple to the god.

The Forum itself was rectangular in shape, comprising a central courtyard, flanked by two long porticoes (A), lined with columns. The porticoes were lined with statues

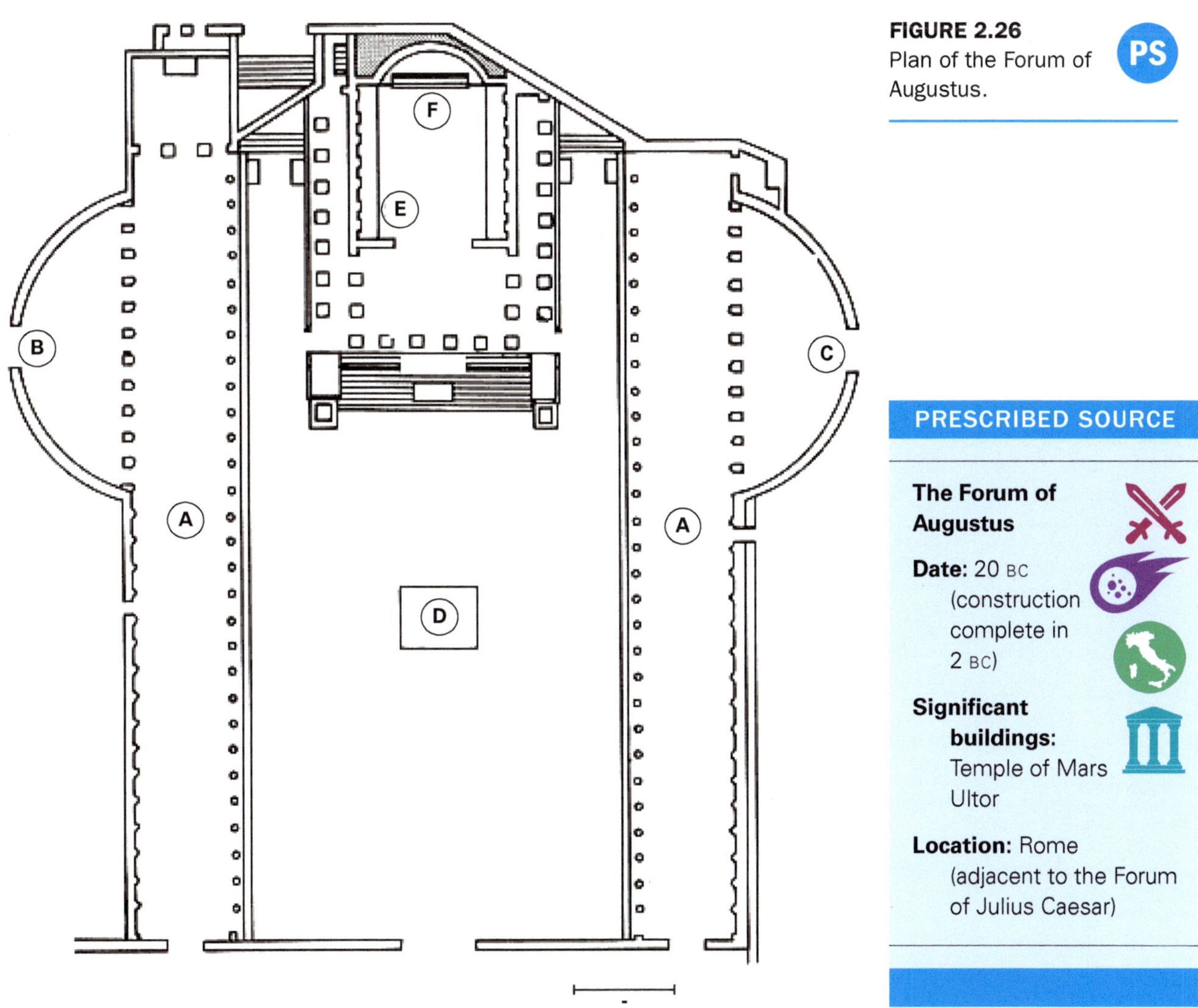

FIGURE 2.26
Plan of the Forum of Augustus. **PS**

of famous Romans. Many of Augustus' ancestors were included, alongside illustrious men from Rome's history – many of them politicians and generals. The west portico housed a colossal statue of Augustus himself, which is now lost but ancient authors describe it as having been significantly larger than the other statues in the porticoes. Each portico had a semi-circular exedra, containing more statuary. The west exedra (B) held a statue of Aeneas and his descendants the Julii, the east exedra a statue of Romulus (C). The central courtyard itself held only one statue. A likeness of Augustus himself, riding a chariot drawn by four horses. The inscription on the statue read simply: 'PATER PATRIAE' (D).

The Temple of Mars Ultor (E) was raised on a platform and accessed by a wide flight of steps. The temple itself would have loomed high above the rest of the Forum and it backed onto a high wall, separating the complex from a neighbouring residential area. As was traditional, the temple contained a cult statue of the deity to whom it was dedicated – Mars the Avenger (F). The cult statue was flanked by a statue of Venus Genetrix (Venus the Mother) and of the Deified Julius Caesar. The temple was dedicated to Mars but this sculptural programme, which featured the gods most closely associated with the Julian clan, indicates that the temple was intended to be a showpiece of Augustus and his ancestors.

None of the forums of the Augustan period have survived completely intact to modernity. The Forum of Augustus is relatively well preserved, however, and archaeologists have been able to compare their material findings with literary evidence (such as Ovid's description in his poems *Fasti* and Suetonius' description in the *Lives of the Twelve Caesars*) to reconstruct a full picture of the site.

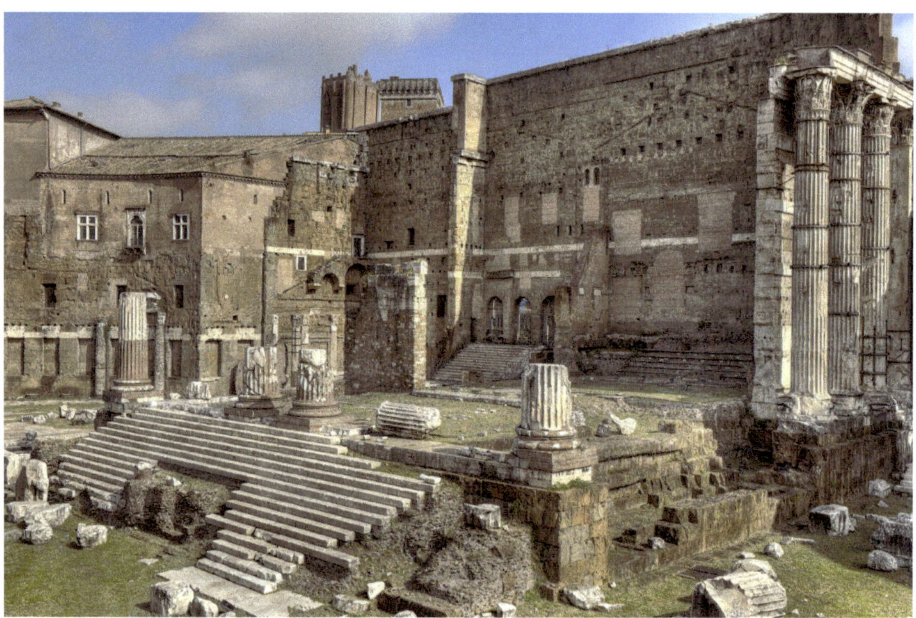

FIGURE 2.27
The ruins of the Temple of Mars Ultor in the Forum of Augustus as it exists today. The steps are still visible and columns have been reconstructed to give a sense of the scale of the temple.

The Ara Pacis Augustae (the Altar of Augustan Peace, usually referred to simply as the Ara Pacis) is a monumental altar complex. Pax, the personification of peace had hardly featured in Roman religion, art or literature before Augustus but, as has been discussed in previous topics, became a central feature of Augustus' regime and propaganda.

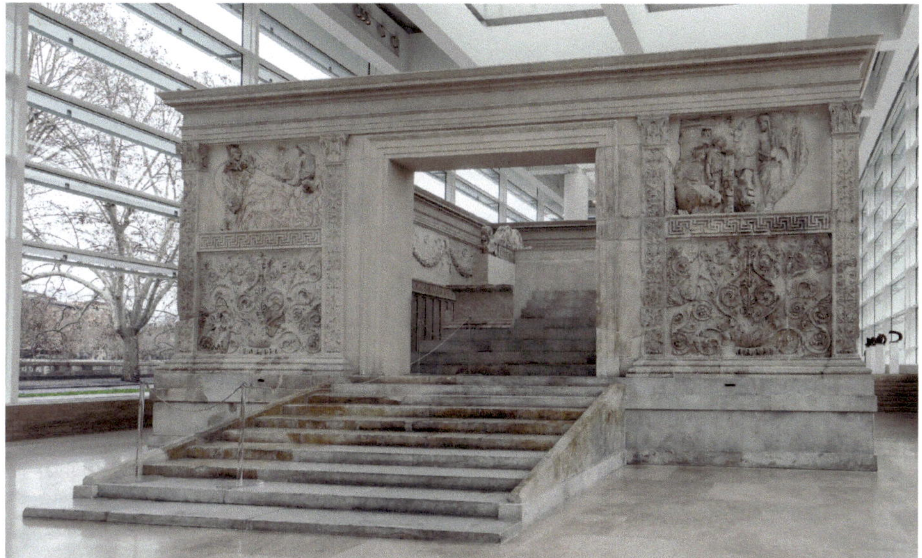

FIGURE 2.28 The Ara Pacis as it stands today, restored and housed in the Museo dell'Ara Pacis on the banks of the Tiber in Rome.

In section 12 of the *Res Gestae*, Augustus states that Senate voted to dedicate the Ara Pacis, following his return to Rome in 13 BC after a three-year absence spent on campaign in Spain. The assertion that the monument was ordered by the Senate is typical of Augustus' style of self-presentation. He maintains an air of humility and seems the perfect Republican by deferring to the Senate on such matters. The subject of the altar, combined with the occasion of its dedication reinforced a central ideal of Augustus' regime: peace through military strength. This was further emphasised by the ceremonial closing of the gates of the Temple of Janus Quirinus at the same time.

Today the Ara Pacis is housed in its own museum complex, which protects the intricate relief sculpture from damage by the elements. Figure 2.28 gives an impression of the entire altar complex. A rectangular building, covered in white marble relief sculpture, is approached by a shallow flight of steps. The altar itself is located inside. The Ara Pacis was certainly designed to be viewed from the outside, as this is where the most intricate and varied decoration is to be found. The interior is adorned with relief sculpture as well, but there is more blank space and the sculptures are merely a regular pattern of garlands. The upper cornice has been lost and the reconstruction visible today is plain. It is likely that the original cornice would have been highly decorated, like the rest of the structure.

The walls of the Ara Pacis are divided into two horizontal halves: upper and lower. The lower half is decorated with a continuous band of panels covered with plant life. The central plant is an acanthus, which is interwoven with vines whose tendrils morph into other plants. Vines were frequently used as a symbol of Augustus' Golden Age as they alluded to fertility and natural bounty. Scholars have noted that the vines on the Ara Pacis are oddly symmetrical, following regular patterns. It is possible that this was merely an aesthetic choice. An alternative interpretation is that the vines represent not only the fertility and plenty of Augustus' Golden Age, but the fact that this blessed state was the result of strict social order. The vines are regular and formal – perhaps a comment on the rigidity of Augustus' regime.

PRESCRIBED SOURCE

The Ara Pacis

Date: 13 BC (construction complete in 9 BC)

Materials: white marble.

Location: Rome (between the Mausoleum of Augustus and the River Tiber)

Significance: an altar to the goddess Pax

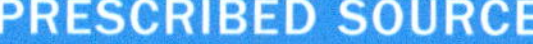

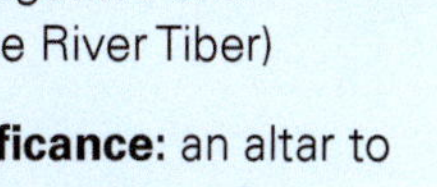

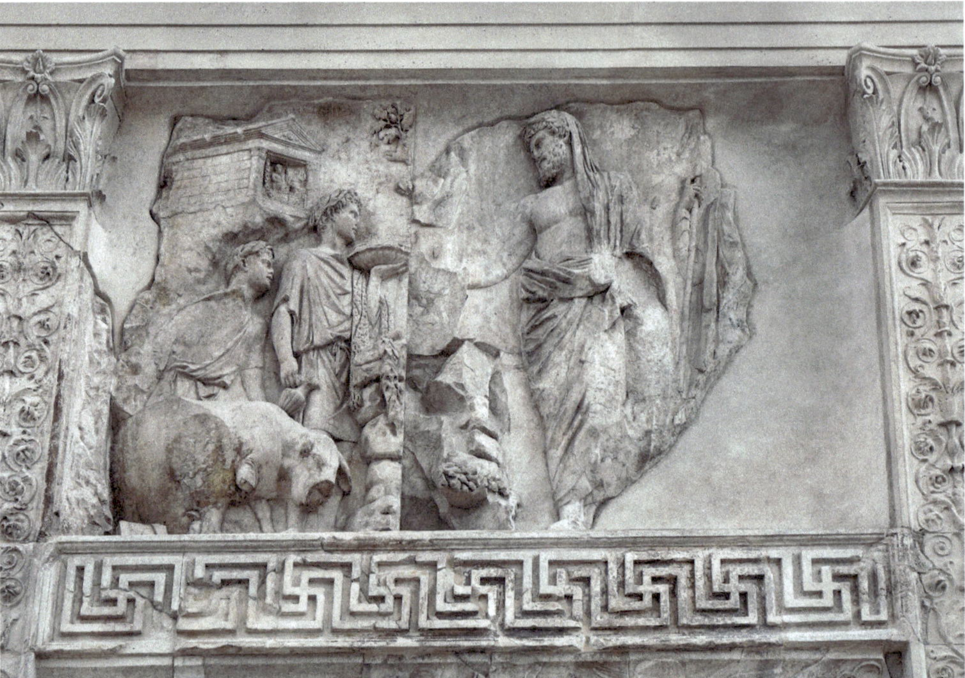

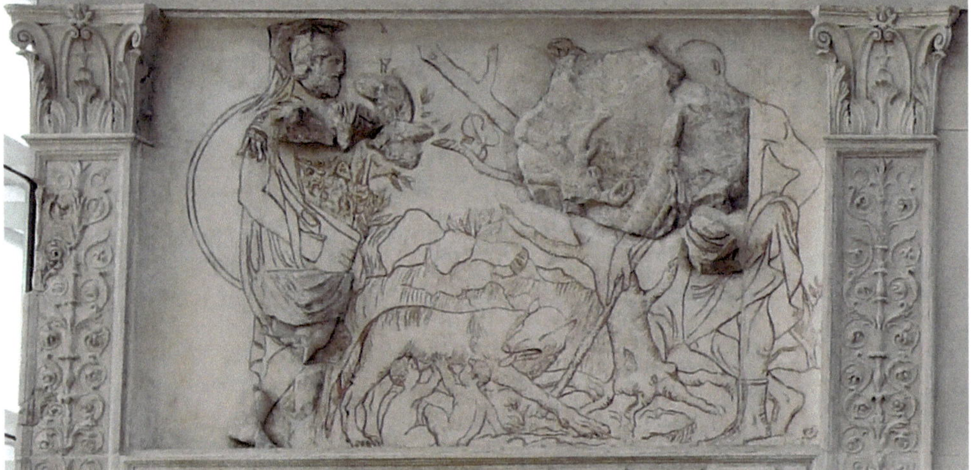

There are then four sculptural panels, two at the front flanking the entrance and two at the rear. At the entrance are depicted Rome's two mythological founders and Augustus' ancestors: Aeneas and Romulus. The Aeneas panel in Fig 2.29 depicts the hero with his head covered, indicating that he is taking part in a religious ritual. This scene takes place as Aeneas arrived in Italy and shows him making a sacrifice of pigs to the household gods of Troy (which he brought to become the household gods of Rome).

The facing panel, widely believed to show Romulus as a baby, has been badly damaged and could only be partly restored. The sketch overlaid in Figure 2.30 is an educated guess at what this panel might have looked like. The two grown men are thought to be Mars (left) and the shepherd Faustulus (right). The twins Romulus and Remus would have been depicted as babies being suckled by a she-wolf, as in the myth of their upbringing.

To the rear of the structure, a panel thought to depict the goddess Roma has similarly been badly damaged. Based on the surviving fragments, she seems to be seated on a pile of armour, a typical representation of the personification of Rome. This also emphasised the link between war and peace in Augustan ideology.

The best preserved of all four panels (Fig 2.31) has, ironically, sparked the most debate. Scholars usually refer to this panel as the Tellus panel, after the earth mother goddess Tellus. There is, however, lively debate as to the identity of the central figure. The female figures are thought to be representations of the sky (left) and sea (right). It could make sense, therefore, for the central figure to be Tellus as a personification of the earth. The domesticated animals at her feet and flowers behind her seem to support this idea. Other plausible suggestions include Ceres (goddess of fertility and especially corn), Venus Genetrix, the goddess Pax or even Livia.

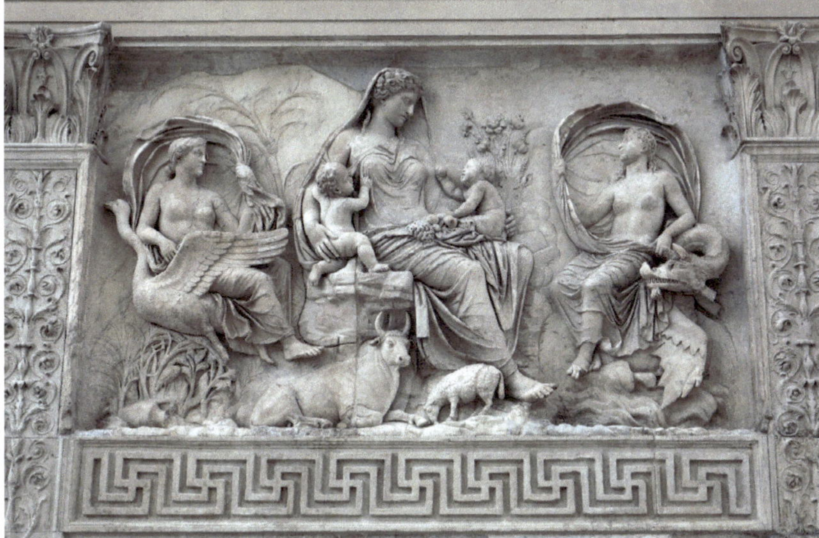

FIGURE 2.31
The Tellus panel. 

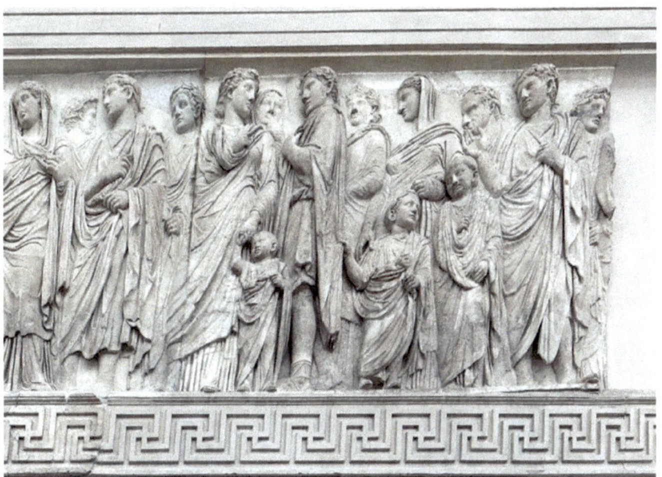

FIGURE 2.32
The imperial family portrayed on the Ara Pacis. 

The upper portion of the side exterior walls are decorated with a frieze depicting a religious procession. The processional frieze shows nearly fifty figures in total and gives the impression of a grand festival. Classicists have attempted to identify the figures in the procession, but there is still debate over some of these. It is generally agreed that the procession includes Augustus himself, along with Agrippa and Livia. Augustus himself is depicted wearing a toga rather than military dress. This presents him as a civic leader. A real innovation in Roman temple art, the frieze depicts children. Almost certainly members of the imperial family, these represent the future of Rome and seem to promise a continuation of the Augustan Golden Age into future generations.

AUGUSTUS' IMAGE IN THE EMPIRE

Augustus' public image within the city of Rome engaged directly with Roman culture and values. The idea of him as a restorer of the Republic, as a champion of traditional values and the mos maiorum, as a religious leader, as Julius Caesar's heir – all of these aspects of his personal brand only made sense within the very specific cultural background of Rome. But Augustus was more than the leader of the city of Rome. He was the leader of the Roman Empire – a massive territory spanning thousands of miles and millions of people from hundreds of different cultural backgrounds. Augustus was well aware of this and he shifted certain aspects of his public image in order to meet the expectations and desires of his provincial audiences.

An excellent example of this shift in action is the representation of Augustus opposite the Egyptian goddess Isis on the Kalabsha Gate (Figure 2.33). Part of a temple complex

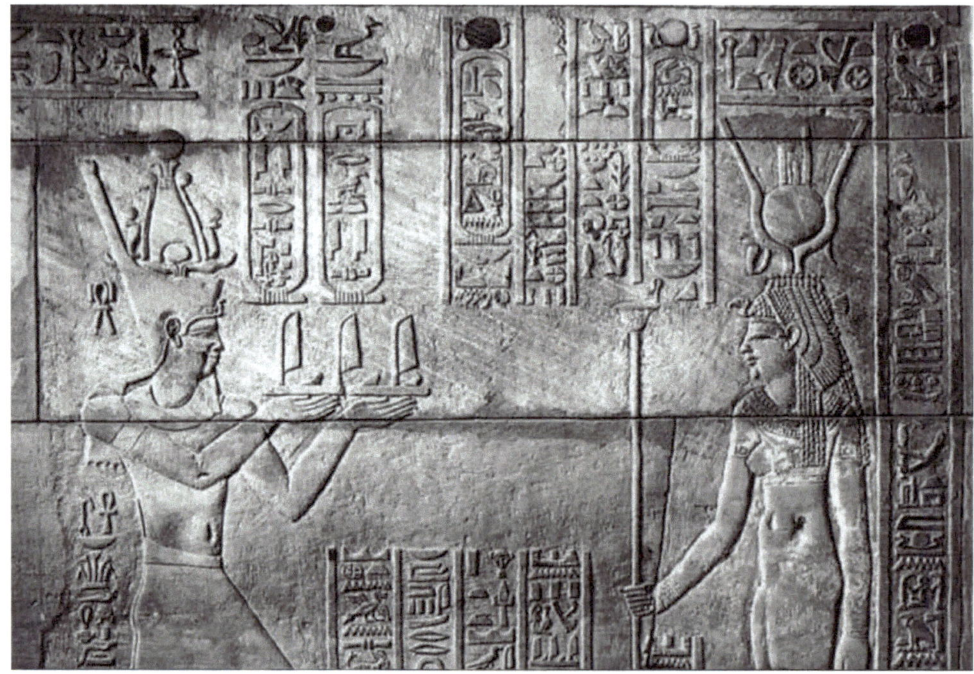

FIGURE 2.33 
Relief showing Augustus from the Kalabsha Gate.

dedicated to a Nubian sun god named Mandulis, this monument shows Augustus embracing gods he did not associate with himself within the city of Rome. The Romans did not automatically impose their religion on the people of their Empire, and some foreign practices were even welcomed into Roman religion. Isis, in particular, was a favourite of some Roman citizens despite her origin as an Egyptian deity. So it was not scandalous for Augustus to identify with these foreign gods, but neither Mandulis nor Isis were used in Augustus' imagery in Rome. Instead he preferred, as we have seen, gods with a direct connection to the Julian clan and the personifications of virtues his regime valued, such as Pax.

Augustus was never crowned ruler of Egypt, but he is clearly depicted here in the style of the pharaohs. He is identifiable as the figure to the left of this image by the cartouches above and to the right of his head. They say 'the Roman' and 'Caesar the god, son of a god'. He is depicted, shirtless but wears a large collar-style necklace, fashionable for Egyptian royalty and wearing an elaborate Egyptian-style crown. His short skirt is also typically Egyptian. Augustus presents Isis with an offering: the hieroglyphic symbol for fields, three times. Finally, it should be noted that this relief sculpture is Egyptian in style, in complete contrast to the idealised realism of most of Augustus' official sculpture in Rome. Other reliefs from around the temple at Kalabsha show other Egyptian deities crowning Augustus, implying that they approve of his rule of Egypt. Still more show Augustus making offerings to the Egyptian deities – he clearly wanted to maintain his pious image but make it work in an Egyptian context.

But exactly how typical was the Augustus and Isis relief at Kalabsha of Augustus' portrayal throughout Egypt? It is difficult to tell, but we can be certain that he did not entirely abandon his usual Classical style. The Meroe Head (Figure 2.34), found in Sudan but believed to have been originally displayed in Egypt, is close to the style of the Prima Porta. The face is highly expressive, a slight deviation from the high Classicism of the Prima Porta, but the careful arrangement of forelocks, the narrow chin and distinctive ears all match. It seems, therefore, that Augustus projected a mixed image of himself in Egypt. Perhaps this was to cater to the native Egyptians and also to the Roman citizens living in and administering the province. Another interpretation is that he had nothing to do with the production of this image, and local people were merely depicting him in a way they thought he would enjoy.

Many provinces of the Roman Empire had long-standing traditions of worshipping their rulers like gods. This was particularly the case in the Hellenistic East, where ruler worship was seen as a sign of devotion and respect (rather than a genuine belief that their rulers were divine). Naturally, many provincials wanted to worship Augustus himself, as their ruler. Augustus did not want to be seen to encourage this, however, as it could play poorly in Rome. It might make him seem more kingly than he was comfortable with and Roman citizens living in these provinces would not abide any state-approved ruler worship.

The solution to this problem was to officially encourage the worship of a new cult: the cult of Rome and Augustus. Officially, the provincials were worshipping him in association with Roma, the personification of Rome. This satisfied the desire for ruler worship, while retaining the impression that no ruler worship was taking place. A particularly fine piece of evidence of this cult is the Temple of Rome and Augustus at Pula, in modern day Croatia, built *c.* AD 2–14 (Figure 2.35).

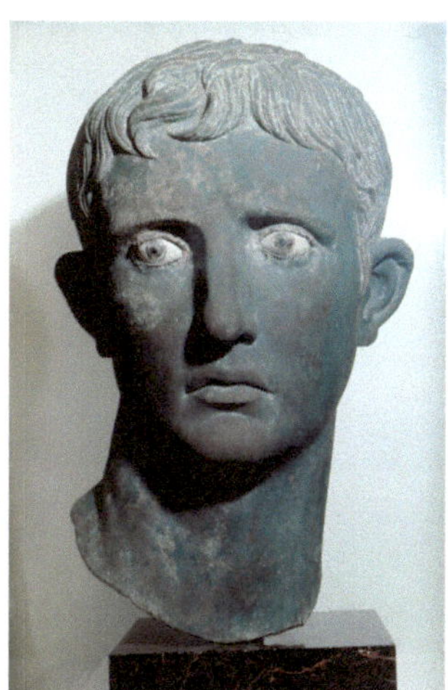

FIGURE 2.34
Meroe Head of Augustus.

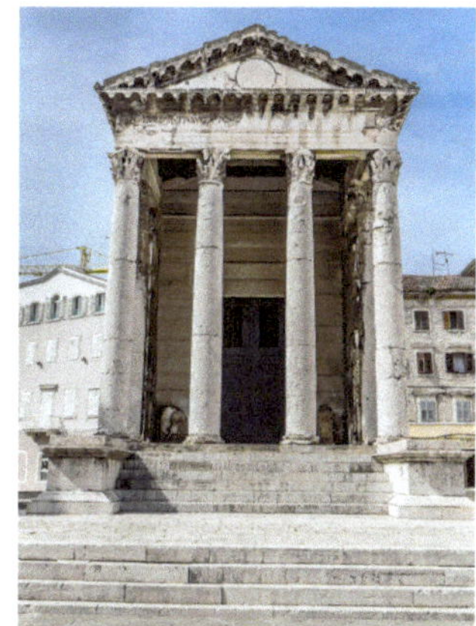

FIGURE 2.35
Temple of Rome and Augustus at Pula.

genius a generic term for a divinity, from a spirit to the major gods; including one's own genius, a cross between a guardian spirit and a soul

Augustus also encouraged the cult of the Divine Julius in the provinces, as well as the worship of his own **genius**. He associated the worship of his genius with worship of the Lares, the household gods of Rome who were worshipped in domestic rituals. This practice was particularly popular throughout Italy, and a number of municipal cults appeared during his reign.

TOPIC REVIEW

These questions should draw on your knowledge of the whole topic, so think carefully about the different things you have learned (check the Topic Overview on pp. 145–6).

1. How did the building programme link with Augustus' image?
2. What did Augustus stand to gain by aligning himself with Saturn as the bringer of a Golden Age?
3. Did Augustus' propaganda campaign address all classes of Romans equally?
4. How successfully did Augustus 'rebrand' himself after he assumed sole power?
5. What was the more effective propaganda tool: coinage, architecture or literature?
6. How important were the ludi saeculares to Augustus' public image?
7. How did Augustus present himself as a religious leader?
8. What played a more important role in Augustus' self-presentation during his reign: peace or war?
9. How similar was the presentation of Augustus' heirs to his own self-presentation?
10. How did Augustus' image in the provinces differ from his image in the city of Rome?

Further Reading

Bradley, P., *Ancient Rome Using Evidence* (Cambridge: Cambridge University Press, 1990), Section 19 (The Principate of Augustus) and Section 20 (The Forums of Rome in the Time of Augustus).

Clarke, M.D.H., *Augustus, First Roman Emperor: Power, Propaganda and the Politics of Survival* (Liverpool: Bristol Phoenix Press, 2010), Chapters 5–9.

Galinsky, K., *Augustan Culture: An Interpretive Introduction* (Princeton: Princeton University Press, 1998), Chapter 3: Ideas, Ideals and Values, Chapter 4: Art and Architecture and Chapter 5: Augustan Literature.

Levick, B., *Augustus: Image and Substance* (Abingdon: Routledge Press, 2013).

Martyndale-Howard, J., *Augustus: Caesar and God. Varying Images of the First Roman Emperor* (Nottingham: University of Nottingham, 2015).

Pollini, J., *From Republic to Empire: Rhetoric, Religon and Power in the Visual Culture of Ancient Rome* (Norman: University of Oklahoma Press, 2012), Chapter 4: From Warrior to Statesman in Art and Ideology and Chapter 5: The Ideology of 'Peace through Victory' and the Ara Pacis Augustae.

Thorpe, M., *Roman Architecture* (London: Bloomsbury, 2001).

Zanker, P., *The Power of Images in the Age of Augustus* (trans. A. Shapiro) (Ann Arbor: University of Michigan Press, 2014), Chapter 3: The Great Turning Point and Chapter 4: The Augustan Program of Cultural Renewal.

Source A: The Prima Porta statue of Augustus

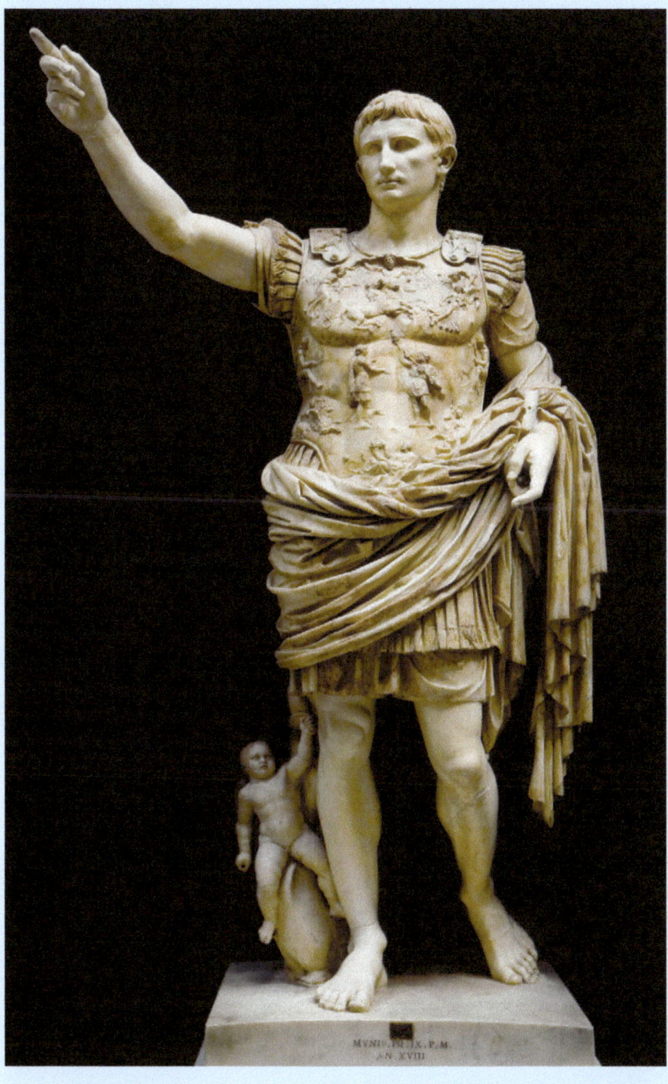

AS Level

1. How does this statue convey Augustus' authority? Make four points and support each with reference to the statue. [8]
2. Discuss how Augustus used the idea of peace throughout his official propaganda. Use the Prima Porta statue, Propertius' *Elegies* 3.4 *War and Peace* and your own knowledge. [16]

A level

1. What impression is given by this statue of Augustus? [10]

Source B: Propertius' *Elegies* **4.6 –** *The Temple of Palatine Apollo,* **lines 21–54**

The enemy fleet was doomed by Trojan Quirinus, and the shameful javelins fit for a woman's hand: there was Augustus' ship, sails filled by Jupiter's favour, standards now skilful in victory for their country. Now Nereus bent the formations in a twin arc, and the water trembled painted by the glitter of weapons, when Phoebus, quitting Delos, anchored under his protection (the isle, uniquely floating, it suffered the South Wind's anger), stood over Augustus' stern, and a strange flame shone, three times, snaking down in oblique fire.

Phoebus did not come with his hair streaming round his neck, or with the mild song of the tortoise-shell lyre, but with that aspect that gazed on Agamemnon, Pelop's son, and came out from the Dorian camp to the greedy fires, or as he destroyed the Python, writhing in its coils, the serpent that the peaceful Muses feared.

Then he spoke: 'O Augustus, world-deliverer, sprung from Alba Longa, acknowledged as greater than your Trojan ancestors conquer now by sea: the land is already yours: my bow is on your side, and every arrow burdening my quiver favours you. Free your country from fear, that relying on you as its protector, weights your prow with the State's prayers. Unless you defend her, Romulus misread the birds flying from the Palatine, he the augur of the foundation of Rome's walls. And they dare to come too near with their oars: shameful that Latium's waters should suffer a queen's sails while you are commander. Do not fear that their ships are winged with a hundred oars: their fleet rides an unwilling sea. Though their prows carry Centaurs with threatening stones, you'll find they are hollow timber and painted terrors. The cause exalts or breaks a soldier's strength: unless it is just, shame downs his weapons. The moment has come, commit your fleet: I declare the moment: I lead the Julian prows with laurelled hand.'

AS Level

3 a. To which battle does this poem refer? [1]
   b. In what year did this battle take place? [1]
   c. Why was this battle significant [1]
4. How does this poem convey the power of Rome's gods and their relationship with Augustus?
   Make four points and support each with reference to the text. [8]

A Level

2. How successfully does Propertius support Augustus and his regime in this poem? [10]
3. How similar was the public image that Augustus crafted for himself to the images that he crafted
   for his heirs? Justify your response with reference to both literature and visual/material culture. [30]

2.4 Augustus' Legacy

The Mausoleum of Augustus 

Date: opened to the public in 27 BC (construction complete in 23 BC)

Materials: brick walls, clad in white marble, large earthen mound, featuring two pink granite obelisks and surrounded by parkland

Dimensions: 90 metres in diameter, 42 metres high

Location: Rome, Campus Martius (between the river Tiber and the Via Flaminia)

Significance: Augustus' monumental final resting place

Augustus carefully managed his public image throughout his lifetime for a number of reasons. First, it enabled him to rise to power and, once that power had been attained, to keep it. He also managed his public image because he wanted to leave a lasting legacy so that future generations, ourselves included, would remember his life and reign in a particular way.

The sources considered in this topic were aimed, not only at Augustus' contemporaries, but toward all future generations. Bear this in mind when studying the sources in this topic. How did Augustus' message change when he was working to secure his legacy?

From as early as 28 BC Augustus had been considering the legacy he would leave on the face of the city of Rome. As discussed previously (see pp. 135–6) he began work on a monumental mausoleum for himself and his family before he had achieved sole power.

The Mausoleum of Augustus was built on a grand scale. It dwarfed even the most lavish funerary monuments that were in Rome at the time, and was even bigger than Mausolus' famous Mausoleum at Halicarnassus (one of the seven wonders of the ancient world and the monument which gave rise to the word 'mausoleum'). Such size was in-line with the majority of the architectural works in the Triumviral Period. What mattered at this time was being seen and heard by the masses. Large monuments made a big enough splash and were sure to get people talking.

Building a mausoleum of such epic proportions could also be interpreted as meaning that Octavian wanted to be viewed as a Hellenistic-style monarch. Massive funerary monuments were common in the Greek east in the Hellenistic period, particularly favoured by the Macedonian royal family. The tomb of Alexander the Great was almost certainly in this style. Such mausoleums were testaments to the power and wealth of rulers who were thought of as heroes: part man, part god.

A further interpretation is that a mausoleum of this size was intended merely to convey the idea of power and authority. Very few Romans had visited or even seen pictures of the tombs of Hellenistic kings – it is possible that Octavian was using a much more simple form of visual language: big = important.

The mausoleum itself stood forty-two metres high, topped with a bronze statue of Augustus himself. Sadly, this statue has been lost, so we cannot infer anything from its pose, but it must have shone like a beacon in the light of the sun and been visible for miles around. It contained multiple burial places, intended not only for Augustus himself but for members of his family and his closest friends.

Burials were not allowed within the city limits, and so the mausoleum was set back from the bustle of the city, surrounded by a public park. This would have given the monument an even greater sense of grandeur. Being separated from the rest of the city meant that it would not be dwarfed by nearby buildings. It also would have given the impression of a Classical Greek temple, which were always separated from the city, surrounded by a holy sanctuary. As the park was open to the public, the mausoleum complex itself could be seen as a gift to the city – yet another way in which Octavian's benevolence improved the lives of everyday Romans.

The position of the Mausoleum on the Campus Martius is also significant to understanding its message. In this position it was close to many other public buildings commissioned by Augustus and his supporters. For example, the Pantheon,

MODERN SCHOLARSHIP

The Mausoleum of Augustus was completed in 28 BC, several decades before his death . . . Given its size and complexity, work on the monument must have begun some years earlier, perhaps in 32 BC, with the tomb playing an important role in the final propaganda battle against Antony, leading up to the naval battle at Actium in 31 BC. By building such a massive tomb for himself at Rome, the young Caesar was eager to highlight the contrast between himself and Antony. Whereas he was demonstrating his commitment to the city, Antony's will (which Octavian illegally seized and made public) revealed that he wished to be buried at Alexandria with Cleopatra. Rumours suggested that he was even contemplating shifting the capital away from Rome to Egypt.

A.E. Cooley, *Res Gestae Divi Augusti: Text, Translation, and Commentary*

Here A.E. Cooley links the building of the Mausoleum with the power struggle between Octavian and Antony. She theorises that it was used to highlight policy differences between Octavian and Antony and that it was intended to highlight his commitment to Rome. If this interpretation is to be believed, then the Mausoleum cannot simply be understood in terms of Augustus' legacy-management, but was instrumental in crafting his public image in his early career as well.

commissioned by Agrippa, was on the Campus Martius. The Forum of Augustus was built on the Campus Martius, as was the Ara Pacis. Also here was an enormous red granite obelisk that had been brought to Rome from Egypt. The shadow cast by this structure combined with the other buildings of the area to create a monumental sundial.

When considering the Mausoleum of Augustus it is important to note that the design was settled and construction began before Antony had been defeated. As such it is typical of the Triumviral Period. The extent to which it represents the lasting impression Augustus wanted to have in his later years is debatable.

Augustus composed an **elogium** for himself, known as the *Res Gestae Divi Augusti* (The Deeds of the Divine Augustus). The text refers to events from the final years of Augustus' life, and claims that at the time of writing the author was seventy-six years old. Assuming this is true, the *Res Gestae* was written in the last year of Augustus' life. As such, we can safely assume that it reflects the intentions and desired messages of the aged princeps, concerned with preserving his legacy.

When Augustus died, the Vestal Virgins revealed that he had left several documents in their care. Among these was his will, which requested that a full account of his achievements be inscribed onto colossal bronze pillars and displayed outside his mausoleum: the *Res Gestae*.

It was not unusual for a Roman nobleman to commission an elogium on their death, to commemorate themselves and their deeds. As such, there is nothing unusual about Augustus' request for an inscription. What was unusual was the length of the text. The

PRESCRIBED SOURCE

Res Gestae

Author: Augustus

Date: AD 13

Significance: autobiographical account of Augustus' life and achievements

Read it here: OCR source book.

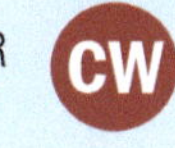

FIGURE 2.36

The Mausoleum of Augustus survives today. Over time some of the walls have crumbled away and the domed roof has degraded. The city of Rome has also encroached on the monument, which no longer sits in the centre of a public park.

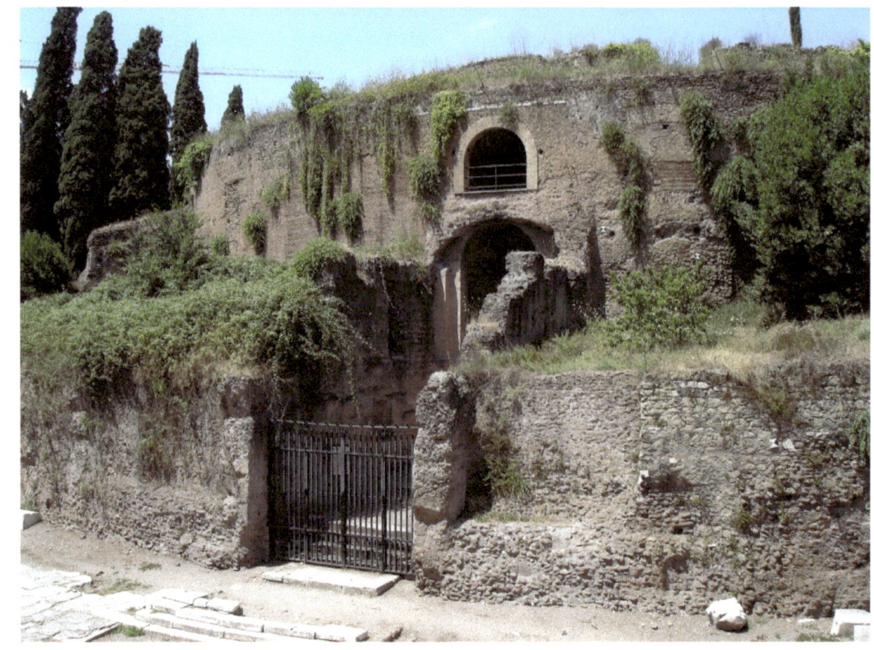

FIGURE 2.37

An artist's impression of the Mausoleum of Augustus, as it would have appeared when it was built.

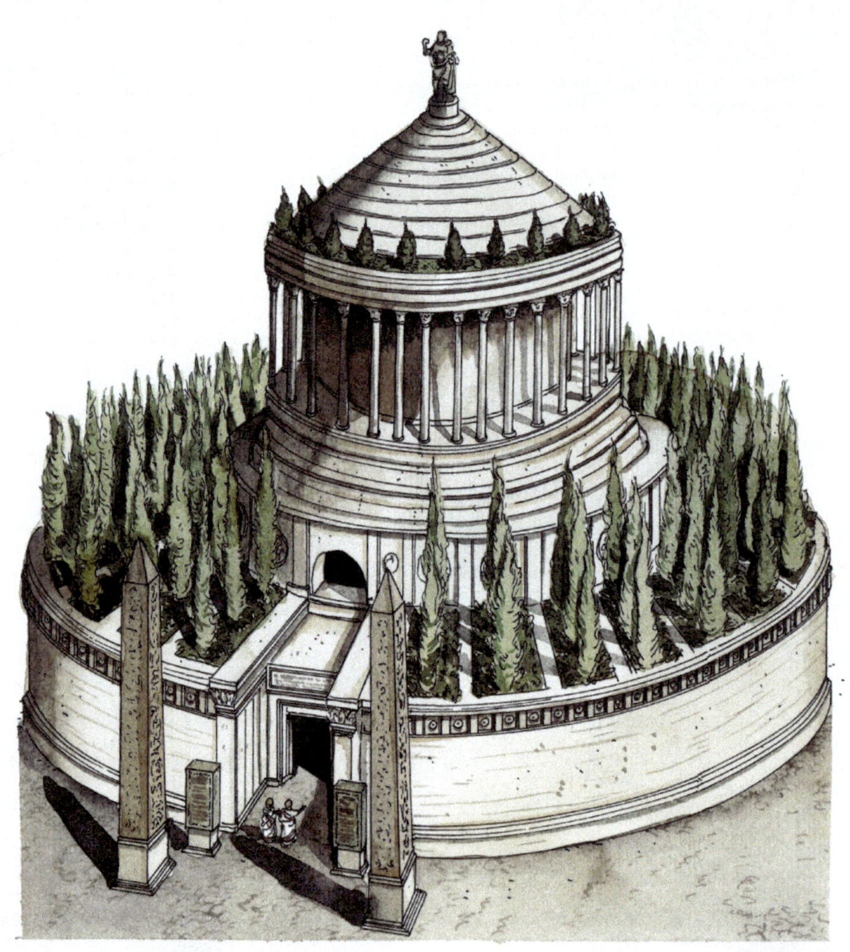

Res Gestae is almost 2,500 words in length, by far the longest funerary inscription we have from this period. This could hint at a certain immodesty on Augustus' part, but one could equally argue that his elogium was so long because he was the only Roman to amass so many achievements in his lifetime.

The text of the *Res Gestae* is somewhat unusual, however, because it focuses almost exclusively on the life and achievements of the deceased (Augustus) and spends no time at all detailing the history of his family and the achievements of his ancestors. In Roman society, which revered ancestors, it was customary for at least a portion of the funerary inscription to be spent on these matters. Augustus gives no mention to his birth family at all and only mentions Julius Caesar by name twice, both times in reference to Julius the god, not the man. Where he refers to Julius Caesar the man, he refrains from using his name and refers to him as 'my father' (*Res Gestae* 1).

Augustus seems to have addressed the *Res Gestae* to the people of Rome, rather than to the people of the Empire more generally. Where he details public works or gifts made to the common people, he exclusively mentions those that took place in the city of Rome. We have good evidence that similar projects were undertaken at various places throughout the Empire, but they are left out of the official account of his achievements. Despite this fact, the text of the *Res Gestae* was reproduced and displayed throughout the Empire after Augustus' death, most often in provincial temples of Rome and Augustus. Indeed, the version of the text that survives to modernity was preserved as an inscription at the Temple of Augustus and Rome in Ankara, (in modern Turkey). The bronze pillars which originally bore the inscription and stood outside the mausoleum were sadly destroyed in antiquity.

Augustus' written style is remarkably succinct and straightforward. Far from the poetic language of his client writers such as Horace and Propertius, Augustus himself chose to write his autobiography with very few adjectives or superfluous words. This is probably because he knew that it would be inscribed. In this medium, every word would have been difficult (and expensive) to carve, so he could have been writing to his medium. It is equally possible that this straightforward style was just how Augustus wrote. He was well known for his dislike of the Asiatic school of oratory – defined by exaggeration, embellishment and unnecessary verbal adornment. Augustus' economical writing style here could be a matter of personal preference. Incidentally, Antony had been well known for his love of the Asiatic style.

The introduction to the *Res Gestae* makes reference to the 'deeds of the divine Augustus'. This reflects a decree made by the Senate in AD 14 shortly after Augustus' death which proclaimed him a god. It is highly unlikely that this phrase was penned by Augustus himself.

It is interesting to note who Augustus deigns to name in the text of the *Res Gestae*. As Brunt and Moore go on to say after the quote on p. 191, in the story of Augustus' rise to power, many prominent players are referred to obliquely:

> At the age of nineteen, on my own initiative, and at my own expense, I raised an army, by way of which I liberated the Republic, which was being tyrannised by a faction.

> *Res Gestae* 1

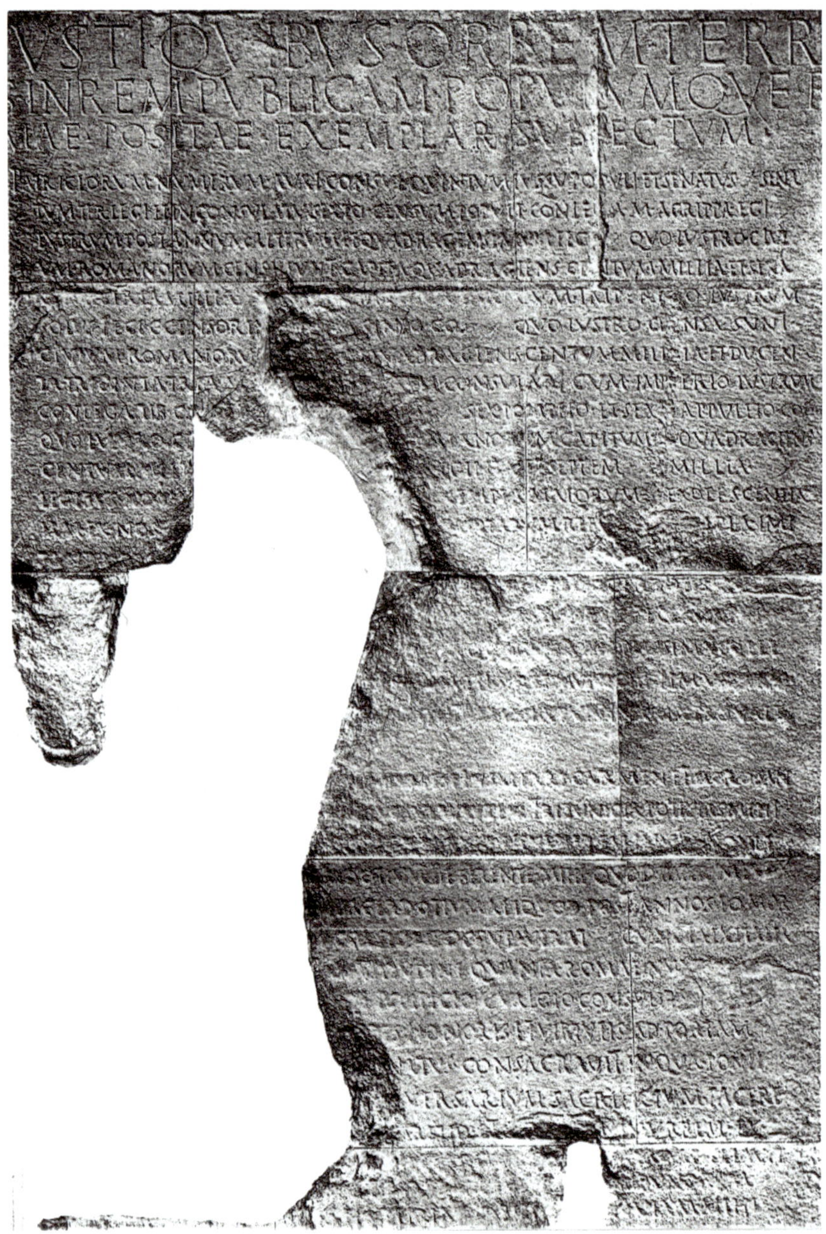

The 'faction' Augustus refers to was Mark Antony and his supporters, whom Octavian had fought against at Mutina with the help of the consuls Hirtius and Pansa (see p. 119). Later in the *Res Gestae*, Augustus refers to his civil war against Antony as 'the war that I won at Actium'. Refusal to name Antony is consistent with Augustus' earlier propaganda and served to encourage the people to forget that this had been a civil war that had cost many Romans their lives.

> I drove into exile those men who had murdered my father.
>
> *Res Gestae* 2

The reliability of Roman *elogia* is disputed. Brunt and Moore argue that funerary inscriptions like the *Res Gestae*, are not likely to contain outright lies. The authors may decide to include or omit certain things to show themselves in the best possible light, or to slightly exaggerate, but they would likely be caught out if they lied outright. Think of funerary inscriptions as a kind of resume or personal statement. The authors wanted to present the very best possible version of themselves for posterity to judge them by. This presentation would be ruined if they were caught in a lie.

Here Augustus refers to Julius Caesar's assassins, led by Brutus and Cassius. By refusing to name them Augustus encourages the reader to forget that they were senators, making it easier to view them simply as assassins. Similarly, by referring to Julius Caesar as 'father' and not using his name, Augustus perhaps encourages the reader to gloss over Julius Caesar's controversial dictatorship and the probable reasons for his assassination.

Augustus' treatment of Sextus Pompeius is less straightforward. He mentions Sextus Pompeius by name in reference to the year of his consulship. However, when referring to the military campaign against him, he refers to Sextus Pompeius and his followers simply as 'pirates' (*Res Gestae* 8; *Res Gestae* 25).

Augustus' accounts of his civil wars are brief and never acknowledge that the wars were, in fact, civil. His accounts of foreign campaigns, on the other hand, are extensive and stress the benefits that these campaigns brought to the Roman people.

When referring to Tiberius' diplomatic mission to Parthia he does not go so far as to claim that it had been a military victory, but his choice of the word 'compelled' when referring to the negotiations does seem to imply the threat or use of force (*Res Gestae* 29). Bearing in mind the fact that many Romans wanted the Parthians to be punished, it seems as though Augustus wanted this episode to be remembered as a humiliating defeat for the Parthians.

Despite the fact that much of the *Res Gestae* is concerned with Augustus' military victories, overall it does not give the impression that Augustus' lifetime was dominated by war and conflict. Indeed, he makes reference to the symbolic closure of Janus' temple in Rome to emphasise the theme of peace:

It was the wish of our ancestors that Janus Quirinus should be closed when there was peace, on both land and sea, throughout the whole of the empire of the Roman people. Before my birth, it had been closed twice in all recorded memory, from the foundation of the city; while I was first citizen, the Senate voted three times that it should be closed.

Res Gestae 13

Augustus' generosity is heavily stressed, in terms of gifts made to the Roman people, buildings he commissioned and games he subsidised:

Four times I helped the treasury with my own money, so that I transferred to those who ran the treasury one hundred and fifty million sesterces.

Res Gestae 17

I rebuilt the Capitol and the Theatre of Pompey, both works at great expense without inscribing my name on either of them.

Res Gestae 20

Three times, in my own name, I gave gladiatorial shows and five times in the name of my sons and grandsons; about ten thousand men fought in these shows.

Res Gestae 22

Throughout the *Res Gestae* Augustus is careful to make frequent reference to the Senate and magistrates. This reinforced his image as a champion of the Republic, who held offices only at the request of the Senate. Indeed, at one point he states outright that all his powers were based on the precedents set by the present generation's ancestors:

I received no magistracies that were not in keeping with the customs of our ancestors. What the senate wished me to do, I carried out through tribunician power. Five times I myself asked for, and accepted, from the senate a colleague in that power.

Res Gestae 6

The *Res Gestae* ends with an explanation of two of his most important titles: Augustus and Pater Patriae. The importance of these titles is emphasised by this prominent positioning, and by the extended explanation of how these titles were conferred upon him, and how they were displayed to the public:

For my service, by senatorial decree, I was named Augustus, and the doors of my house were publicly clothed in laurel, and a civic crown was fixed over my door and a golden shield was put in the Curia Julia.

Res Gestae 34

In my thirteenth consulship, the senate and the equestrian order and the whole people of Rome gave me the title of pater patriae (Father of the Country) and this was inscribed in the entrance hall of my house and in the Curia Julia and in the Forum of Augustus.

Res Gestae 35

AUGUSTUS' DEATH AND THE AFTERMATH

Augustus died on 19 August AD 14. Because his power and position within Roman government was unprecedented, there was no legal or constitutional precedent for what happened next. Over the previous three decades, the Senate had grown used to diminished power and few were prepared to take on the mantle of governing without a new Augustus figure as the princeps. This fact speaks volumes about the way Augustus had been perceived in his lifetime. He had made himself and the role of princeps seem totally necessary to the continued success of the Roman state. Rome would never again revert to being a true republic.

Augustus' stepson Tiberius had been adopted in AD 4 as Augustus' private heir. This, combined with various steps Augustus had taken (see pp. 171–3) to encourage people to view Tiberius as his successor, convinced the army and the Senate to confer the Principate to him. Tiberius was the first man to be formally recognised as the 'Emperor' of Rome, a title that all his successors would hold.

Shortly after his death, Augustus was declared a god. Like the deified Julius Caesar, he was associated with Italy, fertility and Rome herself. His wife Livia outlived him by several years and she too was deified after her death. The divine Livia, sometimes referred to as Augusta, was worshiped as a patron of marriages – perhaps due to her famously long marriage to Augustus himself.

TOPIC REVIEW

These questions should draw on your knowledge of the whole topic, so think carefully about the different things you have learned (check the Topic Overview on p. 185).

1. What impression is given by the Mausoleum of Augustus?
2. Explain why a Hellenistic-style mausoleum might have been problematic for Augustus' public image.
3. Why was the Mausoleum of Augustus set in acres of public parkland?
4. What aspects of Augustus' life are emphasised the most by the *Res Gestae*?
5. From your reading of the *Res Gestae* and your knowledge of Augustus' life, do you notice anything that Augustus chose not to include in his elogium?

Further Reading

Cooley, A.E., *Res Gestae Divi Augusti* (Cambridge: Cambridge University Press, 2009).
Davies, P.E.J., *Death and the Emperor: Roman Imperial Funerary Monuments from Augustus to Marcus Aurelius* (Austin: University of Texas Press, 2004).

PRACTICE QUESTIONS

Source A: Sections 34–5 of the *Res Gestae*

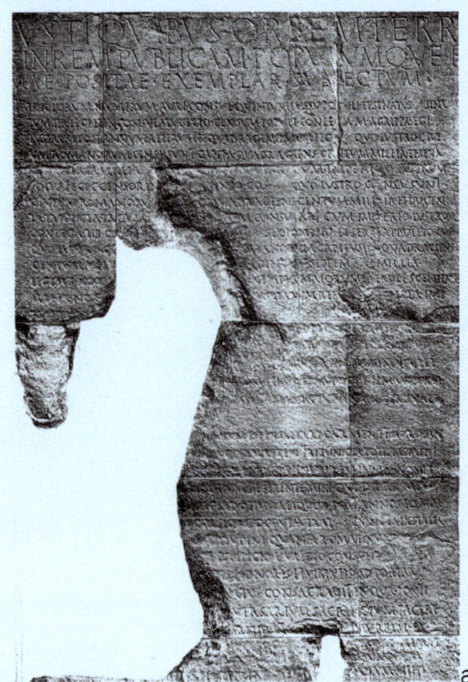

34. In my sixth and seventh consulships, after I had extinguished civil wars, after by universal consent, I was in control of all affairs, I transferred the republic from my power to the control of the senate and the Roman people. For my service, by senatorial decree, I was named Augustus, and the doors of my house were publicly clothed in laurel, and a civic crown was fixed over my door and a golden shield was put in the Curia Julia, which was given to me by the senate and the people of Rome for my courage, clemency, justice and piety, as attested by this inscription. After that time, I surpassed all in influence, although I had no more power than those who were my colleagues in the magistracies.

35. In my thirteenth consulship, the Senate and the equestrian order and the whole people of Rome gave me the title of pater patriae (Father of the Country) and this was to be inscribed in the entrance hall of my house and in the Curia Julia and in the Forum of Augustus below the chariot which had been put there in my honour by senatorial decree. When this was written, I was seventy six years of age.

AS Level

1 a. Who was the author of the *Res Gestae*? [1]
   b. Where was the text of the *Res Gestae* first publicly displayed? [1]
2. What sort of legacy did Augustus leave for us to remember him by? [25]

A Level

1. How does Source A make Augustus seem like a conservative rather than a social reformer? [10]
2. What is the most significant difference between the image of Augustus in the *Res Gestae* and the image that Augustus cultivated throughout his lifetime? Justify your response with reference to a range of ancient sources. [30]

2.5 Later Representations

TOPIC OVERVIEW

The effectiveness of Augustus' self-presentation in creating an imperial image that lasted beyond his life-time through an examination of later sources, including:

- selections from Suetonius' *Lives of the Twelve Caesars*
- the Sebasteion at Aphrodisias

The following prescribed sources are covered in this topic:
Suetonius, *The Lives of the Twelve Caesars: Augustus* : 7–11, 17, 20–2, 26, 28–9, 31, 34, 53, 56–8, 64–5, 68–71, 95
The Sebasteion at Aphrodisias

Don't forget that you will be given credit in the exam if you study extra sources and make relevant use of them in your answers.

In the years since his death in AD 14 Augustus has continued to inspire great works of art and literature. Historians and biographers have been drawn to him as an example of a man whose impact on the world was nigh unparalleled and politicians have looked to him as a model for their own careers and public images. But how has his image changed since his own lifetime? Was Augustus able to craft a public image for himself that endured beyond his own lifetime? If so, how? And if not, why not?

This final topic will explore these questions with reference to a tiny selection of the available later representations, two of which are prescribed sources for this unit.

Each individual looking back on Augustus has brought their own unique viewpoint on the man and his achievements, and this impacted the representations they produced. Each had a particular agenda and was influenced not only by what Augustus did and how he presented himself while he was alive, but by what happened under subsequent emperors as well. The behaviour of Augustus' successors reflects onto Augustus, as he is credited with having established the principate and set the precedent for one-man-rule.

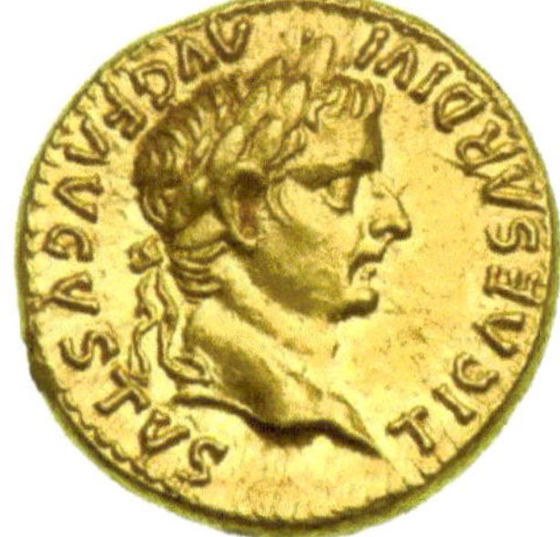

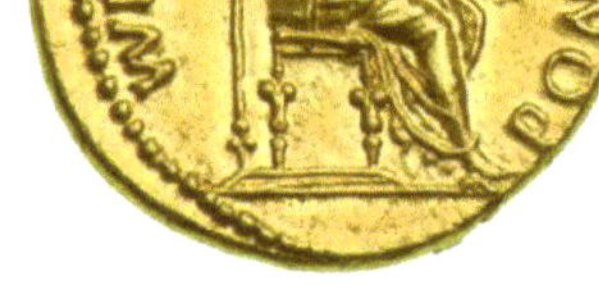

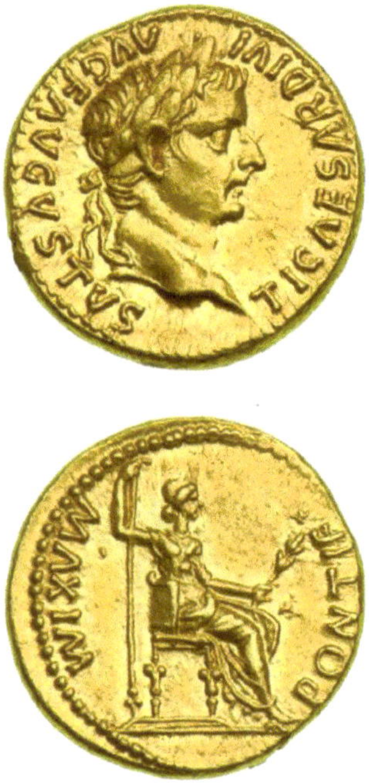

FIGURE 2.39
Aureus of Tiberius.

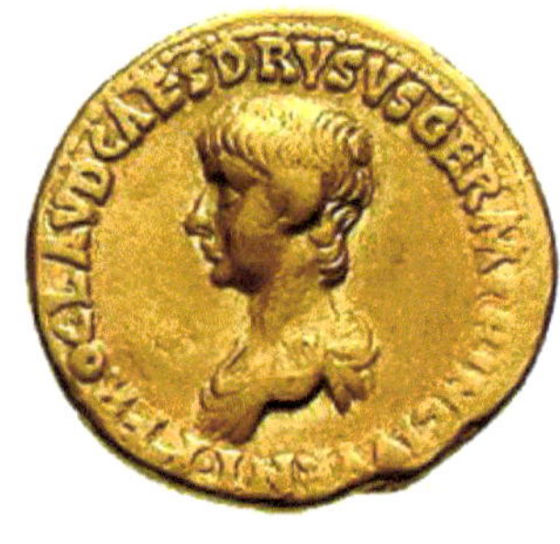

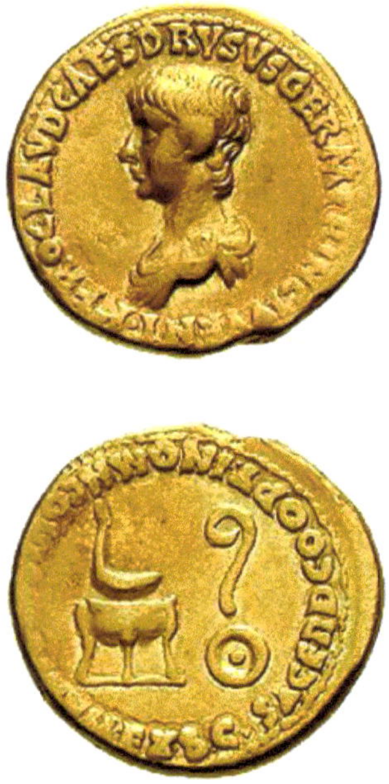

FIGURE 2.40
Aureus of Nero.

S & C

The legacy of Augustus' instigation of sole rule

The four emperors who followed Augustus were members of his family and looking at their reigns can show how the legacy he gave Rome of hereditary rule could be good and bad.

Augustus' son Tiberius' reign (AD 14–37) was characterised by relative stability and peace throughout the Empire. He saved money to leave the state in a strong position and he did not commission many expensive building projects. Augustus must have been a difficult act to follow. Tiberius did not try to compete with his predecessor, but historians generally agree that he governed well. His rule could be said to show how hereditary power could be stable and successful.

Caligula's reign (AD 37–41) was a stark contrast. He lasted only four years before he was assassinated by his own guard. Caligula had a reputation for cruelty and even madness. Under Caligula, Rome experienced the crushing downside of Augustus' legacy of hereditary rule. He practically bankrupted the state by throwing lavish games and took over temples to expand his own palace.

Research the reigns of the final two Julio-Claudians, Claudius and Nero, to see whether they can be said to show the benefits or problems with Augustus' legacy of hereditary rule.

USING AUGUSTUS' IMAGE

Augustus' own style influenced the way in which his successors chose to portray themselves. For example, Figure 2.39 follows Augustus' model quite closely. The portrait image of the ruler with a laurel wreath and very Augustan hairstyle is on the obverse, and the reverse shows a figure, identified as Livia, holding the symbols of Pax. Both in terms of the aesthetic and the messaging, Tiberius' image was clearly informed by Augustus'.

Similarly Figure 2.40, struck nearly forty years after the death of Augustus, bears a striking resemblance to his coinage. The priestly symbols on the reverse are copied directly from Augustus' own coinage. Nero publicly promised to model his own reign on Augustus'. It seems as though Nero made direct visual references to Augustus' coinage to emphasise this aspect of his own public image.

The reason for this influence is unclear. Perhaps Tiberius wanted to stress the link between himself and Augustus to legitimise his rule. Perhaps Augustus, as the first princeps, had become synonymous with power and authority and Tiberius wanted to tap into this feeling.

The period of the Julio-Claudian emperors also saw several depictions of Augustus himself. One of the best preserved is a temple complex dedicated to Venus and to the Divine Augustus known as the Sebasteion at Aphrodisias (in modern day Turkey). The Sebasteion (sometimes referred to as the Augusteum) was started during the reign of Tiberius, at which point Augustus had already been declared a god. The temple complex was paid for by local nobility, so it is likely that it was intended to be a declaration of loyalty to Rome and her leaders, as well as a site for religious devotion.

The southern portico of the temple complex has been restored (see Figure 2.41) and so we can appreciate the type and scale of sculptural decoration that was included in this building. A total of 190 relief panels would have adorned the building originally, some seventy of which survive to us today. The subject of the panels varies massively, from images of the gods, to mythological heroes, to representations of the Julio-Claudian emperors themselves.

The gate of the structure featured two panels, one depicting Aeneas, the other Venus (in her capacity as progenitor of the Julian line). Many panels celebrate the victories of Rome over foreign people, usually depicting a heroic emperor standing dominant over personifications of the defeated places and people.

A similar impression is created by the panel in Figure 2.42, which depicts Augustus stood (left) opposite the winged goddess of victory, Nike (right). Between them stands a trophy, the plundered armour of a fallen enemy and to the bottom of the composition sit a captive soldier and a Roman eagle. Much of the symbolism is very similar to the art of Augustus' reign.

Other shifts in Augustus' presentation following his death certainly did occur. A clear change is his divinity. During Augustus' lifetime, he did not want to be seen to be encouraging others to portray him as a god. Although he associated himself with many gods and encouraged the idea that he was descended from the gods, he was usually only ever directly depicted as a mortal. After his death and deification, however, he was officially

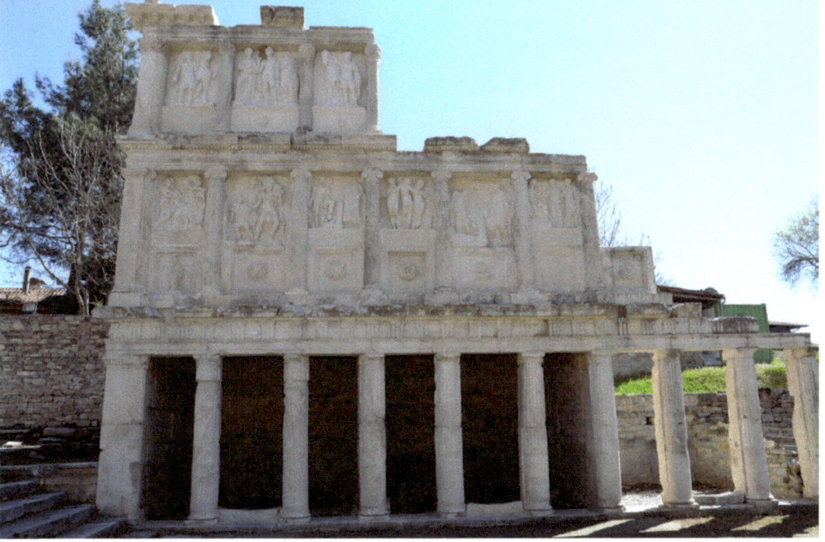

FIGURE 2.41
Restored southern portico. The relief panels here are replicas; the originals are housed in the Aphrodisias Museum.

FIGURE 2.42
Augustus, Nike, trophy and captive.

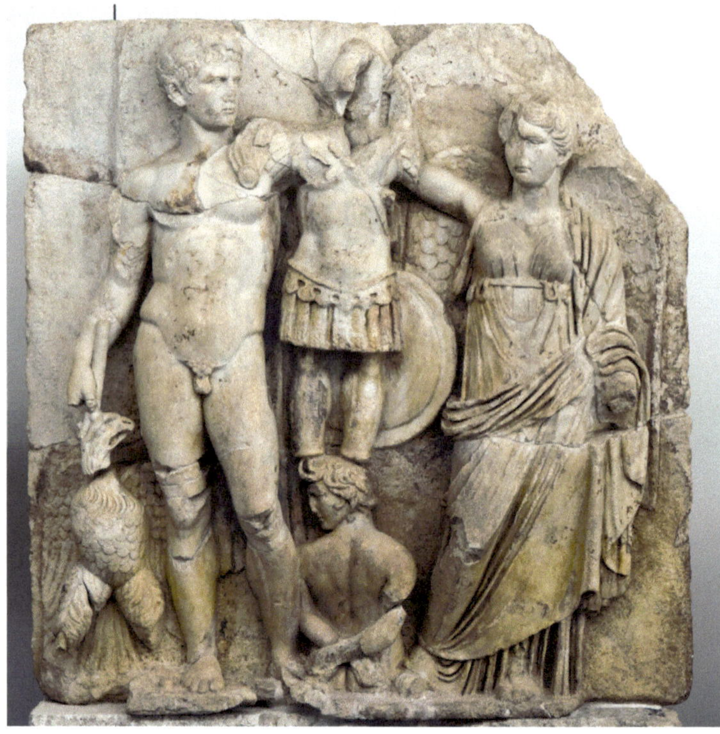

elevated to the status of a god and his depictions often reflected this. For example, this cameo portrait, produced *c.* AD 41–54, depicts Augustus wearing Jupiter's aegis. Jupiter's aegis (a goatskin cloak featuring the face of the gorgon Medusa) was a symbol of his divine authority. The earliest example of literature in the Western canon, Homer's *Iliad*, includes reference to the divine power of the aegis. By depicting Augustus wearing this, it is clear that he was intended to be viewed as Augustus the god, not Augustus the man.

FIGURE 2.43
Sardonyx cameo portrait of Augustus the god.

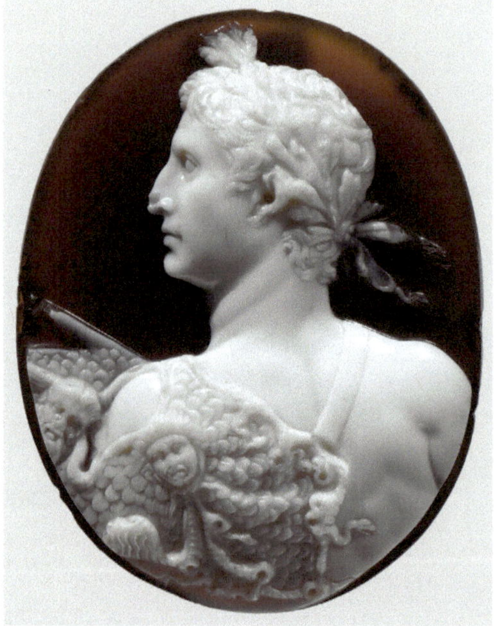

WRITING ABOUT AUGUSTUS: SUETONIUS

Gaius Suetonius Tranquillus (usually referred to as Suetonius) wrote a series of biographies of the Caesars, beginning with Julius Caesar and finishing with Domitian. It became customary for Roman emperors to call themselves 'Caesar', a name which became synonymous with the ruler of Rome. Published in AD 121 in the reign of Hadrian, Suetonius did not have to fear reprisal if he wrote critical things about Augustus. Hadrian was not related to Augustus, and he even competed with Augustus in some ways (for example his own mausoleum was based on Augustus' but slightly bigger). So we can be fairly sure that Suetonius is writing candidly.

Suetonius was a biographer. He based his work on a range of public documents, letters and biographies, but he also used unsubstantiated gossip and hearsay. He loved a good scandalous anecdote, and his biographies contain many of these. That said, Suetonius was not the first to write a biography of Augustus or a history of the period, so he would not have been free to invent whatever he wanted. If he had, then his audience surely would have questioned the accuracy of his account.

Suetonius' work should not be treated as objective fact. As with all other prescribed sources, he merely presents to the reader his own *version* of Augustus. By studying Suetonius' work, we can get an understanding of how Augustus' public image had changed in the century between his death and the publication of Suetonius' work.

When discussing Augustus' time as princeps, Suetonius says he 'ruled the State'. The use of the word 'rule' is significant, since it suggests that Suetonius believed that Augustus played the role of a king or an emperor, not a champion and restorer of the Republic. Suetonius revisits this idea later in his work when he explicitly states that Augustus had considered restoring the Republic, but eventually decided against this move:

> On reflecting, however, that both his own life and the security of the State might be jeopardised, if authority were divided, he decided to retain power in his own hands.
>
> Suetonius, *Life of Augustus* 28

Clearly Suetonius does not believe that Octavian restored the Republic in 27 BC. Perhaps this scepticism was brought about by Suetonius' knowledge that, after Augustus' death, Rome would continue to be ruled by Emperors in a more or less hereditary line. Regardless of the reasoning, Suetonius' account is in stark contrast with Augustus' own propaganda. Suetonius does mention how Augustus campaigned, voted and spoke in the law courts like any other politician, but his conclusion is clear: Augustus was the ruler of Rome, not its princeps (*LOA* 56).

A reasonable portion of Suetonius' account of Augustus' life is focused on his military achievements. The first campaign to be mentioned is his campaign in Mutina alongside Hirtius and Pansa. Suetonius condemns the young Octavian's behaviour as much as he praises it:

> Augustus completed the military task entrusted to him in three months, fighting two major battles. Antony claimed that Augustus took to flight in the first of these, and did not reappear till the following day, lacking his horse and cloak. But all agree that in the following encounter, Augustus not only led his troops, but played the solder's part.
>
> Suetonius, *Life of Augustus* 10

The fact that the source for the account of Octavian's retreat is attributed to Antony invites the reader to question whether it actually happened or not. But if Suetonius had wanted to present a version of Octavian who was a strong and capable military leader, he surely would have left this detail out of his account.

Augustus' decisive battle against Mark Antony at Actium is referred to as a 'great naval victory' (*LOA* 18). This phrase seems to be in accordance with Augustus' propaganda version of the battle, as it indicates both scale and significance.

Suetonius' account of Actium makes no mention of Agrippa's role, letting Augustus take the role of victorious general. He does, however, state that most of Augustus' foreign campaigns were not led by him personally but rather through his generals. The comment that 'Augustus commanded in person in only two foreign campaigns' seems somewhat damning of his military achievements (*LOA* 20). Contrary to this, Suetonius mentions that Augustus was personally involved in the fighting in his Dalmatian campaign and that he visited the front during the campaigns in Pannonia and Germany (*LOA* 20). These inclusions would seem to paint Augustus as a capable leader, willing to put himself in danger alongside his men.

Suetonius does not shrink from calling Augustus' wars against Romans 'civil conflicts', making reference to five separate instances: Mutina in 43 BC (against Mark Antony), Philippi in 42 BC (against Julius Caesar's assassins), Perusia in 41–40 BC (against Mark Antony's brother Lucius Antonius), Sicily in 36 BC (against Sextus Pompeius), and Actium in 31 BC (against Mark Antony) (*LOA* 9). These conflicts are listed, one after the other, serving to highlight the sheer number of battles Augustus fought against his fellow Romans. Suetonius offers an immediate apology after this list, however, stating 'The motivation for all this warfare was that Augustus considered it his duty to avenge Caesar's death, and enforce his decrees' (*LOA* 10).

Augustus' moral legislation is mentioned, and Suetonius' account gives the impression that these policies were unpopular with the people and difficult to enforce:

> He both revised existing laws and enacted new ones . . . to encourage marriage and procreation among the Senatorial and Equestrian orders. He was unable to bring the last of these, which aroused open rebellion against its overly stringent provisions, into effect until he had removed or softened many of its clauses.
>
> Suetonius, *Life of Augustus* 34

This anecdote paints Augustus as an ineffectual leader in terms of social reform, and invites the reader to question whether he was able to direct the behavior of his citizens effectively. Suetonius revisits this idea later in his work when he relates the stories of Julia the Elder and Julia the Younger's respective exiles (*LOA* 65).

Augustus' clemency and respect for religious tradition is conveyed when Suetonius remarks:

> Not wishing to deprive Lepidus of the Chief Priesthood during his lifetime, despite his exile, Augustus waited until the triumvir's death (in 13 BC), to assume the office.
>
> Suetonius, *Life of Augustus* 31

This simultaneously reminds the reader of Lepidus' coup and Augustus' subsequent decision to exile rather than execute his former ally, and also of his significant religious role as Pontifex Maximus. Suetonius goes on to catalogue many of Augustus' accomplishments in the service of Roman religion, including reviving ancient rites, preventing corruption in the selection of Vestal Virgins and restoring temple buildings (*LOA* 31). This section of the *Life of Augustus* seems to be resoundingly positive.

Augustus' admirable qualities are highlighted again by Suetonius with particular emphasis on his reasonableness. He mentions how he adjusted the scale of his planned forum because he did not want to evict the neighbouring residents (*LOA* 56). Similarly, Suetonius reports that Augustus was in the habit of leaving towns and cities at night-time so as to avoid 'troubling everyone with formal ceremony' (*LOA* 53). This paints a picture of a humble princeps, almost embarrassed by his own celebrity.

Suetonius' *Life of Augustus* is peppered with scandalous anecdotes concerning Augustus' behaviour. Suetonius explicitly calls some of these rumours, bringing their reliability into question. For example, the rumour that the young Octavian had arranged for the consuls Hirtius and Pansa to be killed is presented as a rumour (*LOA* 11). Similarly, Suetonius relates a charge made by Mark Antony that Octavian had 'unnatural relations with Julius Caesar as the price of his adoption' (*LOA* 65). The fact that this accusation is attributed to Mark Antony invites the reader to question whether it is true or false. Still, the mere mention of this rumour could be enough to besmirch Augustus' reputation. Other scandals are reported as fact. For example, his own adulteries were apparently so well-known that 'not even his friends denied he was given to adulterous behaviour' (*LOA* 69).

MODERN SCHOLARSHIP

One of the major problems identified by Dieter Flach in his useful critical study of Suet[onius] is that of generalisation, that is, the extrapolation from one specific instance to a repeated action, which is tempting for the biographer who wants to demonstrate character through habitual actions, but which results in exaggeration. This can be done through the use of plurals or verbs in the imperfect or the usual perfect tenses modified by an adverb indicating frequency.

D. Wardle, *Suetonius: Life of Augustus*, p. 28

Wardle here comments on an aspect of Suetonius' writing style that has bearing on his presentation of Augustus. By making statements that imply the frequency or regularity of a certain action, he encourages the reader to make character judgements about his subject based on these. In actual fact, Augustus may only have engaged in a particular action once or twice, but Suetonius can imply that it was much more frequent – thus colouring the reader's interpretations.

Tacitus

Tacitus was a Roman historian who published his work under the Flavian emperor Trajan. He was a successful senator and held the consulship in AD 97. Following this he began a literary career. Probably his most famous work, the *Annals* is a historical work charting the history of Rome from the time of Tiberius' accession to power until Nero's death. Tacitus was anything but an impartial, detached historian and his account is full of biting invective and criticism of the Principate as an institution and of individual rulers. He did not agree with a system which put so much power in the hands of individuals. This, combined with his low opinion of Tiberius, Caligula and Nero certainly biased him against Augustus as the one who established the Principate. Read Tacitus' *Annals* 1.1–15 for a brief account of Augustus' accession to power and an account of his death and the succession. How does Tacitus present Augustus? How have Augustus' successors impacted the way that Tacitus sees him?

Younger Seneca

The Younger Seneca, philosopher and advisor to the emperor Nero, wrote an essay on the subject of clemency, which sought to flatter Nero by implying that he possessed the virtue of clemency in greater amounts than Augustus. The essay points out that Augustus was mild and not quick to anger when he was in power, but that as a young man he had been ruthless and violent. Read the Younger Seneca's *On Clemency* 1.9–11. How does he portray Augustus' character, in particular his virtues? How do you think his writing was influenced by the purpose of his essay?

AUGUSTUS IN THE MODERN AGE

Augustus (called Octavius) is a dominant supporting character in Shakespeare's tragic romance *Antony and Cleopatra*. The play focuses on the love affair of Antony and Cleopatra, played against the backdrop of the breakdown of the Second Triumvirate and civil war. Antony's disdain for Octavius is clear throughout the play and he is discussed several times, although he appears on stage infrequently. He challenges Antony to meet him at sea and it is this that leads to the Battle of Actium, a departure from the real sequence of events. Octavius has the last lines of the play, which bemoan the fact that Antony and Cleopatra have killed themselves and claims that no lovers will ever be as famous as they. He is magnanimous in victory, despite the fact that Cleopatra defied his wishes in killing herself.

Robert Graves' novel *I, Claudius* is a novel in the form of an autobiography. Loosely based on Suetonius' *Life of Augustus*, the narrator of *I, Claudius* is the Julio-Claudian emperor Claudius, who looks back on his life before becoming emperor. His story covers the reigns of the emperors who preceded him, including Augustus'. This book was turned into a television series by the BBC, with the role of Augustus played by Brian Blessed. *I, Claudius* focuses on palace intrigue. Livia, portrayed by Sian Phillips, schemes to have her son Tiberius adopted as Augustus' heir and succeed him to the throne. In this version of Augustus' life, he is depicted as a strong leader, but unable to control his own family. Tiberius disobeys him by having an affair with his ex-wife Vipsania. Julia disobeys him by openly having numerous affairs. In the end, this inability to control his own family is his downfall, as he is poisoned and killed by Livia.

An interesting twist on the *Res Gestae*, Alan Massie published a historical novel in 1986 which claimed to be the autobiography of Augustus. The novel is split into two sections. For the first the narrator is Augustus in his middle age, speaking in a triumphant tone, almost gloating over the defeat of his enemies in the triumviral period. The second section is also narrated by Augustus, but towards the end of his life. The tone here is more subdued, Augustus clearly having been badly affected by the deaths of his grandsons and he reflects on the achievements of his life, as well as his hopes and fears for Rome after his death. A sensitively drawn portrait of Augustus emerges in this work, which emphasises change over his tenure as princeps.

Still another view of Augustus is given by Neil Gaiman, who devoted an issue of his *Sandman* comic series to him. This issue, entitled *August*, sees Augustus disguise himself so that he can go about the streets of Rome unrecognised. He walks through the streets with a dwarf companion named Lycius, talking about his life and achievements. Gaiman's Augustus shows obvious piety towards the gods and respect for the idea of Rome itself and he recognises that he is personally responsible for the deaths of countless people – all in service to Rome. He also reveals that he believed his entire life had been laid out by Julius Caesar and that he is now afraid of Julius the god. Gaiman's Augustus is commanding and self-assured, but at the same time Gaiman shows us his vulnerability and mortality.

TOPIC REVIEW

These questions should draw on your knowledge of the whole topic, so think carefully about the different things you have learned (check the Topic Overview on p. 195).

1. You have seen how later emperors made use of Augustan iconography. What does this say about the effectiveness of Augustus' use of iconography in his lifetime?
2. How did images of Augustus change in the century following his death? What stayed the same?
3. How close is Suetonius' version of Augustus' life to the version that Augustus presented during his own lifetime? What does this imply about the effectiveness of Augustus' propaganda campaign?

Further Reading

Southern, P., *Augustus* (2nd edn) (Abingdon: Routledge Press, 2014), Chapter 9: The Legacy.

Thommen, G., *The Sebasteion at Aphrodisias: An Imperial Cult to Honor Augustus and the Julio-Claudian Emperors* (Chronika: Institute for European and Mediterranean Archaeology, 2012).

Wardle, D., *Suetonius: Life of Augustus* (Oxford: Oxford University Press, 2014).

Source A: Augustus panel from the Sebasteion at Aphrodisias

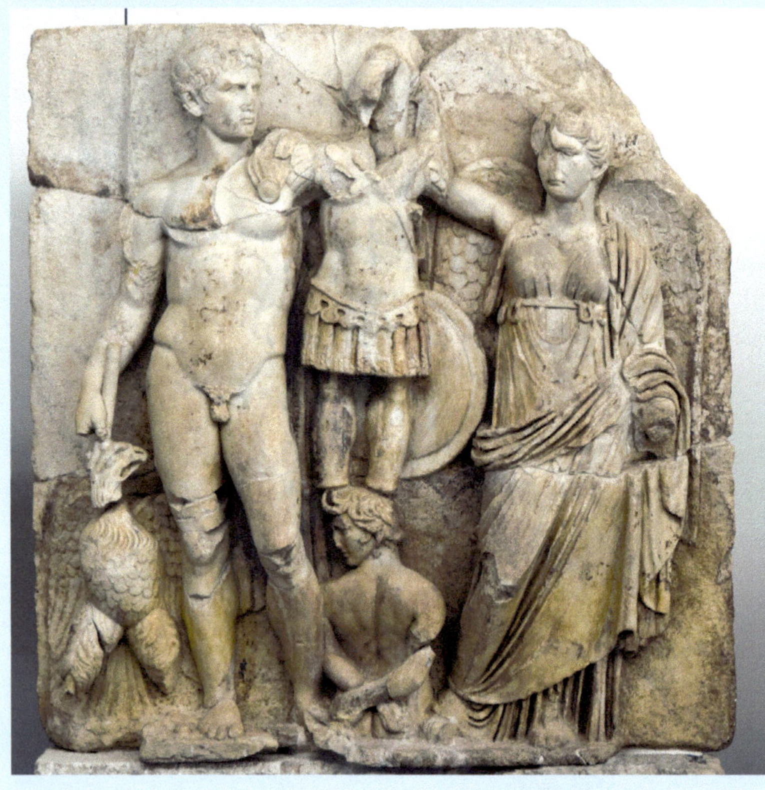

AS Level

1 a. Who is the female figure in this image, depicted on the right? How can you tell? [2]
   b. Explain why this image features an eagle in the bottom left corner. [1]
2. How have later sources depicted Augustus' military campaigns? Use Source A and your own knowledge in your discussion. [16]

A Level

1. What impression of Augustus do we get from this image? [10]
2. Did Augustus succeed in creating a public image for himself that endured past his own lifetime? [30]

What to Expect in the AS Exam for Imperial Image

This chapter aims to show you the types of questions you are likely to get in the written examination. It offers some advice on how to answer the questions and will help you avoid common errors.

THE EXAMINATION

This component of the AS Classical Civilisation examination is designed to test your knowledge, understanding and evaluation of Augustus' imperial image. The examination is worth 65 marks and lasts 1 hour and 30 minutes. This represents 50% of the total marks for the AS Level.

There are two Assessment Objectives in your AS Level, and questions will be designed to test these areas. These Assessment Objectives are outlined in the table below, together with the total number of marks available for each on the paper:

	Assessment Objective	Marks
AO1	Demonstrate knowledge and understanding of: • literature and visual/material culture • how sources and ideas reflect, and influence, their cultural contexts • possible interpretations of sources, perspectives and ideas by different audiences and individuals.	32
AO2	Critically analyse, interpret and evaluate literature and visual/material culture, using evidence to make substantiated judgements and produce coherent and reasoned arguments.	33

Exam structure and question types

The exam is divided into two sections, Section A and Section B.

There are four question types in this exam:

- two sets of short answer questions (four marks in total each)
- 8-mark stimulus questions
- 16-mark shorter essay
- 25-mark essay

Try to plan your time well. The shorter essay question and the essay question together make up 41 of the 65 marks available, and so you should aim to spend the majority of your time on these two questions.

Section A has the following format:

There will be a prescribed visual/material source on the paper. This will be called 'Source A'.

- You will be asked the first set of short answer questions, worth 1 or 2 marks each. Of the 4 marks available, 3 will test AO1, 1 will test AO2
- You will then be asked an 8-mark stimulus question on Source A

There will also be a textual source, which will be an extract from one of your prescribed literary sources. This will be called 'Source B'. The questions follow the same format as above (in fact, the textual source could come before the visual/material source or after it):

- You will be asked the second set of short answer questions, worth 1 or 2 marks each. Of the 4 marks available, 3 will test AO1, 1 will test AO2
- You will then be asked an 8-mark stimulus question on Source B

The final question in Section A will be the 16-mark shorter essay question.

- You may be asked to use one or both of Sources A and B as a starting point for your answer, as well as your own knowledge

Section B has the following format:

- You will be given a choice of two essays, of which you should **only do one**. This is worth 25 marks

Section A

Short-answer questions and visual/material-stimulus question

Let us look at an example. You could be shown the following prescribed visual/material source.

Source A: gold coin (aureus) 2 BC–AD **4.**

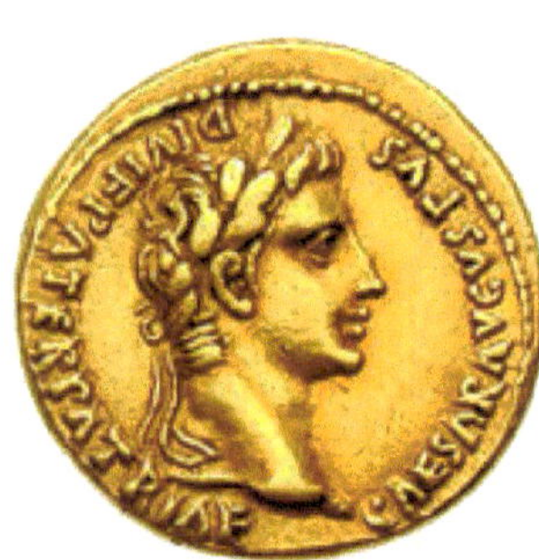

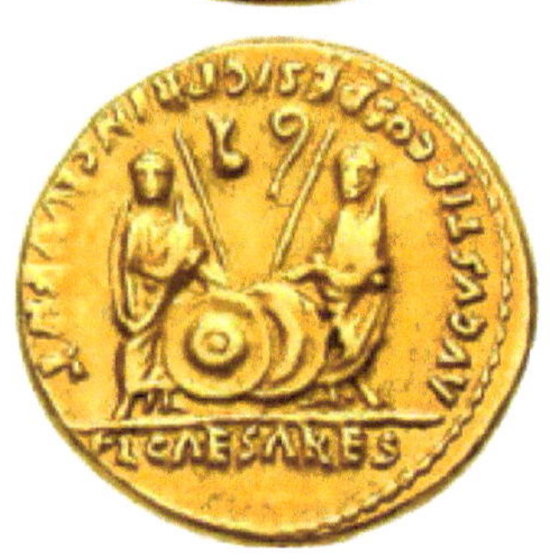

An example of an AO1 **short answer question** would be:

Question: What is Augustus wearing on his head in this image? [1]
Answer: A wreath/the civic crown. [1]

   This mark is AO1 since it requires you to show knowledge and understanding, but there is no analysis or evaluation required.

   By contrast, an example of an AO2 question would be:

Question: Why do you think he had himself depicted wearing this? [1]
Answer: If the answer given to the question above was "the civic crown", then you could make any one of the following points: it was the second highest military honour and so it makes him look like a great general/leader [1]; as it is not the highest possible honour it makes him look modest [1]; it reminds the viewer of his military achievements [1]; as the civic crown is awarded when you save someone it presents Augustus as a saviour [1].

The answer above is AO2 because you are being asked to critically analyse the source, relating this to your factual understanding so as to give your own evaluation of the question.

You will then be asked a **stimulus question** worth 8 marks. Of those 8 marks, 4 are available for AO1 and 4 for AO2. AO1 marks are awarded for the selection of material from the source, AO2 marks for the interpretation, analysis or evaluation of this material.

Therefore, for this coin, you might be asked a question such as this:

Question: Explain what image of Gaius and Lucius is created by this source. Make four points and support each point with reference to the source. [8]

One example of **one** point that you might make is as follows:

Answer: The fact that Gaius and Lucius are surrounded by priestly symbols including the simpulum and lituus [1] evokes the idea that Gaius and Lucius are similar to Augustus in terms of their devotion to Roman religious offices and rituals [1].

In this answer, the key point of interpretation is that Gaius and Lucius are depicted as being involved in religion and in this way are similar to Augustus himself (AO2), and the evidence for this is that they are shown alongside priestly symbols (AO1). Answers will be marked point by point, rather than with a marking grid (as per the following two question types – see below). The four interpretations that you are asked to make are AO2, while the evidence you find to support them is AO1.

Short answer questions and textual stimulus question

Exactly the same principle applies for the questions based on the textual source. For example, look at the excerpt below.

Source B: Horace's *Odes* 4.15 ll. 4–20

> Caesar, this age has restored rich crops
> to the fields, and brought back the standards, at last,
> to Jupiter, those that we've now recovered
> from insolent Parthian pillars,
> and closed the gates of Romulus' temple,   5
> freed at last from all war, and tightened the rein
> on lawlessness, straying beyond just limits,
> and has driven out crime, and summoned
> the ancient arts again, by which the name
> of Rome and Italian power grew great,   10
> and the fame and majesty of our empire,
> were spread from the sun's lair in the west,
> to the regions where it rises at dawn.
> With Caesar protecting the state, no civil
> disturbance will banish the peace, no violence,   15
> no anger that forges swords, and makes
> mutual enemies of wretched towns.

Trans. A.S. Kline

As an example of an AO1 question, you could be asked:

Question: What does it mean when the 'gates of Romulus' temple' are closed? [1]
Answer: There is peace throughout Rome and her Empire [1].

As an example of an AO2 question, you could be asked:

Question: Why do you think Horace chooses to use this as a reference? [1]
Answer: You could give one of a number of interpretations to this question. For example, you could say that the gates had only ever been closed twice before Augustus' reign and so this was a significant and rare event [1]; it links with Augustus' depiction as a bringer of peace [1]; this was a powerful image connoting peace for the original audience [1].

As an example of a stimulus question, you could be asked:

Question: Explain what this poem suggests are the achievements of Augustus. Make four points and support your answer with reference to the passage. [8]

One example of **one** point that you might make is as follows:
Answer: This poem suggests that one of Augustus' key achievements was that he ensured that the Roman people were safe from crime [1]. This is suggested in ll. 7–8 when Horace says that Augustus 'tightened the rein/on lawlessness', which implies that Augustus curbed the activities of criminals [1].

Here, the analysis that he kept people safe from crime is AO2, while the evidence which supports this from the passage is AO1. When you refer to the passage, try if possible either to give line references or quote directly the relevant words or lines.

Shorter essay question

The final question in Section A may ask you to bring together the two sources, as well as asking you to demonstrate your wider knowledge of the Imperial Image topic. There are 16 marks available, 8 for AO1 and 8 for AO2. This question has its own tailored marking grid which you can view on the OCR website.

An example of such a question might be as follows:

Question: Evaluate how effectively Augustus portrayed himself as the protector of Rome. You may use Sources A and B as a starting point, and your own knowledge. [16]
When you **plan** your answer to this question, it might be a good idea to write down some key points of factual evidence which you are going to use for AO1. Some examples might be:

- Augustus conducted several military campaigns, against a variety of opponents including: Julius Caesar's assassins, Marc Antony, Sextus Pompeius and at the edges of the Empire. These campaigns are presented in a variety of literary and visual/material sources
- he was granted the title of 'pater patriae' (Source A)
- he was depicted as protecting the people from crime (Source B)
- he was depicted as protecting the people from war and from famine as a bringer of peace and plenty (Source B)

- he enacted a series of morality laws, which were meant to restore Rome's relationship with her gods. These laws are referred to in Horace's *Carmen Saeculare*

You should also try to write down some key points of evaluation, analysis or interpretation in your plan which you are going to use for AO2. Remember you can give many different interpretations. You might want to spend some time discussing some ways in which he successfully presented himself as Rome's protector, before moving on to consider ways in which he was less successful.

Some examples might be:

Ways in which Augustus successfully showed himself as Rome's protector:

- the civil war with Antony was successfully branded as a war against a dangerous foreign power (Cleopatra)
- Augustus was depicted as a capable commander who could be trusted to safeguard Rome against threats to her military
- Augustus' wars at the edges of Empire protected Rome's image and status
- Augustus' moral legislation and role in official religion protected the religious health of the Roman people
- The title 'pater patriae' links to the idea of a paterfamilias watching over his family unit. This creates a highly paternal and protective image.

Ways in which Augustus did not successfully show himself to be Rome's protector:

- Agrippa's role in planning and executing Augustus' campaigns was well known. Similarly many of his campaigns at the edges of the Empire were conducted by his generals. This could undermine the idea that his military leadership protected Rome
- despite his propaganda campaign, many of Augustus' campaigns were civil conflicts and so it could be argued that his participation in them undermined the idea that he was a protector of Rome.

Try to ensure that you give your essay a clear structure. Perhaps draw up a plan paragraph by paragraph or argument by argument. While it is a good idea to have a brief introduction and conclusion to the essay, try not to make these too long. Your introduction should simply briefly outline the key issues, and perhaps the line you are going to take, while the conclusion should be short and simply summarise the key points you have made to conclude your argument.

Section B

Essay question

In Section B, you will be given a choice of two essays. **You should only do one essay and you will not be given any extra credit for doing both of them!** The essay is out of 25 marks, with 10 marks for AO1 and 15 marks for AO2 (this question also has its own tailored marking grid, which you can download from the OCR website). However, this does not mean that you should be aiming to give evidence and evaluation in exactly that ratio. You should just aim to write the best essay you can, where you back up your arguments with evidence from your studies. What you should avoid doing, however, is over-narrating: telling the examiner the story of what happened in the period, or describing what the sources are rather than analysing them according to the question.

The first thing you need to do then is to decide which question to choose. Make sure that you read both questions carefully and think about what is being asked. It is common for candidates to read the question as they want it to be, rather than as it is. For example, consider the following question:

Question: 'Visual/material culture was essential for the creation of Augustus' powerful public image.' To what extent do you agree with this statement? Justify your response. [25]

It is asking you to evaluate how important visual/material culture was in the creation of Augustus' powerful public image and asking if you think it was essential or not. It wants you to decide whether this image could have been created by literary sources alone or not. A key work here is 'justify'. You should decide on your preferred line of argument and then organise your ideas and evidence such that you are able to support your conclusion with a discussion of the evidence and its impact on the power of Augustus' public image. Various different approaches could be taken, including a consideration of how the visual/material sources reached different audiences, how people interacted with them and the particular messages sent by individual sources. You could also consider what literary sources were able to convey about Augustus' public image and how effectively they created a powerful public image by themselves.

However, notice that it would be very easy to misread this question slightly. You may previously have written a practice essay such as: 'Discuss the contribution of visual/material culture to Augustus' propaganda campaign.' If so, it would be very tempting to reproduce many of the arguments made in that essay. Be very careful not to do this. You must answer the question in front of you, which in this case is about Augustus' powerful public image as a whole.

Therefore, when you make your choice about which essay to attempt, ensure that you have read each question carefully and are very sure about what each one is asking for. It may be that you think that you could answer both. This is a good problem to have! However, try to make a clear decision one way or another and then stick with it. The skills required for this question are the same as those for the shorter essay question, but you have the chance to go into more depth. Make sure you create a good plan which allows you to put forward a well-structured essay.

What to Expect in the A Level Exam for Imperial Image

This chapter aims to show you the types of questions you are likely to get in the written examination. It offers some advice on how to answer the questions and will help you avoid common errors.

THE EXAMINATION

This component of the A Level Classical Civilisation examination is designed to test your knowledge, understanding and evaluation of Augustus' imperial image. The examination is worth 75 marks and lasts 1 hour and 45 minutes. This represents 30% of the total marks for the A Level.

There are two Assessment Objectives in your A Level, and questions will be designed to test these areas. These Assessment Objectives are outlined in the table below, together with the total number of marks available for each on the paper:

	Assessment Objective	Marks
AO1	Demonstrate knowledge and understanding of: • literature and visual/material culture • how sources and ideas reflect, and influence, their cultural contexts • possible interpretations of sources, perspectives and ideas by different audiences and individuals.	35
AO2	Critically analyse, interpret and evaluate literature and visual/material culture, using evidence to make substantiated judgements and produce coherent and reasoned arguments.	40

Exam structure and question types

The exam is divided into two sections, Section A and Section B.

There are four question types in this exam:

- a number of short answer questions (5 marks in total)
- 10-mark stimulus questions
- 20-mark shorter essay
- 30-mark essay

Try to plan your time well. The shorter essay question and the essay question together make up 50 of the 75 marks available, and so you should aim to spend the majority of your time on these two questions.

Section A has the following format:

There will be a prescribed visual/material source on the paper. This will be called 'Source A'.

- one or more short answer questions relating to the source (worth 2 or 3 marks in total). These questions will test AO1 only
- you will then be asked a 10-mark stimulus question on Source A

There will also be a textual source, which will be an extract from one of your prescribed literary sources (in fact, the textual source could come before the visual/material source or after it). This will be called 'Source B'. The questions follow the same format as above:

- one or more short answer questions relating to the source (worth 2 or 3 marks in total, adding up to 5 marks when combined with the earlier short answer questions). These questions will also test AO1 only
- you will then be asked a 10-mark stimulus question on Source B

The final question in Section A will be the 20-mark shorter essay question.

- you may be asked to use one or both Sources A and B as a starting point for your answer, as well as your own knowledge

Section B has the following format:

- you will be given a choice of two essays, of which you should **only do one**. This is worth 30 marks

Section A

Short answer questions and visual/material stimulus question

For example, you could be shown the following prescribed visual/material source.

Source A: gold coin (aureus) 2 BC–AD **4.**

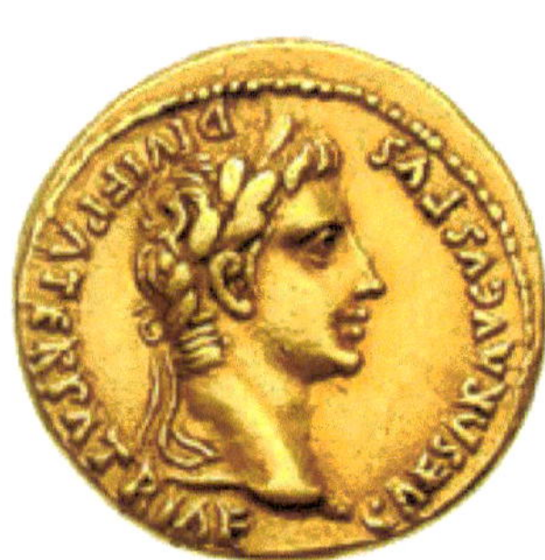

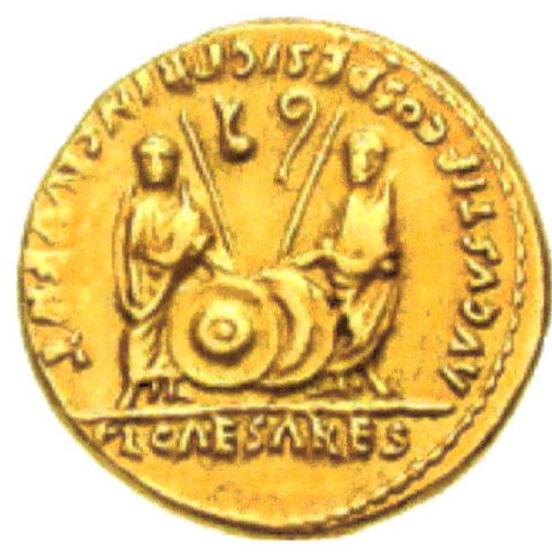

Short answer question

An example of a short answer question would be:

Question: On this coin Augustus is called 'Son of a god'. Which god is Augustus the son of? [1]

Answer: Julius Caesar [1] or the deified/divine Julius Caesar [1].

This question is AO1 since it requires you to show knowledge and understanding, but there is no analysis or evaluation required.

Stimulus question

After the short answer questions, you will be asked a 10-mark stimulus question. Of the 10 marks available, 5 are for AO1 and 5 for AO2. AO1 marks are awarded for the selection of material from the source, AO2 marks for the interpretation, analysis or evaluation of this material. These questions are marked according to a marking grid which you can view on the OCR website.

For example, for this coin, you might be asked a question such as this:

Question: Explain how this coin creates an image of the Imperial family as role models for the Roman people. [10]

Answer: A key word here is 'explain'. You need to think about what the coin depicts and discuss what this suggests about the imperial family. Importantly, as the question directly references the Roman people you should explore how the image created by the coin would have been understood by Augustus' contemporary audience. As the marking grid indicates, you should aim make a range of points which give clear and thoughtful analysis and are backed up with good supporting evidence from the source. Here are examples of two points you could make (you do not need to separate them in your answers):

Point 1: This coin presents an image of an Imperial family that greatly values the importance of the father–son relationship. The obverse of the coin depicts Augustus 'alongside' the reverse which depicts Gaius and Lucius – his adopted sons. This parallel depiction implies a close relationship. Moreover, the words 'father' and 'son' feature prominently on the legend of the coin: 'son of a god', 'father of the nation' and 'sons of Augustus'. In Roman culture the father–son relationship was one of the most crucial kinds of family relationships, thus the closeness of Augustus and his adopted sons, and of Augustus and his adoptive father is presented as an ideal for other Romans to imitate.

Point 2: This coin would have been an effective means to encourage the Roman people to see the Imperial family as role models. This is because of the very fact that it is a coin. Meant for general circulation, it might have passed through many hands, encouraging each new owner to perceive the images and inscription. This would have effectively communicated the coin's message to a broad cross-section of people. Alternatively, one could argue that the potential audience of this coin was limited. It is an aureus, a highly valuable gold coin. Therefore, it is unlikely that this coin would have been seen by many of Rome's poorer inhabitants and in fact only have been an effective means of communicating with the richer classes.

Notice that in each case, evidence from the source leads to a point of analysis. Try to make your arguments as clear and distinct as possible, and always back them up with evidence from the source. In addition, notice that there is room for evaluation of your ideas. The second point gives arguments that both explain how the coin was and was not able to create an image of the Imperial family as role models.

Short answer questions and textual stimulus question

As an example of a literary source, Source B, look at the excerpt below.

Source B: Horace's *Odes* 4.15 ll. 4–20.

Caesar, this age has restored rich crops
to the fields, and brought back the standards, at last,
to Jupiter, those that we've now recovered
from insolent Parthian pillars,
and closed the gates of Romulus' temple,   5
freed at last from all war, and tightened the rein
on lawlessness, straying beyond just limits,
and has driven out crime, and summoned
the ancient arts again, by which the name
of Rome and Italian power grew great,   10
and the fame and majesty of our empire,
were spread from the sun's lair in the west,
to the regions where it rises at dawn.
With Caesar protecting the state, no civil
disturbance will banish the peace, no violence,   15
no anger that forges swords, and makes
mutual enemies of wretched towns.

Trans. A.S. Kline

Short answer question

An example of a short answer question would be:

Question: In what year were the Roman standards retrieved? [1]
Answer: 20 BC [1].

Once again, no analysis is required here, you simply need to show a piece of knowledge and understanding (AO1).

Stimulus question

As an example of a textual 10-mark stimulus question, you might be asked a question such as this based on the passage given from Horace's *Odes* 1.37:

Question: Explain how Horace conveys the benefits of Augustus' reign for Rome in this source. [10]

You should aim to make a range of points, using evidence from the passage. If possible, refer closely to the passage, either by referencing line numbers, or by quoting directly. One example of one point that you might make is as follows:

Answer:
Point 1: This poem suggests that Augustus' reign has reduced the crime rate within Rome and the Empire. The quote 'tightened the reign on lawlessness' suggests that

Augustus has taken some proactive measures to prevent criminals from acting in an illegal manner. This, combined with the assertion that Augustus had 'driven out crime' paints a clear picture of a lawful state. As Augustus is the active party in the case of both of these verbs ('tightened' and 'driven'), Horace clearly implies that this lawfulness is thanks to Augustus' influence.

Point 2: Horace's use of language which glorifies Rome alongside language that denigrates Rome's enemies conveys the idea of Roman superiority. The phrase 'fame and majesty of our empire' is clearly meant in a positive way and would probably have been read, by his original Roman audience, with pleasure since it would have reinforced a sense of nationalistic pride. This comes just lines after the Parthians were called 'insolent', a word which suggests that the Parthians were childish and with an inflated sense of self-importance. In the same short extract Horace breaks down the Parthians and builds up the Romans, encouraging his reader to feel a sense of national superiority.

Once again, these points contain evidence from the source (in this case the passage), which enables a point of analysis to be made.

Shorter essay question

The final question in Section A may ask you to bring together one or both of the given sources, as well as asking you to demonstrate your wider knowledge of the Imperial Image topic. There are 20 marks available, 10 for AO1 and 10 for AO2. This question has its own tailored marking grid which you can view on the OCR website.

An example of such a question might be as follows:

Question: Evaluate how effectively Augustus legitimised his wars. You may use Source B as a starting point. [20]

When you **plan** your answer to this question, it might be a good idea to write down some key points of factual evidence which you are going to use for AO1. You could start by noting the evidence from the source on the paper. Horace's *Odes* 1.37 offers plenty of evidence for this question and could support such ideas as: the idea that peace can be attained through war, the emphasis placed on Caesar as a protector against civil conflicts, and the importance of exacting revenge against the Parthians. In each case, be sure to note down what specific evidence these interpretations are based on. You might then list other examples and pieces of evidence from your wider studies. One important example could be the Ara Pacis, which was dedicated to the personification of Peace. You could also consider how effectively Augustus smeared the images of his enemies in war, from Cleopatra in Horace's *Odes* 1.37 to Sextus Pompeius in the *Res Gestae*.

Think about some of the key words and phrases in the question. The phrase 'how effectively' asks you to assess the success of Augustus' propaganda, rather than merely stating what these sources were trying to convey. As such you should explore the likely responses of his contemporary audience and assess the extent to which they would have been convinced by these messages. There is plenty of flexibility to examine both sides of the argument, and to agree to some extent but not fully. For example, you are not being asked to examine whether Augustus was able to legitimise his wars, but how effectively he was able to achieve this. You really do have the opportunity to give exactly your own opinion on this question! There is no 'right' or 'wrong' answer to a question such as this – you simply need to back up your opinions with strong evidence from your studies.

Section B

Essay question

In Section B, you will be given a choice of two essays. **You should only do one essay and you will not be given any credit for trying to do both of them!** The essay is out of 30 marks, with ten marks for AO1 and twenty marks for AO2 (this question also has its own tailored marking grid, which you can download from the OCR website). However, this does not mean that you should be aiming to give evidence and evaluation in exactly that ratio. A good essay is likely to have more evaluation than evidence in any case, and so you should just aim to write the best essay you can, where you back up your arguments with evidence from your studies. What you should avoid doing, however, is over-narrating: telling the examiner what happened in the period and what the sources are rather than analysing them according to the question.

The first thing you need to do is to decide which question to choose. Make sure that you read both questions carefully and think about what is being asked. It is a common mistake for candidates to read the question as they want it to be, rather than as it is. For example, consider the following question:

Question: Assess the extent to which the public image created by Augustus endured beyond his own lifetime. [30]

You should critically compare and contrast the image that Augustus created during his lifetime with the representations that emerged following his death. However, notice that it would be possible to misread this question. You may previously have written a practice essay such as: 'Do you think Augustus would have approved of the representations of him that arose after his death?' If so, it would be very tempting to reproduce many of the arguments made in that essay. Be very careful not to do this. You must answer the question in front of you, which in this case is about how far the image created in Augustus lifetime was able to remain unchanged following his death. Therefore, when you make your choice about which essay to attempt, ensure that you have read each question carefully and are very sure about what each one is asking for. It may be that you think that you could answer both. This is a good problem to have! Make a clear decision one way or another and then stick with it.

Try to ensure that you give your essay a clear structure. Perhaps draw up a plan paragraph by paragraph or argument by argument. While it is a good idea to have a brief introduction and conclusion to the essay, try not to make these too long. Your introduction should simply briefly outline the key issues, and perhaps the line you are going to take, while the conclusion should be short and simply summarise the key points you have made to conclude your argument. To score good marks in AO1, make sure you choose a range of factual evidence based on a range of sources. Try to include a mixture of literary and visual/material sources. To score good marks on AO2, make sure you examine the issue and weigh up your arguments carefully. You will want to make a variety of points, and again you may find that there are arguments on both sides.

Modern Scholarship

In this essay question, you are required to show knowledge of secondary sources, scholars and academic works in your answer. This requirement of the exam is supported in the textbooks by 'Modern Scholarship' boxes. The OCR rubric says that 'Learners are expected to make use of scholarly views, academic approaches and sources to support their argument'. It is essential that you build in such material in order to do well on this question. How should you do this?

First of all, you of course need to read more widely about the topic. In this book, you have been given suggestions for articles and books to read on a variety of topics relating to Augustus and his public image. Try to follow up as many as possible, and take notes about some of the key arguments that scholars make. It is especially interesting when two authors disagree with each other on a topic, such as whether the art and architecture produced during Augustus' reign was intentionally based on models from the Classical period. When referring to the view of a scholar, you need not quote them directly, although if you are able to remember accurately a few words that they have written, then that will be very impressive. However, it may be that you refer to a general argument that they put forward in a book, an article or a chapter. However, you will not be expected to quote the name of a book or give a chapter reference. For example, you might cite Zanker's view, quoted on p. 129.

Zanker's argument, put forward in his 2014 book, *The Power of Images in the Age of Augustus*, focuses on the idea that Antony's public persona took over his private life. Zanker suggests that Antony did not just project the image of Dionysus for propaganda purposes, but that he started to live as Dionysus incarnate and that this contributed to his downfall. This might well be a view worth putting forward, if the question allowed room for a consideration of the power struggle between Octavian and Antony, or the causes of Antony's eventual downfall. You may wish to reflect more on this view in your essay. You do not necessarily need to quote the details of where you read the ideas, it will be enough to mention the scholar's name and explain what they say.

Above all make your use of secondary sources relevant to the question you are answering. To use a secondary source well you should think carefully about why it is supporting your argument or showing a different argument, and make it clear why you are including it. You might want to agree or disagree with the scholarly view, in which case you will need to explain why you do so. You may not remember everything about the secondary source you have read, but if you ensure the examiner understands what you are using and why, this will strengthen your argument. Using secondary sources in this way gives you a skill that is crucial at university level in many different subjects because engaging with what other people have thought about a particular topic enriches your own understanding.

GLOSSARY

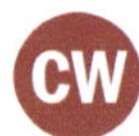

agōn a formal debate in which the playwright can showcase opposing arguments

aulētēs the word for an aulos-player; each chorus was accompanied by one

aulos a double-reed musical instrument similar to an oboe

bacchants female followers of Dionysus

Bacchism cult worship of Dionysus, who was also known by the name Bacchus

catharsis a word meaning 'cleansing' or 'purification' – Aristotle hoped that watching a tragedy would give spectators a catharsis from their fear and pity

chitōn a full-length robe, often ornately decorated

choral odes songs performed by the chorus

chorēgos the financial backer attached to a playwright to support the production of his plays

civic crown the second highest military honour a Roman could achieve, awarded to a citizen who had saved the lives of other Roman citizens

clementia clemency or mercy

crane a device which raised an actor above the level of the skēnē building

deme a village or district of Attica

denarius (pl. **denarii**) a silver coin with a value enough to pay a soldier's wage for three days and buy enough wheat to bake daily bread for a month

dictator a Roman political office chosen by the Senate in times of national emergency as a temporary position with absolute power that was relinquished once the emergency was over

dithyramb a choral dance sung in honour of Dionysus

eisodos (or **parodos**) the entry way into the orchēstra from each side of the theatre

Eleusinian Mysteries an important religious cult in honour of Demeter and her daughter Persephone. Anyone who wished could be initiated into the cult at the annual rites in September

elogium (pl. **elogia**) a funerary inscription

episodes scenes of dialogue between actors

eponymous archōn a leading politician of Athens who was responsible for running the City Dionysia. He is referred to as 'eponymous' since the Athenian civil year was named after him

exodos the final section of the play

games public events held, usually by magistrates or by rich individuals, to honour a particular god or in celebration of an event. Games were a rare chance for the urban poor to enjoy entertainments such as theatrical plays, chariot racing, circus performances and gladiatorial shows

genius a generic term for a divinity, from a spirit to the major gods; including one's own genius, a cross between a guardian spirit and a soul

hamartia a word which meant 'mistake' – in a tragedy, such a mistake led to a disastrous outcome

himation a cloak reaching down to the knees

hybris a range of behaviours from outrageous or excessive behaviour through to physical or sexual assault

iambus (adjective: **iambic**) the spoken sections of a play, also referred to as iambics. Iambic metre is fairly close to the pattern of real speech, and the full name of the metre used in tragedy is iambic trimeter.

iustitia justice, in particular with regard to the law and courts

kommos a formal song at moments of heightened emotion involving dialogue between an actor and the chorus

kōmos a loosely organised revel through the streets with song and dance

kothornoi soft leather boots which reached up to the thigh

legionary standard a pole bearing an eagle (and thus sometimes referred to as 'eagles'), carried into battle by a legion's standard bearer

Lenaea a drama festival held in Athens in late January at which comedy took precedence

liturgy a tax on the super-rich requiring them to contribute to the functioning of Athens

lituus a crooked wand used in religious rituals by the college of augurs

lyric the sung sections of a play. Choral odes are always composed in lyric, and accompanied by dancing, but the characters sometimes also sing in lyric at particularly emotional moments

maenads an alternative name for the bacchants. 'Maenad' means 'frenzied one', because of the madness associated with Dionysus

matrona a married Roman woman

mausoleum a building meant to house at least one tomb

monody a solo song by an actor, often sung at moments of great distress

mos maiorum 'The ways of our ancestors': an unwritten code of behaviour and values, looking to the ancestors as role models

oikos literally 'house', this term is used to describe a household or family unit

orchēstra the 'dancing-area' below the theatron where the chorus performed

parabasis a section of a comedy in which the chorus addresses the audience directly, speaking in the voice of the playwright

parodos the first ode which the chorus perform while coming into the theatre

patron patronage was a social practice in Rome whereby a rich and powerful individual would offer support to poorer, less influential individuals. The kind of support given was variable. Clients were expected to give political support to their patrons

peripeteia a terrible reversal of fortune in a tragedy

physis personal nature, something you are both with, not taught or changed by circumstances

pietas duty to the family, to the state and to the gods

polis (pl. **poleis**) the word for a Greek city-state. The polis of Athens consisted of the city and its surrounding region, Attica

pompē a grand religious procession

Pontifex Maximus Rome's chief priest, a position held for life

princeps senatus (often just **princeps**) the first member of the Senate; a great honour voted by the censors every five years the censors voted for a member of the Senate for this role; they spoke first in discussions, decided when to summon and dismiss the Senate and set its agenda

Principate government by one man, referred to as the 'princeps' or 'first person', with many of the structures of a republican system, such as a Senate and elections, although the power of these is diminished

proagōn an event which acted as a preview and introduction to the festival

prohedria the front row seating in the theatron reserved for VIPs

prologue the opening of the play which sets the scene

Rural Dionysia a drama festival held in the rural demes of Attica in mid-winter

satyr a mythological creature who was a follower of Dionysus. In art, satyrs are depicted as half-human and half-animal

satyr-play a play which parodied tragedy and was presented along with three tragedies by the same playwright

scholion a comment inserted into a manuscript by an ancient commentator

Sibyl a famous priestess of Apollo whose predictions were thought to be the most accurate in the world

Sibylline Books a collection of the prophecies of the Sibyl, kept by the quindecimviri, fifteen priests who would 'translate' the Greek verse into Latin

simpulum a ritual ladle used for pouring libations at sacrifices

skēnē the wooden hut used as a backdrop and for actors to change

sophists a group of influential philosophers in fifth-century Athens, whose interests included religion, ethics, rhetoric and science

stasimon the name for a choral ode after the parodos

stichomythia a dialogue in which two characters speak alternate lines of verse. This makes exchanges punchy, and is particularly appropriate for an agōn. From the Greek *steicho* ('to march in a line' – hence *stichos* means a line of verse) and *mythos* ('word' or 'utterance')

Temple of Janus Quirinus Janus, the double-faced god of transitions and in-betweens, had a temple in Rome whose gates could only ever be closed if there was peace in Rome and throughout the entire Empire. Before Octavian's lifetime the gates had only ever been closed on two occasions in all of Rome's history

theatron the seating area in a Greek theatre

Theoric Fund a fund provided by the Athenian state which ensured that poorer citizens could afford to attend the City Dionysia

thyrsus a ritual staff made of a fennel stalk carried by followers of Dionysus

tragic irony where the playwright contrasts the characters' limited knowledge with the audience's broader understanding

tribe a political division in Athens. All Athenian citizens were members of one of the ten tribes

triumph granted by a Senate vote, a special celebration of a successful military campaign in which the conquering general would ride through the streets of Rome on a chariot with his spoils of war paraded behind

triumvirate 'Rule of three men'

Troy Game an ancient ritual that involved young noblemen showing off their horsemanship with a series of complex manoeuvres

tyrannos a tyrant or king. By the time of tragedy, **tyrannos** could have negative connotations similar to those of the English word 'tyrant' (though the word in tragedy is now always used negatively)

virtus masculine virtue, including courage, strength and general excellence (derived from the Latin 'vir', 'man')

wheel platform a wooden platform on wheels brought on stage which showed a scene from off-stage

SOURCES OF QUOTATIONS

Greek Theatre

11 'Just a word. . .' Aristophanes, *Assembly-Women*, 1154–62, trans. David Barrett, *The Birds and Other Plays* (Harmondsworth: Penguin, 1978); **13** 'Priest save me . . .' Aristophanes, *Frogs*, 297, trans. Judith Affleck and Clive Letchford, *Aristophanes:Frogs* (Cambridge: Cambridge University Press, 2014); **17** 'It would show . . .' Scholion to Aristophanes' *Acharnians* l. 408, trans. Eric Csapo and William J. Slater, *The Context of Ancient Drama* (Ann Arbor: University of Michigan Press, 1995); **18** 'He-e-elp! No, I . . .' Aristophanes, *Peace* 173–6, trans. Alan H. Sommerstein and David Barrett, *The Birds and Other Plays* (Harmondsworth: Penguin, 1978); **24** 'This is one . . .' Csapo and Slater, p. 99; **37** 'Tragedy is the . . .' Aristotle, *Poetics* 1449b, trans. Ian J. Storey and Arlene Allan, *A Guide to Ancient Greek Drama* (Oxford: Blackwell 2006), p. 77; **37** 'What is left . . .' Aristotle, *Poetics* 1453a, trans. Storey and Allan p. 82; **41** '. . . he discovered and . . .' Euripides, *Bacchae*, 279–83 (225–8), trans. David Franklin, *Euripides: Bacchae* (Cambridge: Cambridge University Press, 2000); **44** 'Farce or fantasy . . .' Storey and Allan, p. 174; **45–6** 'Thouriomanteis, iatrotechnas, sphragidonuchargokometas, . . .' Aristophanes, *Clouds* 332–3, trans. Storey and Allan, p. 177; **46** 'It is not really . . .' Paul Cartledge, *Aristophanes and his Theatre of the Absurd* (London: Bloomsbury Academic, 1991), pp. 73ff; **51** 'You could see . . .' Euripides, *Bacchae*, 740–2 (619–20), trans. Franklin; **51** 'One of them . . .' Euripides, *Bacchae*, 1134–6 (965–7), trans. Franklin; **53** 'Come, Muse! Come . . .' Aristophanes, *Frogs*, 674–7, trans. Affleck and Letchford; **59** 'MESSENGER: When she . . .' Euripides, *Bacchae*, 689–711 (583–98), trans. Franklin; **68** 'Nothing is better . . .' *Odyssey* 6.182–4, trans. L. Swift; **71** 'Marriages! O marriage. . . .' Sophocles, *Oedipus the King* 1403–8, trans. Robert Fagles, *Sophocles: The Three Theban Plays* (London: Penguin, 2008); **75** 'To take vengeance . . .' *Rhetoric* 1367a24, trans. L. Swift; **75** 'Making my way . . .' Sophocles, *Oedipus the King* 800–13 (884–98), trans. Fagles; **76** 'Cadmus: Dionysus, we . . .' Euripides, *Bacchae*, 1344–9 (1167–74), trans. Franklin; **78** 'O my children, . . .' Sophocles, *Oedipus the King*, 1–13 (1–15), trans. Fagles; **80** 'I came down . . .' Aristophanes, *Frogs*, 1418–19, trans. Affleck and Letchford; **81** 'of the audience, . . .' Aristophanes, *Frogs*, 1108–14, trans. Affleck and Letchford; **85** 'Euripides: And what . . .' Aristophanes, *Frogs*, 1049–51, trans. Affleck and Letchford; **86** 'Now look at . . .' Aristophanes, *Frogs*, 1013–17, trans. Affleck and Letchford; **88** 'Dionysus: This is . . .' Aristophanes, *Frogs*, 21–34, trans. Affleck and Letchford; **92, 99** 'DIONYSUS + FROGS Bre-ke-ke-kex, . . .' Aristophanes, *Frogs*, 250–78, trans. Affleck and Letchford.

Imperial Image

All quotations are translated by A. S. Kline unless otherwise specified.

129 'At a splendid . . .' P. Zanker, *The Power of Images in the Age of Augustus* (Ann Arbor: University of Michigan Press, 2014), pp. 46–7; **130** 'The relationship with . . .' Zanker, pp. 51–3; **139** 'A Roman – you'll . . .' Horace, *Epode* 9.11–13; **139** 'a maddened queen . . .' Horace, *Odes* 1.37.7–11; **141** 'Cleopatra, who heaped . . .' Propertius *Elegies* 3.11.29–32; **141** 'You fled then . . .' Propertius, *Elegies* 3.11.51; **144** 'A maddened queen . . .' Horace, *Odes* 1.37.7–30; **151** 'O Augustus, world-deliverer, . . .' Propertius, *Elegies* 4.6.37–40; **152** 'I have sung . . .' Propertius, *Elegies* 4.6.69–70; **152** 'Let the Muse . . .' Propertius, *Elegies* 4.6.75–6; **154** 'Men, the rewards . . .' Propertius, *Elegies* 3.4.3; **154** 'I'll begin to . . .' Propertius, *Elegies* 3.4.15–16; **156** 'The high estimation . . .' Zanker, pp. 245–7; **159** 'Postumus, how could . . .' Propertius, *Elegies* 3.12.1–6; **161** 'There is no . . .' Ovid, *Metamorphoses* 15.750–1; **161** 'Therefore, in order . . .' Ovid, *Metamorphoses* 15.758–9; **162** 'Augustus, as heir . . .' Ovid, *Metamorphoses* 15.819–21; **162** 'I beg that . . .' Ovid, *Metamorphoses* 15.868–70; **162** 'Ovid, who . . .' Andrew Wallace-Hadrill, *Augustan Rome* (London: Bloomsbury Academic, 1993), p. 10; **163** 'Romans, though you're . . .' Horace, *Odes* 3.6.1–2; **163** 'Our age, fertile . . .' Horace, *Odes*, 3.6.17–20; **165** 'May his wife . . .' Horace, *Odes*, 3.14.5–9; **167** 'Gentle and peaceful . . .' Horace, *Carmen Saeculare* 33–4; **167** 'Goddess, nurture our . . .' Horace, *Carmen Saeculare* 17–20; **168** 'The Saecular Games . . .' K. Galinsky, *Augustan Culture*, p. 100; **168** 'Phoebus condemned my . . .' Horace, *Odes*, 4.15.1–2; **169** 'With Caesar protecting . . .' Horace, *Odes*, 4.15.17–20; **169** 'we'll sing of . . .' Horace, *Odes*, 4.15.31–2; **172** 'They came to . . .' Horace, *Odes*, 4.4.25–8; **184** 'The enemy fleet . . .' Propertius, *Elegies* 4.6.21–54; **187** 'The Mausoleum of. . .' A.E. Cooley, *Res Gestae Divi Augusti: Text, Translation, and Commentary* (Cambridge: Cambridge University Press, 2009); **189** 'At the age. . .' *Res Gestae* 1, trans. OCR; **190** 'I drove into . . .' *Res Gestae* 2, trans. OCR; **191** 'These *elogia* would . . .' P.A. Brunt and J.M. Moore, *Res Gestae Divi Augusti: The Achievements of the Divine Augustus* (Oxford: Oxford University Press, 1967), p. 3; **192** 'It was the . . .' *Res Gestae* 13, trans. OCR; **192** 'Four times I . . .' men fought in these shows. *Res Gestae* 22, trans. OCR; **192** 'I received no . . .' *Res Gestae* 6, trans. OCR; **192** 'For my service, . . .' *Res Gestae* 34, trans. OCR; **192** 'In my thirteenth . . .' *Res Gestae* 35; **194** '34. In my sixth . . .' *Res Gestae* 34–35, trans. OCR; **199** 'On reflecting, however, . . .' Suetonius, *Life of Augustus* 28, trans. D. Wardle, *Suetonius: Life of Augustus* (Oxford: Oxford University Press, 2014); **199** 'Augustus completed the . . .' Suetonius, *Life of Augustus* 10, trans. Wardle; **200** 'He both revised . . .' Suetonius, *Life of Augustus* 34, trans. Wardle; **200** 'Not wishing to . . .' Suetonius, *Life of Augustus* 31, trans. Wardle; **201** 'One of the major . . .' D. Wardle, p. 28; **207, 214** 'Caesar, this age . . .' Horace, *Odes*, 4.15.4–20.

SOURCES OF ILLUSTRATIONS

1.1 Bloomsbury Academic; **1.2** Bloomsbury Academic; **1.3** DEA / G. DAGLI ORTI / Contributor / Getty images; **1.4** vlas2000 / shutterstock.com; **1.5** James Renshaw; **1.6** Bloomsbury Academic; **1.7** Bloomsbury Academic; **1.8** Bloomsbury Academic after Storey and Allan (2005); **1.9** Carole Raddato / Wikimedia; **1.10** Bloomsbury Academic after Csapo and Slater (1995); **1.11** Bloomsbury Academic; **1.12** Tim Evanson / Wikimedia; **1.13** Bildarchiv Foto Marburg **Source A p. 22** Tim Evanson / Wikimedia; **1.14** Digital image courtesy of the Getty's Open Content Program; **1.15** Alice Wright; **1.16** Alice Wright; **1.17** Alice Wright; **1.18** Antikenmuseum Basel und Sammlung Ludwig / A. Voegelin; **1.19** DEA / G. NIMATALLAH / Contributor / Getty images; **1.20** Leemage / Contributor / Getty images; **1.21** Museum of Fine Arts, Boston **Source A p. 39** DEA / G. NIMATALLAH / Contributor / Getty images; **1.22** DEA / A. DAGLI ORTI / Contributor / Getty images; **1.23** Archaeological Museum Naples; **1.24** Trustees of the British Museum; **1.25** Trustees of the British Museum **Source A p. 48** Trustees of the British Museum; **1.26** Jastrow / Wikimedia; **1.27** Museo Archeologico Regionale 'Paolo Orsi', Siracusa, Italy; **1.28** James Renshaw; **1.29** Michalis Tiverios; **1.30** DEA / G. DAGLI ORTI / Contributor / Gettty images; **1.31** Bolton Museum and Art Gallery, Lancashire, UK; **1.32** Kimbell Art Museum, Fort Worth, Texas / Bridgeman images; **1.33** DEA / G. DAGLI ORTI / Contributor / Getty images; **1.34** DEA / ARCHIVIO J. LANGE / Contributor / Getty images; **1.35** cgb.fr / Wikimedia; **2.1** David Crausby / Alamy Stock Photo; **2.2** Paul Fraser Collectibles; **2.3** accessed www.ljhammond.com **Source A p. 124** Paul Fraser Collectibles; **2.4** Christian Hülsen, *Bretschneider und Regenberg* (1904); **2.5** CNG; **2.6** with permission of wildwinds.com; **2.7** Marie-Lan Nguyen / Wikimedia; **2.8a** Marie-Lan Nguyen / Wikimedia; **2.8b** Glauco92 / Wikimedia; **2.9** CNG / Wikimedia; **2.10** Bloomsbury Academic; **2.11** with permission of wildwinds.com **Source B p. 144** with permission of wildwinds.com; **2.12** Trustees of the British Museum; **2.13** Marjaara / Wikimedia; **2.14** CNG; **2.15** Bloomsbury Academic; **2.16** CNG / Wikimedia; **2.17** Asier Villafranca / shutterstock.com; **2.18** Marie-Lan Nguyen / Wikimedia; **2.19** Bloomsbury Academic; **2.20** CNG; **2.21** with permission of wildwinds.com; **2.22** Bloomsbury Academic; **2.23** CNG; **2.24** CNG; **2.25** with permission of wildwinds.com; **2.26** Bloomsbury Academic; **2.27** Stefano Pellicciari / shutterstock.com; **2.28** Cortyn / shutterstock.com; **2.29** Cortyn / shutterstock.com; **2.30** Cortyn / shutterstock.com; **2.31** Cortyn / shutterstock.com; **2.32** Cortyn / shutterstock.com; **2.33** Margarete Büsing; **2.34** Werner Forman / Contributor / Getty images; **2.35** ZM_Photo / shutterstock.com **Source A p. 183** Asier Villafranca / shutterstock.com; **2.36** ryarwood / Wikimedia; **2.37** De Agostini Picture Library / Contributor / Getty images; **2.38** Theodor Mommsen (ed.), *Res gestae divi Augusti* (1890) **Source A p. 194** Theodor Mommsen (ed.), *Res gestae divi Augusti* (1890); **2.39** with permission of wildwinds.com; **2.40** with permission of wildwinds.com; **2.41** Carole Raddato / Wikimedia; **2.42** William Neuheisel / Wikimedia; **2.43** The Metropolitan Museum of Art, New York, www.metmuseum.org.

INDEX

Numbers in **bold** indicate figures

A

Actium, Battle of 137, 137–43, 152, 190, 200

actors 29, 32, 42

adultery 85

Aeschylus 8, 27, 27–8, 28, 80, 86
Eumenides 36
Persians 24, 28, 36, 87

agōn, the 51–2, 80

Agrippa 126, **127**, 137, 138, 167, 170, 173–4, 180, 200

Agrippa Postumus 170, 171

Alexander the Great 186

Alexandria 134, **135**, 137, 142

Allan, Arlene 44

Apollo 127, 129–31, 150, 151–2, **158**, 159, 167

Ara Pacis Augustae, Rome 176–80, **177**, **178**, **179**

architectural sources 174

Arginusae, battle of 86

Aristophanes 27, 28, 41, 45
Acharnians 17, 46, 47
Assembly-Women 11
Birds 44, 46, 47
Clouds 45–6, 47
Knights 46, 47
Lysistrata 46
Peace 18
Women at the Thesmophoria **20**, 21, 44, 79–81
see also Frogs

Aristotle 27, 56 66, 75
Poetics 24, 36–8, 72, 73–4

Aristoxenus 32

Armenia 134

AS Exam
Greek Theatre 3, 89–95
Imperial Image 107–8, 205–10

Athens 2, 5, **7**
dramatic festivals 4–11
legal system 76–7
political system 70
women in 67

Attica 5, **6 (map)**

Augustus 109–14
arrival in Rome 117
audience 120
Battle of Actium 137–43, 190, 200
Battle of Phillipi 122, 200
becomes Imperator 126
building programme 173–80, **175**, **177**, **178**, **179**
collapse of the Second Triumvirate 126
death 187, 193
defeat of Mark Antony 135–43, 190
divi filius 122, 130
divine patron 127, 129–31
early political career 117–18
enters the Senate 118–19
establishes the Principate 147–8
family background 117
Feast of the Twelve Gods 130
first consulship 119
image in the Empire 180–2, **180**, **181**
later representations 195–203, **198**
legacy 185–93, 196
marriage to Livia 131
mausoleum 135
military leadership 152–9, **153**, **154**, **155**, **157**, **158**
moral standards 164–6
Mutina campaign 119, 199–200
new Golden Age 166–9, 177
as Octavian 116
the peace of Augustus 153
proclaimed a god 189, 193, 197–8
propaganda 120–1, **120**
reign 146–7
relationship with Julius Caesar 117–18, 120–1, 126, 150, 160–2, 189, 191
as religious leader 149–52, **150**
religious role 164, 165
Res Gestae 119, 126, 143, 170, 187, 189–92, **190**
the Second Triumvirate 121–2
sources 106–7, 118
as state father figure 164–6
succession 169–73, **170**, **171**, **172**, 193
support of the urban poor 127
timeline 109–14

aulētēs 30

aulos 30

aureus of Octavian 120–1, **120**, 122, **122**, 147–8, **148**

B

Bacchae (Euripides) 5, 28, 29
the agōn 52
the chorus 30, 57–8
on Dionysus 41
and family relationships 71–2
justice and revenge in 76
messenger speeches 50–1, **51**
music and musicians 32
political ideas and ideals 70
props 33
religious rituals 64–5
the role of the gods 81–2
role of women 66, 68
slaves roles in 69
tragic heroism 74
tragic irony 54

Bacchus 152

Basel Dancers Vase 30, **31**

black-figure chous 43–4, **44**

Brunt, P.A. 191

Brutus 117, 122, 191

building programme, Augustus 173–80, **175**, **177**, **178**, **179**

C

Caligula 196, 202

Cartledge, Paul 46

Cassius 117, 191